THE MOON IN THE WATER

The Moon in the Water

UNDERSTANDING TANIZAKI, KAWABATA, AND MISHIMA

GWENN BOARDMAN PETERSEN

The University Press of Hawaii ☥
Honolulu

Manufactured in the United States of America

Publication of this work was made possible by a grant from the Kalihikai Japanese Language School.

Library of Congress Cataloging in Publication Data

Petersen, Gwenn Boardman.
    The moon in the water.

    Bibliography: p.
    Includes index.
    1. Japanese fiction—20th century—History and criticism. 2. Tanizaki, Jun'ichirō, 1886-1965—Criticism and interpretation. 3. Kawabata, Yasunari, 1899-1972—Criticism and interpretation. 4. Mishima, Yukio, pseud.—Criticism and interpretation. I. Title.
PL747.65.P47   895.6'3'409   79-14994
ISBN 0-8248-0520-8

Contents

Preface

T*he Moon in the Water* is designed as an introduction to Kawabata, Mishima, and Tanizaki. It is intended not as a work of critical theory but as a practical guide meant to increase the reader's enjoyment by revealing layers of meaning that would not generally be apparent to anyone unfamiliar with Japanese literature.

Readers who can enjoy the works of these three authors in the original will appreciate the difficulties of discussing the fiction on the basis of works available in English. They will also understand that since the following pages are particularly designed to increase the pleasure of readers who do not know Japanese (or who read the literature only slowly and with difficulty), I have tried to stay as close as possible to currently available translations, keeping references to untranslated materials very brief.

To avoid confusing the reader who is not familiar with both languages, I have tried whenever possible to conform to the precise wording (usually enclosed in quotation marks) of available English versions, which are listed in the separate authors' bibliographies, rather than using the phrasing of my own readings, even when I regard the published translation as inadequate in minor details. Occasionally, however, I retain my own English versions or substitute more precise wording without indicating such changes. Thus I hope that the reader will be able to enjoy the following pages without the distraction of parenthetical corrections or the confusion of discussions that do not seem to match the available translation precisely. The Japanese language forces the translator to select a precise phrase or detail from a dozen possibilities —often seemingly contradictory, at least to the reader not familiar with Japanese—a fact demonstrated in English discussions of untranslated works and the differences among various versions of a single short story.

The appendix to chapter 1 gives some idea of the range of meanings that three eminent scholars can draw from the Japanese language. The three parallel translations demonstrate the extent to which all the translations under discussion may differ radically from the original Japanese. Because of such inevitable differences, I have not attempted the specialized task of comparing texts and arbitrating disputes here, except when translations may have created a false impression for the reader who lacks firsthand experience of Japanese language, literature, or daily life.

The brief chapter entitled "Contexts" introduces some important names and dates of the historical framework in which modern Japanese writers should be considered. At the same time, it suggests a few of the special qualities of Japanese language and symbolism, recommending helpful collateral readings for anyone who wishes to explore further.

The chronologies give additional information on publication dates (including the intricacies of serial publication whenever possible) to aid readers wishing to make specialized textual studies. I have included some identifying information on content for the reader who does not have access to this Japanese material, as well as a lengthy bibliography for each author's short stories, novels, and other works available in English translation. There is also a general bibliography

listing additional Japanese authors and anthologies and
several useful critical studies.

Dates in these chronologies and bibliographies are sometimes different from those given in other English studies of
Japanese literature, and even from the dates of original
publication given in the copyright information of translations. A few of the errors I have corrected may have occurred
in the course of providing Western equivalents of the Japanese system, in which the reign years "first year of Taishō"
and "last year of Meiji" both indicate 1912 while the last
year of Taishō and Shōwa One both fall in 1926. Other errors may have resulted from the system formerly used in
calculating ages in Japan. A work written "when Tanizaki
was twenty-five years old" (between 24 July 1911 and 23 July 1912 by the Western calendar) might well refer to a work
completed in 1910.

A more frequent cause of difficulty, however, is the system
of serial publication, common in Japan. First publication
may have been spread over several years (and even different
publications), the work appearing as a book—sometimes
under a different title—months or years later. The history of
Kawabata's *Yukiguni* (Snow Country) from the publication
of the first installment in January 1935 through "complete"
versions in 1937, 1948, and later is an extreme example of
the difficulty. Moreover, the various segments—often seemingly "complete" tales—may have appeared under quite different titles and be listed in bibliographies as short stories (a
difficulty compounded by the Japanese habit of using *shōsetsu* as a term for both short story and novel). In this book,
with few exceptions, the publication dates of Japanese titles
given in text, footnotes, and bibliographies are those of first
(often serial) publication. The chronologies provide information on dates of subsequent publication and performance of
plays.

A note in Miyoshi's *Accomplices of Silence* refers to the
reliability of Mishima bibliographies but would apply equal-

ly to the majority of Japanese bibliographies. Therefore, I
have given in my chronologies only those dates I could verify
by consulting the original publications. These dates have
been further checked by three Japanese scholars, to whom I
would like to express my profound gratitude. Nevertheless, I
fear that we may still have been defeated in our attempted
accuracy by some of the factors suggested above.

My extensive footnotes occasionally clarify other points of
scholarly dispute and interpret esoteric allusions in terms
more appropriate for those who have read the novels in Japanese. The primary purpose of my notes, however, is to increase the general reader's enjoyment by identifying specific
ways in which an understanding of Japanese cultural patterns and unfamiliar symbolism can provide added dimensions to the translations. Some of the notes amplify points
mentioned only briefly in the general discussion, while others
draw the reader's attention to variant interpretations, comparisons, and contrasts.

Apart from added paragraphs referring to the deaths of
Mishima and Kawabata, revised sections to reconcile my
discussion of the earlier volumes of the untranslated *Sea of
Fertility* with the complete English translation, and added
comments on Kawabata's *The Lake* and *Beauty and Sadness*,
the following pages were completed in the fall of 1970, not
long after I had returned to Japan. Various studies have been
published since that time, and the list of translations is growing. It has generally not been possible to mention these in my
discussions; I have tried, however, to identify the most useful
of them in my footnotes.

In my discussions of the authors and their works, I have
whenever possible used the phrasing of the many excellent
published translations. For permission to quote from these
sources as necessary (usually briefly), and to make occasional
use of an author's or translator's accompanying notes, I am
deeply grateful to the following: Asahi Shimbun (publisher of
This is Japan and *Japan Quarterly*); The Asia Society, Inc.;

The Atlantic Monthly; Columbia University Press; *The East* Publications, Inc.; Hokuseidō Press; Alfred A. Knopf, Inc.; and Charles E. Tuttle, Co., Inc.

It is impossible for me to thank adequately and by name all those whose kindness and patience contributed in various ways to this book. I should like, however, to express my profound gratitude to the scholar-friends in Japan who helped me unravel knotty questions of syntax and symbolism when we discussed the first draft of my manuscript. I should also like to thank the friends who introduced me to the pleasures of living in Japan—taking me behind the scenes at the Kabuki, to student performances of Mishima's modern Nō plays, and to recitals of classical music and dancing; or introducing me to their professional worlds of medicine, film-making, and Kyoto's geisha and *maiko* during ten delightful years.

The Moon in the Water has been a labor of love. I have not been supported by grants or academic institutions during its preparation, but completed it with the encouragement of my colleagues and students in Japan and California. And I have saved until last a very special thank you to those who shared their homes with me and welcomed me in settings that were often far from my scholarly world—settings as different as a barge in the port of Kobe, a castle of great beauty, and the living quarters of one of Nara's temples, a center of Zen Buddhism.

GWENN BOARDMAN PETERSEN 1975

A Note on Japanese Names

Throughout this book Japanese names are given in the traditional order, with the family name (e.g., Kawabata) followed by the personal name (Yasunari). After a well-known author's death, however, he is often referred to by his personal name alone (e.g., Ōgai for Mori Ōgai, and Saikaku for Ihara Saikaku).

THE MOON IN THE WATER

1
Contexts

*T*he foreign reader coming to contemporary Japanese literature for the first time is apt to be confused by the extremes —on the one hand, evidence of a tradition that includes esoteric elements of Buddhism, tea ceremony, and Bushido (the way of the warrior); on the other, oddly distorted echoes of Western authors and manners. At one moment, readers find themselves in an unfamiliar world of *giri* (duty, obligation, honor), with *tatami* underfoot, and a graceful Japanese garden beyond windows screened by shoji. At the next, they find themselves eavesdropping with pornographers, attending a "gay party" in a Persian-carpeted mansion, and masturbating on a Japanese beach to the improbable accompaniment of visions of St. Sebastian.

Yet the reader who seeks out the familiar in this confusing world is apt to miss the beauty and the full significance of twentieth-century Japanese fiction. So-called influences are apt to reveal themselves as artfully updated versions of centuries-old tradition, while the "quaint" elements derive their significance not from the ways in which they separate East and West but from the ways in which tradition—as in Kawabata's tea ceremony in *Thousand Cranes*—has been subtly distorted in contemporary Japan.

Approaching this bewildering range for the first time, the reader of translations lacks the familiar landmarks. Even if we are accustomed to enjoy "the work itself" and regard biography and history as irrelevant, we need some assistance. Motivation and meaning will be distorted if we are not alert to subtle expressions of cultural differences—attitudes toward love and death, family and individual, everyday realities and remote ideals. Symbolic hints are linked with centuries of poetic sensibility. And because of a Japanese fondness for literary allusion, the reader often needs clues to the literary framework into which modern authors have fitted the novelties of Western literature. It is of course impossible to compress more than a thousand years of literary history into a few pages. Readers whose previous experience has been primarily in Western literatures, however, can at least find in the following pages a brief sampling of relevant "contexts."[1]

Tanizaki Jun'ichirō, Kawabata Yasunari, and Mishima Yukio all draw on this rich tradition in various ways. Like so

[1] In referring to Japan's classics, I have tried whenever possible to cite works excerpted in Donald Keene's *Anthology of Japanese Literature* (New York: Grove Press, 1955). The two volumes on *Sources of Japanese Tradition*, compiled by Ryusaku Tsunoda, Wm. Theodore de Bary, and Donald Keene (in *Introduction to Oriental Civilizations*, edited by W. T. de Bary [New York: Columbia University Press, 1958–1964]), provide the best compilation of primary materials (translated excerpts) concerning many aspects of Japanese culture and history, along with commentary on the context in which ancient documents are to be understood. Particularly helpful are sections on Buddhism, *cha-no-yu* (tea ceremony), and Japanese aesthetics (not just the more familiar terms of *aware* and *yūgen*, but also *miyabi*, *okashi*, and others). Scholarly editions of a number of the classics have been appearing since the 1960s, including Ivan Morris's beautiful translation of Sei Shōnagon's *Pillow Book* for Columbia University Press. Lack of space, however, prevents me from citing all of these and from providing a bibliography of works that would amplify my passing references to the theatrical arts of Nō, Kabuki, and Bunraku (puppets). The nonspecialist will also be helped by Donald Keene's brief *Japanese Literature: An Introduction for Western Readers* (New York: Grove Press, 1955).

many of their contemporaries, they find image, theme, and even characters in their past as well as in present-day Japan. The centuries of poetic tradition include the *Man'yōshū*, the eighth-century anthology containing more than 4,500 poems written between the fifth century and A.D. 759; countless *waka* (a term for Japanese poetry sometimes used interchangeably with tanka, the 31-syllable form); linked verses *(renga)* and haiku. Other sources of inspiration are found in the drama of the Nō, the Kabuki, and the puppet theater (Bunraku) of Osaka. Ancient tales *(monogatari)* include the ninth-century *Ise Monogatari*, told in 31-syllable verses with prose linking segments, and the *Uji Shūi Monogatari* (A Collection of Tales from Uji), probably written about A.D. 1177 to 1244 but including bawdy adventures from Heian Japan as well as fairy tales and even legends linked to the *jatakas* or Buddha birth stories that came from India. Today's writers also find style and form in earlier diaries *(nikki)*, poetic jottings such as the tenth-century *Kagerō Nikki* and the *Tosa Nikki*, as well as the famous *Pillow Book* of Sei Shōnagon (around A.D. 986 to 1000).

An inevitable process of selection operating before 1950 unfortunately left many Western readers with the impression that Japanese literature encompassed only the classic *Tale of Genji*, the haiku verses that delighted our Imagists, and a few Nō plays in Yeatsian transformation. Few modern novels or short stories had been translated, although the tales of Akutagawa Ryūnosuke and others had appeared in scattered publications (many published in Tokyo and not generally available outside Japan). By 1960 the picture was already changing, although even Tanizaki, Kawabata, and Mishima were still quite poorly represented. Western readers could by this time discover the response of Japanese writers to the war in the Pacific—as in Ōoka Shōhei's *Fires on the Plain* (*Nobi*, 1951–1952) or in the short stories collected in Saeki Shōichi's *The Shadow of Sunrise*. They could study wretched wartime existence and the effects of the American occupation in

Hayashi Fumiko's *Floating Clouds* (*Ukigumo*, 1949–1951) and in Osaragi Jirō's *The Journey* (*Tabiji*, 1952) and *Homecoming* (*Kikyō*, 1948). There is even a boy's-eye view of a captured Negro airman in Ōe Kenzaburō's "The Catch" (*Shiiku*—a term that could also be translated as "breeding" or "raising an animal"—in 1958).[2]

Another story of a captive was translated in 1973: Endō Shūsaku's *Umi to Dokuyaku* (Sea and Poison, 1958), detailing the horrors of wartime vivisection. But stories that have not been translated offer sardonic glimpses of resident foreigners, the forces of the occupation, and those Japanese who have relentlessly pursued foreign life-styles. A number of novels reveal Japanese attitudes toward postwar "mixed-blood" children or make impassioned pleas for recognition of the "real" Japan—for example, the Kyoto of concrete buildings and motorcycle clubs and tawdry nightspots rather than the picturesque glimpses of Zen gardens or geisha so anticipated by tourists.

Yet in spite of the continuing inaccessibility of such "popular" works, English-speaking readers can now share the Japanese response to events at Nagasaki and Hiroshima and the aftermath of the A-Bomb, as in Ibuse Masuji's *Black*

---

[2] Bibliographical information on these and other works will be found in the general bibliography at the end of the book. Throughout this discussion, works available in translation are referred to in English with the Japanese title in parentheses at the first reference. Untranslated works are identified in Japanese, followed at first reference by the English equivalent. I have tried to include the major English variants under which works are discussed, but the complexities of Japanese translation (see notes 15 and 17 below) have made it impossible to provide an exhaustive list. *Introduction to Contemporary Japanese Literature* sponsored by Kokusai Bunka Shinkōkai (Society for International Cultural Relations) is a useful reference tool that provides Japanese titles in both *kanji* and *rōmaji*: these are helpful in identifying works that appear in Western discussions under extraordinarily varied "translations," reminiscent of the strange Japanese versions of English-language classics. Unfortunately, many critical studies fail to provide romanized versions of the title under which a work is known in Japan.

Rain (*Kuroi Ame*, 1965–1966) and Hara Tamiki's "Summer Flower" (*Natsu no Hana*, 1947). They can observe the effects of Japanese social pressures in a world of changed needs and values, as in Ōe Kenzaburō's *A Personal Matter* (*Kojinteki na Taiken*, 1964). Western readers can enjoy a classic detective story in the tradition of Holmes and Maigret in the translation of Matsumoto Seichō's *Points and Lines* (*Ten to Sen*, 1957). By 1967, we could enter the surrealistic world of Abe Kōbō's *The Woman in the Dunes* (*Suna no Onna*, 1962) or *The Face of Another* (*Tanin no Kao*, 1966). And now we even have the earthy humor of Nozaka Akiyuki's *The Pornographers* (*Erogotoshi-tachi*, 1967) and Genji Keita's popular tales about the Japanese "salary-man."[3] Names long honored in Japan also appear on American and English library shelves now: Natsume Sōseki, Shiga Naoya, and Mori Ōgai.

Yet even as we enjoy this delightful range of previously unfamiliar fiction, we may forget a fundamental problem—the difficulty of the Japanese language itself. For Japanese is so differently structured and written from our Western languages that the reader of translated works can never approach the original works by Tanizaki, Kawabata, and Mishima as closely as we can approach Russian or French fiction, for instance. Translators struggling with this difficulty have devised various ways of coping with it, but the result

[3] Some of Keita Genji's stories have been collected in two volumes, *The Ogre (Oni-kachō)* and *The Guardian God of Golf (Okashina Yume)*, both translated by Hugh Cortazzi and published in Tokyo by The Japan Times (1972), but unfortunately often difficult to obtain in the United States. In referring to other contemporary short stories, I have tried to select illustrative examples from the two best accessible anthologies—Donald Keene's *Modern Japanese Literature* (New York: Grove Press, 1955) and Ivan Morris's *Modern Japanese Stories* (Tokyo: Tuttle, 1962). In addition to other anthologies cited in the general bibliography, the reader may wish to consult the indexes of *Japan Quarterly*, the journal in which works of Japanese fiction have often made their first Western appearance (sometimes only partial translations, as in the case of Kawabata's *Sound of the Mountain*).

sometimes leaves the reader of the English version with a false impression of a remarkably westernized context—as when a meal having as its major point various special associations with the old capital of Kyoto becomes hopelessly westernized as "baked trout and a salad."

Other Western equivalents can be misleading, too, just as Japanese understanding in turn has failed to grasp aspects of European and American life and literature. In responding to the new and strange during the "reopening" of the Meiji Era, the Japanese adopted aspects of Western literature that suited the traditional Japanese life-style—much as they had selectively adopted ideas in medicine and weaponry from the Dutch traders at Nagasaki during their "closed" period.

Self-consciously modernizing, however, they often hailed as innovations forms and devices they could have looked for in their own past. Such new labels for old forms frequently appear even today in Japanese discussions, where contemporary authors may be oddly identified with the works of Turgenev, Poe, de Maupassant, or Zola, and later D. H. Lawrence, Joyce, Camus, or Sartre. Japanese writers have produced poems "in imitation of Cocteau" and novels supposedly in the manner of Flaubert or Wilde or "the result of my reading Thomas Mann." Yet the results often strike Westerners as intensely Japanese. Sympathetic vibration to congenial aspects of foreign culture can be found in all the modern writers, including Mishima Yukio, whose own tastes led him to ancient Greece for symbol, theme, and attitude. Mishima at least acknowledged that the Greece he found was not necessarily historically accurate: but he said it was what he wanted. In fact, the mostly untranslated essays of his last years show that much of his admiration for things Greek was really a reflection of his obsession with the Japanese samurai tradition.

A Meiji writer who was a self-acknowledged disciple of Poe might similarly be writing in the venerable tradition of Japanese ghost stories—a still popular genre, rich in the horrible and the grotesque. (Such tales and dramas were believed to have a "cooling" effect during the hot summer months—a belief reflected in modern Tokyo, where summer programs at the Kabuki theater include ghastly apparitions to rival anything created in Europe or America.) Many of Akutagawa's tales—like those of Tanizaki—are enriched by such links with the past, including a number in the Uji Collection mentioned above. Both Akutagawa and Tanizaki write with a later psychological insight, and yet the "demonic" and scatological elements of their tales are often to be found in their sources.

Other modern writers have been so eager to espouse the methods of the West that they have praised their own seventeenth-century Saikaku for "conforming" to the standards of French Naturalism! Ostensibly following their French masters, such writers in their own works usually display attitudes that are really closer to Saikaku's world and to his interest in the adventures of *one* man or woman (unconcerned with wider social conditions). Similarly, Japanese critics have praised as "Proustian" contemporaries whose associative techniques could more accurately be placed within the framework of linked verses *(renga)* or haiku (or *hokku*, the starting poem of linked verse).

Critical awareness of the novel form is often dated from Tsubouchi Shōyō's *The Essence of the Novel (Shōsetsu Shinzui*, 1885), at least among Japanese scholars. This work criticizes contemporary writers and "undiscriminating" readers: "It has long been the custom in Japan to consider the novel as an instrument of education, and . . . the novel's chief function [as] the castigation of vice and the encouragement of virtue."[4] Tsubouchi felt that the only books popular at that time were horror stories and works that the West would label "pornographic." As a remedy, he wanted Japanese writers to emulate Dumas (as one writing "cruelly" about "illicit love")

---

[4] In Donald Keene (ed.), *Modern Japanese Literature*, pp. 55–58.

and put an end to "lascivious descriptions of the mysteries of the bed-chamber"—his evaluation of the "vulgar" and "foolish" works of his nineteenth-century Japanese contemporaries.

Yet the Western reader may be forgiven for finding Tsubouchi's ideas strangely familiar. Close reading of his "Essence" shows it to be distilled from the literary criticism of England, Europe, and the United States—in its references to "art" and expressions of a wider range of feelings (although Tsubouchi takes his examples from Japanese contexts, as in his assertion that modern men cannot confine their feelings to the simple range expressed in 31-syllable poetry [tanka or *waka*]).

It is also amusing to note that Tsubouchi's supposedly modern interest in the theory of fiction and his placing of the theory in a Western context fails to give due credit to a famous Japanese predecessor. Lady Murasaki's *Tale of Genji* —written between 1002 and 1020, according to scholarly consensus—shows her hero Genji discussing the *art* of fiction in terms that seem to anticipate Henry James. In Waley's version of "The Glow-Worm" (in "A Wreath of Cloud," part 3 of the *Tale*), Genji says: "The storyteller's own experience of men and things, whether for good or ill—not only what he has passed through himself, but even events which he has only witnessed or been told of—has moved him to an emotion so passionate that he can no longer keep it shut up in his heart."[5] Continuing with words that also seem to anticipate such Romantics as Wordsworth and to paraphrase Matthew Arnold, Genji adds that vice and folly are as proper as

[5] Lady Murasaki (Murasaki Shikibu), *The Tale of Genji*, translated by Arthur Waley (New York: Modern Library, 1960), pp. 500–504. For a recent translation of this passage, see app. 5 of Ivan Morris's *The World of the Shining Prince* (London: Oxford, 1964). By way of contrast, there is an abridged (and extremely literal) translation of the *Tale* by Suematsu Kenchō (1900) reprinted in a Tuttle edition (1974).

"good" or "beautiful" themes. He discusses differences in form related to cultural and historical conditions. Thus, through her character Genji, Lady Murasaki made a case for the *artistic* importance of the novelist nine centuries before Tsubouchi's Western "discoveries."

Yet Western literature continued to provide the major impetus for the Meiji authors, in spite of many fundamental differences in outlook—especially between Japanese and Western attitudes toward family, group, and nation. The individuality that is praiseworthy in the West, for example, remains in much of contemporary Japanese literature as it was at the time of Saikaku's amusing tales written in the 1680s: clearly a fault, and inevitably leading to unhappiness for all concerned.

Paradoxically, the I-novel (*shi shōsetsu* or *watakushi shōsetsu;* and sometimes referred to by Japanese scholars writing in English as "the autobiographical novel") gained enormous popularity and is still practiced in the 1970s, although many scholars have claimed that the Shōwa literature had already turned away from the I-novel and was paying more attention to plot in its earliest years. Novels of this kind are a record of the author's own experiences—not in the sense that Henry James rendered "felt life" or found a "seed" in an after-dinner conversation, but quite literally detailing specific incidents and relationships. It is thus extraordinarily difficult to separate the man from his mask in much Japanese fiction.

Even when the work is not in the first person, it is apt to have the same obsessively self-absorbed quality as Kaiko Takeshi's *Darkness in Summer* (*Natsu no Yami,* 1972) and to be intensely personal and even confessional. Yet the Japanese "confessional" has pitfalls for the Western reader—who should be warned at the outset not to assume that Tanizaki Jun'ichirō is a foot fetishist (as one eminent scholar recently claimed). Tanizaki's earliest work and his last great novel (and many tales in between) include examples of this predilection: but the sources are not in Western psychopathology.[6]

Similarly, Japanese versions of "confession" in the I-novel often seem strange to the Western reader. The assistance offered by such scholars as Etō Jun can provide some clues to fundamental cultural differences.[7] Perhaps we recognize the yearning of our Romantic poets for a kindred soul in Mushanokōji Saneatsu's "a heart [wanting] to embrace another heart . . . exposing one's heart boldly on paper, waiting for another heart to come to it to embrace it." Japanese views of the self and personality, however, usually differ both in kind and degree from their Western prototypes.

Use of the term I-novel (or *Ich-Roman* among Germanic modernists) is not consistent among Japanese critics. Sometimes the author bares his private heart in the first person. Often he provides a third-person hero who shares his own biography—including birthdate, childhood illnesses, and adult experiences as writer, lover, and even potential suicide. Or, like Mishima, the writer may playfully endow his hero with intimate details of his own biography while vigorously

[6] The foot has special significance in Japan, where the traditional "nine points" of feminine beauty include an elegant foot, as well as the line of a delicate neck rising from the back of a kimono, but remain silent on the subject of breasts. A Japanese writer praising a lovely foot might be compared to a Renaissance sonneteer admiring an ivory brow or star-bright eye.

[7] Etō Jun, "An Undercurrent in Modern Japanese Literature," *Journal of Asian Studies* 22 (May 1964): 435; and "Natsume Sōseki: Japanese Meiji Intellectual," *American Scholar* 34 (Autumn 1965): 615, 619. See also Tsuruta Kinya, "Akutagawa Ryūnosuke and I-Novelists," *Monumenta Nipponica* 25 (1970):13–27. Nakamura Mitsuo's discussions include the passage from Mushanokōji (Mushakōji), *Modern Japanese Fiction* pt. 2, pp. 32–33, and *Contemporary Japanese Fiction*, pp. 8–9. The most helpful discussion of the modern Japanese novel is Masao Miyoshi's *Accomplices of Silence*. This study also provides information on a number of works not available in translation; but unfortunately it was published after my own manuscript was completed, and it has generally not been possible to cite Miyoshi in my text.

denying the connection and even disparaging the entire I-novel form.

Attitudes toward individuality and tradition have naturally changed since the first "confessions" of Meiji writers. The tendency to break up the old, large family units, for instance, has resulted in a loss of attendant obligations.[8] Young couples in the 1970s have set up house in modern concrete apartment blocks *(danchi)* far removed both physically and emotionally from the traditional pattern in which the eldest son took his bride home to live under his mother's domination. As family ties weaken, the individual gains in importance, even though Japanese attitudes toward education, business, and recreation remain more group-oriented than those in the West.

Again, the seemingly "new" awareness of self expressed in the I-novel could be linked with Japan's own literary tradition—especially the diary form still favored by so many of today's writers. But it should be remembered that such works as the *Kagerō Nikki, Murasaki Shikibu Nikki* (Lady Murasaki's Diary), and Sei Shōnagon's *Pillow Book* are by no means confessions in the style of a *Portnoy's Complaint*.

The *Kagerō Nikki* was apparently written by the mother of Fujiwara no Michitsuna about A.D. 954–974: seemingly modern in its psychological portrait, it is exquisitely tactful in evading sexual detail. Sei Shōnagon provides a wittily detailed "Aesthetic of Leave-Taking" with a devastating portrait of the uncouth fellow's morning departure from the bedchamber. But she is less concerned with the lovers' physical relationship than with their delicate emotions—hinted as they watch the moon reflected from the snow or share the fragrance of plum blossoms. (Remarkably modern psychological perceptions, however, include an awareness of the

[8] Niwa Fumio's realistic view of the burdens imposed by elderly relatives (in *Iyagarase no Nenrei*, 1947, translated as *The Hateful Age*) is one of many stories showing postwar changes in family relationships and traditional attitudes toward age.

negative effects of a lover carelessly flinging his clothes back on and the positive value of the lover seeming to be reluctant to depart.) The *Tosa Nikki* includes timeless insight (the attitudes of men toward those who are no longer in power) but also reveals characteristically Japanese delicacy of sentiment in writing of a child who has died (and thus cannot share the emotions of the homebound journey).

Such Meiji offerings as Kunikida Doppo's *Shuchū Nikki* of 1902 (called *The Wine-Soaked Diary* in some English commentaries) may at first glance seem closer to nineteenth-century European literature than to these restrained Japanese antecedents. Nevertheless, the intensity of preoccupation with nuances of feeling, and the exquisite convolutions in exploring subtleties of mood and sentiment, are more readily appreciated in the Japanese tradition of diary—and of poetry —than in the world of Portnoy and Herzog. In Natsume Sōseki's 1914 novel, *Kokoro*, as in Mishima Yukio's "confidential criticism," *Sun and Steel* (*Taiyō to Tetsu*, 1965–1968), even the most intimate revelation is a long way indeed from Henry Miller's kind of self-exposure.

The I-novel is sometimes referred to as the confessional novel *(kokuhaku shōsetsu)*. But in spite of the critic who recently read Mishima's *Kamen no Kokuhaku* (Confessions of a Mask) as autobiography, close reading reveals many ambiguities (see chapter 4). Tanizaki's works include *Diary of a Mad Old Man* and twin diaries entitled *The Key*. Several critics have identified parallels between Tanizaki's life and that of his characters in various novels. Yet Tanizaki conducted a well-known literary "argument" with Akutagawa in which he strongly objected to the I-novel on aesthetic grounds. As far as Tanizaki was concerned, one confessional novel was the most that any author should be permitted.

Apparent contradictions—whether in matters of form or questions of source—sometimes seem to be the one consistent element in modern Japanese fiction. Often the borrowings from Western literature seem eccentric: English phrases sprinkled in a traditional Kabuki play or in the *Rōmaji Diary* (*rōmaji:* roman script used in writing Japanese words) or in the surely apocryphal line quoted by one anthologist, "Oh, to be in Yamato, now that October's there."

Although many of these oddities may seem irrelevant to discussion of Tanizaki, Kawabata, and Mishima, some understanding of their Meiji predecessors is helpful. For they were born into a literary world that had numbered Bulwer-Lytton among its Western masters. The first—very loose —translation of a Western novel was Bulwer-Lytton's *Ernest Maltravers* (1878). And critics who fault the West for misunderstanding Japanese literature might well remember this particular example of Japan's own misunderstanding. The novel was given the title *Ōshū Kiji Karyū Shunwa*, Strange Story from Europe: Spring Tale of the Gay Quarters (*Karyū:* the "flower and willow world" or gay quarters of love).

Sir Walter Scott's *Bride of Lammermoor* became *Shunpū Jōwa* (Spring Wind Love Story, 1888). *Resurrection* was enjoyed as "a romantic tale of unhappy love," and Tolstoy was recommended as a writer who could illuminate "Samaritanism." Disraeli's novels were studied as manuals of Western political methods. And later, like the middle-school teacher in one of Akutagawa's stories, men could read Shaw's plays in order to "search out idioms." Even today, school bookshelves may be filled with the complete works of Somerset Maugham ("for their social interest"). Victorian fiction serves as handbook to English manners, and Virginia Woolf is the layman's guide to "the way Western women think."

It was not until the Shōwa period (beginning in 1926) that translators began to provide accurate versions of Western literature. Sometimes even then a Russian or French work was only known through an unsatisfactory English version, although Futabatei's Russian translations and Mori Ōgai's meticulous rendering of German works were notable exceptions. For these and other reasons, the Western reader must be extremely cautious in identifying sources, influences, or "schools" among modern Japanese writers.[9]

In Japanese literary criticism, such terms as "naturalists," "nihilists," "proletarian writers," "aesthetes," "satanists," "neo-perceptionists," and "neo-romantics" rarely mean what the Western reader expects. The terms are ambiguous and even contradictory, often part of a private language employed by half-a-dozen writers united by typically Japanese social bonds rather than true literary affinity.

Western readers, for instance, should avoid even the common classification of Kawabata Yasunari as a "neo-perceptionist" *(Shinkankaku-ha)*.[10] He was a member of the

[9] Many available studies of Japanese literature—including the Kokusai Bunka Shinkōkai volume cited earlier—tend to apply these confusing and misleading labels. Again Miyoshi is helpful. But the reader seeking critical guidance on most of the authors I mention in this chapter will be frustrated by scattered and often contradictory discussions. Headnotes and introductions of the Keene and Morris anthologies cited above, though sometimes reflecting critical attitudes that have been revised in recent studies, are helpful; there is an excellent essay on Dazai Osamu in Keene's *Landscapes and Portraits*. Some translations of Japanese novels also provide critical introductions: but a few include such idiosyncracies of interpretation that the reader would be well advised to ignore the commentary and proceed to enjoyment of the work itself.

[10] Full analysis of the significance of such groupings is beyond the scope of this study. The term *Shinkankaku-ha* (*shin:* new; *kankaku:* sensibility, feeling, perception, sensation), coined by Chiba Kameo, does identify a number of writers who experimented with direct responses or immediate sense perceptions. At a time when proletarian writers were emphasizing content at the expense of form, the *Shinkankaku-ha* insisted on literary values and stressed the role of the novel as art. But a comparison of another member's work with Kawabata's can suggest some of the wide-ranging individual differences among members. The translation of Yokomitsu Riichi's "Time" (*Jikan*, 1931) and Kawabata's *Izu Dancer* (*Izu no Odoriko*, 1926) shows many differences in attitude and technique. One might also compare the function of tea ceremony in Kawabata's *Thousand Cranes* and in Yokomitsu's *Monshō*. Or consider Kawabata's ballet "enthusiast" Shimamura and Yokomitsu's Kaji (in *Shin'en*), who is absorbed in the

Jūsannin Kurabu (Thirteen-Men Club), one of the elements of an ephemeral New Art group. Kawabata also contributed to the publication of a neo-perceptionist manifesto in 1925. But the writers with whom he associated differ from one another quite radically. Their groups changed labels—and membership—with kaleidoscopic frequency, and even groups connected with a particular magazine, such as *Bungei Jidai*, have often been no more than literary equivalents of Japanese business groups. (Such groups reflect the Japanese insistence on "belonging"—an insistence paralleled in the relationship between a modern young worker belonging to and identifying with his petrochemical company or bank in an intimate familial relationship that puzzles Western businessmen.)

The modernization of Japanese literature can, however, be traced through individual writers. Mori Ōgai, for example, is one of many Japanese writers of confessions or diaries. He was the first Japanese writer to live and study in Europe, to experience Western culture at its source, to read German literature in the original, and to make direct and complete translations. The term *Ich-Roman* for the I-novel is also an appropriate expression of his experiences in Germany in the 1880s. The personal note appears in thinly fictionalized accounts of his attachments to European women, as in *Maihime* (Dancing Girl, 1889) and "Under Reconstruction" (*Fushinchū*, 1910). Yet his moral stance remains essentially Japanese.

The range of Mori Ōgai's accomplishment also makes clear the folly of applying a single label to his style, his attitude, or the form of his work. His dual career as doctor and writer resulted in more than fifty volumes in his *Collected*

---

niceties of *kiyomoto* (most moving of the arts—an exquisitely beautiful style of samisen music, part of the Kabuki tradition). Also, like many other Japanese writers, the neo-perceptionists thought of themselves as Western innovators—whereas their technique has obvious affinities with traditional Japanese literature, especially poetry *(waka)* and in particular the devices of linked verses *(renga)* and haiku.

Works—including translations (usually via German) of more
than a dozen European writers; lives of great Confucian
scholars; and his personal *Vita Sexualis* in 1909. He later
became curator and chief librarian of the Imperial Museum
and published the study *Teishi Kō* (Imperial Posthumous
Names, 1921). He wrote Western-style plays; but he was also
intensely interested in the Kabuki. And it is in his work—
rather than in Tsubouchi's derivative *Essence of the Novel*—
that the first authentic Japanese literary criticism appears.
This versatility of one of Japan's earlier literary figures
should be kept in mind when the Western reader is tempted
to find something peculiarly modern in the accomplishments
of Mishima Yukio.[11]

At the same time, when a Japanese critic identifies Mori
Ōgai as the writer to be credited with making his turn-of-the-
century contemporaries conscious of the short story as *form*,
we should not let this identification blind us to Ōgai's own
antecedents in Japan's classical past. It is true that the earliest tales of sad lovers and brave warriors—including most
of those in the Uji Collection—lack sophistication. The humorous anecdotes, the incidents from court and country, and
the cautionary tales of greedy priests and artful politicians
scarcely match the extraordinary artistic unity of the long
and intricate novel *The Tale of Genji* (artistry so finely detailed in Ivan Morris's *World of the Shining Prince*). Yet
many of Ōgai's supposed innovations can be found in the

---

[11] Mishima also has some titles echoing Ōgai's, although Ōgai's *Onnagata* is a play (Mishima's is a short story); and Ōgai's *Kamen* (Mask) is not
an intimate confession by the narrator but a one-act play in which a doctor
gives advice to a patient. Mishima's literary output may seem unique in
range or quantity to Western readers—but only because so much Japanese
literature remains untranslated. Kikuchi Kan (who died in 1948) rivals
Mishima in sheer volume, with over three hundred novels, short stories,
and plays—compared with Mishima's score of approximately two hundred and fifty. (It is impossible to classify some of Mishima's work, which
included such oddities as a song written for a female impersonator friend
and the living art of his movie performance as a gangster.)

works of preceding centuries—just as the frame of mind displayed by the writers of so many of the *shi-shōsetsu* can be linked to the Heian diaries already noted. Moreover, even today, the Japanese find it difficult to identify a *specific* short story form, applying the term *shōsetsu* to novels and short stories alike and only occasionally distinguishing "a short piece" as *tampen*.

Whatever the precise genealogy of today's Japanese short story, it is worth noting how often even the most innovative writers have turned to earlier tales for theme and character. Thus the "demonic" writers may—like Akutagawa Ryūnosuke—have found material for their grotesque fantasies in ghost tales and *jatakas* included in Japan's first anthologies. Even the chamber-pot incident that seemed to shock one Western critic of Tanizaki's works is in reality only Tanizaki's mischievous updating of an incident in the Uji Collection, where the famous lover Heichū (Taira Sadabumi, who died A.D. 923) was delighted by his discovery of ambrosial liquid and "cylinders of incense" in a stolen imperial vessel. Similarly, the lively style of Tanizaki and his contemporaries often suggests the art of traditional storytellers *(hanashika)*, an oral tradition preserved in the popular *rakugo* (humorous stories) today.

For earlier examples of bawdy humor, realistic detail, brisk dialogue, fine psychological perception, and a sense of style and form, we can cite that lively chronicler of the man-about-Osaka, Ihara Saikaku. His *Life of an Amorous Woman* (*Kōshoku Ichidai Onna*, 1686) is still splendidly entertaining—and much funnier than any Happy Hooker. In his handling of colloquial language and his interest in his fellow townsmen, Saikaku could have provided the models that Meiji Era writers sought in the West. Certainly today's readers can still be delighted by his *Life of an Amorous Man* (*Kōshoku Ichidai Otoko*, 1682); *The Life of the Second-Generation Amorous Man* (*Kōshoku Nidai Otoko*, 1684); *Five Women Who Chose Love* (*Kōshoku Gonin Onna*, 1686);

and the *Eternal Storehouse of Japan* (*Nippon Eitaigura*, 1688), in which he offered "New Lessons from the Lives of Wealthy Men."

Two of Mori Ōgai's contemporaries should also be noted here as contributing to modern Japanese fiction: Shiga and Sōseki. Several of Sōseki's novels are now available in translation. And Shiga Naoya is at least represented in several anthologies. Natsume Sōseki's *I Am a Cat* was the first of his novels to become available in the West,[12] although a second translation has been published more recently. In reading this novel, however, it is not necessary to decide whether it has been influenced by European naturalism or whether the term I-novel fits. Nor does Sōseki's association with the Shirakaba (White Birch) group provide necessary clues to meaning. This marvellously detailed view of turn-of-the-century Tokyo is a delight on its own terms.

The sardonic feline narrator announces: "There are two sides to everything"—and then applies this double vision with devastating effect. In artfully matter-of-fact tone, the cat tells of the self-important teacher bemoaning the hard life —even as that teacher stuffs himself with New Year soup (*zōni*) or lies snoring on the *tatami*. Later the cat offers comments on wives who have been ruined by attendance at modern girls' schools and on men who have misunderstood Western culture "and blindly accept all imported ideas,

[12] *Wagahai wa Neko de aru* (1905–1906). Quotations are from the translation by Shibata Katsue and Kai Motonari (Tokyo: Kenkyūsha, 1961). Although the Western reader can appreciate many of the ironies of this tale, perhaps it should be pointed out here that there is also humor in the cat's use of the elevated *wagahai* form of "I." Other titles similarly carry additional significance for Japanese readers. Sōseki's *Kokoro* (1914) means both "heart" and "mind" rather than "the heart of things" suggested by one translator. *Kusa Makura* (1906) is literally *Grass Pillow*—a poetic term for travel that is scarcely suggested by the translator's choice of *Three-Cornered World* for his version. A brief but helpful study of these and other works is Edwin McClellan's *Two Japanese Novelists: Sōseki and Tōson* (Chicago: University of Chicago Press, 1969).

believing that by accepting them, they are becoming true gentlemen." But the attack is not a simple campaign either against false Japanese values or the dangers of modernism. Thus the reader can respond with a smile when this valuable commentator comes to an untimely end. Hoping to cheer himself by lapping up two glasses of beer, the wise cat miscalculates his own capacity and tumbles into a rain barrel. We are offered the fantastic spectacle of a drunken, diary-keeping cat drowning—and doing so with the Buddhist words of acceptance on his tongue, as he most properly invokes Amida Buddha.

But what does this witty cat have in common with the characters of another so-called I-novelist, Shiga Naoya? As with Sōseki and Mori Ōgai, the label offers no clues. And as with those authors, the Japanese critics have provided a dazzling array of alternative—and equally unhelpful—labels. We are told that Shiga is a "neo-idealist," a "naturalist," a "humanist." He is also identified as one of the Shirakaba (White Birch) group, who were supposedly influenced by Tolstoy but were all graduates of Gakushūin (The Peers' School) and were apparently in an alliance as much social as literary.

None of these labels offers guidance to Shiga's eloquent meditation on death in *Kinosaki Nite* (At Kinosaki, 1917). Nor are labels needed when we read "Seibei's Gourds" *(Seibei to Hyōtan,* included in Ivan Morris's *Modern Japanese Stories).* This ironic little tale describes a boy whose beautifully polished gourd is the subject of a moral lecture by his teacher: it is a Worthless Object. As his scorned art passes successively through the hands of the school porter, an antique dealer, and a wealthy collector, its value in commercial terms rises—priced according to the standards of the acquisitive beholder—until the despised zero is raised to 600 yen. Yet if this is a writer's statement about his art, it is an ambiguous one: the value of art may be negative. The other gourds are smashed. The boy Seibei has turned to pictures. And already his father has begun scolding the boy about his new interest in painting.

Shiga's novel *An'ya Kōro* (The Dark Road, 1921–1937) offers a different view of boyhood experience. It is filled with a sense of solitude and tragic yearning for affection. Kensaku's experiences range from a rather sordid relationship with Oyei to dialogues on Zen Buddhism and responses to Chinese poetry. His responses to the beauty of the Japanese scene and the melancholy mood of this novel resemble those found in centuries of Japanese poetry.

Such modern versions of ancient philosophies are in startling contrast to Japan's first truly socially conscious novelists: the proletarians, whose literature grew out of contemporary unrest (such as riots over the price of rice after the First World War). Here a label at least serves to identify several writers, among them Kataoka Teppei, Fujimori Seikichi, Hayama Yoshiki, and Kobayashi Takiji. Identified with the movement at various times, all were active in politics and frequently subjected to official abuse and persecution. Kobayashi Takiji, in fact, died in prison as the result of police torture.

Yet even these ideological lines are not clear: Kataoka Teppei, author of "Linesmen" and a member of the Labor Farmer party, was also regarded as one of the *Shinkankaku-ha*—a strange kind of relationship if we remember that the poetic Kawabata was also supposed to be one of that group.

A better idea of the proletarian line can be found in the titles of such tales as "Letter Found in a Cement Barrel," "The Factory in the Sea," "The Efficiency Committee," and "For the Sake of the Citizens." Most famous is Kobayashi Takiji's *The Cannery Boat* (*Kani-Kōsen*, 1929). *Cannery Boat* tells of former coal miners and factory hands, children of the Hakodate slums, and students—all tricked into a supposedly profitable job and all confined aboard a 3,000-ton boat ripe with the stench of sweat and stale sake, piled with garbage, and infested with lice, bugs, fleas, and the bosses.

The politics of the author are clearly symbolized in the contrasts: cracked cups, filth, and cruelty below decks; and white-coated stewards bringing elegant glasses to the saloon (where the captain entertains the maritime police and "big shots of the seamen's unions"). For readers in Japan, where no one is too poor to share the ritualistic enjoyment of the daily bath, public or private, the horrors of the capitalistic system are further symbolized in a captain and boss who continue to enjoy their daily *ofuro* while the crew and the factory hands must make do with a once-a-month ration of dirty water.

Unlike the earlier Japanese experiments with European naturalism—generally restrained—proletarian literature is rich in the stinking and the specific. *Cannery Boat* has students who talk about European literature: but aboard this vessel men get beri-beri, their teeth are smashed in, they are tortured, they resemble maggots. They also learn to use the vocabulary of "capitalist," "exploiter," and "proletariat"— especially after a group are washed up on the Kamchatka shore, where they enjoy a fortuitous encounter with Russians and, conveniently, a Chinese interpreter.

In such tales it would seem that traditional Japanese values have vanished and literary forebears are forgotten. Workers in dye plants, telephone linesmen, printers, factory hands in cement plants, transportation workers, and silk mill employees are pitted against scabs, brutal policemen, cruel bosses, luxury-loving capitalists, fat landowners, and absentee landlords. Surely this is Western rhetoric.

Yet the world remains profoundly Japanese. The rallying cry—"Japanese workers, act!"—is greeted with "Banzai!" A special boat comes with mail, Japanese delicacies, and movies (Western and Japanese, however) to celebrate the ten-thousandth can off the assembly line. A pay envelope is displayed before a dead father (it is placed on the family altar). We hear the nostalgic notes of the samisen and biwa. Even the brutality of the police is rendered in terms of their bad manners—when they invade the union hall, they rush in "without even taking off their shoes."

But the literary value of these stories is invariably low. The emphasis is on propaganda, and often the Japanese tradition is debased for this purpose. A man chops off his little finger: this is not the traditional gesture, as of a lovelorn geisha, but part of a put-up job to discredit the communist leaders. A Korean worker's ghost roams through a factory: Japanese readers recall the return of badly treated lovers in Kabuki dramas or the ghost of a loyal retainer who had been buried alive with his dead lord—but this ghost was a worker who had been buried alive in cement as the result of a contractor's graft.

Such workers had rarely appeared in Japanese fiction before the influx of Western ideas and literature. Saikaku's "common man" was several rungs up the social ladder, and workers were quite beneath the notice of Heian writers. Yet even in the first decade of the twentieth century Japanese writers were looking at their unmentionable outcast group (*eta:* a term no longer acceptable in Japan), as in Shimazaki Tōson's *The Broken Commandment* (*Hakai* ["transgression"], 1906), while the hardship of city life provided theme and content for many of the new generation of writers.

These writers included women, among them Higuchi Ichiyō. Her *Takekurabe* (Comparing Heights or Growing Up, 1895–1896) describes the life of children on the fringes of the old Yoshiwara licensed quarters. After the Second World War, Hayashi Fumiko wrote *Shitamachi* (Downtown, 1948) and *Ukigumo* (Floating Clouds, 1949–1951), showing the harsh life of Japanese women in the 1940s. There is little in such a life or in these works to remind the reader of the elegant Heian contexts of Murasaki Shikibu and Sei Shōnagon. *The Tale of Genji* is justifiably described as "the world's first psychological novel" by many critics—yet that achievement was not matched in later years, no "feminist" school arose among the women writing in the modern period, and in spite of other individual accomplishments, including the sensitive studies of women by Enji (Enchi) Fumiko, there are no women writers with the stature of Tanizaki, Kawabata, or Mishima.

Miyamoto Yuriko wrote socialist novels, and in the early decades of the twentieth century a number of women—like their male counterparts—made self-conscious attempts to adopt Western ways. Such experiments produced little lasting fiction; and some of their radical life-styles sound more like scripts for Hollywood than real life in Tokyo. One of these "new" women reacted to personal failure with a traditional gesture—drawn perhaps from the puppet and Kabuki plays of Chikamatsu (based on early eighteenth-century events)—and attempted love-suicide. Unlike the figures in Chikamatsu's popular dramas, however, she survived . . . and even wrote about emancipated women.

There was little chance for emancipation in the 1930s and 1940s, of course. Japanese writers both male and female were repeatedly censored—and censured—when their work struck the military-minded bureaucrats as subversive or occasionally depraved. Some intimidated writers remained silent rather than have their work suppressed by the police and other agencies or face orders from the Board of Information to omit scenes that might corrupt manners. And a number of foreign writers whose works had been popular models were now rejected as bad influences, that is, apt to encourage, liberal or democratic attitudes.

It is not surprising that postwar writing revealed violent reactions to the restraints of those years. Prostitution, homosexuality, pornography, and other topics that had previously been treated with restraint were now more often described in explicit and violent detail. The label "postwar nihilism" is no more helpful, however, than such earlier tags as "naturalist" or "neo-romantic." And Japanese discussions of "postwar nihilism" can be of use only if they are understood in the context of Japanese attitudes toward death and suicide, the many varieties of Buddhist thought, and the vagaries of earlier literary group postures. Today's writers—like their Meiji predecessors—often make claims of doubtful authenticity when they affiliate with Western movements. Existentialism, for instance, may for a Japanese writer be little more than evidence of reading one or two essays by Camus or Sartre.

Some postwar trends and fashions, however, can help the foreign reader evaluate Tanizaki, Kawabata, and Mishima. Many of Mishima's works seem pathologically bizarre. He has rewritten history in terms of deliberately abnormal psychology, as in his tale of the Priest of Shiga and the Imperial Concubine (*Shigadera Shōnin no Koi*, 1954; translated as "The Priest of Shiga and His Love"). His modern Nō plays substitute cigarette butts and shabby relationships for the poetic and evocative understatements of the original dramas.

But many of Mishima's contemporaries were similarly reexamining their traditions. Some took a sardonic view of military "heroes"—as in the stories of Saeki Shōichi's anthology, *The Shadow of Sunrise*. In poetry, the "doughty Yamato warrior" had become a machine-gunner. In modern Nō imitations by other writers, lyrical glimpses of long-ago lovers were transformed into sensational or soap opera versions of such contemporary events as the fall of Rangoon.

Some writers produced enormously popular lyrical evocations of the past—such as Fukazawa Shichirō's "Songs of Oak Mountain" (*Narayama-Bushi Kō*, 1957), a work that sold more than a quarter of a million copies. But this "lyrical" writer also produced a story, ironically titled "Dream of Love" (*Fūryū Mutan*, 1960), dealing offensively with the Imperial Family. The editor who published that story had his life threatened, and Fukazawa himself made a strategic retreat from the literary scene to a life of farming.

Another postwar iconoclast is Dazai Osamu, whose *Setting Sun* (*Shayō*, 1947) is available in translation. A kind of culture hero for many years, even after his suicide in 1948, Dazai Osamu was admired as much for his personal life of "splendid dissipation" as for his writing. His sensational blend of liquor, sex, and drugs had the kind of appeal enjoyed by an earlier group of satanist writers. And questions of his supposed idealism and sense of purity on the one hand and heightened appreciation of evil on the other cannot be fairly answered on the basis of material available in English.

Mishima's preoccupation with cruelty can be viewed in the light of the contemporary fashion for the sensational, a fashion reflected in the number of films with *zankoku* (cruelty) even in their titles. One of the best ten films of 1962 dealt with *seppuku* (ritual suicide) by an Edo *rōnin* (masterless samurai) who performed the act grotesquely with a blunt bamboo sword. This film was widely regarded as a criticism of the samurai code, however, whereas Mishima's 1966 film *Rite of Love and Death* (based on his short story, "Patriotism") was but one aspect of his obsession with military vigor.[13]

In the film—in which he himself "performed" *seppuku*— Mishima emphasized the juxtaposition of beauty and ugliness suggested in his short story "Patriotism." He rendered the young couple's love in lyrical terms, using the traditional Nō stage for his setting and concluding with an image of a raked-sand Zen garden. But intervening scenes were filled with horrifying specific closeups of blood and bowels and the agony of the "noble" ritual suicide.

Mishima's attitude toward both the erotic and the ugly aspects of his strangely rendered "beautiful" cruelty—in his fiction as well as in this film—is one aspect of his own genius. But Japanese films and fictions have often linked the cruel with the erotic. Foreign readers were unaware of such aspects of contemporary Japanese life as the erotic movie and tape industry until 1968, when Michael Gallagher translated Nozaka Akiyuki's *The Pornographers*. Yet that amusing

[13] See Gwenn R. Boardman, "Greek Hero and Japanese Samurai: Mishima's New Aesthetic," in *Critique* 12(1970):103–115.

work is only a reflection of contemporary Japanese taste, revealed in the themes and plots of popular novels and magazine features too. It is a pity that we lack translations of the everyday reading of today's commuting businessmen, seemingly demure office girls, and quite conventional housewives. These stories are often even more frank than those of Genji Keita in revealing Japanese cultural differences.

In the novels of Kawabata, Mishima, and Tanizaki, the reader will find two of these cultural differences to be of major importance: attitudes toward sexual conduct and attitudes toward suicide—quite different in Japan from our Judeo-Christian taboos. In contrast to the Western abhorrence of suicide, for instance, the Japanese have for centuries accepted suicide as an honorable solution to problems ranging from offended (military) honor to failed examinations and love relationships. Lovers who could not be united in this world—for "family considerations" and other reasons—committed love-suicide in anticipation of being reborn together on the lotus leaf of Buddha's paradise. This was a favorite theme of Chikamatsu's plays (written between 1683 and 1725 but still performed both on the puppet stage and in Kabuki versions). Modern executives and students still commit suicide to atone for failure, although other suicides—including Kawabata's—remain unexplained. But Mishima's dramatic death was deliberately conceived in the samurai tradition of *seppuku* (even with a hint of homosexual love-suicide according to some commentators).

Full treatment of Japanese attitudes toward love and sexual relationships requires a separate study. But a few clues will help the Western reader avoid misunderstanding the writers under discussion here. The historical context includes the influence of Shintō beliefs and continuing phallic reverence—as seen at Takata, a few miles from modern, industrial Nagoya, for instance, where a six-foot phallus of startling realism is on permanent display and the souvenirs include peppermint-flavored candy of unmistakable masculine ("mushroom") shape.

The Japanese assume that sexual activity is but one normal and pleasurable aspect of life. For centuries, devices, pictures, marriage screens detailing the forty-seven basic positions (such as "the moon through the window," "fishing for dragonflies," and "the carp going up the waterfall"), and marriage manuals have been available to enhance this pleasure. In addition, there has been a long history of erotic literature, quite unlike Western ideas of what is pornographic or obscene.

The earliest examples include "pillow tales" (*makura-zōshi*, but not to be confused with the Heian "pillow book" or journal of Sei Shōnagon). One of today's Japanese marriage manuals, titled in English *How to Love* and picturing the classical positions as well as more recent sexual advice, was given as a free supplement with the Japanese equivalent of *Ladies' Home Journal* or *Good Housekeeping*. The frank advice in such a modern publication, however, is not really new: it is simply the most recent version of the ancient marriage screens provided to help the novice lovers or the early *Koshibagaki-zōshi*, in which the "rites of initiation" were demonstrated by a well-endowed Heian gentleman and his lady.

In fiction, these straightforward attitudes are found in Saikaku's "amorous" men and women, whose rollicking adventures provide an amusing picture of seventeenth-century life. Even *The Tale of Genji* is, beneath its exquisite fabric of moon viewing, carefully chosen poems, and court etiquette, a splendidly picaresque tale.[14] Genji's adventures—and those of his friends and, later, his younger relatives—lack the detail

---

[14] For full and scholarly discussion of these and other aspects of the *Tale*, the reader is directed to Ivan Morris's *The World of the Shining Prince*.

of those of Fanny Hill or Tom Jones. They are to be understood in a different social and aesthetic context. Yet they are,
after all, a series of artful dodges for enjoying "the dew of
woman" beneath the quilts of ladies-in-waiting, of princesses, and even of a victim of ghostly possession.

In *The Tale of Genji*, though, as in most subsequent treatments of sex in Japanese literature, the terms are poetic
rather than clinical, the pleasures are invariably accepted as
natural, and physical detail is often deemed unnecessary. But
the naked human body—quite acceptable in the world of
public baths—did not particularly interest these writers. Like
the artists of *Shun-ga* ("spring pictures" of erotic intent), the
writers could suggest more by an artfully draped kimono. In
Heian times, if we are to judge from the words of Lady Murasaki's personal diary, the naked appearance of ladies (recently robbed of their clothes) was "unspeakably horrible."

Japanese attitudes may also be deduced from haiku, for
although these delicate 17-syllable verses are not concerned
with sex, even the great master Bashō in one haiku places
courtesans and *hagi* (bush clover—a favorite poetic image in
Japanese literature) under one delicately moonlit roof.
Western views of right and wrong in matters sexual are irrelevant here—except in those instances where the author has
acquired, or perhaps only read about, Christian views of
morality. It should be noted, too, that when he takes the lovely little Murasaki into his palace for "training," Genji's
methods are far indeed from those to be found in *Lolita*.

Homosexual relationships are similarly treated rather differently in Japan than they have been in many Western coun-
tries. But in evaluating aspects of Mishima's stance in his fictions and in his essays, we should keep in mind his differences
of *attitude* from such earlier works as Saikaku's *Danshoku
Ōkagami* (The Great Mirror of Sodomy or of Manly Sensual
Pleasures).

The reader knowing Kawabata's work only in translation
might think that the Nobel Prize winner is a more "poetic" or

delicate writer than Mishima. Yet it is worth noting that he too wrote many intensely sensual tales. Hallucinatory elements of Kawabata's story "One Arm" (*Kata-ude*, 1963–1964) might seem related to problems of sexual pathology—although a number of his contemporaries wrote similarly experimental pieces. But the reader assuming "One Arm" is a piece of sick modern surrealism should recognize that there are antecedents in Japan's literature long before the introduction of Western writing. There is, for example, the story of Kannon told by Shiba Zenkō in the eighteenth century, recounting that when times were hard the Goddess of Mercy would remove one of her arms and rent it out. The imagery of Kawabata's story is deeply indebted to centuries of Japanese literature: yet the story also offers a perception of loneliness that is valid in today's world of Freudian and Jungian analysis.

Traditional Japanese images, the terminology of Japanese aesthetics, and the nature of the Japanese language itself can deepen our understanding of contemporary works in translation. Concepts of *aware*, *yūgen*, *sabi*, and *miyabi* admittedly require volumes of interpretation for full understanding, of course, yet a summary hints at some profound differences from the attitudes of the West.

The term *aware* (or *mono-no-aware*) is perhaps known to Western readers as a result of haiku anthologies. The term refers to sensitivity, qualities of transience, and delicate perceptions of inherent sorrow. At one level, *aware* includes the association of a falling cherry blossom petal with the inevitable death of a samurai (the cherry blossom being a symbol of samurai virtues in its tenacity as well as in the suddenness of its eventual fall). But it is more than that: *aware* also encompasses an intense awareness of beauty in a briefly perceived instant, perhaps accompanied by an unvoiced sigh as we recognize that it *is* but a moment.

Whether or not *aware* is an expression of Buddhist thought need not concern us here. Yet the sense of transience permeates Japanese literature and life in ways that it is difficult for us to understand. Even the *hiragana* syllabary is memorized by a poem—the *iroha* syllables forming a meditation on the color and fragrance (of flowers) that are—like other aspects of life—*not* everlasting. It ends with the thought: "I have overcome life's material aspects and will dream no more (shallow) dreams."

Other terms of Japanese aesthetics may seem to offer little help in interpreting modern fiction. Yet consider the term *yūgen*—meaning *mystery*, but more than that. It refers also to the emphasis that Japanese aesthetics places on subtlety and suggestion: the veiled moon's beauty is more exquisite than the shining *meigetsu* (full moon). It is also the mystery of that "ineffable" quality that Zeami discussed in his treatise on Nō drama. *Sabi* is an "antique look" in modern translation but it alludes to the appreciation of the harmony of age —an appreciation found in the haiku of Bashō, for instance, or in the accessories of the tea ceremony. The quality of *miyabi* (refinement) epitomized in Heian culture is only rarely referred to now.

In addition to these traditional aesthetic terms, traditional literary and dramatic forms provide clues to appreciation of modern fiction—in spite of the fact that Japanese writers as different as Natsume Sōseki and Mishima Yukio have either denied that there *is* a tradition or have claimed that their own pages are filled with "thoughts from across the sea."

Modern fiction and poetry remain very rich in literary allusions—to a line found in a poetry anthology of a thousand years ago, to an image in a seventeenth-century haiku, to passages in one of Chikamatsu's puppet plays, to scenes of the Nō and Kabuki stages, to incidents in court journals or feudal chronicles. This is the literary habit of mind demonstrated in the traditional New Year's Day game of the Hundred Poems, in which players must match halves of well-known verses in the *Hyakunin Isshu* compiled by Teika (1162 to 1241). Today's families may prefer to spend the day watching variety shows on television. Modern readers may miss allusive phrases in the works of Kawabata or Mishima. And yet the persistence of the poetic sense in Japan may be gauged by the continuing popularity of the Emperor's annual poetry-writing contest: thousands of Japanese citizens submit *waka* or tanka.

The seasonal associations of such poetry are part of every person's vocabulary and can be traced back over a thousand years to the "four seasons" lore of Heian culture. The seasonal sense is maintained in everyday life: in the care with which materials and colors of kimono are still selected and in the discrimination employed in choosing appropriate *kakemono* (hanging scrolls) for the *tokonoma* (alcove) of the Japanese home. Many contemporary writers make use of these seasonal associations. A single reference to plum blossom (the first winter flower), to the sound of the cloth-beaters' mallets (autumn), or to a certain variety of grass, is sufficient to evoke a mood, to introduce a cluster of enriching associations, or to imply a character's feelings and actions. Kawabata is particularly adept at employing such words, as in *Snow Country* or *Sound of the Mountain*.

Sometimes the symbolic effect can be carried over into the translation. But attempts to find equivalent imagery may prove disastrous. In Japanese, "seven (autumn) grasses" *(nanakusa)*—or any one of these grasses—can suggest the whole "sad season." But if the translator replaces the symbolic flowering grasses with "seven wildflowers," nothing remains.

The cuckoo has none of our Western connotations of cuckoldry and sexual adventure. Instead it suggests "the bird of the other world," singing in the fifth month to warn the farmer that now is the time to plant his rice; or it is the "dusk-singing" bird, evocative of sadness. But one translator, apparently regarding the cuckoo as not sufficiently poetic for Western sensibilities, boldly rendered it as "skylark" (meaningless in that context). Similarly, an ingenious series of puns

on salt—relevant in the context of salt-gathering maidens—
loses all flavor in the translation to a series of sugar puns.

This brings us to some problems of the Japanese language
that must be understood if the foreign reader is to appreciate
how translations differ from the originals and from each
other (see appendix): problems of idiom, syntax, and connotation and—in the visual qualities of ideograms—one absolutely untranslatable element.

Japanese is written in a combination of *kanji* (ideograms
derived from the Chinese but differing in many respects) and
a syllabary (*hiragana* or *katakana*, the *katakana* being reserved for writing of foreign words and telegrams). The
foreign reader may not care that each character has multiple
readings, including the Chinese literary *on* and the native
Japanese *kun* reading. But such knowledge helps the reader
to understand why Tanizaki's short story "Tattoo" is sometimes listed in *rōmaji* as *Irezumi* and sometimes as *Shisei.*[15]

---

[15] *Irezumi* is the *kun* reading of two characters read as *Shi-sei* in the *on*
pronunciation. *Ire (ira)* or *shi* means "to prick" or "pierce," but there is a
hint of a homophone: *iro (shiki)*, meaning *color.* Tanizaki preferred the
reading *Shisei* (although he has also been quoted as saying that he preferred *Irezumi!*). Such variant readings of titles are among the many
bibliographical problems in Japanese fiction. Another is the system of
serial publication—often the parts (as of Tanizaki's *Makioka Sisters* and
Kawabata's *Snow Country*) are spread over several years, appearing under
varying titles and even being drastically rewritten before publication of a
hardcover edition. Japanese titles given in *rōmaji* (especially when diacrit-
ical marks are omitted) can also trap unwary readers, as with the Eikō of
Mishima's novel *Gogo no Eikō (The Sailor Who Fell from Grace with the
Sea).* Mishima often used obscure *kanji*, reaching beyond the 1,850 essential *kanji* of common usage and the 6,450 found in most dictionaries to the
obsolete 5,500 of classical literature. The translator cannot really convey
this exotic vocabulary even by using unfamiliar English words; nor would
such devices as printing the exotica in Gothic script quite create the *visual*
effect of the Japanese. An excellent discussion of Japanese language problems is Masao Miyoshi's "The New Language" in *Accomplices of Silence*,
which also discusses the significance of abandoning earlier, literary
language.

The Japanese reader responds to the visual qualities of these characters—a dimension lost to the Western reader. For example, the Japanese looking at the ideogram for *nowaki* feels refreshed: he sees in the two characters the wind "dividing a field." Our English language cannot convey the emotional response to the iris pictured by *kanji*. We have no equivalent to the pleasures to be found in contemplating the table of contents of the classic *Tale of Genji*.[16]

Yet just such an emotional response to *kanji* is an essential part of the Japanese reader's experience, even as it is part of our understanding of the disturbed Mizoguchi's response to the "Golden Pavilion" in Mishima's novel. Elsewhere, the elements making up an ideogram may carry associations that simple translation cannot hope to offer—as in the case of the ideogram for scenery, made up of the two characters for mountain-water *(san-sui)*: a more tightly controlled and yet more vividly evocative expression than any our own vocabulary can offer.

The average Western reader is handicapped by an inability to *look* at the beautiful language. When the Japanese speak of a person "writing" a poem, the term includes both the calligraphy and the words. But this emphasis on the way the language is written, or looks, is difficult for most foreigners to comprehend. In Japan, however, the scrolls hung in the *tokonoma* often do not bear a picture in our sense: instead, there is a beautifully written poem. References to the calligraphy displayed in a person's home—as in many of Tanizaki's novels and Kawabata's—thus define character and set tone in subtle ways that are difficult to annotate.

Another hidden delight of the Japanese language is the multiple readings of characters *(kanji)*. The language is also extraordinarily rich in homophones—there are more than

[16] I am indebted to my friend Professor Hisao Kanaseki, who first opened my eyes to these pictures. See also his "Haiku and Modern American Poetry," *East-West Review* 3 (Winter 1967–1968):229–230.

sixty different characters read as *ko* and close to two hundred read as *kō* (and with a range of *meanings* almost as great). These provide literary possibilities unimagined by most Western authors and offer, moreover, extraordinary opportunities for puns and other forms of wordplay.

The way of writing the language—run on without breaks between ideograms, syllables, and words (although modern printed texts provide breaks not used in older volumes or even in modern correspondence)—also permits words to ricochet off one another in infinite variety. In verse and drama, "pivot words" change their meanings in relation to the reading of the preceding and following syllables—nuances that fail to reach the modern Japanese ear. Western readers who have forgotten the delightful wordplay in the works of Renaissance poets, and the puns that Shakespeare makes even at solemn moments, may also be puzzled by the many-layered meanings of Japanese literature. Yet even the reader who has not yet mastered the Japanese language can find some fine examples hidden in the notes of various scholarly translations of Japan's classics. Two of the best sources are the notes provided by Ivan Morris for his translation of Saikaku's *The Life of an Amorous Woman and Other Writings* and those furnished by Donald Keene in his translation of *Four Major Plays of Chikamatsu* (both cited in my bibliography).

Sometimes even a single ideogram carries a range of meanings and symbolic associations too rich for translation: the (literally) correct word cannot convey its extended symbolic values. An example is the "color" of Mishima's novel *Forbidden Colors (Kinjiki)*, which immediately hints to the Japanese reader that the content will be erotic. "Color"—the character that is read as *shiki (jiki)* in the Chinese *(on)* pronunciation and as *iro* in the Japanese reading *(kun)*—carries an inescapable link with sex or sexuality in ways much more specific than our familiar references to a girl "coloring" or "blushing." Whole scenes in Kabuki are built around the "colors" of the Yoshiwara courtesans. And when a woman "colors" —as in Kawabata's *Beauty and Sadness* or *Thousand Cranes* —the Japanese reader is alerted to hints that the woman is becoming increasingly *desirable* to the man who is looking at her.

The *kanji* for "color" can also be read as "complexion," "love [affair]," "sweetheart," "sensual pleasure," and "tint," becoming in its verb forms and compounds "to be amorous," "to be stirred," and "sex appeal," as well as referring simply to "fall (leaf) colors." The man who is "fond of color" *(irogono [mu])* is lustful. *Iro-ke* is both simple "shade" and a term for "romance." *Iro-me*, "a soft glance," clearly hints at sexuality. Arriving at puberty is expressed with the verb *iro-kezu (ku)*. *Iro-banashi* (color-talk) is a love story. Such associations enrich the meanings of Tanizaki's story "Tattoo" *(Irezumi* or *Shisei)* and suggest the newly awakened passions of the tattooed girl—especially in the description of her disordered hair falling over "colored" cheeks (although this part of the narrative has unfortunately been omitted in the two versions of the tale provided by Western translators). The translator of Mishima's *Kinjiki*, however, permitted us to share the subtlety of the Japanese words. Lacking the Japanese reader's sensitivity to such varied "colors," we are at least spared the false crudity of earlier English references to *Forbidden Colors* as *Forbidden Sex*.

Other erotic hints or connotations similarly escape Western readers unfamiliar with Japanese life and literature. Yet such hints of sexuality are an essential aspect of Kawabata's delicately lyrical passages, as well as of Tanizaki's more earthy humor. For instance, one of Tanizaki's stories is titled *The Key*. Its twin diaries of sexual adventure are related to the key *(kagi)* of the title. But *kagi* is also a term used for the penis—thus providing an additional ironic note to the story.

Another homely object with hidden Japanese meanings is the pillow *(makura)*. "Two pillows" provide a specifically sexual reference. *Makura-e* are "pillow-pictures," splendidly specific in their rendering of the ways of love. Komako in Kawabata's *Snow Country* offers "fire for a pillow." And centuries of Japanese poetry reveal the pillow's rich erotic tradition.

Alas, the Western reader is not stirred by the hints of a Japanese pillow. Nor does the gesture of "untying the obi string" excite the Western reader, especially when the translator interprets the kimono's heavy, decorative obi as a mundane "belt" or "girdle." But unfastening or loosening the obi cords is by no means the equivalent of making oneself comfortable. As in the *obi-hiki* (scenes of sexual violence in the Kabuki), it is a prelude to intimate sexual encounter. The mechanics of the Japanese kimono, with its elaborate system of sashes, undergarments, and fasteners, make it impossible to suggest a Western equivalent. It is rather as though unfastening a blouse button in a Western novel immediately suggested a rapid-sequence striptease followed by immediate intercourse. Loosening the obi is more subtle both in form and implication. Similarly, plucking the sleeve is not mere commonplace importuning in the Japanese context: it is a specifically erotic invitation.

Of course, Japanese wordplay and symbolic gestures are not always erotic. As with the seasonal symbols already noted, the hints may be clues to feelings of sadness, to Buddhist belief, or even to death. The number four in one reading is *shi*, a homophone for death. Thus the visitor to hospitals and the comforter of invalids must meticulously avoid the local equivalent of thirteen. Japanese readers receive ominous hints from four objects. They find a different meaning from ours in the color white—a symbol not of virgin purity but of death. The blue of Mishima's *Ao no Jidai* (1950) is not that of blue movies. Nor does the supposed link with Picasso's Blue Period inform the English-speaking reader that the novel focuses on a group of university students and that their blue *(ao)* period *(jidai,* also read as "age") is also a reference to youth.

Such points can be annotated. But Japanese syntax often defies translation. The translator must sometimes add details, while at other times he or she is forced to be specific when the Japanese writer has deliberately only hinted at meaning. Tanizaki thought that writers should exploit the various aspects of the Japanese language—he developed his theory in fictions that are exercises in ambiguity. At the same time, he often inserted specific details of clothes, medicines, or meals, providing Japanese readers with clues to action, mood, and meaning—details that often disappear from translations.[17]

Another element that is lost in translation is the Japanese use of levels and kinds of language. In his *Snow Country*, for instance, Kawabata makes use of the customary Japanese distinctions between masculine and feminine speech—and these are essential to our understanding of the relationships of Komako, Shimamura, and Yōko. Writers also exploit regional differences in language, such as the contrasts between

---

[17] A case in point is that of the meal of trout and salad referred to earlier. In *Some Prefer Nettles* (*Tade Kuu Mushi*, 1928–1929), the doll-like Ohisa is developed as the epitome of traditional Kyoto womanhood. At the novel's end, she serves esoteric Kyoto specialties, dishes that Tanizaki carefully names (such as *waka ayu no shioyaki* and *gobō no shira-ae*). He does not specify the regional significance (in Japan, the hint suffices). Unfortunately, the translator's "baked trout" and "salad," while partially identifying the ingredients, give the false impression that Ohisa has become westernized after all. Moreover, the gourmet specialty is reduced to the commonplace—as though crêpes suzettes had been rendered as "hot cakes and syrup." A more fundamental problem is the Japanese failure to distinguish singular from plural or definite from indefinite. Thus Kawabata's novel translated as *The House of the Sleeping Beauties* has a title with a wider—and more subtle—range of meanings for the Japanese reader in the ideograms for *nemureru* (sleeping) *bijo* (beauty). The two characters used in writing *bijo* allude to the quality of beauty *(bi)* or grace, or sweetness, or loveliness of one woman *(jo)* or of several, of a specific woman or perhaps Woman incarnate.

The appendix to chapter 1 illustrates the problems of translation, in the versions by three eminent scholars of passages in Tanizaki's *Shisei* (Tattoo).

Osaka and Tokyo speech in Tanizaki's *Makioka Sisters*.
Other writers too have used Kyoto speech, in characterizing
a graceful geisha, for instance. And to these distinctions of
educated speech the writer can also add tricks of common
speech. The dialect of Osaka *(Osaka-ben)* is used to marvelously vulgar and comic effect in Nozaka's *Erogotoshi-tachi
(The Pornographers)*—but this effect can scarcely be approx-
imated in the translation.

Tanizaki and his contemporaries also make use of the rich
variety of levels of language used in Japanese to establish the
speaker's "rank" in relation to others and provide clues to attitude. Thus in *The Makioka Sisters* the way in which people
speak to Taeko suggests how damaging her conduct has been.
In Tanizaki's *Portrait of Shunkin*, the Japanese reader can
draw conclusions about the ambiguous relationship from
nuances in the terms that Shunkin and Sasuke use in speaking
to one another. Similarly, a modern Japanese college faculty
can be amused by a reference to the computer when the
speaker "addresses" the computer in language supposedly
reserved for an inferior speaking to his superior. Similar
subtleties permit the author to show his characters insulting
one another. And he can indicate shifts in intimacy in ways
far more subtle than the simple *Sie-du* or *vous-tu* shifts of
German and French.

In modern fiction, levels and kinds of language can expose
a character's idiosyncracies or pretensions, perhaps in the
author's use of old-fashioned or "literary" language (as in the
use of elevated language for comic effect in *I Am a Cat*). During the early years of the Meiji Era, of course, such literary
language was the only acceptable one for the novelist, and
one achievement of the modern writers was their breaking
away from this language—so radically different from spoken
Japanese.[18]

---

[18] Futabatei Shimei is given much of the credit for this break, especially
for his experiments in the incomplete *Ukigumo* (Drifting Cloud,
1887–1889; translated by Marleigh Grayer Ryan as *Japan's First Modern*

Many modern writers, however, have not broken away from the old habit of literary allusion—leaving younger Japanese readers as puzzled as their Western counterparts and continually challenging the translator. Allusiveness often begins with the title, as in the subtlety of Kawabata's *Suigetsu*, literally Water-Moon, an image carrying rich literary and even metaphysical implications.[19] Kawabata's *Chirinuruo* (1933–1934), "The leaves have fallen . . . ," is an allusion to a famous verse (a particular *waka* formed out of the Japanese syllabary). One recent biographer of Mishima declared the title *Chinsetsu Yumiharizuki* "untranslatable." Actually *Yumiharizuki* refers to the new crescent moon, which resembles a bent bow—and that image in turn is an allusion to Tametomo, renowned as an archer. Fortunately, few modern works approach the literary allusiveness of Heian times: an allusiveness that has led to centuries of scholarship and fat volumes devoted to phrases and images in *The Tale of Genji*.

Today's Western readers do not have to feel themselves unduly handicapped by these esoteric elements of the Japanese language, thought, and attitude. Yet there are a number of important cultural differences to keep in mind—ranging from standards of beauty to attitudes toward sex and suicide. The Western reader will find such contexts valuable in reading Tanizaki Jun'ichirō, a Meiji Man first published in 1910; Kawabata Yasunari, noted for his remarkable economy of

---

Novel: Ukigumo [New York: Columbia University Press, 1967]), a novel that should not be confused with the later *Ukigumo* (1949–1951) of Hayashi Fumiko, translated as *Floating Clouds*. Futabatei Shimei moved away from the earlier preference for aristocratic and military heroes and created the prototypical antihero of New Japan, the timid and ineffectual Utsumi Bunzō. Another landmark in the move away from traditional style, subject, and language was Tayama Katai's 1907 novel *Futon* (*futon:* quilts—traditional Japanese bed and bedding), a work that is also sometimes identified as the prototype of the Japanese I-novel.

[19] See Gwenn R. Boardman, "Kawabata Yasunari: A Critical Introduction," *Journal of Modern Literature* 2(1971):86–104.

words, whose forty-year literary career culminated in a Nobel Prize; and Mishima Yukio, whose work did not appear until the end of the Second World War.

These three writers demonstrate the full range of Japanese tradition—from "noble" violence to the delicacy of Japanese aesthetics, as well as the paradoxes of crude colors appearing in a world of subtly discriminated scents and sounds, of haiku poetic theory applied to Freudian practice, and of Western evils shadowing a serene world of Buddhist thought. These pages of "Contexts" can unfortunately only hint at some of the names moving through the Japanese landscape and provide some helpful markers. For more detailed guidance the reader exploring this landscape can turn to some of the studies suggested in my footnotes—for example, Miyoshi on the Japanese language, Keene discussing Dazai, McClellan's study of Sōseki, and Morris describing the long-ago world of the Shining Prince.

Ideally, readers would approach Kawabata, Mishima, and Tanizaki only through the Japanese language. For those who cannot do so, there is some consolation in the fact that most Japanese commentators were as puzzled as their Western counterparts when they tried to interpret Mishima's death. Their confusion came not from an inability to read Mishima's words but from ignorance of the *contexts* in which his words and actions should be understood. And even in translation the careful reader can find the clues provided by Mishima's cultural heritage and personal aesthetic. Mishima might seem to be just one more Japanese writer incongruously seeking Western inspiration when he made a bizarre suggestion that a body-building "ethic" and Greek perfection could replace the lost samurai code, or developed a theory of "actionism" through a private army costumed in Ruritanian splendor. But in making his ultimate gesture of heroic death, *seppuku*, Mishima was reconciling personal aesthetic and ancient ideal—fusing art and life with a perfection that can only be appreciated in terms of his intensely Japanese contexts.

APPENDIX

The difficulties of arriving at a satisfactory English version of a Japanese text may be judged from the following paragraphs. These three excerpts from Tanizaki's *Shisei* are from translations by Howard Hibbett,[20] Matsumoto Ryōzō,[21] and Ivan Morris.[22]

First, the description of the tattooer's first face-to-face meeting with the girl of the beautiful foot:

> Seikichi's long-held desire turned into passionate love. One morning late the next spring he was standing on the bamboo-floored veranda of his home in Fukagawa, gazing at a pot of *omoto* lilies, when he heard someone at the garden gate. Around the corner of the inner fence appeared a young girl. She had come on an errand for a friend of his, a geisha of the nearby Tatsumi quarter. [Hibbett]

> One morning in the late spring of the fifth year of his quest, as toothbrush in mouth, he was inspecting his *omoto (Rhodea japonica)* in a pot on the open bamboo verandah of his small house at Sagachō in Fukagawa, a girl he had never seen before came in through the rear wicket of the garden. Passing by the screen-fence attached to the house, she walked up to him. She was a messenger from a singer at the Tatsumi-house which Seikichi frequented. [Matsumoto]

> One morning a year later Seikichi received a visit at his house in the Fukagawa district. It was a young girl sent on an errand by a friend of his, a certain geisha from the Tatsumi quarter. [Morris]

[20] From *Seven Japanese Tales*, by Tanizaki Jun'ichirō, translated by Howard Hibbett, pp. 163, 168, and 169. Copyright © 1963 by Alfred A. Knopf, Inc. Reprinted with permission of Alfred A. Knopf, Inc.

[21] From *Japanese Literature New and Old*, by Matsumoto Ryōzō (Tokyo: Hokuseidō Press, 1961), pp. 110, 115, and 116–117. Reprinted with permission of the publisher.

[22] From *Modern Japanese Stories*, edited by Ivan Morris (Tokyo: Tuttle, 1962), pp. 87, 90, and 91. Reprinted with permission of the publisher.

Second, the tattoo is completed:

In the full light of the spring dawn boats were being rowed up and down the river, their oars creaking in the morning quiet; roof tiles glistened in the sun, and the haze began to thin out over white sails swelling in the early breeze. Finally Seikichi put down his brush and looked at the tattooed spider. This work of art had been the supreme effort of his life. Now that he had finished it his heart was drained of emotion. [Hibbett]

Soon, the spring morning dawned; more and more barges were afloat on the water, their sculls grinding noisily and their white sails swelling before a fair wind in the dispersing fog, while the roof-tiles of the houses over the wide area of Nakasu, Hakozaki and Reiganjima glistened in the sun. Seikichi laid down his paintbrush and looked at the spider [identified as a *jorō-gumo*, a courtesan spider, in the preceding paragraph]. It was indeed his life and soul. Having finished it, he felt as empty as a shell. [Matsumoto]

The spring night was almost over. Already one could hear the dip of the oars as the rowboats passed up and down the river; above the sails of the fishing smacks, swollen with the morning breeze, one could see the mists lifting. And at last Seikichi brought himself to put down his needle. Standing aside, he studied the enormous spider tattooed on the girl's back, and as he gazed at it, he realized that in this work he had expressed the essence of his whole life. Now that it was completed, the artist was aware of a great emptiness. [Morris]

And third, the girl comes from the color-intensifying bath:

As she left the tub, too weak to dry herself, the girl pushed aside the sympathetic hand Seikichi offered her, and sank to the floor in agony, moaning as if in a nightmare. Her disheveled hair hung over her face in a wild tangle. The white soles of her feet were reflected in the mirror behind her. [Hibbett]

Getting out of the bath, the girl pushed Seikichi away when he tried to help her. Instead of drying herself, she threw herself on the bath-room floor, groaning as though crushed under a giant burden. Her disheveled hair fell over her flushed cheeks in hideous confusion. Behind her was a mirror stand reflecting the white soles of her feet. [Matsumoto]

But when she stepped out of the bath, she did not even have the strength to dry herself. She pushed aside Seikichi's helping hand and collapsed on the floor. Groaning, she lay with her long hair flowing across the floor. The mirror behind her reflected the soles of two feet, iridescent as mother-of-pearl. [Morris]

2
Tanizaki Jun'ichirō

*T*anizaki Jun'ichirō's career spans the full age of contemporary Japanese literature, from Meiji through Taishō and into our own Shōwa period. He was born in 1886, the year after publication of *The Essence of the Novel,* and his earliest work was appearing in little magazines beside other tales that have become landmarks of Japanese fiction. He has been linked, tenuously and often incorrectly, with many of the period's literary developments and claimed by many of its "schools." Japanese critics have carefully identified his "satanic" elements, for example. They point to his I-novels (ignoring Tanizaki's own aesthetic attack on the genre). They admire examples of "love-talk" literature, though apparently disturbed by his supposed worship of women. Yet Tanizaki should not be confined by such labels and categories.

Fifty Years of Meiji Man

The range of Tanizaki's work does embrace most of the fashions of the time, including the writing of historical novels. But that is only one aspect of his varied work. He also shows the traditional qualities of Japanese literature, such as literary allusion and poetic ambiguity. Even his titles offer hints of multiple and ambiguous meanings. Or they exploit the characteristics of the Japanese language in ways that frequently serve as ironic commentary on the ensuing narrative.[1] Yet Tanizaki's work does not fit neatly into any of the categories or sources. Nor can it be accounted for by other widely accepted clichés.

Tanizaki's work is often said to reflect his moving from Tokyo to the Kansai after the Great Kantō Earthquake of 1923. According to various commentators, this geographical change is linked with alleged changes in style, attitude, and themes. Tanizaki's change of domicile is even linked with "evidence" of an "East-West conflict" or with some sort of changed allegiance from "modern" Tokyo to "conservative" Kansai. Close reading of Tanizaki's works, however, will show that the move to "traditional" Kansai was neither so lengthy nor so influential as has been claimed. As he wrote: "The tryst [his 1923 move to Kyoto] was brief. I was back in Tokyo shortly afterwards."[2]

---

[1] *Sasameyuki* (1943–1948) is the Japanese title of *The Makioka Sisters.* *Sasame-yuki* is a term for dampish, thin snow *(yuki)*—hinting at the ambiguities of the central character, Yukiko. Another term for thin snow, *usuyuki,* is traditionally symbolic of evanescence. Thus the title may also refer to the "thinning" of the old culture, the warmth of the Ashiya climate, or even beautiful Yukiko's nature. The poetic ambiguities of *Ashikari* (1932) defeated the translators of that story. But the Japanese reader recognizes an allusion to a Nō drama and various homophones. *Ashi-kari* is literally reed-cutting, but the more usual term for cutting (*kiri—kari* is used only for cutting grasses) has a homophone reading "mist," especially appropriate for the misty many-layered narrative. The stories translated as "The Thief," *Some Prefer Nettles,* and "The Bridge of Dreams" are additional examples of titles that are many-faceted in Japanese.

[2] In "Kyoto: Her Nature, Food . . . and Women," *This Is Japan* 12(1965):222–225. It is true that Tanizaki lived both in Kyoto and later (with his third wife) in Okamoto, between Osaka and Kobe. His complaints against Kyoto, however, were concerned with the climate, not with the inhabitants, and the balanced tone so characteristic of Tanizaki's fiction is evident in his other essays on Tokyo, Osaka, and Kyoto alike—including the untranslated essays *Watakushi no mita Ōsaka oyobi Ōsakajin*

Interpretations of a Tokyo-Kansai dichotomy oversimplify widespread Japanese attitudes toward these two areas, and the foreign reader needs some assistance in interpreting the statements of native Osakans and Tokyoites as well as the fictional manifestations of supposed differences of attitude and temperament. The Osaka dialect *(Osaka-ben)* will always produce the same kind of hilarity that Brooklynese can provoke in the United States. On the other hand, Osaka has been a center of Japanese commerce for more than three hundred years (even during the centuries when Tokyo was the feudalistic military seat of government). This is not the place for an extensive discussion of such differences, but the reader unacquainted with Japan must recognize that any reference to Osaka-Tokyo "contrasts" is as fraught with subjective interpretation as American clichés about North and South or English stereotypes of Home Counties and Midlands idiosyncracies.

Among foreign writers there is a further tendency to interpret Osaka-Tokyo contrasts as synonymous with Kansai-Tokyo. The Kansai area, however, encompasses not only commerical Osaka but also the old Imperial capital of Kyoto and international Kobe (now Japan's busiest port). In modern Japanese fiction, we often find Tokyo contrasted with "conservative" Kansai, too. We also find statements about money being a favorite topic of Osakans—perhaps resulting from attitudes developed when Tokyo was a city of samurai. Three centuries ago, Chikamatsu's puppet plays revealed the

---

(Osaka and the Osakans I Know, 1932). Osakans are "frugal" in comparison with Tokyo extravagance in *Portrait of Shunkin*. They speak to strangers with "free and easy manners" quite different from Tokyo formality in *Ashikari.* Yet at other times "formality" becomes a praiseworthy "reserve," while Osakan "openness" appears as a tactless way of "pushing one's own ends" in *Some Prefer Nettles.* Moreover, commentators on Tanizaki's attitudes often fail to distinguish between the opinions expressed in his own voice on various occasions and those that are closely tied to demands of fictional characterization.

tragedies of Osakan businessmen ruined by their expensive pursuit of courtesans. Today the Tokyo businessman can spend a fortune wooing "hostesses" (though these are usually on his expense account). And Osaka and Tokyo are now the twin commerical giants of Japan.[3]

The Kansai dialect—in contrast to the rough *Osaka-ben* —is a soft, "feminine" language, of which Tanizaki has made excellent use in delineating character. In his essay on Kyoto he described a "Kyoto type" of woman: "softer, more elegant, warmer than Tokyo's" and with a beauty that is "a product of art, tradition, elegance, and sophistication."[4] She is the elegant figure seen at her best in kimono. Today she is still somewhat more conservative than her Tokyo cousin in adopting Western fashions. In contrast, the "Tokyo type" would be the girl adopting French-made *midis* at a time when the average American woman still looked at such fashions askance.

Tanizaki's fiction, however, is constricted neither by fashions nor by clichés. The maturity of style and theme so often linked with Tanizaki's Kansai residence can be shown as a qualitative development from his earliest work, with its fine understanding of paradoxical human behavior. At the same time, his early work foreshadows attitudes and even specific characters found in his novels more than twenty years later. Close examination of *Some Prefer Nettles* (*Tade Kuu Mushi*, 1928–1929), the novel usually identified as marking the new (Kansai) Tanizaki, will reveal attitudes and techniques found even in his "demonic" tales.

The facts of Japanese history have made it difficult to express unqualified judgments about any writer's progress—the

---

[3] Tanizaki's own background was that of Tokyo's commerce rather than government, although accounts differ as to whether his family were printers or rice brokers. In writing of his mother and grandmother, Tanizaki clearly links them with "Old Edo."

[4] Tanizaki's delight was not confined to this elegance, however, as his remarks on the jolly custom of *zakone* indicate (see note 21).

years of censorship imposed limitations no one could escape. During the 1930s and the war years, hampered by politico-social restraints, Tanizaki like other writers produced a number of historical novels and tales, including *A Blind Man's Tale* (*Mōmoku Monogatari*, 1931), *Ashikari* (*Ashikari*, 1932), and *A Portrait of Shunkin* (*Shunkinshō*, 1933). He began the difficult work of translating Lady Murasaki's *Tale of Genji* into modern Japanese (1936–1941). Throughout the war, Tanizaki worked on his twentieth-century equivalent of a Heian chronicle, too: *The Makioka Sisters*. And when publication of this novel of contemporary life in the Kansai was halted as "not in the national interest," Tanizaki published part of *Sasameyuki* himself.

Tanizaki's work was later rewarded with the Asahi Culture Prize for Literature and the Imperial Cultural Medal (1949). This might seem to mark the end of his "historical" period, culminating with *Shōshō Shigemoto no Haha* (partially translated as "The Mother of Captain Shigemoto," 1949–1950). Yet it should be remembered that Tanizaki's apparent participation in a fashion for historical narrative is also a manifestation of his very earliest interests. He studied Japanese literature at the Imperial University; his first published work, the play *Tanjō* (Birth, 1910), was historical; and he used period settings for many other stories and plays. Among the works not translated are *Zō* (Elephant, 1910), with an Edo setting; *Hosshōji Monogatari* (Story of Hosshō Temple, 1915), with a Heian setting; and *Okuni to Gohei* (Okuni and Gohei, 1922), set in the Tokugawa period.

Nor do Tanizaki's "historical" works display a quasi-romantic yearning for the vanished past. As in *A Blind Man's Tale*, he shows a fine sense of historical perspective, and he demonstrates his interest in the vagaries of human behavior, especially (as in *The Makioka Sisters*) in the complexities of love and marriage. This psychological perception also distinguishes Tanizaki from other writers with whom he is linked

as one of the "love-talk school." In particular, Tanizaki's frequently ironic tone and his universal appeal cannot be over-
emphasized both in evaluating Japanese views of Tanizaki's
"worship" of women and in comparing his use of autobiographical material with the undiscriminating confessions of
the I-novelists.[5]

Critics have busily identified specific illnesses and partial
self-portraits in Tanizaki's work, claiming *Itansha no Kanashimi* (Sorrows of a Heretic, 1917) and a number of other
stories for the I-novel genre. Yet in all essential points, Tanizaki's fictions are quite different from the I-novels. Where
such works include relevant and irrelevant material alike,
and simply record events and feelings (often in sentimental
tones), Tanizaki's work is carefully plotted and has the essential qualities of distillation and organization of experience.[6]

In Tanizaki's fictions, events may be foreshadowed in inci-

----

[5] Etō Jun is a representative modern Japanese critic, and a number of his
essays are available in English. Nakamura Mitsuo comments on Tanizaki's
"worship" of women and even declares that Tanizaki regarded men as
manure for nurturing women's beauty (Nakamura's *Modern Japanese Literature*, pt. 2, p. 13 and *passim*). Nakamura's critique also identifies as
"the epitome of aestheticism" in Tanizaki's work the episode in *Akuma*
(Demon, 1912) in which the lover licks the woman's dirty handkerchief.
Discussions of the early "aesthetic" and "satanic" Tanizaki, however,
tend to ignore the consistency of theme and characteristic devices to be
found in his earliest as in his last works.

[6] Tanizaki's own experiences are nicely reworked, as in the incidents re-
called from teaching in a friend's home (used in *Shindō*) or the way in
which the medicines he required in old age provided Tanizaki with amusing properties for *The Diary of a Mad Old Man*. Comments on Tanizaki's
view of women are frequently illustrated with "parallel" anecdotes from
his life—for instance, the much-quoted anecdote of Tanizaki acting as go-
between for his own wife. Seidensticker in the introduction to his translation of *Some Prefer Nettles* tells of Tanizaki turning to the novelist Satō
Haruo and asking: "How would you like to marry Ochiyo?" Other versions, differing only in minor details, were long-time favorites of Tokyo literary gossip.

dents as slight as a delayed train and meaning may be gauged by a letter-writer's choice of paper or by *kanji* written with a fountain pen instead of with elegant brush strokes. Moreover, as a master of point of view and multiplicity of meaning, Tanizaki does not play the intrusive author. Unlike the aphoristic Mishima, insisting on commenting on the action, Tanizaki employs many artful dodges to separate himself from the reader—as in the ambiguous perspectives of *Portrait of Shunkin* or the mist-shrouded narrative of *Ashikari.*

It is admittedly difficult for the reader who does not know Japanese to evaluate Tanizaki's work properly and compare him with his contemporaries. Nakamura's comments on Tanizaki's "aestheticism," for instance, serve as reminders of the many works not available in translation. The foreign reader cannot even make such a commonplace comparison of studies of women as Chikamatsu Shūkō's *Kurokami* (Black Hair, 1922) might afford. Nevertheless, Tanizaki's works available in English do offer a representative sample of his writing. Although the Nobel Prize Committee felt that too little of his work was available in translation in 1960, when his name had been mentioned for the award in literature, the situation had been largely remedied by the time of his death in 1965. Today a score of his novels, short stories, essays, and plays are available in English and various European languages.

From these works, we can see that *The Key* (*Kagi*, 1956) and *The Diary of a Mad Old Man* (*Fūten Rōjin Nikki*, 1961–1962) are both reminiscent of the earlier *Some Prefer Nettles.* Both also include details that might have appeared at the start of his career in "Tattoo" or during his "historical" period in *Portrait of Shunkin.* Both show that discrimination in theme and attitude which early marked Tanizaki out from his contemporaries, as well as his awareness of the sociopsychological problems of the modern world and the traditions and values of his Japanese heritage. Yet the more we examine Tanizaki's supposed debts either to this heritage or to various

European and American fashions, the more we become
aware of the unique qualities of Tanizaki Jun'ichirō's own
voice.

In 1911 Nagai Kafū wrote an appreciative essay on
"Tanizaki Jun'ichirō's Works."[7] This early critique in *Mita
Bungaku* included a comparison of Tanizaki with Anatole
France. Other Japanese criticism has at various times praised
Tanizaki as "Wildean," compared his work with that of
Baudelaire, and commented on his "coloring of Poe." All
these links, however, are no more than the tenuous relationships already noted in the works of so many Meiji writers and
their successors. Random identifications of Tanizaki with
neo-romantics, satanists, or aesthetes are similarly misleading oversimplifications.

Tanizaki's indebtedness might as readily be found in such
Japanese classics as the Heian *Tale of Genji*; the fourteenth-
century Chronicles; the eleventh-century *Konjaku Monogatari* or the later compilation of Tales from the Uji Collection
(some tales are found in both collections); and the fourteenth-
century *Masukagami* (Mirror of Clarity or Increase) and the
Ōkagami (Great Mirror). Anyone looking at *The Tale of
Genji*, for example, will soon recognize that the Japanese of
Heian times had a very fine visual and olfactory sense more
than eight centuries before Poe began to write, though applied in rather different ways (in appreciation of clothes of
many-colored opaque layers, for example, and of *kōdō*, the
art of incense "listening"). Proustian evocations—as of

[7] Born in 1879 but sufficiently well established to be a discoverer-
mentor of Tanizaki, Kafū later occasionally found himself the target of his
protégé's criticism. After publication of Kafū's *Tsuyu no Atosaki* (Beginning and End of the Rainy Season, 1931), Tanizaki (whose own Collected
Works had appeared in 1930) attacked Kafū for handling characters as
though he were a puppeteer manipulating dolls. Tanizaki makes amusing
reference to his friend in *Diary of a Mad Old Man*, where the old man
quotes a Chinese verse by Kafū and adds: "Kafū has always been one of my
favorite novelists, though his calligraphy and his Chinese poetry leave
something to be desired."

childhood crickets, occasioned by the sweet-sour smell of
starch in one Tanizaki story—have their true antecedents not
in a European model but in the allusive technique of *renga*
(linked verse).

A pair of stories from the beginning and end of Tanizaki's
career should illuminate these points. Although the short
story "Tattoo" (*Shisei*, 1910) and the novel *Diary of a Mad
Old Man* (*Fūten Rōjin Nikki*, 1961–1962) were written fifty
years apart, both can introduce the reader to Tanizaki's
recurrent themes, to his characteristic tone, and to his very
sensitive use of the Japanese language (especially his use of
Japanese "vagueness" to reinforce ambiguities of word, gesture, and action).

In both these stories, three themes are clear—and all three
recur throughout the entire Tanizaki canon, including his
stories, plays, and essays. One is the aesthetic theme: an interest not only in the relationship of art and reality but in the
qualities of perception itself. A second is the significance of
gesture: not examining gesture and meaning in the sensational terms of Mishima's *Confessions of a Mask* but using
nuances of daughter-in-law Satsuko's approach to a piece of
fish (in *Diary*), or the way the girl stumbles from the tattooer's bath, to hint at the character's intention. Such clues
are designed to prod the reader into making his or her own
interpretation, rather than being instructed by an intrusive
author. The third theme might be described as values: Tanizaki's interest in social and philosophical perspectives,
hinted in his context of psychologically ambiguous word and
gesture.

"Tattoo" focuses on Seikichi, a man noted for his voluptuous tattoos, who rather enjoys the groans of pain that accompany the flow of blood from his needle-pricks. Hence the
comparison with Poe. But Tanizaki carefully recreates a
world in which the norm was the pursuit of beauty—at a
time when courtesans were roused by the beauty of the tat-

toos decorating an admirer's body. Then—as Tanizaki stresses in his narrator's opening paragraphs—a client would willingly endure the agonies of a scalding hot bath to bring out the richness of the prized demitint work and cinnabar shades that were also "most painful to administer."

Into Tanizaki's finely drawn world of exotic color and experience steps a white foot: a bare, delicate foot peeping from beneath a palanquin curtain and suggesting to the tattooer the spirit of Woman "stepping" on men. This is the beauty and this the spirit he has sought for his "perfect subject." He follows the palanquin but loses sight of it. Five years later a messenger comes from a nearby geisha. Apparently only about seventeen years old even now, this messenger is the Woman of the Foot.

Yet he does not immediately tell her of their earlier encounter. First he tests her spirit by showing her two picture scrolls—both of female onlookers or instigators of the tortures of men (Chinese tortures, including such refinements as binding to fire-filled copper pillars, and so on). Tanizaki again carefully distinguishes the quality of the painted scenes: the first, for instance, inspires a sense of mystery rather than the "coarse feelings" one might expect, while the second ambiguously suggests both a spring flower garden and the terrors of battle.[8] Here the girl's face is reflected, and here too is a glimpse of her innermost self.

Drugged by Seikichi, the girl lies asleep while he creates his masterpiece. Tanizaki renders both the scene and the passage of time with Japanese poetic sensibility. Sunlight reflected from the river beyond the windows bathes the sliding screens and the body of the girl in golden ripples, and as Seikichi "paints" upon the "canvas" of the girl's back, the spring sky darkens, the moon rises beyond a distant mansion,

---

[8] This ambiguous suggestion is rooted in Japanese tradition, including the already-noted comparison of the samurai and the cherry blossom.

and he works on by the light of a candle. As the spring morning dawns, Seikichi looks down on the completed spider that
sprawls on the girl's back, "embracing" her. Tanizaki has
already described the flowing of the tattooer's "spirit"
through his colors into the girl's body. Now Seikichi feels
quite empty.[9]

As the girl returns to consciousness, the tattooed spider
seems to writhe with her body's movements. It is now time
for the color-intensifying bath. Already her dreamy voice has
a note of menace. She drives Seikichi from her, not wanting a
man to see her suffer; and Tanizaki renders her transformation in terms of coloring cheeks and disheveled hair. She
groans as though burdened.[10] The mirror stand meanwhile
reflects the soles of those white feet that had first inspired
Seikichi.

"Tattoo" ends with Seikichi gazing at the transformed girl
(now suitably calm and combed). Looking at the scroll titled
"Victims," she comments that Seikichi is her first victim. He
responds to her triumphant voice with a request that she let
him see the tattoo once more. She uncovers her back, and the
reader's final view of the scene is the dazzling picture of the
sun reflected from her shining skin. This fire image may remind us of the infernal flames of Akutagawa's "Hell Screen"
(another story with a system of thought and aesthetics different from our own).

To link such a story as "Tattoo" with *Diary of a Mad Old
Man* might at first seem perverse. Yet the similarities help the
reader perceive not only the essential unity of all Tanizaki's
work but also the subtleties frequently lost in translation (as
in the erotic connotations of the *spring* day on which the tat-

---

[9] "Emptiness" is another quality with different meanings in Japan from
those we are familiar with in the West. Rather than suggesting "drained of
emotion" or "exhausted" in our terms, Emptiness may (like Buddhist
"Mindlessness") be linked with philosophical Enlightenment.

[10] Both Western translators of "Tattoo" offer a rather disappointing version of this passage: see appendix to chapter 1.

tooer creates his spider, the *coloring* of the girl's cheeks, and
the tattooer's feelings as he injects his *colors* into her body).
The central characters of both stories are Artists with a
Dream, although the diarist's dream might at first appear to
be only the ambition of a lecherous old man.

The major part of the *Diary of a Mad Old Man* is the
record of Utsugi Tokusuke, seventy-seven years old. There is
also a multifaceted postscript, his nurse's report, Dr. Kat-
sumi's clinical record, and a note written by Utsugi's
daughter-in-law—three perspectives for ambiguous interpretations of the supposedly final deterioration that is foreshadowed in the closing passages of the old man's own report.

Utsugi himself reports in a matter-of-fact tone that adds
ironic commentary to his extraordinary narrative.[11] In telling
of his relationship with his ex-chorusgirl daughter-in-law Satsuko, with his own daughter, with his wife, and with his son,
Utsugi's character gradually emerges. He fancies the Japanese past—delicate Kyoto dishes, the exquisite femininity of
Kabuki *onnagata* (men who play women's roles and are said
to distill the very essence of feminine nature), and his
daughter-in-law's feet. He scorns his own children, knows
nothing of his son, despises his wife, and showers the
daughter-in-law with gifts. He is also ailing, partially crip-
pled, and tended by a nurse.

The narrative traces the adventures of Utsugi in pursuit of

---

[11] In the course of this narrative, the reader observes the old man favor-
ing his daughter-in-law: giving her a three-million-yen tiger-eye ring, for
instance, although he refuses to give his daughter as much as twenty thousand yen (less than sixty dollars) for a desperately needed house payment.
These glimpses hint at the reliability of later passages in the daughter's
final account of her father: the reader should ask some questions about the
figure in the garden she describes. (She shows Utsugi sufficiently recovered
to be up and about, as Satsuko leads him by the hand, and dutiful son
Jōkichi declares that they should humor the old man in the matter of his
swimming pool.) Tanizaki's use of multiple points of view and unreliable
narrators in this novel can be compared with many other examples in his
work.

his dream—this artful daughter-in-law who "innocently" entices the old man as he in turn supplies her with an imported purse, a foreign car, an expensive ring, and even, he proposes, a swimming pool in which she may twinkle those tempting little toes. It is not precisely the "dew of woman" of long-ago literature that Utsugi seeks. Nor does he seem unduly troubled when Satsuko makes clear to him that she is sleeping with his nephew. Utsugi's lure to hell, like that of the tattooer, is a delicate white foot.

Like Seikichi, Utsugi is also attracted by cruel faces, even those of foreign film stars. He, too, has his art: in a remarkably funny scene he frantically dashes about his Kyoto hotel room while attempting to make footprints of the girl. These rubbings are made with meticulous fidelity to tradition—on fine paper, with special ink, using carefully prepared tools—as a first step toward the remarkable grave marker he plans. Utsugi in death will have Satsuko's pretty feet "stepping on his departed spirit" in place of a carved Bodhisattva, Kannon, or Seishi.

On the way to this final enlightenment, however, Utsugi suffers for his art. The reader is spared none of the old man's physical problems: pain, swelling, a stroke, the number of his bowel movements, his rising blood pressure. These ailments are balanced by his amatory progression—a progression always encouraged by the daughter-in-law (a point to be kept in mind later in evaluating her protests about the "horrid" foot-rubbings incident).

This balance is typical of Tanizaki's characteristically ironic tone, which distinguishes Tanizaki's psychologically valid studies from those of his poetic contemporary Kawabata. Yet because Tanizaki maintains a careful balance in his presentation, the reader invariably is persuaded to respond with sympathy as well as laughter to even the most grotesque of the old man's postures. This is the human comedy of Shakespeare acted by a Japanese cast.

Utsugi plays many parts, especially to gain more favors

from Satsuko.[12] At one level, this offers the humor of appearance belying the reality of meaning. At another, it reveals
Utsugi as a man of confused values. His fancy for Satsuko—
whom he sees with a travesty of the artist's eye, perhaps—
blinds him to the meaning of both her actions and his own.
His visions of his own puny work of art as a latter-day "Buddha's Footprints" are simultaneously pathetic and absurd.

Perverted artist Utsugi nevertheless enjoys his image of
Satsuko while he gradually approaches his own version of
reality. Like a Renaissance lover advancing from physical to
divine Beauty, Utsugi at first enjoys only hints of the lady's
eventual condescension—and since this drama is, after all,
Japanese, the first sign of her favor comes when Satsuko offers to share a dish of *hamo* (sea eel). Later she offers bare
toes for him to see and touch—a seemingly Western piece of
coquetry that nevertheless might well have been drawn from
Japan's geisha tradition.[13] Her thinly veiled invitations to the

---

[12] Tanizaki leaves the reader to discover the boundaries of Utsugi's art
and philosophy, to appreciate fully both the man and the role-player. For
instance, Utsugi's diary is dotted with reflections on death, on Buddhist
sects, on Old and New Japan—Tanizaki's artful way of showing the old
man's preoccupation with form. The nature of Utsugi's art must also be interpreted through such hints as his nostalgia for "The Moon at Dawn."
Rather than being a moment of poetic *aware,* this leads Utsugi to visualize
his own plump and repulsive face framed by his coffin. Of course, the
irony of his ambition is heightened in the Japanese context (for those, that
is, who recognize the customary deeply philosophical associations of
"footsteps of the Buddha").

[13] As already noted, the foot is one of the traditional nine points of feminine beauty in Japan. Its poetic associations are hinted at in "Tattoo,"
where Seikichi sees the girl's lovely toes as "shells on the shore of Eno-
shima." As we are reminded in *Some Prefer Nettles*, the geisha might
please her customers with her delicately perfumed feet. Lovers in contemplation of a lady's lovely foot appear in a number of Tanizaki's stories. In
Portrait of Shunkin, Sasuke recalls Shunkin's dainty foot as it nestled in his
palm, "its heel so soft and smooth"; he regularly clasped Shunkin's feet to
his bosom. Similarly, Oshizu's devotion to her sister in *Ashikari* is symbolized in part by her willingness to act as personal foot-warmer.

bath are followed by permission to kiss her leg. That leg extended from behind a shower curtain becomes as great a lure for Utsugi as any vision of the Pure Land. Enhancing her elegant foot with a high-heeled sandal at one point, letting Utsugi run his tongue along her shower-wet calf and instep at another, Satsuko teases the old man along with various "special privileges,"[14] until his diary ends with the ultimate sacrifice (his health for a footprint) and the ambiguous postscripts noted above.

In both *Diary of a Mad Old Man* and "Tattoo," Tanizaki tells more about his characters than he is willing to state directly. Often this revelation is as indirect as the implications of a choice of medicine or the preference for a particular dish. Often, too, the mundane detail must be balanced against some poetic ideal—as in Utsugi's romantic pursuit of Beauty and his very unromantic route. In "Tattoo," at the moment of meeting Beauty incarnate Seikichi is not simply looking at a pot of *omoto (Rhodea japonica)*. "Gazing at lilies" in one translation suggests an epiphany that is quite different from Tanizaki's intention. At that "romantic" moment, in fact, Seikichi has his toothbrush in his mouth—a detail unfortunately omitted by the two Western translators.

The house across the river in "Tattoo" is illuminated by the moonlight of many poetic associations; but this

---

[14] Although Satsuko tells Utsugi that his kisses remind her of a garden slug, the privileges she grants include a necking session in exchange for the three-million-yen ring. Perhaps events in the bathroom require a further footnote for Western readers. It is true that the scenes of foot-loving are set in a Western bathroom, one of Utsugi's "improvements." Satsuko's conduct, however, must also be measured according to the Japanese tradition in which women are quite accustomed to assisting sons and husbands (and not just lovers) in the bath. But Satsuko progresses from a surrogate sicknurse-wife (who "never comes round in front" when she dries the old invalid after his bath) to a relationship indicated when her leg emerges from the cover of a shower curtain in a hint of the days when she had performed in the Nichigeki Revue.

ephemeral rooftop belongs to the mansion of the Lord of Jōshū. Rather than being an undercutting of the poetic and aesthetic tradition, as such fragments of "reality" are in Mishima's work, in Tanizaki's they are essential aspects of his aesthetic of harmony. Just as pain and cruelty are close to beauty, and as hate is akin to love, so the mundane is never far from the poetic. This once again shows Tanizaki's insistence (as in *In'ei Raisan:* "In Praise of Shadows") that "Beauty must grow from the realities of life."[15]

If sometimes the realities seem excessively detailed, the impatient reader should beware. The catalogue of the diarist's medicine cabinet, for instance, is a long way from Arnold Bennett and the pleasures of "reading the label on the bathroom shelf." The Western reader, however, is apt to miss the subliminal message imparted to his Japanese counterpart, although each product is a specific that comments on the diarist's self-view, exposing his attitude toward both himself and his world.

Other details in the two stories are similarly revealing in ways characteristic of Tanizaki's writing. Such mundane details may be used for ironic counterpoint. They may also illuminate character. Or they offer a social statement that places the characters in their world. Yet it must be remembered that even when details seem more characteristic of a naturalist's work, for instance, in Tanizaki's pages the stage is set by a master designer. It is a pity that translators often omit these details as meaningless for foreign readers or substitute details with connotations different from Tanizaki's. For Tanizaki selects even a spider as carefully as a Heian lady selected her kimono colors.

The spider of the tattooer's masterpiece has neither the

[15] This quoted sentence and another on page 68, as well as a number of words and phrases, are reprinted from Seidensticker's "adaptation" in the *Atlantic Monthly*, January 1955, pp. 141–144 (reprinted with permission).

simplicity of one translator's "great" spider nor the connotations of the other's "black widow." Tanizaki's *jorōgumo*[16] can be linked with Japanese legends of evil enchantment— the great earth spider mentioned in his essay "In Praise of Shadows" or the seven-foot "spider fiend" immortalized in the favorite Kabuki drama *Tsuchigumo* (The Ground Spider). But "courtesan spider" *(jorōgumo)* is doubly appropriate in the geisha context of the story, while also carrying hints of the Chinese way of reading the characters for courtesan as "destroyer of the castle." Thus Tanizaki underscores the power and pride of Seikichi's ideal Beauty, while subtly hinting of the imperious women in the tattooer's two Chinese scrolls.

Seemingly tiresome details of food similarly reinforce Tanizaki's artistic purpose. The narrator of *Ashikari* eats two bowls of *kitsune-udon*. To the Japanese reader these "fox noodles" are inescapably linked with enchantments (the fox frequently appears as a beautiful woman, to trap the unwary traveler, for instance); the noodles thus help to create this particular story's ambiguous, shadowy atmosphere. In *Diary of a Mad Old Man*, not only the choice of food but the way of eating it helps to define relationships and delineate character. The wife's leaving her plate as clean as though a cat had licked it and the daughter-in-law's messiness and uncouth handling of *ayu* (sweetfish) and plum sauce also hint at their profound psychological differences. These go far beyond any clichés about "past and present" or "traditional and modern."

Tanizaki is examining values here, too. He is not concerned with criticism of foreign cheese, or dogs, or dress, but

---

[16] The term *jorō* covers all classes of courtesans (and one scholar has counted more than 450 terms), from the magnificently costumed, attended, and talented *tayū* (at the top of the old hierarchy) to the cheapest prostitute. Today's geisha (a term coming into use only in the nineteenth century) continues the tradition of artistic, musical, and social accomplishment of the higher-ranking *jorō* of the past.

with the (inadequate) reasons why people follow a fashion or cling to an outworn mode. It is in this context that we read of the wife's preference for the traditional Japanese toilet and Satsuko's enthusiasm for French movies, Filipino boxers, and a Negro film star appearing in *Black Orpheus.*

One more point about "Tattoo" and *Diary of a Mad Old Man* can serve to introduce the reader to another pair of Tanizaki's stories and to his recurrent protagonist, the artist seeking Beauty.[17] Seikichi the tattooer sees the human body as his canvas, and as a former *Ukiyo-e* artist he is also described as a tattooer of uncommon sensibility. Utsugi, too, has an artist's obsession with an idea of Beauty, wishing to create Eternal Beauty with a red-inked footprint. However grotesque his plan and however amusing its details— especially that frantic pursuit of the Perfect Image of the Foot—Utsugi is clearly more driven by his illusion of Beauty than by the reality of a greedy, manipulating daughter-in-law.

In *Portrait of Shunkin (Shunkinshō,* 1933) and in *A Blind Man's Tale (Mōmoku Monogatari,* 1931), Tanizaki again examines ideas of Beauty and of Art and Reality. Here his device for examining the very essence of Seeing is the creation of blind protagonists. These two stories also display the

[17] The number of artists and would-be artists in Tanizaki's work is remarkable. Another is Kawai Jōji in *Chijin no Ai* (A Fool's Love, 1924–1925), who tries to create his Ideal out of the waitress Naomi (a woman resembling Mary Pickford). The father in "Bridge of Dreams" (*Yume no Ukihashi,* 1959) creates a second wife in the beautiful image of the first and then, as death approaches, passes on his role to his son (much as a great actor might hand on his role to a favorite pupil or as today's Kabuki actors entrust tricks of performance and specific roles to their sons). The girl in *Shōnen* (1911) is an artist in the creation of fear in her playmates. The father-in-law of *Some Prefer Nettles* attempts to create an Ideal Woman, to be manipulated as though she were a puppet and to minister to him, caring for his every need. The Beauty of these artists is usually given physical—and feminine—form and is often linked with a dream in Tanizaki's fictions.

rich sensory appeal characteristic of Tanizaki's work (and especially appropriate in the context of the perceptions of the blind). As in the two stories already discussed, we learn something about the feel of reality. At the same time, we reexamine values: the personal feeling lying behind such grand abstractions as Love, Honor, and Duty.

The sense of touch in these two stories of the blind is both a psychological perception and a metaphysical statement. Sensitivity to touch even renders the precise quality of inhumanity in the artist Shunkin. When Sasuke caresses Shunkin's skin, he feels her flesh (always warm, real flesh in Tanizaki's fictions). Sasuke's action, however, is linked with an image of Shunkin caressing the (inanimate) trunks of old plum trees, perhaps hinting at Shunkin's own inhumanity. In other stories, a girl finds pleasure in "cool, slippery fabrics" or the texture of a heavy silk robe reminds a man of the feel of his beloved's limbs.

Characters in Tanizaki's novels do not respond only through their sense of touch. They are aroused by every kind of sensory appeal: the warmth of the *futon*, the chill of an old-style theater; smells that include the scent of cloves from Ohisa's hair, a theater atmosphere redolent of "penetrating pungent mint," burning incense, chrysanthemum mosquito coils, bathwater perfumed by cloves; even Chinese garlic and the smoke of cigars. There is, too, the smell of the prostitute Louise's powder permeating Kaname's clothes and preserved in the palm of his hand as a "voluptuous secret." Nor does Tanizaki forget sounds—not just those sounds registered by the acute ears of his blind men but also the delicate click of fingernails, the ubiquitous temple bell, the ringing of a dog's chain, or the ugly sound of an old man's breathing that somehow manages to be transformed into childhood reminiscences of the cry of crickets and the comfort of a mother.

Tanizaki's sensory appeal includes color. In his essay "In Praise of Shadows," Tanizaki asserted: "We Japanese find it hard to be really at home with things that shine and glitter."

Often in his pages, colors have the muted tones of Japanese tradition. Yet in stories both early and late we find brilliant colors of sapphire gloves, a saffron *furoshiki*, an emerald-colored vase, the cinnabar inks of the tattooer and the footprint-making old diarist, and the bright kimono of the cherry-viewing Makioka sisters.

Reality and Illusion: Dream and Shadow

Portrait of Shunkin begins as an episode in the narrator's life: he seeks Shunkin's grave in the grounds of a temple of the Pure Land sect in Osaka following his acquisition of a slim volume bound in the old Japanese style. What follows is only in part a "discovered document" that might be linked with the "discovered" documents of Swift and Defoe or with the artfully fictionalized diaries of Japan's past (such as *The Tosa Diary*). The anonymous volume or *Life* is "perhaps" the work of Shunkin's devoted pupil Sasuke. And "perhaps" is the keynote of the ensuing action, just as ambiguity of all kinds is characteristic of Tanizaki's fiction.

Throughout the narrative, perceptions of truth waver. Sometimes the insight is metaphysical, sometimes psychological, sometimes aesthetic, sometimes ironic. Passages from the old volume are alternated with the narrator's interpretations and with generalizations on human nature and on the qualities of art. The narrator comments, he describes a photograph (itself ambiguous), he records scraps of conversation. We have, too, the words of an old woman who tends the graves of Shunkin and Sasuke, the strange "lovers" whose true relationship is but one aspect of the mystery; and her judgments must be qualified by the revelation that she not only helped the couple after they were both blinded but continued to take care of Sasuke during the ensuing years. Thus fact and fiction interweave as in life itself.

In such a context, to recount the plot of *Portrait of Shunkin* is obviously not going to tell what it is about. We might say that the story is "about" Shunkin, a blind woman musician, her relationship with pupil-lover-vassal Sasuke,[18] and his memories in "garrulous old age" when he lives on as a music teacher himself (for twenty-one years after her death). The relationship begins when the boy is apprenticed to a family pharmaceutical business in Osaka and is appointed to escort the recently blinded daughter of the house to her music lessons. Though always keeping a proper social distance (nicely rendered in such details as the boy's precise posture when he leads his young mistress through the streets), the boy must also perform quite intimate tasks (as in washing her hands after she comes from the toilet).

Yet the boy is no ordinary apprentice. Inspired by the beauty of the girl's playing upon koto and samisen, he saves money for an inexpensive instrument. Then he sacrifices his sleeping hours to practice.[19] Shunkin offers to become his teacher, and the family indulges this whim. The relationship becomes increasingly ambiguous. Shunkin sets up as an independent music master, taking Sasuke along as her "servant." Later, he blinds himself—apparently in response to her distress after an intruder has poured scalding water on her face. Each episode, however, is presented in terms that question its meaning, and psychological readings of this portrait would reduce Tanizaki's finely drawn meditation on perception to the level of sadomasochistic casebook.

[18] It is impossible to define the relationship. Hints of it are given in Tanizaki's use of levels of language (in Shunkin's occasional use of "Sasuke" in speaking to her "servant," for instance). But she denies their intimacy even when she becomes pregnant, and except for occasional and tantalizing hints, Tanizaki seems to stress the master-servant rather than the teacher-pupil relationship.

[19] Again there are hints of multiple meanings. We wonder why Sasuke selected the samisen, for we have been told that it takes three months to master the fundamentals of koto playing, whereas the samisen requires three years. Perhaps he chooses the samisen for the most readily apparent reason: his samisen costs less and is easier to conceal. Or perhaps he prefers the samisen because even so early in life he seeks perfect beauty by the more difficult route.

Tanizaki in fact is most careful to offer multiple interpretations even of Shunkin's "cruelty." He details the harshness of other music masters, artists, and puppeteers. But he also shows her cruelty of word and gesture toward the devoted boy, her rapacity, her lack of feeling for an impoverished blind student, and her mean-spirited behavior toward servants and students alike. Perhaps she displays tender emotion in the tears she sheds after Sasuke is blinded, but as in other episodes we see this portrait of Shunkin without ever being sure of the underlying "reality."

We are told that Sasuke found an inner vision when he became blind.[20] A priest comments that Sasuke was an example of Zen spirit making the ugly into the beautiful: "nearly the act of saint." Yet this idealized view, like other glimpses of perfection in Tanizaki's work, may as logically be read as an example of selfishness or cowardice—going to any length to pacify Shunkin and preserve his quiet life. Sasuke may be sacrificing his sight only for an illusion of the beautiful: or his action may hint at the ultimate meaning of Beauty itself.

Beauty is linked with cruelty in *Portrait*; often it seems only an illusion; it involves suffering. At the same time, ideas of beauty in *Portrait* reveal something of the role of the imagination. At various times Sasuke uses the real Shunkin before him in everyday life to call to mind the Shunkin of his memories. In his blindness he finds compensations: and the narrator hints that among them are undreamed-of ecstasies in art and love. When Sasuke could no longer *see* Shunkin, he could enjoy a finer appreciation of the softness of her body and the sound of her exquisite voice.

---

[20] This blinding is ambiguous, too. Sasuke merely suffers from cataracts in the *Life*, although the narrator's account includes quite horribly specific details of Sasuke's self-inflicted blindness, describing even the soft texture of the eyeball as he sits before a mirror and drives a needle into this sensitive spot. We might compare this action with that of a traditional Japanese hero blinding himself for love—but Sasuke's weakness, tears, and humility are scarcely marks of nobility. Moreover, in context Sasuke's feudal gesture is anachronistic, borrowed from an age that has already passed.

Blindness may not help Sasuke to see Shunkin's true nature: Tanizaki's insistence on presenting many points of view urges the reader not to expect such a single truth. But in *A Blind Man's Tale* the sightless narrator helps us to see history in a new way. All the characters of this story—except for the narrator Yaichi—are found in contemporary historical accounts of the Civil War Era and Ieyasu's great victory of 1600. History in this story, however, is rendered through the quality of a woman's flesh, the changes perceived by the blind masseur's sensitive hands.

The action of this *Tale* is drawn from the sufferings of the beautiful Lady Oichi, first torn between love for her husband, the Lord Nagamasa, and for her brother Nobunaga. Later she endures a difficult second marriage. Finally she dies in the noble-romantic tradition of the feudal world. Thus we watch the making of history through the not-so-blind eyes of a man who observes: "Maybe even great heroes in their innermost hearts are no different from ordinary men."

This narrator—masseur to samurai, entertaining them with his samisen, then sent to entertain the embattled ladies—is a wonderful device that again offers multiple perspectives on "reality." There are examples of the blind man's "sharp intuition," such homely commentaries as his views on know-it-alls, and the intimate view of history when the Lady Oichi opens her heart to her masseur, rather as her twentieth-century counterpart might confide in a favorite hairdresser. Yet only a man in his peculiar position of intimacy as blind masseur could possibly offer this common view of uncommonly heroic ideals. Thus he can comment on Lord Hisamasa's "foolish notion of duty" without forcing the reader to choose between a foolish judgment and a heroic principle.

The tone of the narrator, however, encourages the reader to accept the idea that Lord Hisamasa was really a blunderer whose lack of good judgment brought the House of Asai to ruin. Similarly, defeat can be inevitable because of Nagamasa's "filial piety" (commonly regarded as a virtue, not a handicap). Again the reader is offered both the no-nonsense response of the ordinary man like himself and the historical-heroic climate in which such piety was also a tool of familial self-preservation. The historical version accepts the necessity of Nobunaga's cruelty in killing his sister's son (heir of the dead and defeated Lord Nagamasa); the masseur qualifies the heroic convention by observing that these acts had "fearful consequences." Elsewhere he finds hints of an explanation of historical events in the personal relationships he observed within castle walls. A man's cruelty, for instance, is carefully linked with its possible source: Lady Ochana's view that he was an outcast.

A final point is worth noting. This narrator, who has seemed to hint at the weaknesses of "honor," "duty," and "filial piety" in the feudal framework, is himself a man of that feudal ethos. Because of his role in the fire in which Lady Oichi finally perished, and in spite of the clearly rendered explanation of his actions there, he feels himself "in shame and dishonor," with no function now that his lady is dead. At thirty-one, he steals away to atone by living in poverty. Now —thirty years later—he is recounting past events, begging the man he is massaging to put something down in writing. He has given the reader the benefit of his own insight: a fresh perspective on history. But we cannot forget that at the end he has also come to see the past as "an empty dream."

In other stories, too, Tanizaki presents a world of dream or of shadows. Often this shadowy quality is related to his theory of fiction, the idea that may be expressed in the words of the father-in-law in *Some Prefer Nettles:* "Isn't it better to leave things only hinted at?" This is the traditional Japanese attitude, the aesthetic finding beauty in the veiled moon, in the merest glimpse of a woman (even of her calligraphy, in *The Tale of Genji*), or in the misted landscape. It is also, of course, a manifestation of the most sophisticated twentieth-century "ambiguity of meaning."

Tanizaki's own statement on the traditional aesthetic can

be found in his "In Praise of Shadows."[21] In this essay Tanizaki meditates on the subtle darkness of old buildings and the
harsh illumination of the modern. Noting the impossibility of
building an uncompromisingly Japanese house in the modern
world, yet wanting the comfort of modern conveniences, he
inevitably discovered that the "snarling electric fan" essential to comfort at the same time wrecks the harmony.

Such differences are clearly much more than a matter of
convenience: the real distance between past and present is
aesthetic. This point is made clear even in Tanizaki's examination of the visual and tactile qualities of articles found in
the East as compared with those in the West: the relative
whiteness, even the texture itself, of paper; the qualities of the
brush compared with those of the pen; the function of the
house roof. He would "call back at least for literature this
world of shadows we are losing"—but we should keep in
mind that it is in literature, not in life, that he would revive
the past.

One of Tanizaki's most shadowed stories begins with the
"realities" of life, as he maintained beauty must always do.
Then he artfully leads the reader farther and farther from the

---

[21] E. Seidensticker's adaptation of *In'ei Raisan* (1933–1934) in the
Atlantic Monthly 195(see note 15, above) gives the main points. Tanizaki's
essay has often caused misunderstanding. One commentator, for instance,
wondered why Tanizaki did not extend his aesthetic to plans for a new
house (Tanizaki was apparently horrified at the prospect of his architect
actually providing him with such a gloomy place as the one "praised" in
his essay). Tanizaki's admiration for the unrivaled, shadowed beauty of
old Kyoto houses is linked in the essay with his appreciation of a young girl
viewed in wavering lantern light, smiling through lips "green as enchanted
fires" (a reference to long-ago green-black lipstick). Recalling that women
still blackened their teeth and shaved their eyebrows when he was a boy,
Tanizaki describes the intensity of the beauty of this white "face alone"
(without such distractions as red lips and glistening teeth). In practice,
however, he preferred jolly young Kyoto *maiko* (apprentice geisha) tumbl-
ing in *zakone*. He described this practice in "Kyoto: Her Nature,
Food . . . and Women": customers, geisha, and *maiko* spread their bedding in one room; then they all jumped in together.

familiar world into a world where dream and reality are indistinguishable and we, too, may meditate on Beauty and consider the truth of seeming illusion. This masterpiece of aesthetic distancing is *Ashikari* (*Ashikari*, 1932). It begins with a journey that persuades us to travel with the narrator: we move in space and in time on an adventure simultaneously geographical, psychological, mystical, and aesthetic.

Ashikari begins with the narrator embarking on a journey "of no interest to my family," a deceptively simple progression through the countryside and by ferry—a journey also rich in poetic allusion[22] and with hints of traditional symbolic meaning. This journey is designed to lure us into an atmosphere beautifully created: a stage setting for the dramatic appearance of a mystifying stranger and the ambiguous account of events that the stranger's father had described to him long ago. We find ourselves in a mystical and mythical past, our enchantment as assured as if we too had shared those bowls of fox noodles. We know the landscape is "like a picture in an old book," but we are willing to suspend our disbelief and step into that world when we hear the rustle of the reeds and a man comes forth "like my own shadow."

We have come with the narrator along his road of "wild boars and brigands" into a timeless setting "scarcely changed in a hundred years." We too have sat beside the silent river. And we are ready for the stranger's story. This shadowy figure offers us yet another picture: a misted long-ago scene like something from the pages of *The Tale of Genji*. As he describes this remembered scene, we glimpse a beauti-

[22] These allusions may escape the Western reader and modern Japanese alike. But they include references to the Shrine of Minase; to lines by the Emperor-Poet Gotoba (who died in 1239), "forever lovely falls the twilight" (in turn an allusion to an incident in *The Tale of Genji*); to historical events celebrated in poems, stories, and dramas. The poetic mood is enhanced by the landscape (the mountain silhouetted by the moon), by the narrator's recitation of appropriate Chinese verses, by his songs for the lute, and by his recollections from a thousand-year-old book on courtesans.

ful woman and hear the music in a remote garden to which this mysterious figure and his father traveled beneath the light of the moon—a kind of ritual pilgrimage they made each year. Lulled by this poetic setting, we find ourselves confronted by another kind of shadow: complex relationships of men and women in love.

It is a peculiar triangle the stranger presents: Oyū is a beautiful widow who according to social custom belonged to her husband's family (she must raise her son and never think of remarrying). Her admirer is Seribashi, only much later revealed as the shadowy figure's father. Her sister Oshizu marries Seribashi only for Oyū's sake: she will never consummate the marriage, but willingly devotes her life to offering the cover under which sister Oyū and Seribashi may meet. Oshizu and Seribashi will be true to Oyū by never living as man and wife.

Subsequent events are narrated with the mistiness of a dream filled with ambiguity. We glimpse Oyū visiting the couple and occasionally traveling with them (sometimes with the "wife" sleeping in a separate room). Although the relationship appears tenuous and Oyū seems an unattainable "ideal of womanhood" that makes Seribashi think of a figure in an old picture (brocaded and playing the koto), eventually Seribashi and Oyū become "too intimate."

We are told that their "physical purity" is kept. The dream, however, must end. Her late husband's child dies, and Oyū is forced to marry a sake merchant—a man with a villa beside Lake Biwa (a place with its own poetic associations). In the feudal context of Love and Honor, Seribashi and Oyū might at this point commit the double suicide of lovers (*shinjū*, as in the love-suicide plays of Chikamatsu; but *jōshi* since the Meiji Era). They are prevented, however, by their feeling of responsibility (in its deepest Japanese sense) to the devoted Oshizu. Moreover, the passing of Oyū's loveliness from the world would be unbearably pitiful.

The triangle must be broken. Oyū's new life in its luxury

suggests "an old and mellowed picture"—a deliberate evocation of our first glimpse of her beauty. She returns to the
framework in which she was introduced: a scene by moonlight, an isolated garden in which the stranger and his father
glimpsed a beautiful musician.

This is not the end of the narrative. The decline of Seribashi's fortunes follows. "In a flood of gratitude," he at last
lives as husband to Oshizu (fathering the teller of the tale).
That tale-teller remains a mysterious figure himself, as he
later vanishes into the reeds again. Yet neither triangle nor
dream can be said to end with the final rustle of the reeds. We
have been told that the son of Seribashi is on his way to make
another annual pilgrimage—repeating the tradition of moon-
viewing and Oyū-watching shared with Father Seribashi in
his boyhood. The voice of reality, the narrator of this twice-
told tale, who first lured us into this enchanted landscape,
asks: "Surely Oyū is now past eighty?" To such a prosaic
question there can be no answer. The grass rustles in the
wind, and the man vanishes "like a wraith in the light of the
moon." We must not ask whether that tale-teller and those
lovers were of spirit or of flesh.

Whether or not the tale is over when the tale-teller
vanishes in ghostly silence, the beauty of the story—like that
of the lovely Oyū herself—is enhanced by our seeing it
through this "delicate veil of gossamer silk." Our first
glimpse of Oyū at the theater, her inaccessible quality, her
resemblance to a long-ago picture, the setting remote in both
time and place, the dreamlike quality of events—these are
elements of a fantasy that is both poetic and mythic. There
may be hints of Freudian reaching into the unconscious and
at one level there are details suggesting psychopathology; yet
to reduce Ashikari to a casebook would be to destroy the
dream, and the beauty.

To understand the complexity of the recurrent search for
Beauty in Tanizaki's work, we can compare Ashikari with a
later story, "The Bridge of Dreams" (Yume no Ukihashi,

1959). Again beauty is both illusory and sexual. Again the title offers links with the past through literary allusion. *Yume
no Ukihashi* is the title of the sixth and final section of *The
Tale of Genji. Ukihashi*, moreover, is not simply a bridge; it is
specifically a floating *(uki)* bridge. Thus *Ukihashi* is linked
with various Japanese phrases for the transient world *(ukiyo)*,
that "floating world" linked in turn with the "flower and
willow" world of pleasure.

Again the story opens with uncertainty. The beautifully
written lines on the bridge of dreams hang as we in the West
would hang a picture. Contemplating the calligraphy (a traditional aesthetic pleasure), the narrator wonders: "Who
wrote these lines?" His question hinges on the *style* of the
calligraphy. But as Tadasu wonders "which mother" wrote
the characters we discover that his "real" mother has died
and his stepmother has been meticuously fitted into the role,
even assuming the "real" mother's name of Chinu.

In *Genji*, "a dream linking dream to dream" does indeed
refer to the insubstantial beauty of life, but in Tanizaki's
story the dream is focused in a woman's milky breast. At the
same time, nothing is what it seems. The second mother is not
the innocent duplicate of the first: she began life as a geisha
(after her family's bankruptcy), married a cotton merchant,
and was divorced at eighteen and sent back to her parents.
Later she taught tea ceremony and flower arranging.

When this second mother eventually gives birth to a son,
the child (Takeshi) is put out for adoption—again an incident
rich in hidden meanings, puzzles that the narrator cannot
solve by visiting the family retainers in whose care the baby
is supposed to have been placed. The mystery of the stepmother's actions, of the unresisted lure offered the boy, is
never solved—not even when it is revealed that the father,
suffering from a fatal illness, had requested Tadasu to take
his place with the stepmother, marry the gardener's com-
pliant daughter (so that she would be available to help in this
"care"), and send away any children they might have.

The reader is offered various hints and questions. What is the significance of the dying father's repetitions of the phrase "the bridge of dreams"? Which mother does his cry for "Chinu" refer to? What are the real circumstances of the stepmother's death following the bite of a centipede? Tanizaki gives us only an entry made by the narrator three years later: he has divorced the gardener's daughter (hinting that this was perhaps to settle his nagging doubts about the stepmother's death); he has sold the house associated with "The Bridge of Dreams" (linked with *Genji* both by the written words and by the events of history); and he has brought back the lost brother, Takeshi. We find that young Takeshi looks exactly like the mother.

But which mother? And who was Takeshi's father? (There are hints that the narrator might have fathered this boy.) We only know that the narrator plans to live with Takeshi, "hoping to spare him the loneliness I knew." The remembered loneliness, the narrator's ambiguous memories of his two mothers, and the comfort of a woman's breast might all seem to point to a Freudian interpretation and abnormal psychology. But Tanizaki is not a clinical psychologist. The reader who regards this story as an example of Tanizaki's "strange" interests is ignoring the tradition. For the relationship of boy and stepmother is but another version of a traditional theme, one found in *The Tale of Genji* itself. The reader puzzled by Tadasu's relationship with the second Chinu should remember the world of *Genji*, in which the Shining One fathered an exquisitely beautiful son by his father's concubine Fujitsubo (that is, by his stepmother, who was one of the Emperor's wives).

A closer look at scenes in *Ashikari* and "Bridge of Dreams"—and some footnotes on Japanese custom—will help the foreign reader appreciate Tanizaki's careful balance of poetic and prosaic here. The Japanese context is essential if we are to avoid misinterpreting these and other stories in which dreams of beauty are linked with memories of mother (often more lovely than in life),[23] and if we are to avoid oedipal readings of different social patterns.

Traditionally (and even today) the Japanese boy is *physically* much closer to his mother than his European or American counterpart. It is not just a matter of being carried around on her back (sophisticated city mothers may frown on this practice and prefer to push a baby carriage). But in the Japanese bath (public *sentō* or home *ofuro*), she does not simply stand outside the tub and sponge her infant. On the contrary, and often until long after he has entered primary school, she is in the bath with him. Afterwards she holds him close to her (unclothed) breast while she dries him. Later, if the family still sleep on *futon* rather than in Western beds, she will take the boy into her bed or place his *futon* between hers and her husband's.[24]

It is unusual for a boy to continue to sleep in this way when he is as old as ten, as the boy does in Niwa Fumio's *The Buddha Tree* (*Bodaiju*, 1955–1956). That boy seeks comfort by placing his hands inside his mother's kimono or lying with her nipple in his mouth (her dry breasts seeming like "toys to play with"). This is the ten-year-old's custom when he returns from school each day—and it is his *age* not his action that occasions comment. This scene, though quite different in function from Tanizaki's, serves as a reminder that late weaning

[23] A double for a deceased mother appears in *Yoshino Kuzu* (The Arrowroot of Yoshino, 1931): a man falls in love with and marries a woman who is the image of his deceased mother. *Haha o Kouru Ki* (Reminiscence of My Beloved Mother, 1919) records Tanizaki's own dream two years after his mother's death. In the dream, as a boy of seven or eight, he seeks his mother and finds her walking along a seaside road: she is playing the samisen and weeping. Then the 34-year-old Tanizaki wakes.

[24] Consciously modern Japanese are apt to argue that today's children do not come between their parents in this particular way. Yet many modern stories present scenes in which the traditional Japanese placing of the child's bed or *futon* is obviously taken for granted. In addition, many recent marriage manuals discuss the practical—and psychological—difficulties that are apparently still encountered as a result of this widespread custom.

is also a Japanese tradition which is still commonplace in remote and rural areas. Perhaps this tradition is the origin of Tanizaki's dreams—or of a fantasy such as *Kiseki* (1717) in which a girl takes her wet nurse with her when she goes to the marriage bed.

It is in this context that Tanizaki uncovers the female breast: a world far removed from the heroic male breasts and the female breasts rendered in terms of animal imagery and bloody fangs in Mishima's pages. In Tanizaki's tales, scenes of boy or man and breast do not indicate sexual aberration. Whatever Freudian elements there are in the origins of these scenes, they are wonderfully poetic in expression.

With this in mind we can return to "Bridge of Dreams" and scenes in which Tadasu as a child was lying beside his mother. The occasion is specifically *not* erotic if we observe the clue of the traditional obi. For we are told that Tadasu's mother did not remove her obi. We see Tadasu seeking out his mother's nipples, playing with them as though he were still an infant, running his tongue over them, taking them between his lips—childhood reminiscence mingled with scents of her hair and of milk. These are part of his "sweetly white dream world."

When the young orphaned Tadasu is later offered his step-mother's dry breast, this dream seems lost. But after she in turn has given birth to a son (that child so mysteriously sent away), Tadasu finds her milking her breasts in the Silk Pavilion. The difference between this relationship and that with his own mother is nicely rendered in her comment: "It tickles." The dream world sometimes seems to return, although now she speaks of Tadasu's "real" mother (perhaps stressing her own personality or self and thus separating herself from the dead mother, that first Chinu whose identity she had been asked to assume). Now Tadasu is about thirteen years old and several inches taller than his stepmother. Yet he suckles for half an hour and does so in repeated sessions. His father makes no objection.

In *Ashikari*, too, breast and dream are linked—as when the

devoted Oshizu sucks Oyū's full breasts and then gives a cup-
ful of the milk to her "husband." In context, this is a beautiful fulfillment of Seribashi's dream of courtly womanhood. It
links him symbolically with Oyū, in a scene that provides us
with a measure of the distance between Tanizaki and Mishima. Not only is the tone different in Mishima's scene of a
woman milking her breast into a soldier's tea bowl in *The
Temple of the Golden Pavilion*; but Mishima deliberately and
meticulously strips away the illusory first impression of his
scene.

The Ambiguities of Love and Marriage

The poetic implications of the female breast in Tanizaki's fiction cannot be denied. Its role as symbol of the dreamworld
at times suggests a metaphor for imagination itself. Yet this is
not the poetry of Kawabata's fictional universe, in which our
essential loneliness is a recurrent theme. In Tanizaki's balancing of opposites and his ironic tone we share the point of
view of an urbane observer, and as in *Ashikari* and "Bridge
of Dreams," the reader—like the protagonists—moves from
dream to mundane aspects of daily life without any sense of
discord.

Tanizaki's gently ironic tone also distinguishes him from
the exponents of "love-talk" literature with whom his name
is so often linked, just as it distinguishes him from the self-
absorbed I-novelists. The "love-talk" literature by aesthetic
and neo-romantic writers had its antecedents in the erotic literature already mentioned, in pillow pictures, and in the
scenes of sexual violence *(obi-hiki)* of the Kabuki stage. It can
also be linked with the vast popular literature of the Genroku
period (late seventeenth to early eighteenth centuries), including the stories of Saikaku already cited, and the amusing
range of *ukiyo-zōshi* (floating world stories).[25]

---

[25] Several *ukiyo-zōshi* are reprinted in Howard Hibbett's *The Floating
World in Japanese Fiction* (New York: Oxford, 1959). The critics' use of

In earlier erotic literature, as in the "gay quarters" stories of Tanizaki's contemporaries, including Nagai Kafū, love and marriage tend to be two mutually exclusive states. Tanizaki, however, often brings them together under the same roof, as in *The Key*. In that novel, as in the earlier *Some Prefer Nettles*, the tone is ironic. Yet the meditations on love and marriage are both perceptive and "modern." Again, before examining Tanizaki's treatments in detail, the Western reader needs footnotes on Japanese custom, especially as expression of attitudes so different from our Western tradition.

Readers of *The Makioka Sisters* generally regard the emphasis on family and the scant credit its characters give to love as symptomatic of a stifling and anachronistic tradition. Readers of contemporary Japanese magazines, on the other hand, might conclude from letters to the editor, from "confessions," and from intimate views of news personalities that in Japan today attitudes toward marriage differ little from their Western counterparts. The truth lies somewhere between. For although the modern girl enjoys freedom unknown to her mother, many conservative families give their daughters freedom only to say no to prospective husbands carefully checked by the family. Love marriages *(renai kekkon)* are advocated by Tokyo's modern college students and salaried workers. Nevertheless, love still tends to defer to family judgment. Love is still not regarded as a prerequisite for marriage . . . and may still be only a fringe benefit. The women of Tanizaki's pages for the most part belong to a generation that at least hoped love would develop at some time after the exchange of the ritual sake cups at the wedding ceremony. Yet most of them would not expect the kind of freedom enjoyed by some of the modern girls coming to maturity after Tanizaki's death.

---

the term "love-talk literature" is derived from *jōwa-bungaku* (*jō*, meaning *sentiment*, and *jōwa*, *love story* and *lovers' talk*, also being encompassed by the Japanese term). Some examples of the "love-talk literature" and the "stories of the Gay Quarters" are given in note 39.

In the past, love was entirely excluded from marriage. Marriage was the family affair indicated in the careful "marriage investigations" of the Makioka family—investigations still made by Kansai families thirty years after Tanizaki wrote his novel. When Tanizaki himself was born, however, there were none of today's opportunities for informal meetings in hiking clubs, ski lodges, or student coffee shops. Then love was to be found only outside marriage in teahouses and pleasure quarters. Often such love led to disaster—as it still does occasionally today. And this is the Japanese tradition commemorated in the plays of love-suicide written by Chikamatsu or in racy Genroku accounts of a young merchant "ruined for love."

This traditional separation is not the ideal of Tanizaki's fictional world, although it has to be admitted that when he puts love and marriage under the same roof it is not always in relation to the same person. The triangles and other multisided figures in Tanizaki's pages often lead to tragicomic denouement. Moreover, he portrays a number of seemingly "un-Japanese" wives with modern demands for sexual fulfillment. Again, though, the reader of Japanese fiction in translation needs to proceed with caution. There are many Japanese stories of such modern women among fiction not translated (although few demonstrate Tanizaki's skill of characterization and accuracy of psychological perception).[26]

Unfulfilled love or impossible love can be poetic in Tanizaki, as in *Ashikari*.[27] But it may also be vastly amusing, as

---

[26] Examples of the women portrayed by Tanizaki's contemporaries are presented above and in note 39.

[27] Among the characters devoted to a dream in one way or another are the masseur of *A Blind Man's Tale*; Shunkin's devoted servant-lover-slave Sasuke; the boy of "Bridge of Dreams"; the two men and a woman of *Aisureba Koso* (Because of Love, 1921–1922); the young man of *Yoshino Kuzu*; and Shōzaburō, protagonist of *Itansha no Kanashimi* (Sorrow[s] of a Heretic, 1916–1917). Kaname in *Some Prefer Nettles* also has "a vague dream."

when various women love Shōzō, while he loves only his cat (in *Neko to Shōzō to Futari no Onna*, 1936). The theme receives similarly humorous treatment in the diarist's pursuit of his tantalizing daughter-in-law and in the adventures of the once-plump lover of *Aguri* as he sets out to buy his play-mate her first Western clothes.

Once again, a pair of Tanizaki's novels can introduce a characteristic element of his work; and once again they come from the beginning and the end of his career. *Some Prefer Nettles* (*Tade Kuu Mushi*, 1928–1929) and *The Key* (*Kagi*, 1956) are both novels on the theme of marriage. Both depict men wrapped up in illusion. At the same time, these stories are enriched by psychological insight, showing Tanizaki's sensitivity to the appalling distance between our hopes and our accomplishments. They also show Tanizaki's under-standing of women, often ironic, and the realistic attitude quite at odds with that popular image of Tanizaki as Wor-shipper of Women.[28]

Some Prefer Nettles might be read as an open-ended medi-tation on marriage. Apparently "cultural" difficulties are no more than outward signs of the profound psychological dif-ficulties of Shiba Kaname and his wife Misako and the role of her scarcely glimpsed lover Aso. Kaname and Misako would like a divorce: he had been relieved when she took a lover. Kaname now tolerates this relationship, and we find him and his wife reluctant to take any further action. Their reluctance is only tenuously related to their ten-year-old son or to the larger "family" responsibilities of marriage (though if Misako decides she wants to marry Aso, Kaname offers to in-tercede with her father, who would naturally raise objec-tions).

---

[28] Even in his very earliest novels and plays Tanizaki shows an acute and realistic awareness of female psychology. The woman of "Tattoo" who likes men as victims is not found only in manuals of psychopathology. The wife who willingly devotes herself to a weak husband may be com-monplace, but she is sketched with uncommon skill as Sumiko in *Aisureba Koso*.

Such family considerations are part of the Japanese tradition, while the father-in-law himself cultivates tradition in the person of Ohisa. A widower, he is cared for by this "old-fashioned" Kyoto girl, his personal puppet trained to perform the refined and proper gestures of an earlier time. Yet in spite of this elegance, she is flawed by bad teeth. As far as Misako is concerned, her father is simply "an old lecher whom she found generally repulsive."

At one level, *Some Prefer Nettles* explores yet another artist in pursuit of Beauty—or an illusion. The father-in-law has attempted to create Ohisa in the image of *his* needs, but rather than making a frontal attack on the father-in-law's false values, Tanizaki gives several perspectives on the nature of a puppet's life. The sequence of events in the marriage of Kaname and his wife, leading to the moment when they seem to be on the eve of divorce, must finally be evaluated through the metaphor of the puppet stage and Kaname's perception at the end of the novel that his father-in-law's Ohisa is no puppet.

At the beginning of the novel, all four of them attend a performance of the Bunraku puppets in Osaka.[29] Just as some qualities of the "mad" old diarist were perceived in the context of traditional theatrical illusion (Kabuki), so now the puppets help to expose the relationships of Kaname and his wife. Kaname is drawn into the first puppet performance and sees the domestic scene as having "telling authenticity." Lines on "nourishing a serpent" seem terribly apt in reference to his own marriage. At the same time, when a puppet is lifelike, it is *disturbingly* so, while Kaname sees Ohisa and the puppet figure of the geisha Koharu as not so unlike each

---

[29] These puppets are three or four feet tall. Each is manipulated by a master puppeteer who moves the head and right arm while a second man operates the left arm and a third moves the legs (or the skirts of the female doll, which tradition decrees to be a figure without feet). To the accompaniment of samisen music and *jōruri* chant, the puppeteers move these dolls through dramas of love, honor, and war—as well as domestic crisis (popular stories that have in many cases also been adapted to the Kabuki stage).

other: both are "at a distance from humanity," and Kaname himself tends to retreat from humanity, as when he finds this quality in the Kobe prostitute Louise.[30]

Yet this is no oversimplified illusion-and-reality, puppet-and-woman equation. There are other puppets—again the object of a family excursion. We share an appreciation of the "innocence" of the more naive audience watching the Awaji puppets, the different quality of the Awaji puppets, and the "crudity" of episodes in their dramas (episodes usually omitted from the Bunraku's Osaka stage). Crudity is a quality linked with the "reality" of Louise, and the "reality" of the second audience eating and joking reminds us of Kaname's disturbed response to a "lifelike" Bunraku puppet.

At the same time, Tanizaki offers perceptions of the reality of marriage. These include Kaname's sad recognition of the part played by the "small ministrations" of marriage, as in the wifely duty of selecting his kimono accessories. Kaname and his wife are already so far from intimacy of contact that her touch seems "as cool and impersonal as a barber's," and it seems "almost immoral" when they sit close together on a train. When they are free of the restraint of preserving false marital face, as with their friend Takanatsu, they can laugh and joke like two friends. True to life, Kaname and Misako can no longer talk to one another, although she feels she can talk over her problems more easily with this outsider, Taka-natsu. The final perception is infinitely sad: Kaname recognizes that even his lifeless marriage, "like the sheen of wood-work seen and remembered . . . was something so near and so familiar that it would continue to pull him even after it was gone."

This, then, is the reality of marriage—to be measured

[30] Louise is often misinterpreted as simply representing the foreign (with Ohisa and Misako representing two varieties of the homegrown) woman. Although she is Eurasian in appearance, Louise is also clearly identified as half-Korean—a significant aspect in the Japanese context (where anti-Korean prejudice in the twentieth century is far removed from close cultural links in the past).

against Kaname's own illusory response to doll-like Ohisa in the final scene. He waits to spend one last night with Misako (they have come to the point of divorce and the father-in-law, reluctant to agree, has taken Misako out to dinner). As he takes a bath and is fed and cossetted by this geisha-doll Ohisa, Kaname reflects on his secret dream of a "type Ohisa." Earlier he had thought: "One does better to fall in love with a woman who can be cherished as a doll." He had felt a spiritual peace in his father-in-law's pilgrimage to various holy places in the company of correctly costumed doll-like Ohisa and in the old man's search for a wooden puppet to contemplate at home.

Now Kaname can take a closer look at his dream. As he waits for Ohisa to bring him some old books (to help pass the time until Misako and her father return), he notices a doll in the corner. This is the female Awaji puppet, the father-in-law's other memento of a lost art. As Kaname watches, the door slides slowly open. We see the old Japanese books. We know who had gone to fetch them. But Tanizaki does not find it necessary to name Ohisa now. He only lets us share Kaname's ambiguous perception—of a figure that is *not* a puppet dimly perceived in the shadows beyond his mosquito net.

The dreams, the perception of the importance of small "comforting" ministrations in marriage, the sexual distance between a husband and wife who seem unable to fulfill one another's needs, the wife seemingly modern yet wishing that her husband would make her withdraw from the relationship with Aso—out of these elements Tanizaki fashions a timely view of marriage. Yet this modern marriage screen is brightened by many ironic touches, as in the episode when Takanatsu brings a rare volume of *The Arabian Nights.*[31] Our final

---

[31] This unexpurgated English edition of *The Arabian Nights* leads Kaname to praise Occidental women (incidentally ignoring his own response to Kyoto-beauty Ohisa). Kaname's comment on the loneliness and deprivation of the Japanese man who lacks the "worshipful" appreciation

impression of gestures and meaning is ambiguous. We are not quite sure what the pictures are supposed to tell us—although there are clues in the literal title: *Tade-Eating Insects*, from a proverb suggesting that tastes do differ. (Qualities of *tade* [smell and taste], however, differ from the quality of the translator's "nettle" [touch].)

The Key, like *Some Prefer Nettles*, may be read both as a study in ambiguity and as a many-sided commentary on domestic life and illusion. Its title refers to the key that the husband *seems* to use in locking up his diary, although *kagi* is also a specific Japanese term for the penis. The novel consists of alternating diary entries by the husband (referred to only as "Papa") and his wife Ikuko. The cast includes their daughter Toshiko and her future husband Kimura (who is later revealed as the mother's lover, with strong evidence that the daughter had been virtually pimping for her mother).

A bare outline of events in *The Key* sounds merely like a pornographer's sketch. The wife secretly regards her husband's face as extraordinarily repulsive; she responds to him with both love and hate. She drinks too much, faints in the bath, is hauled out by her husband, dried with the aid of friend Kimura, and later cries out Kimura's name during passionate semicomatose interludes in the domestic *futon*. She eventually takes Kimura for a lover. And this "modest" wife even entertains her lover Kimura in one room while her husband lies dying in another.

The husband for his part encourages his wife to drink and asks the friend's help (while suspecting Kimura's "attitude")

---

of women found in Western literature has unfortunately led critics to the belief that this is Tanizaki's own philosophy. Kaname, however, names his examples of such worship: Greek goddesses, the Virgin Mother, and Hollywood movie stars. This ironic trinity he then links to attitudes found in Japanese court literature but lost in the Buddhist decline under the Edo shogunate. Again the comparison is ambiguous. (And readers seeking more information on the relative importance of Confucian and Buddhist thought under the shoguns may wish to consult de Bary.)

both in rescuing her from the bath and later in processing intimate photographs. The daughter moves out of the family home, apparently to facilitate her mother's meetings with her own would-be husband Kimura. First Toshiko supplies the brandy-and-bath complex (the mother's route to erotic interludes) at her rented cottage. Later she finds mother and lover a convenient hotel. The young man, though officially recognized as "marriage prospect" for this daughter, admires the mother, offers the lecherous father a Polaroid camera with which to photograph semicomatose Ikuko, accidentally lets the daughter discover nude photographs of her mother, meets the mother in secret, and after the father's death plans to marry daughter Toshiko, who will "make the sacrifice for the sake of appearances" as the three survivors live together.

The entries we read cover a period from New Year's Day to the eleventh of June; and until this New Year entry "Papa" had carefully omitted entries concerning sexual relations from his diaries lest his wife read them. (Paradoxically, although he locks the diary up, he secretly hopes that she *will* read what he has written.) Entries in his diary, as in hers, also reveal their mutual efforts to hide, or reveal, their secret thoughts. The key to understanding might well be the husband's March entry: "The four of us—all the while deceiving one another—are cooperating quite effectively."

Both diarists, however, are very unreliable narrators.[32]

[32] The unrealiable narrator is another favorite device for ambiguity in Tanizaki's stories. An outstanding example is *Watakushi* (I or Myself in Japanese, but unfortunately made specifically "The Thief" in translation). This narrator, too, announces "I have not written a single dishonest word here"—but all his words are deliberately ambiguous. At the opening, boys preparing for entrance to Tokyo's Imperial University are discussing love and crime. They say that they might "perhaps" commit murder, but a thief is "a different species." The narrator records a suspicious look directed at him and comments on the resemblance of the thief's coat to his own. He jots down notes on his own nature until at last he shows himself taking a ten-yen note and heading for the weed-filled area "where I always buried the things I stole." In his comments on his feeling of a "criminal's

Papa stresses his sincerity and describes the diary as his way of talking to his wife indirectly. This point has to be kept in mind in following his entries about her "natural endowment" and his notes concerning the stimulating effect of jealousy on his own sexual powers (for this he is grateful to Kimura). At first he pictures his wife as a woman of "old-fashioned Kyoto upbringing"—although we also learn that modest little Ikuko has a sexual vigor that far outstrips her husband's (a man who is exhausted but really does not mind).

The wife's adherence to convention is obviously a matter of form only. And the forms are to be observed only when they are in her favor—as in the traditional "First Auspicious Night" for intercourse, the second of January. But all her assurances that she would "never dream of touching" her husband's diary, even when he leaves the key out as a hint, and all her protestations about "things too shameful to mention" are eventually shown to be the words and gestures of a deceitfully masked actress.

While she is pretending in her own diary that she is unaware of the way she calls out Kimura's name, unaware of her husband's illness, and unaware of her husband's photoerotic sessions by fluorescent light, the final entries show she has known more than she admits. She has been reading the husband's diary. Moreover, this demure figure has some remarkably clear recollections of the occasions when she had supposedly fainted in the bath. It should be admitted, however, that the husband's entries hint that he found such deceits infinitely comforting. He records his shock at the daughter's clear explanation of events: upset at "being confronted with something that I had done my best to ignore" (a very traditional Japanese response).

The real interest of *The Key*, however, is not in its appar-

_____

anxiety and isolation," however, the narrator has done more than play an unreliable part. He has been Tanizaki's instrument for once again dissecting human self-deception and showing how close are the feelings of innocence and guilt.

ent actions but in the extraordinary ambiguities of gesture
and meanings. Reasons for the actions are questioned in various ways throughout the narrative; they are never given
unequivocally. We are constantly aware of the husband's uncertainties and the wife's tendency to protest too much—
especially in notes on her own virtue, innocence, and sensitivity. Even such entries as the husband's assertion that each
had a scheme (all "doing our best to corrupt Ikuko") must be
measured against evidence of Ikuko's own role-playing, as
she acts the part of "a woman carefully brought up, who
wouldn't dream of infringing on anyone's privacy."

Ambiguities of the daughter's actions are not confined to
the mother's written doubts in her final diary entries. Readers
have gathered their own evidence from the father's notes on
Toshiko's casual inquiry about her mother's activities or her
pointed reference to having left the (drunken) Ikuko alone
with Kimura "a half hour ago." Dutiful daughter points out
to father that in spite of her mother's later meetings with
Kimura in hotel rooms, "Mother is still faithful"—and then
makes a qualifying allusion to "unnatural method . . . [and]
nastier ways."

The wife's frank admission of lies in her own diary (these
range from her pretended illness to her "true" relationships
with husband, daughter, and lover) does not necessarily negate such statements as "I haven't the faintest desire to pene-
trate [my husband's] psychology." Tanizaki has shown us a
woman more interested in her own combination of lustful-
ness and "shyness" than in the feelings of those about her.
Yet the distortions of her entries serve also to cast doubt on
her husband's diary protestations of not reading his wife's entries. Moreover, if the daughter really is wily and does have
"a touch of Iago," such apparently minor matters as outfit-
ting her mother in new (unfamiliar) Western clothes must be
reinterpreted in deeper symbolic terms.

Ultimately, the only truth in *The Key* seems to be the
wife's comment: "How we deceived and ensnared each other
until one of us was destroyed." Even that must be footnoted

by the patent absurdity of a March entry declaring that she had thrown off the mask of self-deception. Nor is there adequate evidence in support of her claim that "anyone, no matter how gentle, would have been warped by the steady pressure of that degenerate, vicious mind" of her husband. The final entry on the future triangle of mother, daughter, and Kimura (that relationship in which Toshiko plans to "sacrifice" herself) is the ultimate ambiguity. "That is what he tells me," writes Ikuko. In view of the lies and partial truths that are the custom in that household, such an entry tells nothing. The ultimate lie may after all be a mask for Kimura's intentions. It may also be a mask with which Ikuko can comfort herself.

Many of the perceptions of *The Key* relate to the deceptions and self-deceptions by which we all survive and which are indeed the stuff of comedy. We might be impressed by Papa's thought: "To be startled after more than twenty years together by a first awareness of the physical beauty of one's own wife—that surely is to begin a new marriage." We think what a modern husband he must be (in the Japanese context: seeing his wife in terms of sexual pleasure rather than familial duty). He then observes the "terrible misfortune for a married couple's tastes to conflict so bitterly." But this bitter conflict does not spring from profound difficulties: the trouble is that they cannot agree whether intercourse is more proper in the dark or by electric light.

The humorous aspects of this relationship are reflected in an extraordinary Wife's Progress in which she begins modestly, in darkness, with "silence during the act." This old-fashioned figure, as she dreams of Kimura, gradually adopts a more ardent tone. Soon she begins to bite her husband's tongue and earlobe. Eventually, she initiates the ill-timed encounter that is climaxed by her husband's stroke. Tanizaki is both wonderfully and tactfully funny in his account of Ikuko extricating herself from what is undoubtedly a most embarrassing position.

Yet in spite of his fondness for clinical detail—as in the ail-

ments of the Makioka family or the deterioration of the mad
old diarist—Tanizaki often renders details of sexual encounter in delightfully indirect ways. He can write of a lover's repeated visits simply: "At eleven, footsteps in the garden." In
The Makioka Sisters, he says all that is necessary about the
second honeymoon of Teinosuke and Sachiko in a single line
of bedtime dialogue.[33]

Tanizaki can take one of Japan's traditionally erotic gestures (untying the obi string) and use it simply as a prelude to
lying down, alone, to rest. He can also take potentially erotic
and even pornographic material and make it unexpectedly
comic, as he does in many details of *The Key*. Not the least
amusing among these details is the remarkable vignette of the
comatose diarist stretched out beneath the probing chopstick
of his physician (obviously an emergency tool and not standard Japanese medical equipment). Testing for reflexes, the
doctor applies the chopstick to the husband's testicle: to
Ikuko's fascinated eyes, it moves "like the squirming of a live
abalone." (To appreciate fully the point of Tanizaki's joke,
the Western reader should note that the Japanese enjoy eating
raw fish, or *sashimi*, a delicacy that includes "squirming" or
"dancing" raw prawns).

Tanizaki's fine discrimination in the use of sensory appeals
operates also in his treatment of sex, where the sound of a fingernail tying the obi, the scent of a girl's powder, the texture
of silk cloth, and above all the feel of flesh are more erotic
than any modern clinically oriented novel could possibly be.
He continues the Japanese poetic tradition, in which sexual
encounters can be rendered as "dew on the hairy caterpil-
lar," "the night pledge," and "the dew of woman." He also

[33] Similarly, although that novel is "about" marriage, the mark over
Yukiko's eye (a hormonal problem expected to clear up when she marries)
is as close as Tanizaki comes to sexuality. The most explicit sexual allusion
(in spite of all the references to Taeko's illegitimate relationships and baby)
is perhaps the little German girl's game with dolls. We approach no closer
to Yukiko's sex life than her husband-to-be's anticipation: he will enjoy
watching the dark spot disappear.

writes from the amusing perspective of centuries of *senryū*, the wittily earthy versions of haiku with a satiric tone.

The blind masseur feels history as he feels the lady's body beneath his sensitive fingers. Even women are enchanted by Oichi's beauty (unlike the woman who contemplates pouncing on another woman's flesh in one of Mishima's stories). But apart from the philosophical dimension of rotting flesh in *The Mother of Captain Shigemoto*, flesh is a source of pleasure linked with dreams rather than nightmares. And if there is an element of terror, it is more apt to be balanced—as it is in the short story "Aguri"—by quite ironic perception.

"Aguri" (*Aoi Hana*, 1922) is a tale of a man and his mistress: Okada, drained of life by the vampirish demands of his mistress, and Aguri, this pleasure-loving girl. The incident itself is slight: Okada is on his way to a "foreign" shop in Yokohama to fit Aguri out in her first Western clothes. But this is only the surface of a funny and sad view of maid-mad man. Okada, now aware that his fine rich flesh is "melting away," was until a year ago coyly pleased when friends at the public bath commented on his feminine sort of figure. He would be quick to retort: "Don't get any funny ideas."

Now, instead of having white buttocks, "plump as any girl's," he is a positive skeleton, a sick man—especially in his own eyes. Sick indeed, as Tanizaki offers the delightful spectacle of Okada gamely carrying on mundane conversations with Aguri about clothes and trains while visualizing her casual "Oh, are you dead?" should he yield to impulse and collapse on the sidewalk. *Her* mind is happily absorbed with visions of silks and satins, and jewelry. *His* hallucinatory interior monologue is absorbed with her promises to love his ghost and with his own sensations of giddiness, as well as glorious memories of being crushed by Aguri's excessively solid weight.

Like other Tanizaki characters, Okada feels himself to be squeezed, cramped, and pressed by Western clasps, leather, and straps. "Held together" by Western clothes, he struggles bravely along, cheered by the prospect of playing leopard

with Aguri after the shopping is over—although the only action we see is in Okada's mind as he visualizes his mad collapse on the sidewalk. Gathering crowds, and his demand
that Aguri carry him piggyback, herald the entrance of his
deceased mother and a policeman to this hallucinated scene.
Aguri—the voice of reality—breaks in with a question about
a watch: and off he goes again, this time in a fantasy of himself as a Chinese gentleman with Aguri-singsong-girl beside
him. As they approach the store, he is lost in an imagined
scene of museum galleries and statues.

Finally, we see Okada in the dressing room, preparing to
cover his statue-Aguri in all these strange European clothes
(clothes "like a second skin," not something to wrap the human body in from outside but "a kind of tattoo to be absorbed into the skin"). She unties her obi, that ancient erotic
gesture: the statue of Okada's imagination stands naked. At
that moment of enlightenment, Aguri smiles. But Okada,
hopelessly tangled in the unfamiliar silks and accessories, his
illusion fading in the confrontation with real clothes, merely
finds that his own head begins to swim. . . .

Amusing though such a story may be, it reveals Tanizaki's
unfailing craftsmanship. Here as in other stories, he balances
various opposites—especially prosaic appearances and hidden fantasy—for effects both ironic and illuminating. As accurate in its perceptions as a clinical report, this story, seemingly so slight, also shows Tanizaki's gift for the selection of
telling details. And while these details are, as already noted,
devices for characterization, footnotes to the action, and
clues to meaning, they might also serve to remind us of Tanizaki's role as a chronicler of modern Japan.

Chronicles of Modern Japan

In *The Makioka Sisters* (*Sasameyuki*, 1943–1948) Tanizaki
—like his predecessor Lady Murasaki—chronicles in affectionate detail a way of life entirely unfamiliar to the foreign

reader. Tanizaki is not content to describe the masks and record the words and gestures of convention in the Makiokas' "main house" and "second house." These may appear no more than modern equivalents of the mansions found in *Genji*. He also transforms them into devices for expressing gently ironic perceptions, while he lifts the masks of social and psychological usage to hint at the underlying motives of uncertain modern man.

Tanizaki's understanding of his Japanese scene provides both theme and setting for the world of *The Makioka Sisters*—a society in which emphasis is still placed on "face" and on strict adherence to form, and where the individual is trained to suppress private feelings, molding the self and subordinating emotions to the demands of family and group. But Tanizaki is not writing a novel of manners in the usual sense, and his account of the arranging of a marriage actually provides a metaphorical view of tradition in all its personal, national, and even international aspects.

All of Tanizaki's writing is at one level a chronicle of modern Japan (or, in the case of his historical stories, modern man's perspective on the "romantic" past). But as with the medicine cabinet of the mad old diarist, the details always function in terms of the *craft* of fiction. Ambiguities of meaning are apt to be explored through styles of calligraphy, food, or dress. Characters are defined according to their setting—Western or Oriental incongruities in the choice of accessories, for instance. *The Makioka Sisters* has its share of apparently trivial details that are actually artful clues foreshadowing coming events or interpreting past actions.

At the same time, we must acknowledge that careful annotation of *The Makioka Sisters* by some future scholar might illuminate a whole age in the way that *The World of the Shining Prince* has taken us behind the screens and the carriage blinds of Genji's world. The social historian may well gain more helpful information from the pages of Tanizaki's work than from up-to-date samplings of opinion: Tanizaki is very meticulous in recording the scenes and properties of his dramas, whereas the average Japanese regards the opinion pollster as a bad-mannered fellow to be outwitted by false information if necessary.[34]

As in his historical tales, Tanizaki recreates a time and place in terms that even a non-Japanese may understand. The behavior of characters may differ in degree but not in kind from the norms of that world. And this is quite different from the characters of Mishima's fictions, who are often grotesque exceptions to the norms and values of their time or setting. Tanizaki is careful to show even such eccentrics as the imperious Shunkin and the single-minded tattooer in terms of comparison rather than contrast with their time (comparing, for example, Shunkin's cruelty with that of other puppeteers, musicians, and artists).

Tanizaki's careful re-creation of the Makioka world reveals how marriages are arranged and what attitudes the Japanese have toward family, business, and friends. In this world he shows the importance of rank (even within the family) and of social obligations—and the appalling consequences of living only for oneself. The collector of minutiae can study seasonal variations in kimono here, observe the proper plants for a modern garden, and even learn to distinguish as the Makiokas do between arrivals on the *Tsubame* (Swallow) Express and the *Kamome* (Seagull). Readers who happen to have lived in the Kansai or in Tokyo recently will be more familiar with the superexpresses *Hikari* and *Kodama*, the world's fastest trains. Yet they will also be startled to realize how little attitudes have really changed behind the superficial scene shiftings of the past thirty years.

[34] Tanizaki's pages provide countless footnotes on Japanese culture and custom: the choice of kimono according to age, season, and occasion; the selection of suitable scrolls for hanging in the *tokonoma*; even the full range of entertainment, including Kabuki, puppets (Bunraku and Awaji varieties), and such modern pleasures as boxing matches, foreign movies, and nude revues.

Many of the scenes, the words, and the actions, in fact, have not changed at all. Even the contemporary tourist can find helpful hints in the details of Makioka life in spite of minor changes (for instance, the Oriental Hotel in Kobe and the Imperial Hotel in Tokyo both have new buildings). The reader discovers the name of a restaurant serving those wriggling prawns or a *sushi* shop offering the best rice delicacies topped with fish or rolled in *nori* (seaweed or laver). One might even obtain helpful hints on where to find the most comfortable beds.

The reader is led, moreover, through a veritable course in home medicine, beginning with techniques for giving shots of vitamin B and continuing with instructions for a rough-and-ready method of peeling scarlet fever scabs. One is introduced to the customs of private hospitals and the attitudes of doctors, while enjoying an internship at the Makioka bedside. There are distinctly clinical accounts of dysentery, miscarriage, gangrene, vomiting, and even childhood nervous disorders. These realities are not a simple catalogue, however, but a device for providing marvelously ironic counterpoint, balancing the exquisite formalities of genteel husband-hunting or exposing the pretensions of characters whose perfection in other matters may thus be called in doubt.

In terms of plot, *The Makioka Sisters* is the story of the arranging of the marriage of Yukiko, third of four sisters in an old Osaka family. At the beginning, she is the subject of a conversation: "We have another prospect for Yukiko." Five marriage meetings *(miai)*, four cherry-viewings, and five hundred and thirty pages later, we get our last view of Yukiko. At last she is aboard a train bound for her Tokyo marriage ceremony. She is on her way: but in what terms! That modest, retiring, and immaculate figure of the opening paragraphs is at the end described as "peevish." At the heroic moment when she is destined for marriage with Mimaki (a man "whose tastes were turning toward the Japanese"), "Yukiko's diarrhea . . . was a problem on the train to Tokyo."

Yet in the context of Tanizaki's narrative, such an ailment serves to humanize rather than to satirize the impeccable Yukiko.

Sasameyuki is a narrative of enormous scope, moving between the main house in Osaka and the second house in Ashiya—two seats of the old but deteriorating Makioka family. The husbands of these two eldest girls have taken the Makioka name, as men in Japan may still do when the family lacks sons. Tatsuo, husband of Eldest Daughter (and a man who "thought only of general principles, never of the people concerned") heads the main house. His transfer to the bank's office in Tokyo means that the main house must move away from its traditional Kansai base. But apart from the few months Yukiko spends unwillingly in Tokyo, the two younger sisters remain unconventionally at the second house (headed by Teinosuke and Sachiko).

At the center of the action stands enigmatic Yukiko, distinguished by unusual reticence, shyness, hints of an older Japan —a sad, slender figure. Appearances, however, can be misleading. Although she looks as if she would come down with tuberculosis (one cautious marriage prospect even insists on a chest X-ray), she is "really the strongest of them all." Silent through the various marriage meetings, even when social form would require her to make at least token conversation, Yukiko can on occasion burst out with vehement reproaches against the youngest sister Taeko. (These outbursts are, however, much-needed lectures that the two elder Makioka girls have been quite unable to give.) Moreover, when niece or sister falls ill it is Yukiko who is practical, enduring, and a source of strength.

Yukiko's responses to the marriage prospects are apt to be ambiguous. One prospect is an old fisheries clerk. We are uncertain of her reasons for rejecting him. Perhaps it is because, as she says, in leading the group to look at pictures of his deceased wife and children he betrayed that "he understood nothing of woman's finer feelings." On the other hand, Sachiko's interpretation of Yukiko's words and gestures hints at quite different possibilities on this as on other occasions. Nowhere, however, are Yukiko's real thoughts revealed: Tanizaki never plays all-seeing author. Once again the reader must guess from the evidence offered.

As counterpoint to Yukiko, we have Taeko or Koi-san ("small daughter"), the youngest sister. In contrast to Yukiko (seemingly representing the refined past, though extremely practical on occasion), Taeko is a "brisk, enterprising modern girl who went ahead quite without hesitation." Thus she is seen in willful involvement first with Okubata (their short-lived "elopement" some years earlier being the first of the episodes potentially damaging to Yukiko's prospects, as their later escapades are similarly ill-timed). Next Tanizaki shows Taeko's relationship to the photographer Itakura, a man indebted to Okubata's family (hence deviating from a proper sense of duty in his relations with Taeko); moreover, his motives are questioned, as in a glimpse of him "making a show of hesitation" yet contriving to accept Taeko's proposal. Finally, there is the bartender Miyoshi, by whom Taeko has an illegitimate daughter whose death-at-birth precedes this unmarried couple's first venture in housekeeping. Ironically, this venture gives Taeko "her own establishment" ahead of Yukiko after all.

These details, however, fail to show the multiple layers of narrative and meaning in this novel. For it is by no means a simple tale of the Good Sister and the Bad or of Gentle Kansai Maiden Yukiko pitted against Self-Willed Modern Miss Taeko. Yukiko's modesty and propriety are shown not merely as handicaps in the marriage mart but as qualities uncomfortably lacking in human warmth. Though never outwardly condemned (that is not Tanizaki's method), Yukiko—seemingly the old Japanese ideal woman so modest and retiring—can be stubborn (a much more serious flaw in Japan than in the West). And for all the efforts of family and friends in her behalf, we find "they can expect no help from her."

Yukiko's apparent acquiescence frequently masks an iron determination—as in the incident of the cherry-viewing kimono, which she quietly unpacks when she is coaxed to stay on in Ashiya. This detail reveals that when she left Tokyo for a short visit to Second Sister, Yukiko had already determined precisely how long she would stay. Moreover, when Yukiko ultimately agrees to marry Mimaki, impoverished son of the nobility (in Tanizaki's blunt Japanese, a viscount's *shoshi* or bastard), she is not merely "peevish" about it: she also takes care not to show any pleasure. And as the translator so nicely puts it, she even takes care "not to let slip a word of thanks to those who had worked so hard for her." But whether Yukiko actually *feels* either pleasure or gratitude remains a mystery.

Similarly, Taeko's conduct is not always clearly wrong. She can be entertainingly bright at an awkward *miai* (marriage meeting) for Yukiko. This may be Taeko's positive response to the self-respect she gains from the considerate behavior of the other guests, although in Sachiko's eyes, when she is later annoyed by Taeko's ill-timed pregnancy, this positive view changes to the thought that Taeko was merely drunk. In spite of her modern yearnings toward a career as seamstress (any work for a girl being anathema to the conservative head of the family), it is Taeko who devotes herself to learning the Snow Dance in its most traditional Osaka form. There is even a hint of an explanation for her behavior to satisfy a Freudian critic: the relationship with a father who viewed her as dark and plain, the death of her mother, and the attitude of a stern brother-in-law continually judging her a heretic and a nuisance.

Similarly, Okubata and Itakura are balanced. On one side, there is Okubata, weak son of an old family. On the other, there is the self-made photographer Itakura, whose family position is defined as a step below the Makiokas. For all his flaws of character, Okubata is considered by the main family as an acceptable marriage prospect because of his family's "position." Yet the reader finds it is hard to share even this weak enthusiasm when Okubata appears at the height of the flood in immaculate clothes, armed with a tourist camera, and obviously "quite unwilling to sacrifice the crease in his trousers for his future wife." It is Itakura who rescues Taeko: and however sly and opportunistic he may seem to Sachiko, Tanizaki also insists on depicting him as a dutiful son, an amusing as well as a courageous friend, and a young man more hardworking than the majority of his contemporaries.

Beyond the personal relationships, the households that provide the setting for events in *The Makioka Sisters* also offer deeper social (and psychological) commentary on households in Japan. Tsuruko of the main house may be taken as the norm. People who do not know her well are overcome with admiration for this "thorough industrious housewife" and praise her self-less industry—unaware that her gestures are merely the signs of her own (selfish) feelings of excitement or childish delight in surprising her sisters. She always manages to look neat and unruffled, although she is surrounded by a swarm of children. She lives up to the rigid standards of her husband in an atmosphere that makes it plain why the two younger girls prefer the less formal Ashiya house.

Yet Sachiko at the Ashiya second house is no paragon: she enjoys delicate health, sheds sentimental tears, and sees the whole world in relation to herself. The critical illness of her sister makes Sachiko think of her daughter's scarlet fever the preceding year. But this memory only activates concern for herself: she wonders if this year she must again miss the performance of Kikugorō, the Kabuki actor. Nor is she slow to wangle free photographs from Itakura when he comes to take pictures of Taeko's dance recital—although she is the one who condemns *him* as opportunistic. There are, too, hints of the ways in which she has dimmed Yukiko's marriage prospects, always by "accidents" that might have been avoided:

her own livelier appearance at a *miai*, a tactless question about an obscure literary allusion, even the particular circumstances of her miscarriage.[35]

Through the various marriage prospects for Yukiko, Tanizaki explores Japanese attitudes in full range—from the most conservative old families, with their rigid adherence to protocol, to those who have experienced European or American "freedom." These free types, however, tend to revert to traditional attitudes; and Tanizaki makes it clear that changes in dress or accent or eating habits do not necessarily indicate a change in outlook at all.

The family backgrounds of the prospects mirror the declining fortunes of the Makioka family. But Tanizaki's interest is by no means limited to the social commentary. As in other novels, each character is limned in telling psychological detail. Like a meticulous scroll painter from Japan's past, Tanizaki puts them all in his picture—but he sees them with modern eyes. There is, for example, the man on the train. Yukiko recognizes the vaguely familiar figure as a marriage prospect of ten years ago: but she could not have been happy with "a man who spent his life on slow trains between one out-of-the-way station and another."

---

[35] There are other housewives in Tanizaki's *Makioka* gallery—the smart wife of a broadcasting company executive, newly returned from abroad; Niu and Itani, the aggressive "lady gangsters" pestering Hashidera to get married again; Tokyo and Osaka matrons in a comedy of manners that excels the finest of Jane Austen; and even foreign housewives, such as the German neighbor, Mrs. Stolz, whose frankness in relations with her husband is a wonder to Sachiko and who is "a woman outstanding even among Germans." The cast also includes the Russian Kyrilenkos, with their "astonishing set of stomachs" and their "old one," whizzing around the skating rink, upright and confident, passionate in anti-English quarrels with her daughter. Ironically, this daughter later goes to England and makes a fine marriage. This incident leads Sachiko to meditate on Western ways of love and marriage, as she wonders if such cases are common in the West. But she concludes that Japanese common sense simply would not permit such unconventional alliances.

We do not see the world exclusively through the well-bred Makioka eyes, of course. There is also Oharu, herself described in rough terminology suitable to the view of her fellow servants: "It wasn't only that she was unwashed—she ate incessantly, she had chronic dyspepsia, and her breath was really enough to make one hold one's nose." Through such remarks, Tanizaki offers a maid's-eye view of the proprieties of Japan.[36]

These proprieties in turn help to define character, even as incidents reflect on larger philosophical or sociological questions. The quality of Sawazaki's lack of respect for the Makiokas' position is symbolized in his letter refusing Yukiko: he writes in pen and ink on a sheet of very ordinary paper, in contrast to his acceptance of Mrs. Sugano's invitation to the meeting (in brush on elegant paper). The magpie quality of Taeko's links with the traditional arts emphasizes her effi-

---

[36] The effect of such naive observers in Tanizaki's fictions is often enhanced by lower-class or rough dialect (such as Osaka-ben), impossible to reproduce in translation. Sometimes we see the action through a child's eyes, as in The Mother of Captain Shigemoto, one of Tanizaki's explorations beneath the surface of history. The young and very beautiful wife of an old man is stolen away by the trickery of a ninth-century prime minister. The boy Shigemoto is puzzled by his father's actions (when he at last does see his mother again, she is a nun). We follow the boy, sharing his mystification as he watches the father in the darkness of night. We share his feelings as he watches the father who seems to be abasing himself in contemplation of rotting female corpses, stinking, maggotty. Tanizaki carefully withholds inappropriate analysis of meaning or the intrusion of adult judgment here. The impersonal narrator simply footnotes what the boy *sees* with what has been *said*, linking this "contemplation of foulness" with Buddhist sources (texts that outlined a route to salvation). We hear the father speak to the boy of his feelings. But the boy knows nothing of the philosophy of the Buddhists or the psychology of his father. Thus—as the blind masseur provided a different perspective on the heroics of history in A Blind Man's Tale—so here we see the grand principles of history reduced to a boy's simple emotions: he would prefer the father to preserve his mother's beauty. The voice of the narrator merely speculates on "ordinary human sentiment"—sentiment that might include the idea that the father should love his son more.

cient modern character: she picks up exotica from the past—
rather as the mad old man of the *Diary* and the father-in-law
of *Some Prefer Nettles* make a hobby of assembling congenial
fragments of tradition. She discovers, for instance, the precise method used by geisha to avoid spoiling heavy lip
makeup. But has such a gesture any point in Taeko's world?

When Taeko is glimpsed as "a tenement woman" or trades
coarse jokes with the kimono maker—or when there is a
shadow of dissoluteness in her appearance as she lies ill with
dysentery at Okubata's house, though this feeling gives way
to her customary gaiety—Tanizaki hints of things to come.
Resembling in Sachiko's eyes "a charity patient picked up in
the gutter" or a servant in a teahouse ("not too proper an
establishment"), Taeko eventually becomes such a woman:
at the end of the novel she is living, unmarried, with her bartender in an upstairs room in Kobe.

The care with which Tanizaki always prepares the reader
to respond to characters through subtle clues is again evident
in this novel. The circumstances of the marriage meeting
with Sawazaki provide an excellent example. There are social hints that he is flawed: his willingness to participate in
an unconventional *miai*, the improbability of a man with his
millions actually wanting for his bride the third daughter of
an impoverished (though old) Osaka family. To these are
added psychological preparation, incidents foreshadowing
the coming disappointment: the ominous unexplained halt of
the train carrying the sisters to the meeting, a firefly hunt
that does not quite live up to the historic, courtly ideal. Then
we see the man himself, his dress a little too careless for the
occasion (suggesting that he is not taking this *miai* seriously),
his ordinary gestures, his unhealthy complexion hinting at a
glandular disorder.

Sachiko's response confirms the reader's: there is something a little furtive, effeminate, timid in his manner. His
character is summed up in the passage describing Sawazaki
as a man who "hated to be asked something he didn't know

the answer to." His flaw is established through his facile praise of calligraphy ("whether or not he had finished reading"—although it is customary to *contemplate* the beautiful brushwork). Moreover, the frown with which he responds to an allusion to a poem he does not know hints at Sawazaki's vanity.

In other episodes, Tanizaki uses conventional Japanese symbols such as seasonal images to illuminate word or gesture in both social and psychological terms. Sachiko reflects on the ancients grieving over fallen cherry blossoms. She recognizes that this is "something more than a fad or a convention"—and Tanizaki would certainly agree. But when Sachiko responds to the blossoms with "pleasant sorrow," she is not experiencing the delicate *aware* of a haiku poet. Her sorrow is limited to her own little world: regret for her sisters' passing youth and for her own. For the old aesthetic sense, Sachiko has substituted a modern and personal involvement.

In *The Makioka Sisters*, Tanizaki also uses seasonal images as a calendar recording the deterioration of sensitivity. And tradition itself disintegrates through the cherry-viewing parties of the Makiokas. At first a group so beautiful that even strangers beg them to pose for photographs, the girls return to Kyoto each year. Each year the scene is subtly dimmed. One by one the girls are missing from the group, until the last two years when Taeko's absence from the picture is a symbol of a more profound change. The seasons that mark the passing of time indicate the psychological change—from delightful "small daughter" to shabby mistress a of bartender.

It is true that in Tanizaki's world the song of the thrush, the double globeflower's bloom, and the fall of the pomegranate blossom come at the appointed time, as in Kawabata's scenes, and the old arts have not been lost. Even Taeko studies the dance, and the uncouth maid can write haiku and play a few tunes on the koto. Unfortunately, as Tanizaki hints, neither tradition nor participants are quite at their best.

Occasionally flaws in character are hinted through the inversion of traditional symbols—as when snowflakes are hinted by falling cigar ash. Etsuko listens to insects not in a palace garden but in the weed-choked yard of foreign neighbors. The firefly hunt is not a picture-book affair of long sleeves, the dance movement of fans, and the poetic image of a quiet river: it is a disorderly progression in *yukata* (cotton kimono) beside a ditch through the rice fields. Yet this is not the mocking and deflating allusion found in Mishima's pages. Rather Tanizaki seems to be gently suggesting that the traditional symbols—though no longer at their best—can survive (and delight).

The courtly illusion of princesses on firefly hunts is gone. Nevertheless, families do still write haiku. Even the impassive Yukiko is moved by the autumn moon-viewing verses sent from the Ashiya house. These lines are not the elegant brushwork of a Genji sending his perfumed fan to the lady behind the screen: one verse is written by the slatternly maidservant! Yet perhaps there are values in preserving the tradition. For it brings an emotion that is sadly lacking from the room in which Yukiko, lonely in Tokyo, sits watching the moon.

Again the question seems to be related to Tanizaki's interest in the *meaning* of forms. Tanizaki is familiar with a world in which a man is judged by the kind of twelfth-year memorial service he holds for his parents; where the correct form of a *miai* often seems to obscure the true meaning of the meeting; and where Yukiko, Teinosuke, and Sachiko seem all to have been made unhappy in order to save face for Tatsuo, head of the main household.

Too often in such a world, individuals become "thralls to the family name." Values are confused: the main house is more upset by Taeko's wish for a career than by her very irregular relationship to Okubata. Yet form may also at times offer a valuable way of protecting both appearance and reality. The elaborate precautions for masking Koi-san's love affairs may also be the only way of protecting "innocent" Yukiko, although Tanizaki again avoids unqualified approval. Yukiko's own formal mask—her detachment from events—is shown as ambiguous. She is so rank-conscious that she would sooner stand in the rain than enter a cab ahead of her sister. In her insistence on the proprieties, she misses one marriage opportunity after another. Yet Western readers may feel she is not so innocent. For although Taeko's own nature contributes to the youngest sister's downfall, and in spite of her willfulness and preference for unsuitable friends, we feel a certain sympathy. We find it difficult to avoid the suspicion that much of Taeko's trouble stems from the fact that she must wait for marriage until the will of that "pliant" elder sister Yukiko has been bent to fit the customary forms.

Once more, Tanizaki urges the reader to withhold either-or judgments. He shows us Itakura "sly" in Sachiko's eyes: but this is "childlike innocence" to the admittedly prejudiced Taeko. Itakura is conspicuous in his leather jacket, displaying the "peculiar coarseness of emigrants returned from America"; his motives are called in question. Yet it is he who rescues Taeko from the flood. The maid Oharu is careless in her work, unclean in her habits, and unreliable in her words. Nevertheless, she is the one whose strength helps bring the child Etsuko through the torrent, who finds shelter for the Tokyo family during a typhoon, and who first helps Taeko through the discomfort of dysentery and later shares Taeko's isolation during the surreptitious pregnancy. Even Yukiko, for all her reticence, her apparent coldness, and a shyness that seems totally inappropriate in the modern city, has her moments of action, strength, and speaking out.

Again we hear Tanizaki's characteristically balanced tone; again he takes a reflective look at things as they are. Once more he probes the masks of "seeming," yet qualifies implied criticism with layers of alternative interpretation: his ideal of ambiguity and shadows. At the same time, Tanizaki compares disparate ways of life, primarily in terms that expose clichés about Tokyo-Kansai contrasts, yet always with universal implications. In *The Makioka Sisters*, Tanizaki reveals more clearly than in any of his other novels how unreliable clichés are (and incidentally gives the lie to clichés about his own preference). Early in the novel, remarks on gestures and facial expressions and authentic Tokyo speech lead to the remark that Mrs. Niu has been cheapened and has betrayed her Osaka self. Yet when Elder Sister moves to Tokyo we see that the elegant Kansai way has its faults too: a dependence on things or ways of the past can keep the individual at a deadening distance from life.

Tsuruko has never even seen Tokyo. Thus her arrival could provide Tanizaki with a wonderful opportunity for innocent commentary in the tradition of a Swift or a Goldsmith. But Tanizaki is not concerned with a foreigner's-eye view: he is not interested in satiric destruction. His observer may be a foreigner in Tokyo; but she is also an adaptable Japanese housewife. To our surprise, as to her sisters', rather than being thoroughly distressed she settles down very well. She is not a particularly reliable observer: Tanizaki has already stressed her fondness for role-playing and her unusually narrow experience. Yet she is a fine vehicle for that middle way, the compromise of which Tanizaki seems so fond.

Tokyo is a place where even the *tatami* comes in an inferior size, where the winds are harsh and dry, and where the people seem cold. Yet it is a very convenient world with its shops, pleasant with its amusements for children, and invigorating with its clean air (obviously not the smoggy Tokyo of the 1970s). Differences run deep, though. Tanizaki is not blind to the difference between lonely Yukiko looking at that moon alone from her upstairs window in Tokyo while the family in Ashiya shares in the writing of haiku. But he also makes it clear that such disadvantages must be balanced against the Tokyo advantage of not having to worry over appearances (the "unknown" Makiokas of Tokyo do not have to keep up appearances as they had to in their role as an old

Osaka family). Tsuruko is free to retain her accent while adopting a new freedom of dress and of diet, while for the next generation—her children—there is no sense of loss at all.

The house in Tokyo may open wide cracks during a typhoon. Its shabbiness may be increased by contrast with the treasures from the dark Osaka home. Yet it provides a bright and busy setting, perhaps after all a more suitable environment for the growing family (recalling that Tanizaki's own lyric memories "In Praise of Shadows" were *not* his personal design for modern living). Rather than offering Osaka and Tokyo as signs of the changing times, Tanizaki uses their contrasts to footnote the concept of change itself: a point suggested by the subtle differences between the Tokyo of the novel's "now" and the Tokyo the sisters remember from childhood visits with their father.

The Makioka Sisters defines Tanizaki's interest in the world beyond Japan. Seidensticker, writing several years after publication of this book, claimed that Tanizaki was indifferent to the problems of the time.[37] Tanizaki might be offering his own response to that in Teinosuke's thought: "Times being what they were it seemed better not to let reckless talk invite trouble." After all, much of this novel was written during a period when direct commentary on the environment—national or international—was absolutely proscribed.

The climate of the times would thus account for the absence of political commentary, while social questions were the province of the proletarian writers to whom Tanizaki was opposed on aesthetic grounds. Moreover, Tanizaki is a master of point of view, and the world outside is *not* a world of which the Makiokas are generally aware—or a world about which most Japanese cared before the 1950s. When Tanizaki does look at the problems of the day, it is clear that his

---

[37] Edward Seidensticker, "Modern Japanese Literature," *Atlantic* 195 (January 1955):169.

real interest in the larger politico-social scene is its traditional function in defining the role of the individual.

The tiny world of the Makiokas does not necessarily lose
importance by virtue of the comparison. On the contrary, the
significance of personal dignity grows in our world of shifting values, conflicting judgments (such as the Kyrilenkos' attitudes toward England or the Japanese view expressed in
Sachiko's letter to Germany, when she is "overcome with
pleasure at the military successes of a friendly nation"), and
an uncertain future in which even Sachiko has to take an active part in air raid drills and bucket brigades. Once more we
enjoy Tanizaki's multiple and often unexpected points of
view.

There are in fact several references to the world outside in
The Makioka Sisters, but these are always most relevant to
the plot or to developing characterization. A comment on the
China Incident links with remarks on training "strong"
women; Taeko's dolls are a "disgrace . . . so far from everyday life," but what of *her* life? Study in Europe is delayed because of the worsening war situation. These allusions to
events beyond the Makioka world all function within the
story. At the same time, they hint at a broader philosophy of
human conduct, as in conversations about the possibilities of
friendship between Japan and China. Through the Makiokas'
comments on news items and international events, Tanizaki
offers continual reminders that for the ordinary man it is not
the grand army but the welfare of friends (in this context, the
Stolzes and Katharine) that counts.

The Makioka Sisters shows Tanizaki's characteristic preoccupation with the individual. As Meiji Man he may sometimes strike the foreigner and the Japanese alike as rather
self-conscious about the dichotomies of his world: the past-
present, Eastern-Western, traditional-modern contrasts already noted. Yet these were the problems of his time—as they
are for anyone caught between two cultures of conflicting
values. And it is in his fictional examinations of values that
Tanizaki excels.

To speak of his progress (writing style before and after his move to the Kansai) is to speak only of the natural growth of a superb craftsman whose themes and treatments remained remarkably consistent. The balanced tone, with a prosaic recounting of often quite outrageous material, offers a restrained irony that should not blind us to underlying meanings. Not that meaning is ever a simple matter—for Tanizaki's balance is also that of a master of ambiguous perspectives and multiple points of view, in early and late works alike.

Looking at *The Makioka Sisters*, we can see all this. We can also look back to earlier work for resemblances and to his last novels in which the irony at last roars out in the hearty laughter of *The Key* and *Diary of a Mad Old Man*. The psychological perceptions of these late works, however, are not evidence of new development (to be contrasted with Tanizaki's early "satanic" work, for example) but an outgrowth of earlier studies revealing Tanizaki's understanding of the motives of men—as well as of women and children.

Among the children are those of *Shōnen* (Youth, 1911), in which Mitsuko is teased by her timid half-brother Shin'ichi and his friends, grows masochistic, and learns to create terror; the twelve-year-old boy in the play *Kyōfu Jidai* (Age of Terror, 1916) who thinks that his brother has murdered his wife in order to marry his mistress; and the young Shigemoto (in *The Mother of Captain Shigemoto*, 1949–1950), missing his beautiful mother and puzzled by his father's response to the loss. Tanizaki examines the fears and dreams of ordinary men, too, sometimes by the indirect means of an *abnormal* state, as in *Watakushi* (1921), focusing feelings of guilt and innocence in the person of a thief, or in "Terror" (*Kyōfu*, 1913), where the man's clinically correct claustrophobia with its German terminology hints at the panic of Everyman himself.[38]

---

[38] In addition to the women mentioned in note 28, above, there is Shunkin, for instance. Tanizaki shows her streak of cruelty and stubbornness as

Since it is in connection with "female psychology" and "worship of women" that Tanizaki's name is so often mentioned, it might be as well to take one more look at his treatment of women and note that Tanizaki is primarily interested in woman's relationship with man. Often, seemingly small incidents comment on the difficulties of relationships, on the fact that no man or woman can truly know the heart of another. Thus Misako (in *Some Prefer Nettles*)—able to talk over her problems only with an outsider, Takanatsu—tells as much about the difficulties of marriage as any account in *The Makioka Sisters*, written twenty-five years later, or in *The Key* at the end of his career.

The European features of the waitress who attracts Kawai Jōji in *Chijin no Ai* (A Fool's Love, 1924–1925) have led to critical emphasis on possible East-West conflicts that Tanizaki was here working out. It is true that their relationship seems masochistic, that he is unable to break with this dream girl who resembles Mary Pickford—even when she takes innumerable foreign lovers—and that he humbles himself in order to keep her. But any modern marriage counselor will concede the validity of Tanizaki's case history, while any ordinary reader should be able to recognize that the *contrast* is artfully rendered in contemporary terms (at a time when Tanizaki's fellow Japanese were consciously concerned with changes in behavior—changes focused by the much-quoted earlier words of Emperor Meiji, who wished that Japan might take the good and not follow the bad of the promising new cultures of Europe and America).

For Tanizaki, differences in culture are only one aspect of

"common to the handicapped" (a realistic view at odds with the usual sentimental clichés). But the perceptions are usually enriched by humor (as when the fellow in *Kyōfu*, much to the distress of his companions, nips from a pocket flask), and by irony (reinforced in this case by the homophone *kyōfū*: moral reform). Tanizaki's understanding of women can be further appreciated in comparison with the works of his contemporaries (note 39, below).

his metaphors for the human condition, one manifestation of his favorite device of pairing opposites and letting the readers decide for themselves. In *Ashikari*, for instance, the narrator recalls a writer alluding to a community of courtesans as "a deplorable state of affairs," although to another man they offered "an earthly paradise." An ironic modern response to these courtesans assuming Buddhist names (seeing their labors as being in "a spirit of sacrifice") is balanced by the observation that these women (assailed by priests for creating a moral climate at variance with the teachings of the Buddha) were at least not taking life—whereas in the strictest of judgments, surely a "good" fisherman was, contrary to the injunctions of the Buddha, in fact taking life.

Here as in *The Makioka Sisters* and *The Key* the various perspectives (parallel subjective and objective comments, contradictory interpretations, ambiguities of word, gesture, and meaning) may remind us of the words of Natsume Sōseki's *I Am a Cat*: "There are two sides to everything." But in Tanizaki these two sides are apt to increase to half a dozen.

Other modern Japanese writers have exploited the ambiguities of meaning in their life and language, of course. They, too, have provided multiple points of view. Their fictions include "new" women in love and marriage—even as early as the 1930s women are playing the stock market, or sampling one another's husbands, or forming a club dedicated to "no more birthdays after thirty-five." The Western reader, however, may find some of the stories of bourgeois housewives, or slum women, or ladies of the Gay Quarters substituting sentimentality and clichés for the insights we find in Tanizaki.[39]

[39] For those who cannot read Japanese, there are useful summaries of works about "new" women in the Kokusai Bunka Shinkōkai *Introduction to Contemporary Japanese Literature* (1939). Stories by Tanizaki's contemporaries, including the view of married life in Kishida Kunio's play *Kami Fūsen* (The Paper Balloon, 1925) offer instructive comparisons. There is also the work of Tanizaki's mentor Kafū (whose characters in *Tsuyu no Atosaki* had struck Tanizaki as "puppets"). Kafū depicts a

Even the most successful story does not match his artful blendings.

Akutagawa, for example, is like Tanizaki a master crafts-man. Like Tanizaki he has been credited with satanic horrors and aesthetic style. In "Kesa and Moritō" he gracefully re-solves our anticipation of violence with the sound of a shutter opening and a glimpse of a shaft of pale moonlight. In "Gra-titude" *(Hōon-ki)* he offers multiple points of view ingenious-ly through three confessions: one by a notorious thief, Amakawa Jinnae; another by the man to whom he plays ben-efactor; and a third by the man's scapegrace son Yasaburō. These three interpretations of events, and the author's voice giving stage directions on facial expression and gesture, how-ever, lack the subtlety and nice balance of *humor* that en-liven Tanizaki's work.

Many of Tanizaki's contemporaries ended their stories with a question: "When and where will these two meet again?"—or as in the play by Fujimori Seikichi flashing a sign that reads "What made her do it?" But Tanizaki's ques-tions are unvoiced, though often related to specific incidents. Just what *did* the prostitute do to the author in *Itansha no Ka-*

---

waitress, Kimie, with uncommon sexual drive. But Kimie—like the waitress Sayoko in Hirotsu Kazuo's *Jokyū* (1931)—is very different from the waitress in Tanizaki's *Chijin no Ai*. We do not *feel* the emotions of these other women or the troubles of the three wives in Kikuchi Kan's *San Katei* (Three Families, 1934) as we understand their counterparts in Tani-zaki's pages. (The Western reader who can enjoy the original Japanese ver-sions of the works cited above feels no more empathy than does the reader confined to the Kokusai Bunka Shinkōkai synopses.) In Kafū's *Ude Kurabe* (Trial of Strength, 1916; translated by Kurt Meissner as *Geisha in Rivalry*), we find a fascinating account of the behind-the-scenes mechanics of a geisha's life, but emotions and motives are described rather than felt. Moreover, some of the "love-talk" tales are self-consciously literary in origin. For example, characters in Yamamoto Yūzō's novel *Onna no Isshō* (Life of a Woman, 1933) are modeled on de Maupassant's, and they ex-change Heine verses instead of traditional Japanese poems. In many stories, too, the "new" love is either stickily sentimental or aggressively ideological—as when "love" is expressed in a joined cry of "Workers, arise!"

nashimi? Who poured the scalding water on Shunkin and why? What is the nature of the "snake" in the untranslated *Shōnen* (where critics tend to focus on the presence of another cruel female—Mitsuko, the girl who frightens the other children)? Only marginally of Freudian significance, this focus of horror ultimately leaves the reader, like the boy, uncertain as to the nature of the threat. Was the snake real or carved from wood? And was the terror any less real or the domination more perverse if the beast's only life was in the imagination of a frightened boy?

Tanizaki's ambiguities may be poetic in the Japanese tradition or prosaic in the manner of a mystery story. His perceptive psychological studies are rendered with great artistry and always leave room for the reader to exercise imagination. His careful delineation of the past implies—but never makes explicit—a judgment of those who are merely fanciers of tradition.[40] At the same time, Tanizaki fashions from the past a commentary on the distance between dream and reality: between our hopes and "the way things are."

It might be tempting to read the voice of *Ashikari*'s narrator as Tanizaki's, "trying to embody the idea of my sense of loss that all these days are past," recognizing that many of his words seem "nothing but whimsical fancy to a young man," yet hinting that they are an essential means by which older people can endure the present. Tanizaki, however, has a full appreciation of modern ways and conveniences— though he continually exposes the weaknesses of those who use the modern marvels not because they are superior but simply because they are new. Again he implies a criticism of false values and superficial judgment.

But Tanizaki's fiction of ambiguity, his mastery of point of

---

[40] Tanizaki's fanciers of tradition include the old diarist, who dazzles his relatives with a knowledge of Heian and Kamakura pagodas and Buddhist sculpture—although his own Nirvana would be eternity beneath his daughter-in-law's footprints. The father-in-law of *Some Prefer Nettles* also plays with the past, acting it out with doll-Ohisa, while failing to recognize (as Kaname ultimately does) that she is not a puppet but a woman.

view, his understanding of both past and present, and his psychological insight illuminate the *in-yō* (yin and yang) of twentieth-century Japan without attempting to award the prize to either of the elements that must eventually settle into proper harmony. Tanizaki's essay "Kyoto: Her Nature, Food . . . and Women" demonstrates attitudes that provide clues to this balance and to his theory of fiction.

His aesthetic of shadows—his preference for vague language and meanings hinted at rather than specified—is one aspect of Kyoto, as his essay "In Praise of Shadows" revealed. He finds "art, tradition, elegance, and sophistication" in Kyoto's women now. But he also recalls the jolly custom of *zakone*, that occasion when customers, geisha, and *maiko* (young apprentice geisha) spread their bedding on the floor and "all jumped in together," sleeping happily in one room. A jolly custom, indeed, although "one would often wake up the next morning with a splitting headache."

That headache should remind us of the outstanding quality, the realistic touches, that help to maintain the balance in Tanizaki's chronicles of Japan. Recognizing the exquisite past and enjoying the often confusing (although convenient) present, he hints at the need for *values* upon which the future can depend. If Tanizaki's reflective, tentative tone seems reminiscent of Buddhist "acceptance" on some occasions, on others it is an intensely modern irony not to be confined within national attitudes but having a universal appeal.

Viewing tradition objectively, while gently mocking all empty conventions of word and gesture, Tanizaki illuminates a world that is, in final analysis, still the intensely Japanese home of Meiji Man's sons and grandsons. The Western reader needs some footnotes on the social and psychological context, of course. Often Tanizaki provides all the necessary clues—as in his carefully inserted perspectives on a time that valued Beauty in terms of a painful tattoo, an artist who produced exquisite sounds by following a tradition that included many cruel masters and suffering pupils, or a marriage that must consider family ahead of personal feelings. We can appreciate Tanizaki's role as chronicler in his recording of the minutiae of these unfamiliar worlds. At the same time, appreciating his craftsmanship, we can come to recognize his true role in recording the paradoxical ways of modern Japan.

The actors in Tanizaki's fictions are trained in a tradition—just as ninth-generation Kabuki actors proudly carry on the art of their ancestors. They are related, however tenuously, to Saikaku's amusing Men (and Women) Who Loved Love. But they are not so closely tied to time and place as Saikaku's seventeenth-century heroes. Their actions are sometimes linked with attitudes that differ from those in the West. Their eye for beauty is still more apt to be focused on the exquisite line of the back of the neck or on the delicate foot than on the curves of Western breasts. Telling detail, rich in connotation for the Japanese, may seem only tiresome cataloguing to the uninitiated. At the same time, words and gestures may seem impossibly vague to the Westerner demanding familiar conciseness and logic. Yet in the final analysis, Tanizaki has succeeded in the seemingly impossible. In his finely constructed chronicles he has set the universal Human Comedy upon a truly Japanese stage.

Works Available in English

"Aguri" (*Aoi Hana*, 1922). Translated by Howard Hibbett. In *Seven Japanese Tales* (below).

"Ashikari" (*Ashikari*, 1932). In *Ashikari and Story of Shunkin*, translated by Roy Humpherson and Okita Hajime. Tokyo: Hokuseidō, 1936.

"A Blind Man's Tale" (*Mōmoku Monogatari*, 1931). Translated by Howard Hibbett. In *Seven Japanese Tales*.

"Bridge of Dreams" (*Yume no Ukihashi*, 1959). Translated by Howard Hibbett. In *Seven Japanese Tales*.

Note: An explanation of seeming discrepancies in dating in both bibliography and chronology is to be found in the preface.

The Diary of a Mad Old Man (*Fūten Rōjin Nikki*, 1961–1962).
Translated by Howard Hibbett. New York: Knopf, 1965.

"The House Where I Was Born" (*Umareta Ie*, 1921). Translated by
S. G. Brickley. In *The Writing of Idiomatic English*, edited by
S. G. Brickley. Tokyo: 1951.

"In Praise of Shadows" (*In'ei Raisan*, 1933–1934). Translated by
Edward Seidensticker. *Japan Quarterly* 1(1954):46–52.
[Adapted by Edward Seidensticker in *Atlantic* 195(January
1955):141–144.]

The Key (*Kagi*, 1956). Translated by Howard Hibbett. New York:
Knopf, 1961.

"Kyoto: Her Nature, Food . . . and Women." *This Is Japan*
12(1965):222–225. Tokyo: Asahi Shimbun, 1964.

The Makioka Sisters (*Sasameyuki*, 1943–1948). Translated by Edward Seidensticker. New York: Knopf, 1957.

The Mother of Captain Shigemoto (*Shōshō Shigemoto no Haha*,
1949–1950). Parts 9 and 10 translated by Edward Seidensticker in *Modern Japanese Literature*, edited by Donald
Keene. New York: Grove Press, 1956.

"A Portrait of Shunkin" (*Shunkinshō*, 1933). Translated by Howard Hibbett. In *Seven Japanese Tales*. [Hibbett's translation,
annotated by Hayakawa Hiroshi, also appears in the bilingual Modern Japanese Authors series (Tokyo: Hara, 1965).
The story is summarized in *Introduction to Contemporary
Japanese Literature* (Tokyo: Kokusai Bunka Shinkōkai, 1939)
as *Shunkin: An Extract of Her Life*. It has also been translated
as *Story of Shunkin* (below).]

Seven Japanese Tales. Translated by Howard Hibbett. New York:
Knopf, 1963.

Some Prefer Nettles (*Tade Kuu Mushi*, 1928–1929). Translated by
Edward Seidensticker. New York: Knopf, 1955. [Summarized
in *Introduction to Contemporary Japanese Literature* as
Tastes Will Differ.]

A Springtime Case (*Otsuya-goroshi*, 1915). Translated by Iwado
Zen'ichi. Tokyo: 1927.

Story of Shunkin (*Shunkinshō*, 1933). Translated by Roy Humpherson and Okita Hajime. In *Ashikari and Story of Shunkin*.
Tokyo: Hokuseidō Press, 1936.

"Tattoo" (*Irezumi* or *Shisei*, 1910). Translated by Ivan Morris. In

Modern Japanese Stories, edited by Ivan Morris. Tokyo: Tuttle, 1962. [Tanizaki preferred to read the *kanji* as *Shisei*, and this is the reading given by Hibbett in *Seven Japanese Tales*, where the translation is titled "The Tattooer." A third translation of *Shisei* ("Tattoo") is that of Matsumoto Ryōzō in *Japanese Literature New and Old*. (Tokyo: Hokuseidō Press, 1961). Some scholars maintain that Tanizaki told *them* he preferred the reading of *Irezumi*. But I am afraid that there is no way of reaching final agreement on this subject.]

"Terror" (*Kyōfu*, 1913). Translated by Howard Hibbett. In *Seven Japanese Tales*.

"The Thief" (*Watakushi*, 1921). Translated by Howard Hibbett. In *Seven Japanese Tales*.

The White Fox (*Shirogitsune no Yu*, 1923). Translated by Eric Bell and Ukai Eiji. In *Eminent Authors of Contemporary Japan: One-Act Plays and Short Stories*. 2 vols. Tokyo: 1930–1931.

A Partial Chronology

1886   24 July: Born in Tokyo.

Studied classical Japanese literature at Tokyo Imperial University but did not graduate. Several little magazine pieces, including *Gakuyūkai Zasshi*, published before 1910.

1910   September: *Tanjō* (Birth), a historical play published in *Shinshichō*.

October: *Zō* (Elephant), a play with Edo setting, published in *Shinshichō*.

November: *Shisei* or *Irezumi* (Tattoo) published in *Shinshichō*. Collection of seven short stories and plays with this title published by Momiyama-shoten in December 1911.

December: *Kirin* (*Kirin*: mythical beast, symbolizing a genius), a story about Confucius, published in *Shinshichō*.

1911   January: *Shinzei*, a play, Tanizaki's first paid piece, published in *Subaru*.

June: *Shōnen* (Youth), the story that won Tanizaki critical recognition from Ōgai, Ueda Bin, and others, published in *Subaru*.

September: *Hōkan* (*Hōkan:* an entertainer, sometimes compared to a jester, who accompanied geisha) published in *Subaru*.

October: *Taifū* (Typhoon), a novel, published in *Mita-Bungaku*.

1912   February: *Akuma* (Demon) published in *Chūō Kōron*. Collection of short stories with this title published by Momiyama Shoten in January 1913.

July–November: *Atsumono* (Hot Soup; Stew), his first long work—but unsuccessful and incomplete. Serialized in *Tokyo Nichinichi Shimbun*.

November: *Himitsu* (Secrets), a short story, published in *Chūō Kōron*.

1913   January: *Zoku Akuma* (Second Demon) published in *Chūō Kōron*.

Kyōfu (Terror) published in *Osaka Mainichi Shimbun*.

May: *Koi o Shiru Koro* (Age Susceptible to Tender Sentiment), a play, published in *Chūō Kōron*.

1914   September: *Jōtarō* (Jōtarō: man's name) published in *Chūō Kōron*.

Haru no Umibe (Beach in Spring), a play.

Zōnen (Hatred) published by Hōneisha in a book titled *Iraka*.

1915   January: *Otsuya-goroshi* (The Murder of Otsuya; translated as *A Springtime Case*) published in *Chūō Kōron*. Published as book by Senshōkan in June.

June: *Hosshōji Monogatari* (Story of Hosshō Temple), a play with Heian setting, published in *Chūō Kōron*. Also staged in this year.

September: *Osai to Minosuke* (Osai and Minosuke), a novel with Edo setting, published in *Chūō Kōron*. Book published by Shinchōsha in October.

1916   January: *Shindō* (Wonder Boy), an autobiographical novel, published in *Chūō Kōron*.

March: *Kyōfu Jidai* (Age of Terror), a two-act play with Edo setting, published in *Chūō Kōron*.

1916–
1917   *Itansha no Kanashimi* (Sorrow[s] of a Heretic) written in 1916 and published in *Chūō Kōron* in July 1917.

1917   January: *Ningyo no Nageki* (Mermaid's Grief), set in Chinese palace, published in *Chūō Kōron*. Book published by Shunyōdō in April.

Uguisu Hime (Lady Nightingale), a play.

1918   August: *Chiisana Ōkoku* (Little Kingdom), a novel about a school group (construction resembles a mystery story), published in *Chūgai*.

October: *Kin to Gin* (Gold and Silver) published by Shunyōdō.

1919   January-February: *Haha o Kouru Ki* (Reminiscence of My Beloved Mother) published in *Tokyo Nichinichi Shimbun* and *Osaka Mainichi Shimbun*.

June-July: *Fumiko no Ashi* (Fumiko's Foot), a novel, serialized in *Yūben*.

Aru Shōnen no Obie (A Boy's Misgivings).

1921   *Umareta Ie* (The House Where I Was Born), a reminiscence, published in *Kaizō*.

March: *Watakushi* (I or Myself; translated as "The Thief") published in *Kaizō*.

1921–
1922   First act of *Aisureba Koso* (Because of Love; but translated into French as *Puisque je l'aime* by C. Jacob [Paris: Editions Émile-Paul Frères, 1925]) published in *Kaizō* in December 1921. Second and third acts, titled *Daraku*, published in *Chūō Kōron* in January 1922.

1922   March: *Aoi Hana* (Blue Flower; translated as "Aguri") published in *Kaizō*.

June: *Okuni to Gohei* (Okuni and Gohei), a play with Tokugawa setting, published in *Shinshōsetsu*. Staged at Teikoku Gekijō (with Tanizaki directing) in July.

Hommoku Yawa (Hommoku Nocturne [*yawa:* night talks]).

1923   January: *Shirogitsune no Yu* (Hotspring of the White Fox;

translated as *The White Fox*), a play, published in *Shin-chō*.

January-December: *Kami to Hito tono Aida* (Between God and Man), a novel, serialized in *Fujin Kōron*.

Ai Naki Hitobito (People without Love).

1924   March: *Mumyō to Aizen (Avidya* [Illusion] and Attachment; French translation: *Mumy et Aizen)*, a two-act play, published in *Kaizō*.

1924– *Chijin no Ai* (Fool's Love), a novel, serialized in *Osaka*
1925   *Asahi Shimbun* from March to June and in *Josei* (Pratonsha) from November 1924 to July 1925.

1925   July: *Akai Yane* (The Red Roof), a novel, published in *Kaizō*.

1926   January-May: *Tomoda to Matsunaga no Hanashi* (About Tomoda and Matsunaga), a novel.

1927   February-December: *Jōzetsuroku* (My Chattering Note; or My Voluble Note), an essay on techniques of fiction and popular novels, published in *Kaizō*.

1928– March 1928–April 1930: *Manji* (Buddhist Swastika), a
1931   novel with conversation in Kansai speech, published in *Kaizō*. Tanizaki later revised *Manji*—apparently with some assistance from persons native to the area. The narrator of the final version, published by Kaizōsha in April 1931, uses feminine Osaka speech forms and vocabulary throughout.

1928– December 1928–June 1929: *Tade Kuu Mushi (Tade*-Eat-
1929   ing Insects; translated as *Some Prefer Nettles*) published in *Tokyo Nichinichi Shimbun* and *Osaka Mainichi Shimbun*. Published by Kaizōsha in November 1929.

1930   March-September: *Rangiku Monogatari* (Chrysanthemum Tale), a story with Muromachi setting, serialized in *Tokyo* and *Osaka Asahi Shimbun*.

Tanizaki Jun'ichirō Zenshū (Collected Works) published in twelve volumes by Kaizōsha.

1931   January-February: *Yoshino Kuzu* (The Arrowroot of Yoshino), a novel, published in *Chūō Kōron*. Book published by Sōgensha in 1937.

September: *Mōmoku Monogatari (Mōmoku:* blindness; translated as *A Blind Man's Tale)* published in *Chūō Kōron.* Book published by Chūō Kōronsha in February 1932.

1932 February-April: *Watakushi no mita Ōsaka oyobi Ōsakajin* (Osaka and the Osakans I Know), essays, published in *Chūō Kōron.*

November-December: *Ashikari* (Reed Cutting; translated as *Ashikari)* published in *Kaizō.* Book published by Sōgensha in 1933.

1932– September 1932–March 1933: *Seishun Monogatari* (Mem-
1933 ories of My Youth), later retitled *Wakaki Hi no Kotodomo,* published in *Chūō Kōron.*

1933 June: *Shunkinshō* (Portrait of Shunkin) published in *Chūō Kōron.* Book published by Sōgensha in December.

Kaoyo (Kaoyo: a woman's name), a play in five acts.

1933– December 1933–January 1934: *In'ei Raisan* (In Praise of
1934 Shadows), an essay, published in *Keizai-ōrai.*

1935 Began translating *Genji Monogatari* into modern Japanese. (See 1936–1941 entry, below.)

1936 January-July: *Neko to Shōzō to Futari no Onna* (A Cat and Shōzō and His Two Women) published in *Kaizō.* Book published by Sōgensha in July 1937.

1936– January 1936–July 1941: *Jun'ichirō Yaku Genji Monoga-*
1941 *tari* (Tanizaki's modern Japanese version of *Genji Mono-gatari)* published in twenty-six volumes by Chūō Kōron-sha.

1937 Elected member of Japan (Imperial) Academy of Arts.

1943– First installment of *Sasameyuki* (Thin [or Light] Snow;
1948 translated as *The Makioka Sisters)* published in *Chūō Kōron* in January 1943. Work was "censured," but Tani-zaki himself published early part of *Sasameyuki* in July 1944. Chūō Kōronsha published early sections in June 1946 and the middle section in February 1947. Last part serialized March 1947 to October 1948 in *Fujin Kōron.* Book published by Chūō Kōronsha in December 1948.

1947   Mainichi Prize for Publication and Culture awarded for
        Sasameyuki.

1949   Awarded Asahi Culture Prize for *Sasameyuki.* Awarded
        the Imperial Cultural Medal.

1949–   December 1949–March 1950: *Shōshō Shigemoto no Haha*
1950   (*Shōshō:* major-general, or sometimes "court noble"; pts. 9
        and 10 translated as "The Mother of Captain Shigemoto")
        published in *Mainichi Shimbun.* Book published by Maini-
        chi Shimbunsha in August 1950.

1955–   April 1955–March 1956: *Yōshō-jidai* (Boyhood) published
1956   in *Bungei Shunjū.* Book published by Bungei Shunjūsha in
        March 1957.

1956   January-December: *Kagi* (The Key) published in *Chūō*
        Kōron. Book published by Chūō Kōronsha in December
        1956.

1959   *Tanizaki Jun'ichirō Zenshū* (Collected Works) published
        by Chūō Kōronsha.

        October: *Yume no Ukihashi* ([Floating] Bridge of Dreams)
        published in *Chūō Kōron.* Book published by Chūō Kōron-
        sha in February 1960.

1961–   November 1961–May 1962: *Fūten Rōjin Nikki* (Diary of a
1962   Mad Old Man) published in *Chūō Kōron.* Book published
        by Chūō Kōronsha in May 1962.

1962–   October 1962–March 1963: *Daidokoro Taiheiki* (Life
1963   Around the Kitchen—his maid) published in *Sunday Mai-*
        nichi. Book published by Chūō Kōronsha in April 1963.

1964   Elected honorary member of American Academy and
        National Institute of Arts and Letters.

1965   "Kyoto: Her Nature, Food . . . and Women" published in
        This Is Japan 12(1965):222–225. Tokyo: Asahi Shimbun,
        1964.

        30 July: Tanizaki died.

        September: *Nanajūkyūsai no Haru* (The Spring of My
        Seventy-Ninth Year), Tanizaki's last writing, published
        posthumously in *Chūō Kōron.*

3

Kawabata Yasunari

*K*awabata Yasunari, awarded the Nobel Prize in literature in 1968, was born in Osaka in 1899. Son of a physician
who wrote Chinese poems, he was orphaned as a small child
and raised by grandparents and (after they, too, had died) by
an uncle. At one time, he wanted to be a painter, but by the
time he was a sophomore in middle school Kawabata had determined to become a writer. His first magazine publication
was *Shi no Hitsugi o Kata ni* (Carrying My Teacher's Coffin
on My Shoulder, originally titled *Kuraki Sensei no Sōshiki*) in
Danran, a little magazine, in 1915. While he was still a
schoolboy, Kawabata also saw some of his work appear in
Keihan Shimpō (a local newspaper of Ibaragi). These publications included several tanka and such short pieces as *Awayuki no Yoru* (Night of Light Snow) and *Murasaki no
Chawan* (Purple Teacup).

In 1920 Kawabata entered the English Literature Department of Tokyo Imperial University, but he transferred to the
Department of Japanese Literature because the attendance
requirements were less strict and he wanted to write.[1] After

---

[1] Accounts of Kawabata's difficulties in college are to be found in Volume 4 of *Kawabata Yasunari Zenshū* (Collected Works, in the sixteen-

getting permission from novelist Kikuchi Kan to revive the title *Shinshichō*, Kawabata and a group of university friends published this little magazine, in which his *Shōkonsai Ikkei* (Memorial Day Scene) appeared in April 1921.

Kikuchi and other writers praised this story, and Kikuchi continued to recommend Kawabata's work. Much of Kawabata's early work was literary criticism, however, and it was as a critic rather than a novelist that many of his contemporaries saw this "young lover of literature." His first paid article in fact was a book review, *Nambu-shi no Sakufū* (Mr. Nambu's Literary Style) in *Shinshichō*, for which he received ten yen in December 1921. After graduating from the university, Kawabata joined Yokomitsu Riichi and others in publishing *Bungei Jidai* (Literary Age), the magazine that served as focus for the *Shinkankaku-ha* (neo-perceptionists). The friendship with Yokomitsu was particularly close, as diary entries, the postscripts in the *Zenshū* (Collected Works), and Kawabata's words when Yokomitsu died all testify.

The Japanese themselves, although at first surprised that the Nobel Committee had recognized such a very "Japanese" writer, are unanimous in praise of the quality of Kawabata's work—as they have been since his *The Izu Dancer (Izu no Odoriko)* was published in February and April 1926. They have praised his poetic language, spoken of his "calm and thorough Japanese eyes," and admired his "pursuit of Japanese beauty." Yet there is a remarkable range in interpretation of Kawabata's work in Japan. One critic declares

---

volume edition of 1948 to 1954). The *Zenshū* include a number of postscripts that illuminate Kawabata's theory and practice of the art of fiction and offer clues to interpretation of many of his stories. There are also many biographical notes on his financial difficulties as well as on his literary and psychological development. For instance, Kawabata tells of giving the manuscript of *Umi no Himatsuri* as security for a loan, pawning a watch to buy paper and ink, and lacking money to pay his rent. Even when he was writing these postscripts for the volumes published in honor of his fiftieth birthday, he was still plagued by unpaid bills.

that *Snow Country* is characterized by abstractionism and surrealism; another finds the structure of the Nō in Kawabata's work, comparing the narrator of *The Izu Dancer* with the *waki* (second player) and seeing the dancing maiden as the *shite* (first player). One critic declares that Kawabata's favorite theme is that of a woman who lives by selling her artistic talent. Others identify a recurrent motif of "traveling." Kawabata's colorful protégé, Mishima Yukio, examines Kawabata's work in *Eien no Tabibito*, and in his introduction to *House of the Sleeping Beauties* declares that Kawabata's theme is "the worship of virgins"—a theme that Mishima regards as the source of Kawabata's "clean lyricism."

Western observers have been similarly challenged to find approaches to meaning in Kawabata's work. One has even gone so far as to find affinities with both Ernest Hemingway and Henry James. Western surprise at the time of the Nobel award, however, was based on the very small number of Kawabata's works then available in translation. One of the works mentioned by the committee, *Koto* (Ancient City, 1961–1962), has not yet been translated into English,[2] although the other novels mentioned by the committee had both been translated: *The Izu Dancer* and *Snow Country* (1935–1937, 1947, and 1948).

Only a handful of other works were then available in English: the novel *Thousand Cranes* (*Senbazuru*, 1949–1951); "The Mole" (*Hokuro no Tegami*, 1940), "The Moon on the

---

[2] *Koto* has been translated into German by Walter Donat as *Kyōto* (1968). It is a novel variously read as "a pastoral symphony" and a modern fairy tale in the tradition of the *Bamboo Cutter's Tale* (a Japanese classic of an abandoned baby). Enriched by familiar seasonal images and by contrasting light and dark women (twin sisters eventually reunited at a Kyoto festival), this is another of Kawabata's lyrical evocations of time and memory. One more lyrical treatment of recurrent themes is *Beauty and Sadness* (*Utsukushisa to Kanashimi to*, 1961–1963). Unfortunately, this was not translated until 1975, after my manuscript had been completed, and it has therefore not been possible to discuss this work at any length. (See Note 32, below.)

Water" (*Suigetsu*, 1953), and "One Arm" (*Kata-ude*, 1963–1964) in various anthologies and *Japan Quarterly*; excerpts from *The Sound of the Mountain* (*Yama no Oto*, 1949–1954) in *Japan Quarterly*; and a short story, "Reencounter" (*Saikai*, 1946), published in a bilingual anthology in Tokyo. Seidensticker was working on a translation of *Nemureru Bijo* (Sleeping Beauty or Beauties, 1960–1961), later published with *Of Birds and Beasts* (*Kinjū*, 1933) in *House of the Sleeping Beauties and Other Stories*; he completed a full translation of *Sound of the Mountain* in 1970.

At the press interviews following announcement of the Nobel Prize, Kawabata said that he felt rather uneasy because the decision was not based on his work in Japanese. *Snow Country*, for instance, had been translated into Swedish from Seidensticker's English version, and English has been the medium through which Kawabata's work has most often reached the West, a point that Kawabata himself made clear in paying gracious tribute to his various translators.

The translators in turn have spoken eloquently of their difficulties. One is the familiar problem of levels and kinds of speech, found even in the straightforward prose of Tanizaki. In *Snow Country*, for instance, there is no way for the translator to share with Western readers the effect in Japanese of the "masculine" talk of Shimamura and the correctly "feminine" speech forms of Komako—although this makes the problem of *who* is speaking rather less for the Japanese reader. Nor can the Western reader absorb on the one hand the nuances of Shimamura's shifting from *ko* (girl) to *onna* (woman) as he talks to Komako or, on the other, Komako's responses to those nuances.

Sometimes Western critics sound as though they are faulting Kawabata for not using a familiar narrative technique. It must be understood at the outset, though, that Kawabata does not employ the usual techniques of narration and that his prose style—especially in its use of wordplay and highly allusive imagery—does not quite survive translation. Never-

theless, patient interpretation of his symbols and some understanding of Kawabata's technique can be gained even from
the admittedly limited materials now available in English.

One other difficulty must be noted, and that is a bibliographical one. Other Japanese novelists have published their
work in serial form and under various titles, but Kawabata is
further noted for his habit of rewriting, adding segments, and
making changes in titles and content alike. Some future
scholar will doubtless meet the challenge with a Variorum
Kawabata. In the meantime, we can only note such examples
as *Snow Country*. Its first segment, titled *Yūgeshiki no
Kagami* (Mirror of the Evening Scene), appeared in *Bungei
Shunjū* in January 1935. According to Kawabata's own version of subsequent publications, he had more to say than
could be written in time for the *Bungei Shunjū* deadline. But
the *Kaizō* deadline was later, and he could make revisions
and additions to his original idea, titling this (second) version
Shiroi Asa no Kagami (Mirror of a White Morning). Other
segments, variously titled *Monogatari* (Story), *Torō* (Futile
Efforts), *Hi no Makura* (Pillow of Fire), and *Temariuta*
(Handball Song) were published from November 1935
through May 1937. A "complete" *Yukiguni* appeared in
June 1937; and another version appeared in 1948.[3] *The
Sound of the Mountain (Yama no Oto)* was published in seventeen segments from September 1949 through April 1954,
although the titles of these segments were sometimes changed
before *Yama no Oto* appeared as a "complete" novel of sixteen chapters.

[3] There were numerous textual changes in the magazine segments when
they reappeared in the 1937 *Yukiguni*, especially changes in characterization and in style (from more realistic and straightforward to lyrical and
symbolic). Further changes were made in the 1948 version. And yet
another revised manuscript of *Snow Country* was found among Kawabata's papers after his suicide, with the notation: "Finished writing this
February 1972." He had made more than one hundred changes (words
and phrases) and had deleted some passages.

Many single stories similarly changed titles. For instance, *Ochiba to Fubo* (Fallen Leaves and Parents, 1925) becomes *Ochiba to Chichi* (*Chichi:* father) and appears under several other titles as well. "The Mole" (*Hokuro no Tegami*, literally "The Mole's Message" or "Letter," 1940) is in some versions "The Mole's Diary" (*Nikki*), and it first appeared as *Akusai no Tegami* ("Bad Wife's Letter"). The titles are often richly allusive, as in the case of *Chirinuruo*, already noted, and *Suigetsu* (discussed below), so that the reader wishing to truly understand Kawabata's meaning must track down the multiple hints contained even in title changes. Finally, Japanese and American publishers, editors, scholars (and even Kawabata himself, as in his Collected Works) often disagree on dates.

Acknowledging these difficulties at the outset, the Western reader can, however, find a useful frame of reference in the classical literature of Japan. For here, rather than in supposed links with individual French writers, or European movements, or the Scandinavian literature he is said to have read in high school, are the true sources of Kawabata's delicate prose. In his *Who's Who Among Japanese Writers*,[4] Kawabata makes clear his interest in such classics of the Heian period as *Genji Monogatari* (*The Tale of Genji*) and *Makura no Sōshi* (*The Pillow Book* of Sei Shōnagon). In *Japan, the Beautiful, and Myself* (*Utsukushii Nihon no Watashi—sono Josetsu*),[5] Kawabata describes *The Tale of Genji* as the pinna-

[4] Compiled by Kawabata and Aono Suekichi for the Japanese National Commission for UNESCO/PEN Club (Tokyo, 1957).

[5] Kawabata's Nobel Prize acceptance speech of 12 December 1968— published by Kōdansha in Japanese and English (Tokyo, 1969). (The volume is printed Japanese-style from the "back," with pages numbered accordingly—and thus making the English translation "begin" at p. 74 and end at p. 41.) In his public lectures at the University of Hawaii in 1969, Kawabata similarly asserted that no Japanese novel has ever measured up to *Genji;* and in "Undying Beauty" (1969) he wrote that he chose *The Tale of Genji* and the literature of the Muromachi period (1335–1572) "to help me forget the war and endure the defeat."

cle of Japanese literature: he says that it was his principal
boyhood reading. Kawabata also refers to the suggestions,
the inferences, and the evocative qualities of Japanese poetry.
He writes eloquently of characteristic Japanese art, in which
the "heart" is space, succinctness, and "what is left out." He
concludes with references to a thirteenth-century priest-poet
who wrote of the Buddha, the manifestation of ultimate
truth, being found in the empty sky.

Kawabata finds in this emptiness with its spiritual or Buddhist foundation the "nothingness" of his own works—a
point that critics speaking of nihilism in its Western sense
should remember. Kawabata's words in the essay "Undying
Beauty" are also helpful, especially his discussion of the affinity of beauty and sadness in Japan (a theme echoed in the
title of the last complete novel to be published in his lifetime:
Utsukushisa to Kanashimi to [Beauty and Sadness, 1961–
1963]).[6] During the wartime years of violence, Kawabata has
told how he found consolation in the works of poets who
lived in earlier times of unrest; and in "Undying Beauty" as
in his other essays we find references to the *waka* of Saigyō,
the *renga* of Sōgi, the haiku of Bashō, and the various diarists
attempting to preserve a literary tradition (for example,
Teika's *Meigetsuki:* Chronicle of the Harvest Moon). He
speaks too of his affinity with the art and literature of the period of Ashikaga Yoshimasa, whose fifteenth-century Silver
Pavilion expresses an aesthetic different from Kyoto's earlier
Golden Pavilion.

All these references are reinforced by Kawabata's use of
phrases and images from centuries of Japanese poetry, his
new expressions of the traditional feeling of *renga* (linked
verses). He has repeatedly spoken of his intention: to preserve
the "traditional taste," that is, the poetic sense, of Japan—a
sense that he reminds us has always linked beauty with sad-

---

[6] In *This Is Japan* 17(1970):57–58 (published by Asahi Shimbun in
1969).

ness. This tradition is more helpful in understanding Kawabata than any discussion of his association with the neoperceptionists.[7] Of course, one cannot ignore this association, but the shifting interests and allegiances of the group, and the ways in which Kawabata differs from Yokomitsu, for example, suggest that his appreciation of "the deathlessness of Japanese beauty" is the more helpful approach. This beauty in its poetic expression (the seasons, the moon, the snow, the hints of meaning) is especially important. Beauty is frequently symbolized in the person of a girl—sometimes passive, sometimes aggressive, but always passionate, although the passions may be only hinted at and expressed through traditional erotic symbolism. Yet Kawabata also conveys the sexuality of these girls and their older counterparts with richly sensual images as varied as a sheaf of rice, a "voluptuous" tea ceremony bowl, and a glowing pink nipple responding to a man's—or a woman's—touch.

The images do not always survive transposition into alien languages. But even in translation Kawabata is clearly a poet, steeped in tradition, yet viewing contemporary life with an extraordinarily perceptive eye. Close reading shows that his intensely Japanese scenes—a mountain resort with its geisha, a tea ceremony cottage with its centuries-old utensils, a room illuminated by generations of moon-conscious poets —provide settings for sensitive portrayals of timeless and universal human feelings. It is unfortunate that difficulties of the

---

[7] Other writers of the *Shinkankaku-ha* (neo-perceptionist) group use a challenging syntax in which sentences are linked by traditional associations rather than narrative logic—as Kawabata uses mirrors, autumn grasses, tea ceremony utensils. But comparisons of Kawabata and Yokomitsu will show the ways in which Kawabata's fiction is invariably more *deeply* allusive and richer in implication. Readers unable to appreciate nuances in the Japanese original, however, should remember that Japanese scholars themselves offer varied (and contradictory) interpretations of Kawabata's links with the neo-perceptionists and neo-romantics (as well as the characteristics and membership of those groups).

Japanese language itself and of Kawabata's own poetic, highly allusive style result in our seeing but a thin reflection of his
work in the West. Yet in just that image—the reflected moon
—we may find illumination, an introduction to all those
qualities of Japanese aesthetics already discussed.

The Moon in the Water: Tradition and Myth

The best introduction to Kawabata's work is the short story,
Suigetsu, translated as "The Moon on the Water." An understanding of its imagery can suggest the depths of meaning in
longer and more complex stories. Even the title is so richly allusive that a whole volume of annotation would scarcely do
justice to all its possibilities. Also, we have to admit at the
outset that not all Japanese readers will be aware of the more
esoteric hints of *sui-getsu*, literally water-moon, and more
properly translated as "The Moon *in* the Water" to make the
allusions clear.

Japanese readers will at least *see* the familiar picture of the
moon and may think of moon viewing, even if this is only a
modern autumn moon-viewing party like those of Tanizaki's
Makioka Sisters. September is the focal time of the *Suigetsu*
narrative, while autumn is the "sad season," appropriate to a
story that is a meditation on the qualities of death and beauties of (transient) life. Japanese literature is rich in poetic images of the moon. Moon, flowers, and snow together are a
synonym for beauty, three pictures frequently depicted in the
calligraphy on the scroll hanging in the *tokonoma*, especially
of tea ceremony rooms. Kawabata himself quotes many such
lines in his essays and fictions. In *Japan, the Beautiful, and
Myself* he quotes two thirteenth-century poems on the moon.
He adds that he likes to write these lines when he is asked to
provide examples of his calligraphy.[8]

---

[8] One of these is from Dōgen: "In the spring, cherry blossoms, in the
summer the cuckoo./ In autumn the moon, and in winter the snow, clear,

There are scores of phrases used in describing the moon: these range from *kan-getsu*, the ice-cold winter moon, to *mei-getsu*, that glittering, richly luminous full moon of autumn. But even more important, there are countless allusions to the specific image of the moon in the water. Lines by Chōshū, Buson, Saigyō, Bashō, and other masters immediately come to mind; whole episodes in *The Tale of Genji*; the closing words of the Kabuki play *Sesshū Gappō ga Tsuji* (1773) in which the dying Tamate is a model of womanhood, "her mind as clear as the moon reflected on the inlet . . . she is pure"; and Nō plays such as *Izutsu*, in which two lovers look at their reflection in a well. Chikamatsu's puppet play *Nebiki no Kadomatsu* has a much-quoted line on "the basin that holds no more moonlight" (a triple-layered allusion to a courtesan's ransom). Favorite scenes of Japanese dance include the salt makers, as in *The Makioka Sisters* (where Tanizaki describes the old dance teacher urging her pupils to concentrate on "the unreal moon in the brine buckets"). Every literate Japanese knows the lines in Kannami's Nō play *Matsuka-ze:* "The moon is one, the reflections two" and "to dip up the reflected moon —how poetic." Kannon, Goddess of Mercy, is

---

cold." It is in Dōgen's words that we find one of the most beautiful interpretations of the moon-in-the-water image. Kawabata also refers to the work of Myōe, "the poet of the moon," and reads one of Myōe's 31–syllable poems as a work of "compassion" and "deep Japanese spirit." It should be noted, too, that even in today's transistorized and skyscrapered Japan, businessmen, housewives, and students occasionally hold autumn moon-viewing parties and write haiku while they listen to insects. The more "progressive" may scorn the habit as old-fashioned and artificial, but the department stores on Tokyo's Ginza still do a thriving trade in chirping insects. Tokyoites wishing to write autumn haiku today may have to carry their beetles and crickets home in plastic cages: it takes a hardy bug to survive Tokyo smog. In *The Lake* (*Mizuumi*, 1954), Gimpei hangs one of these modern cages on the back of a girl's dress—the fireflies being part of a commercialized "ceremony" in Tokyo but also, in Kawabata's story, serving as a link between Gimpei's memory and the poetic hints of meaning.

frequently depicted looking at the moon in the water. Yet these examples by no means exhaust the lyric richness of the title *Suigetsu*.

For "the moon in the water" is also an established phrase in Buddhist literature: "something without substance." In the *Zenrin Ku-shū* (Anthology of Zen Poems), the idea is expressed in the lines: "A pair of monkeys are reaching / For the moon in the water." This is a poem to admonish the student who seeks truth in something without substance, yet its "twisted" meaning (the paradox typical of Zen logic) reverses the apparent significance. The student should not differentiate apparent opposites and contradictions—Buddha and sentient beings or enlightenment and delusion (the moon in the water). The real is unreal and the unreal is real. So in the Zen interpretation, the moon in the water *is* a real moon.

Or one might refer to the words in the Dōgen conversations recorded by the disciple Ejō in *Shōbō Genzō Shakui:*

> Our attainment of enlightenment is something like the reflection of the moon in the water. The moon does not get wet, nor is the water cleft apart. Though the light of the moon is vast and immense, it finds a home in water only a foot long and an inch wide. The whole moon and the whole sky find room enough in a single dewdrop, a single drop of water. And just as the moon does not cleave the water apart, so enlightenment does not tear man apart. Just as a dewdrop or drop of water offers no resistance to the moon in heaven, so man offers no obstacle to the full penetration of enlightenment.[9]

[9] From Tsunoda Ryusaku, Wm. Theodore de Bary, and Donald Keene (compilers), *Sources of Japanese Tradition* (1964, copyright 1958 by Columbia University Press), vol. I, p. 246 (quoted by permission of the publisher). An instructive contrast to the deeply apprehended Buddhist sensibility of Kawabata's work can be found in *The Buddha Tree*, written by a former Buddhist priest, Niwa Fumio. Niwa tells of esoteric ritual, of the conflicts in the life of a priest (for example, private versus public duty), and of his relationship with wife and mother-in-law (the protagonist sleeps with his mother-in-law rather than with his wife). Whereas Niwa talks about the loss of meaning in Buddhist ritual, Kawabata *shows* loss of meaning, as in

None of this of course is intended to imply that Kawabata is a Zen writer. Zen Buddhism is only one aspect of the cultural heritage of which he makes such subtle use in his allusive prose.

Certainly not all Japanese readers will be aware of all the Buddhist allusions: nor will they immediately link the title of this story with the name of the young wife, Kyōko, or the mirror held by her bedridden husband. Yet the echoes are there for anyone who will listen. In Zen literature *kyōka* (the flower reflected upon the mirror) may be used instead of *suigetsu*. The *kanji* that is *kagami* in its Japanese reading (when it is written alone) becomes *kyō* in the Chinese reading (in compounds), so that the sound of Kyōko's name is linked with the differently written *kyōdai*, the mirror stand of this story, and with *kyōmen*, the reflective surface of a mirror.

The linking of moon and mirror, moreover, is a traditional association found as far back as the seventh-century verse in the *Man'yōshū*, where the lines to a princess temporarily enshrined include this memory: "Walking hand in hand, your eyes / Fondly fixed upon your lord as upon a mirror, / Admiring him ever like the glorious moon."[10] There may even be hints in the title of Kawabata's story of another *sui*, the

_____

the tea ceremony of *Thousand Cranes*. In *Thousand Cranes*, Kawabata again makes use of the moon-in-the-water image of *Suigetsu* (in this case a star reflected in the garden's stone basin). In *Sound of the Mountain*, Kikuko is linked with the reflection of the new moon in the well water. And in *Beauty and Sadness* the lesbian lovers participate in a ceremony that includes the drinking of sake from a bowl in which the full moon is reflected.

[10] The mirror of the water-moon image has literary-cultural allusions rooted both in Buddhist and in Shintō thought. Legends of the origins of Japan tell of the three Divine Treasures: Mirror, Sword, and Jewel, today guarded in the Grand Shrine of Ise and Atsuta Shrine in Nagoya. The mirror is thus a link with Japan's ancient gods of sun and moon. In addition, according to Shintō belief the mirror is a sacred embodiment of the *kami* ("spirit" or "god[s]"). It suggests the unstained mind and is "the source of honesty," hiding nothing, according to generations of scholars and priests. Also, the phrase "the moon in the water" and its equivalent "the flower in the mirror" are part of the Zen philosophy of swordsmanship—but the sword is Mishima's symbol, not Kawabata's.

homonym meaning "essence," as well as the colloquial reading of *sui* as "knowledge of the world."

The foregoing may seem like excessive delving into a
two-*kanji* title, yet these are only a few of the hints contained
in the deceptively simple image of water-moon. These possibilities deepen a meaning that is never made specific,
enriching the implications we find even in a simple outline of
the story. One might also keep in mind the lines by Bashō
that Kawabata quoted in "Undying Beauty": "In what is
meditated upon is nothing that is not of the moon." For the
whole of *Suigetsu* is a third-person reverie or meditation told
from the point of view of Kyōko, the wife.

We begin with Kyōko's recollections of letting a bedridden
husband see her garden reflected in a hand mirror. Gradually, Kawabata reveals that she has married again, this new
husband being a divorced man fifteen years her senior and
father of a young son. When the bedridden husband died,
Kyōko secretly placed in his coffin the hand mirror and a
mirror from her never-used honeymoon case. After the cremation, people wondered what the "shapeless mass" could
be. Kawabata does not make explicit the hint of esoteric
meaning, the resemblance of these melted mirrors to *shari*,
the gemlike substance supposed to be found in the ashes after
cremation of a Buddhist saint. Nor does Kyōko tell either
family or second husband that the answer to this mystery lies
in her own gesture.

There are other mysteries. Kyōko, outwardly still childlike, feels "as if her husband . . . had been a child inside her."
When she becomes pregnant in the second marriage, she is
deranged—a confusion reflected in such incidents as providing her stepson with two rice lunches. Only at the end, when
she revisits the old mountain home once shared with the sick
husband, does Kyōko startle herself with the thought: "What
if the child should look like you?" Only then does she turn
back to life (with her second husband), "warm and at
peace."

As in other Kawabata stories, events and relationships are

gradually unfolded in a series of memories linked with a specific image. Like the water jar and cups for the tea ceremony in *Thousand Cranes* or the red maples in *Sound of the Mountain*, there is in *Suigetsu* a mirror. A first look at this mirror shows only a secular object: a part of Kyōko's (unused) trousseau. At the beginning, the reflection offers only a fresh perspective of Kyōko's (unawakened) beauty, as her young husband perhaps finds "something new in the mirror." By the time she thinks of letting the now-sick husband see her garden, the mirror's surface has become cloudy, its rim smeared with face powder and dirt. Kawabata delicately sketches "the world in the mirror." For the husband, it is a world of sky, clouds, snow, distant mountains, and nearby woods. He sees the moon, and the flowers, those other elements of the image "beauty." But that is not all: "Men walked down the road in the mirror and children played in the garden." Eventually, as she and her husband look into the mirror together, Kyōko cannot distinguish between the world seen directly and the reflection. "Two separate worlds came to exist. A new world was created in the mirror and it came to seem like the real world." The mirror even reflects a silver sky —though the sky itself looked grey. The mirror becomes "the eye of their love."

After her second marriage, Kyōko does not lose "that unique feeling her former husband had planted in her toward the beauty in the mirror," although her own reflection seems to lack the special bright quality of reflected sky. She comes to yearn for the separate world shared with the first husband —an "almost physical yearning" that for the sake of her new husband she tries to interpret as "something like a distant view of the celestial world."

This interplay between sexual and metaphysical is in fact one of the charms of this story—as of so much of Kawabata's work. The sexual overtones are inescapable: the mirror stand (matched by the cremated hand mirror) is likened to a widow; hand mirror and toilet-case mirror carry a variety of bridal associations; Kyōko's musty and (neglected) toilet case is contrasted with the "large and strong . . . [but] not new" case of the twice-married new husband. The first husband dies of tuberculosis, traditionally associated with unrequited or unexpressed love in Japan.

But the worlds reflected in the mirror are more than physical. There is, for instance, a terrifying instant when Kyōko perceives that she can see her own *self* only in the mirror. Out of this comes an appalling vision of her first husband seeing "death itself" in his reflection and committing psychological suicide. Yet even as Kyōko suspects herself of committing psychological murder, she remembers: "He would have sacrificed his life to keep the world in the mirror."

Reflections in Japanese literature, however, are not to be confused with our Western (Platonic) deceptions, as the Zen paradox has already made clear. Also, Japanese aesthetics would find the "reflection of a reflection" that lingered in Kyōko's heart even more beautiful than the shining world. Misty qualities—and even empty vases (as in the accounts of a tea master's empty vase hinting that guests should look outside at the [snow] "flowers")—always suggest much more than they reveal at first glance. The water-moon of this story is just such a subtle image: "After heavy rains he and Kyōko would gaze at the moon through the mirror, the reflection of the moon from the pool in the garden."

The beauty of the mirror must nevertheless be balanced against its terrors: Kyōko's perception that her very face changed when she became pregnant and her belief that she could "see straight through" the mirror. Kawabata sketches Kyōko's moments of madness in richly symbolic terms: prosaic on the surface (she consents to hospitalization), yet layered with hints of the cold air bringing control "as if the devil possessing her had gone." At one level, she sees that the old house now has new tenants; at another, she hears again the bird whose melody has offered a recurrent counterpoint. Kawabata asserts that she is "warm and at peace" after she has thought, "What if the child should look like you?" But whose image, whose reflection will that be? We do not know the answer to such questions in Kawabata's work.

In *Snow Country*, too, the delicate imagery provides our hints of meaning—and again there is the mirror. To this mirror Kawabata adds other evocations of beauty, especially the snow and images of Woman.[11] Here as in many other Kawabata stories there are contrasting "dark" and "light" women, although these are far indeed from the bad and good women of the Western cliché. Once more the plot is of the slightest: Shimamura is a middle-aged amateur scholar "too plump for running." He is a specialist in Western ballet, with but one qualification: he has never seen a performance. Coming from Tokyo, this dilettante had met his mountain geisha. (As a hot-spring geisha, Komako might seem essentially a vulgar one-nighter to the Japanese, a woman not to be confused with the skilled and respected professionals of Kyoto, Tokyo, and Osaka. But when Shimamura first meets her, she has not yet become a professional, and he is especially attracted by her "purity" or "cleanliness." Again, though, there are hidden Japanese clues. For although *seiketsu* does indeed mean "purity," there is a homonym *sei* meaning "sex.")

The slight narrative of *Snow Country* focuses on Shimamura's three visits to the snow country during a two-year period. It subtly indicates changes both in Komako and in Shimamura, including his attraction to Yōko, a figure ren-

---

[11] The third element in the trio of Beauty (moon:snow:flower) is the flower, *hana*, often used to mean woman, as in *hana no iro* (flower's color, or woman's beauty). The snow is indebted to a snow cult that can be traced back through centuries of Japanese literature to ancient China. It is seen in the snow that lies deep in the *waka* of the *Kokinshū* (A.D. 905), in countless later tanka and haiku, and even in verses by present-day housewives. It is the snow linked with blossoms in images of transcendental beauty and such familiar phrases as *hana-no-yuki* (cherry-blossom snow: *hana*, flower, also being used as a specific reference to cherry blossoms). It is to be found in such metaphors as "to tread snow," meaning to undergo a hard experience.

dered in images of dazzling light. There is no resolution at
the end: only the haunting picture of Komako walking from
the scene of a fire. She is carrying the body of Yōko, while
Shimamura falls and the Milky Way flows "with a roar."

Although Komako is only a mountain geisha, for Shimamura she retains the quality of *seiketsu*, simultaneously
"pure" and "clean," even when she staggers to his bed so
filled with sake that she is more inclined to vomit than embrace. Shimamura still finds her "clean," even exquisitely so.
This evaluation, however, must be balanced against his notions concerning Chijimi linen and his own illusory feeling of
being "bleached clean." We read about his taste for this rare
linen: he carefully collects pieces and has them fashioned into
summer kimono that are later sent to be "snow-bleached"
every year. What a beautiful image: he thinks of the white
linen spread out on the deep snow, the cloth and the snow
glowing scarlet as the sun rises. It is at this moment that Shimamura feels "bleached clean." And it is at this moment that
we discover that a Tokyo shop takes care of all the details:
Shimamura does not even know where the work is actually
done.

As with the ballet, Shimamura has simply read about
snow bleaching in an old book. This romanticism, always responding to the "attraction of the unreal," inspires him with
a view of silver white flowers on a far mountainside. Shimamura can quote passages about the lovely autumn grasses.
Yet when mountain women stand before him, their backs
bowed under the weight of bundled grass, he recognizes
neither the plant of his literary memories nor the mountain
flowers viewed at a (romantic) distance.

Such a summary, of course, does not convey even a hint of
the true nature of *Snow Country*—a novel in which action is
rendered in images and symbolic clues rather than in
straightforward account. These hints may be as indirect as
the sound of a bird or the color of a moth's wing; or they may
be detected in shifting perspectives—as when the finely

grained wood and vermilion lacquer of furniture that was once aesthetically "correct" in Tokyo is next seen in a room resembling a brightly papered box and is finally, awesomely, incongruous in a room that resembles a fox's or a badger's lair.

Other symbols in *Snow Country* are as complex as the mirror of *Suigetsu*, as the title of an early segment *(Shiroi Asa no Kagami: Mirror of a White Morning)* has already suggested. Again the mirror images focus the narrative and pose symbolic questions. The opening scene introduces Shimamura and his "strange angle of vision" (at this point, simply the reflection of the girl Yōko in the train window). But that "evening mirror" becomes a recurrent image, its spell and the intensity of the otherworldly power of "the mirror in the evening landscape" also helping to define the characters of Yōko and the Woman (Komako, but not named until almost a third of the way through the novel) whom Shimamura is going to visit. The mirror foreshadows the link between Yōko and Komako: Shimamura wipes the window with the one finger that "remembers" the woman of the snow country and is startled by an eye that floats in the mirror-window. As the evening light shines in Yōko's mirrored face, Shimamura feels his chest rise at the "inexpressible beauty" of it.

Later, when he sees the mountain geisha Komako reflected in the mirror at the hotel, Shimamura contrasts her bright red cheeks with the snow reflected white in the depths of the mirror. Yet at the end of the episode, as he returns to Tokyo, Shimamura looks at Komako in the station window and recognizes that red-and-white moment as the instant when he "parted from reality." This image in turn is linked with the unreality of his taste for Western ballet. At the same time, it is linked with the unreal beauty of Yōko.

Mystic reflections merge with psychological: and the world in the mirror further reflects the seasonal hints so essential to Japanese poetry and classical literature. Sometimes Kawabata's season words are taken directly from Bashō's haiku. At others, he uses traditional associations of persimmon, cricket cry, or snow to enrich characterization, to render the passage of time, even to substitute for narrative while implying subtle emotional changes, and to foreshadow action in a curling petal or a dripping icicle.

The opening of *Snow Country* is permeated with the intense cold of mountain winter, expressed even in such homely detail as bundled-up stationmaster and shivering hotel porter. But the white depths of that "mirror filled with snow" make it essential that the reader look beyond the familiar. Kawabata's sensory—and sensual—images depict a cold that strikes at the core of Shimamura's being and sounds of the freezing of snow over the land (sounds that seem to "roar deep into the earth").

The quality of Shimamura's first encounter with Komako is rendered in a flashback of spring imagery. This is Kawabata's recurrent device, in which an image *is* a memory (cf. the red maple of *Yama no Oto*, below). It is a relationship made especially clear by two yellow butterflies—seen in a rare moment when Shimamura goes running and laughing down a mountain-side. Such butterflies flash in and out of centuries of springtime verses. They are also called *ichinichizuma:* "one-day spouses," suggesting the fleeting nature of the Komako-Shimamura relationship. (In earlier literature, *tsuma [zuma]* referred to either partner, although it is now used only to refer to a wife.)

Part 2 opens with an autumn scene, always connoting sadness in the context of classical literature, *renga*, and haiku. The mood is deepened when Shimamura thinks of Bashō's lines on "A crow / perched on a bare branch / autumn evening." Each detail of setting helps to build the mood: even the departing geisha is named Kikuyū (*kiku* is the chrysanthemum, an autumnal image). Autumn grasses, insects, colors —all might have been taken from a manual for aspiring haiku writers. But there is a profound difference: the seasonal changes parallel deeply perceived personal relationships that go far beyond mere seasonal convention.

Shimamura sees autumn maples reflected in the mirror:

earlier he had seen the red of Komako's cheeks against the cold, clean white of the snow. At that time, he had heard a voice calling. It was Yōko's. But now he hears another voice: a hint that he will hear Yōko no more in this world. Even the colors of Kawabata's world make subtle seasonal-psychological shifts here. The spring green, so fresh when glimpsed behind a young geisha at the resort, becomes dusky when it is mirrored in Komako's flesh. And in the closing section's mood of autumn sadness, Shimamura focuses on a moth's wing: it is green, too, but a green that is "almost the color of death."

As autumn deepens toward winter, as the insects die, and as the guests gather for maple viewing, Kawabata foreshadows the "freezing roar" of the final paragraph. The first hints are given through winter symbols, carefully inserted into the autumn landscape. Then Shimamura lies in bed listening to a Nō recital after the first snow has fallen. As winter comes, he makes an excursion into the deeper mountains, where villagers tell of the "roaring at the center," a sound that is a prelude to the coming mountain cold.

While the seasons change, Kawabata depicts shifting and ambiguous relationships. We had shared Shimamura's view of that young couple on the mountain train in the opening scene. Yet the relationship between these two (Yōko and Yukio) is never made more explicit than when Yōko declares she can never again nurse a man or visit anyone else's grave. The question of whether the young man (son of the music teacher with whom Komako lives, and at one point identified as the reason for Komako becoming a geisha—to pay for his treatment) was or was not Komako's fiancé is never answered. We are never sure of Komako's feelings toward Yōko. She dislikes talking of Yōko, yet is always thinking of her (as a "heavy load," impossible to get rid of, although at one point she urges Shimamura to take over the burden: "If she were to fall into the hands of someone like you she might not go crazy after all"). Yōko's attitude toward Komako is similarly ambiguous. She refers to Komako as "a fine person," but "not lucky," and asks Shimamura to be good to her. Yet Yōko also wants Shimamura to take *her* back to Tokyo with him.

In his introduction, Seidensticker states that Shimamura is drawn to Yōko through Komako. At one point Komako does say, "Try seducing her!" But the symbolic value of the reflection in that evening mirror of the train window is part of a poetic study that is not concerned with two overlapping triangles. The opening images suggest Shimamura's otherworldly excitement, and his premonition of something linking the mirrored faces on the train with the woman he is going to visit is not to be reduced to a relationship through Komako. The attraction clearly begins long before he discovers they are all bound for the deep snow.

The attraction is related to a quality in Yōko herself. From the beginning, Shimamura responds to Yōko with a deep excitement; he feels an unnamed attraction that is contrasted with his intensely physical and sensual response to Komako. Komako is vital, urgent, strong, warm. Her small mouth, essential for a Japanese woman's facial beauty, is sometimes described as a sign of passion. Komako also offers "fire for a pillow." If she does seem momentarily lonely, the effect is "seductive." Even her reaction to a sheaf of rice is sensual: she half-closes her eyes with pleasure, just as she had done in Shimamura's arms. Every physical detail is there, from her bare feet ("clean to the hollows under her toes") to her strangely cold hair and her full warm breasts (subject of a teasing dialogue in which Shimamura notes they have been caressed into unequal development). At heart, she seems the very essence of "a woman of the pleasure quarters," one who invariably comes reeling drunk from geisha parties to Shimamura's bed. Even as she races with Shimamura to the concluding holocaust, she pauses to offer a later meeting at his inn.

Kawabata never lets the reader forget that Komako is

Woman. (In Japanese this generic term is always before one, since the language does not distinguish number or article.) There is an animal quality about her, sometimes made specific as "a restless night beast." Yet this does not prevent both the hollow Shimamura and the cold snow country itself from being mantled with the scent of woman. All the senses are brought into play from the first moment when Shimamura's finger bends and unbends as it "remembers the woman" until he trembles with wanting to touch her when they race toward the fire.

In contrast, Yōko is unreal, eternal, otherworldly—that phosphorescent eye of the evening mirror. Repeatedly her voice echoes with a strange sad resonance, she is strangely beautiful, there is a piercing quality in her look, her voice is "like an echo of love." Shimamura feels that she is at the very center of some remarkable occurrence, as he had imagined Yōko and Yukio on that train as "going on forever, farther and farther." In this early view, Yōko seemed a character in an old romantic tale: at the end, her body falling through the flames seems "a phantasm from an unreal world." She, too, can seem voluptuous; but when she does, the dominant impression is still one of her burning glance, "cold as a very distant light."

Shimamura feels that Yōko's eyes for all their innocence could send a probing light to the heart of his relationship with Komako, and this is one element of the attraction. But it is only in the imagery of the terrible closing scene that Kawabata hints at what that probing light might reveal, and the anguish of that revelation.

Kawabata's characterization is so subtle a web of allusion and suggestion that such summary can never do full justice to his fiction. Relationships, as in *Snow Country*, may also be expressed in terms quite foreign to Western thought, although at other times they are apparently universal. There is little difficulty when Shimamura's treatment of the ballet is compared with his treatment of Komako, for instance. Yet in the midst of the discussion between Yōko and Shimamura on the possibility of their meeting in Tokyo, when his affection for Komako wells up violently, Shimamura thinks: "To run off to Tokyo as if eloping with an obscure girl [Yōko] would somehow be in the nature of an intense apology to Komako, and a penance for Shimamura himself." This expression of very Japanese attitudes simply cannot be rendered into Western equivalents.

Komako's talk of jealousy, and Shimamura's reluctance to call Komako to his room after Yōko begins working in the kitchen of his inn, seem universal. But how shall we react to the incident in which Shimamura calls Komako "a good girl"? She had been "the girl at the music teacher's" until their first meeting; then she was "the woman," unnamed until late in the narrative (in contrast to the early naming of Yōko). Later, at the meeting that foreshadows their parting, Komako is momentarily "girl." Almost immediately, though, Shimamura says "You're a good woman." The implications in that shift ("girl" is an endearment appropriate in addressing a girlfriend, whereas "woman" is often used for a mere sexual partner) are sufficient to provoke a quarrel—as well as so moving Komako that even during the excitement of the terrible fire she turns aside to chide him about it.

Only rarely does Kawabata offer more than symbolic hints of meaning—as when Komako refuses to go to Yukio's bedside, saying "I don't want to see a man die." The reader is permitted to speculate with Shimamura whether the reluctance comes from "coldest heartlessness" or "too warm a passion." Yet even when the hints are to be found in many-layered symbolism, Shimamura is seen as contemporary man: universal in implication though intensely Japanese in detail.

Most challenging is the conclusion of Snow Country— Komako literally takes up the burden of the earlier metaphor, and the Milky Way is both setting and symbol for the strange snow country love. It enfolds Komako and Shimamura as they race toward the fire, a vast presence, a radiance in which Shimamura feels himself floating. It wraps the night earth in a naked embrace, "voluptuous," yet also reminding Shimamura of Bashō's haiku on the Milky Way arched over a stormy sea. The stars flow over Shimamura and the woman as they run on, until images of fire and stars merge—the sparks spreading off into the Milky Way and seeming to pull Shimamura with them. Even the firefighters' water turns to a white mist, mirroring the stars.

• Here Japanese allusions become too dense for annotation, while offering infinite varieties of temptation to the symbol hunter. For instance, *setsujoku* (to "clean" one's shame) is written with characters that hint of the "melting snow" around the fire. Fire (known as "flowers of Edo" from the time when Tokyo's wooden houses continually fell prey to flames) contrasts with the snow and may be linked with the already noted flower image of "cherry blossom snow." Or perhaps there is a hint of one of the three Buddhist evils: the flames of lust. More important, however, is the density of allusion to the Milky Way itself. Coupled with the preceding scenes describing Shimamura's pilgrimage to the countryside of the Chijimi weavers, these allusions inevitably suggest the legend still celebrated in Japan's festival of Tanabata.

Tanabata Matsuri marks the one day each year when *amanogawa* (Heaven's River, that is, the Milky Way) is bridged by the magpies who have come to reunite the lovers, the stars Altair *(Kengyūsei)* and Vega *(Shokujo,* also the guardian of poetry and music)—the Herdsman and Weaver Princess stars. Kawabata has emphasized Shimamura's interest in Chijimi linen and its weavers. Komako had only reminded Shimamura of the fabric and its cool quality.[12] Their

---

[12] Note, however, that the coolness is also said to be the play of the principles of light and darkness—hinting of yin and yang *(in'yō).* Yin signifies qualities of dark, cold, heaviness, the female image, associated with water; while the complementary yang indicates male, the left, lightness, and fire. The light and dark also suggest Komako's association with darkness and

love would leave "nothing so definite as a piece of Chijimi; human intimacies have not even so long a life." It was Yōko whom Shimamura imagined "long ago [singing] . . . as she worked over her spools and looms." Yōko, then, is the Weaver Princess with whom the Herdsman shall be reunited. At this point the symbol hunter is further tempted to see hints (in the venerable Japanese tradition of "pivot words" that change their meaning according to preceding and following syllables) that the *mura* of Shimamura should be linked with the herding *(muragaru)* of the Herdsman himself.

But of course this would force meanings that do not belong in the delicate world of Kawabata's prose. When Komako literally takes up her burden of Yōko at the end and Yōko's face is "vacant" there is no more than a simultaneous hint of death and of the Mindlessness of Buddhist enlightenment. While the crowd presses closer, attempting to take this burden from Komako, Shimamura trips and falls, his head back. It is at this moment that "the Milky Way flowed down inside him with a roar." Here two levels of meaning merge. Shimamura's romanticism ("the attraction of the unreal") and Yōko's otherworldly quality (the "probing light" of her mirrored and mystical eye) flow together. Beginning with a fragment of erotica—Shimamura and the geisha—we find that we have participated with Kawabata in the making of myth.[13]

Yōko's with light. Light and dark women are found not only in *Koto*, as already noted, but also in the sleeping virgins of the *House of the Sleeping Beauties*. In *Thousand Cranes*, Chikako is associated with dark qualities, while "the girl of the thousand cranes" is always seen in terms of light: a vein of light, a flash, or brightness. In "One Arm," there are additional hints of the five elements, of Confucian harmony, and of the left-right symbolism of esoteric Buddhist lore (as there may be in the primarily erotic movement of Shimamura's left index finger). In *The Lake* the contrast is seen in terms of two worlds—the pink-tinged view through a taxi driver's open window and Gimpei's "blue" world, seen through glass and hence "cleaner": but it is the open view that is linked with the touch of a girl.

[13] There is an interesting contrast here with Mishima's use of the Milky

Yet Kawabata with his lyric prose has not forced such a mythic extension. There are only symbolic clues to such readings, as he makes maximum use of the ambiguity of the Japanese language, its multiple meanings, and its verbal and visual hints. He also makes the fullest possible use of familiar symbols—although the Western reader may miss the delicate eroticism. The associations of the pillow *(makura)*, for instance, reinforce the hints found in the comment that Shimamura enjoyed Komako's "fire for a pillow." The hints of untying the obi string—prelude to sexual encounter—are neatly rendered in *Snow Country* when Shimamura is wakened by the sound of Komako *tying* her obi string. This is not only a tactful rendering of the morning after. It may also suggest the eventual ending of their relationship.

The Bean and the Tea Ceremony:
Old Symbols and New Meanings

Kawabata's fiction carries more symbolic layers than most foreign readers can hope to appreciate. But an understanding of his technique of allusive narration will reveal the ways in which old symbols take on new meanings while never losing their traditional Japanese values. A short story and a novel available in translation illustrate this point very well. In the short story, "The Mole," a familiar Japanese symbol, the bean, takes on new meanings. In the novel, *Thousand Cranes*, the form and accessories of the tea ceremony tell more than can be read in its narrative line.

"The Mole" *(Hokuro no Tegami*, 1940) is a message or letter *(tegami)* from Sayoko, written as though to the husband from whom she is now separated. The letter focuses on a

---

Way image. In *The Sailor Who Fell from Grace with the Sea*, genitals are for "copulating with the stars of the Milky Way" and pubic hair is to "tickle coy stardust" when this "rape" occurs.

birthmark that is shaped like a bean, a female sex symbol found, for instance, in *manjū* (bean-jam cakes that also serve as a precise anatomical symbol) and in bean-planting and bean-harvesting folksongs of lusty double meaning. As in other Kawabata stories, the flow of time washes back and forth through a series of associative images. Sayoko's narrative begins, "Last night I dreamed about that mole." As she recalls various incidents involving the mole, the reader too travels back to the early days of Sayoko's marriage and even to her childhood. Sayoko reveals fragments of a deteriorating relationship in which the husband chides, grows violent, and finally becomes indifferent.

At first the husband had described Sayoko's mole as "wonderfully round and swollen"; it was "bigger than a bean." Yet when she was first scolded for playing with her "bean," Sayoko was still "more child than wife." The memory that after she was thirteen she kept the habit to herself further suggests how closely the symbol is tied to her developing sexuality.

In the dream, the symbolism becomes even more explicit: "Like a spoiled child" she clamors, clutching at her husband's sleeve—that Japanese gesture symbolic of sexual importuning. She asks him to put her mole in the pit of his own birthmark. (Only at this point does Kawabata reveal that the husband, too, has a mole.) "What a fine fairy story it would make if your mole really were to swell up because you put mine in it." This odd reversal of the usually female bean (the swelling of the husband's mole hinting at the phallic transformation of Sayoko's) suggests the faults in Sayoko's marriage. That marriage shows a progress from meek agreement, through unwomanly "fighting back," to the trembling speculation that *other* men might find her habit charming.

After the dream, in which the mole "like a black bean" comes off in her hand, Sayoko feels "tired through and through" and light, as though she had "laid down a burden."

This is reminiscent of occasions when Sayoko's husband beat her, in an effort to end the habit, and she experienced "a feeling of relief."

The bean then is a metaphor for a sexual relationship.[14] At the same time, it serves as focus for a meditation on the meaning of marriage, though in tone and in technique very different from Tanizaki's meditations on the same subject. Sayoko reflects on the need for accommodation—even as she seems to suggest that she expected her husband to do all the adapting. One by one she catalogues the possible interpretations of her own symbolic gesture: a memory of her family's love, a confession of love for her husband that could not be put into words, or perhaps only a sign of preoccupation with her own small self. There she is, then, alone with her precious self, free to do with it as she will. But only the cold tears come.

Thus an ancient symbol offers commentary on a modern dilemma. Rather than suggesting conflicts between an "old-fashioned" and a "modern" approach to marriage, Kawabata uses familiar symbols to offer new and even universal meanings. The faults in Sayoko's relationship are rendered metaphorically through the bean and the dream. Kawabata is not simply updating a convention. He is making a vanishing literary and cultural heritage work in a contemporary environment.

He can take a child's tale and make it a metaphor of doomed adult love, as he does in *Snow Country*—not only in the already noted use of legendary Tanabata figures but also in the sound of a tea kettle.[15] This sound is gracefully linked

---

[14] Later, in an author's note to the translation (by Edward Seidensticker) in *Japan Quarterly* 2(1955):93, Kawabata said that it was his intention to tell of the process of loving and being loved and of how they differ for a man and a woman. He also commented on the story's hint of the love of the woman for herself and the sadness this brings. Another "portrait of a marriage," *Suishō Gensō* (Crystal Fantasy, 1931), has not yet been translated.

[15] This is another of Kawabata's philosophical-poetic hints also. In the

through a bell-like tone to the sounds of Komako's footsteps: it is a warning that Shimamura must leave the mountains. But the tea kettle has other, older associations; it is linked with the badger in Japanese legend and thus offers a double link with Komako, since her room has been compared to a badger's lair.

Such hints enrich *Snow Country*, where past symbol and present meaning are woven together as delicately as a piece of that exquisite Chijimi linen. But when we come to *Thousand Cranes*, we find that the tea-ceremony utensils have been worked out of extraordinarily difficult clay. *Thousand Cranes (Senbazuru*, 1949–1951) was awarded the Japan Academy of Arts Prize, and the entry in *Who's Who Among Japanese Writers* (compiled by Aono Suekichi and Kawabata himself) describes it as illustrating "the highest reach of Japanese feeling." The Western reader, however, needs considerable assistance in interpreting that delicate feeling, the subtleties of tone, and the more esoteric aspects of its significant gestures.

Footnotes on the ritual of *cha-no-yu* (tea ceremony) are of no more help to the novice than a one-sentence definition of Zen Buddhism would be to a seeker after Enlightenment. And even beyond the problems posed by a novel in which the tea ceremony defines character and interprets action, there are questions of ambiguous relationships and attitudes that are apt to have connotations for the Western reader quite different from those of Kawabata's intention.

Buddhist philosophy of music (Avamska doctrines), a moment has communion with eternity at the intersection of sound and silence (when sound meets silence to create music). *Aware* is frequently linked with a specific sound, too, as Heian literature in particular shows. In Kawabata's other stories there are many examples: the bird's song linked with Kyōko's realization in "The Moon on the Water"; the birds that Kikuji hears in *Thousand Cranes* as he lies beside Mrs. Ōta, awakens, and feels his mind "clean" (clearly implying Zen Emptiness); the multiple sounds of *Sound of the Mountain* (among them an electric shaver and a vacuum cleaner as well as more traditional images and familiar sounds of crickets).

At one level, *Thousand Cranes* is a story of sickness—a theme made clear by the title's allusion to the paper birds of origami (the art of paper folding). The Japanese say that anyone who can fold a thousand paper cranes—even on his deathbed—will surely recover from his malady. The sickness here festers in Mitani Kikuji, a young man obsessed by dark images from his father's past. These are focused in the birthmark, "concrete as a toad," on the breast of Chikako, who had once briefly been the elder Mitani's mistress. Chikako —in person, or through symbolic manifestations of her birthmark—poisons all Kikuji's later moments of seeming happiness. Moreover, Chikako is the one who introduces him to Inamura Yukiko (thus foreshadowing a sad ending).

Yukiko carries a *furoshiki*[16] patterned with the thousand cranes (the bird is also symbolic of longevity: the "thousand-year-bird"). She flashes in and out of the narrative as "an impression of light." She is fresh, clean, healthy; she alone is in proper aesthetic relation to the tea ceremony, performing the ritual with no personal quirks. Yet her light casts its own disturbing shadows on Kikuji's enjoyment of Mrs. Ōta, transforming her warmth into images of weeping and ugliness.

[16] This *furoshiki* itself is a very simple example of the difficulties of rendering Japanese into equivalent English. The translator's "kerchief" may suggest to the Western reader either a peasant headdress or a workman's bundle. But this peculiarly Japanese carrying cloth is a silk square (though there are also cotton and outsized versions for tradesmen). It is not out of place at weddings, where each guest is given souvenirs of the occasion wrapped in a *furoshiki*. It is used on formal visits to carry the mandatory gift for one's host. Interpretations of the tea ceremony in this novel require much deeper knowledge of Japanese custom, however—including the whole aesthetic of *cha-no-yu* and its philosophical (Zen) implications. Some "flaws" are no more than subliminal hints (such as using a pair of cups that usually signify *conjugal* felicity for a man and his mistress here; or evidence of loss of poetic feeling in the maid's choice of morning glory for the centuries-old gourd vase not because of the customary poetic associations but "because they are both vines"). Others (using the wrong door or serving *black* tea in tea ceremony bowls) are more obvious breaches indicating that the "sickness" is beyond the curative powers of the Inamura girl's thousand cranes.

Here it should be noted that the darkness of the encounters with Mrs. Ōta is not the "blackness" of Western evil/good contrasts but the specifically sexual *koi wa yami* (love is darkness) and another hint of the feminine aspect of *in'yō*. Similarly, the darkness of Chikako's birthmark has an added sexual dimension. Elsewhere "color" has its erotic connotations: on each occasion when color rises in Mrs. Ōta's daughter Fumiko, the Japanese reader is alert to the growing attraction felt by Kikuji (the hint of *iro-ke*, sex appeal, and other aspects of *iro* [color] already noted). And a number of passages describing Mrs. Ōta and Fumiko suggest the poetic use of "bedewed with rain," meaning exposed to sexual love.

Similar subtleties are found in the tea ceremony itself. At the outset, the foreign reader needs to know that the treasured, centuries-old tea bowls are not the delicate porcelain one might suppose. The bowl is a handleless cup that comes in various sizes from the small ones found in traveling sets to those—often measuring more than six inches in diameter —used in the tea ceremony's most formal practice. Part of the philosophy of the tea ceremony—its linking of man and nature, its insistence on simplicity—is found in the bowl itself. Fashioned out of sturdy pottery, deliberately rough in form and texture, though its muted colors and uneven qualities are part of its beauty, the bowl's origin in the clay of earth is of deep philosophical significance. Its very form is a focus for meditation.

Disorders in the tea ceremony—insensitivity to its accessories, neglect of its philosophy, intrusion of personal considerations—symbolize the sickness of *Thousand Cranes*.[17] The extent of the malady is even underscored by the occasion of the first ceremony: the *fourth* memorial service for Kikuji's father and hence for the Japanese carrying the doubly fatal

[17] After I had written this interpretation of *Thousand Cranes*, I read Kawabata's own interpretation—in his Nobel Prize acceptance speech *(Utsukushii Nihon no Watashi—sono Josetsu)*—in which he described *Thousand Cranes* as a negative work and an expression of doubt and warning on the vulgarity into which the tea ceremony has fallen.

connotations of *shi* (the homonyms *four* and *death*). Guests drop in casually at this memorial tea ceremony, behave selfishly and tactlessly, or accord the accessories only perfunctory glances instead of the mandatory and meticulous inspection. Hostess Chikako, a master and teacher of tea ceremony, nevertheless conducts ceremonies that are a travesty of the ideal. Not only are accessories apt to be "slightly out of season"; throughout the novel she selects them for personal and emotional rather than aesthetic reasons. Chikako uses the Art of Tea as a tool in managing Kikuji's affairs. And, in the ultimate perversion, she brings tea in the manner of a waitress filling an order.

Full awareness of the complications of Kikuji's malady requires extensive knowledge of Japanese attitudes. Although there is danger of destroying the delicacy of Kawabata's lyric hints, annotation is essential in pinpointing significant details. For instance, Kikuji neglects his garden: but the garden should be tended as an integral part of the teahouse. Or Mrs. Ōta sheds a tear on the kettle: although passions are appallingly out of place in the world of tea.

In *Thousand Cranes*, a centuries-old Oribe-ware tea bowl (used at the opening tea ceremony) serves as a subtle link between the characters. Later, a Shino tea ceremony water jar that had also belonged to Mrs. Ōta comes to represent for Kikuji the flesh both of the mother and of her daughter Fumiko. A pair of Raku bowls used by Mrs. Ōta and the late Mr. Mitani deepen the sorrow that Fumiko and Kikuji have in common after Mrs. Ōta's suicide. The little cups that have traveled with the parents serve as ironic center for the tragic ritual in which Fumiko and Kikuji finally purge the emotions of the past.

Use of the 300-year-old tea-ceremony water jar as a flower vase—for Occidental flowers, moreover, and not even in the *tokonoma* (alcove) of a tea cottage—and the "man-wife" pairs of cups offer symbolic parallel to the action. At the end, Fumiko breaks the little "female" Shino cup with obvious desperation. This symbolic gesture, however, is apt to puzzle the Western reader. Fumiko has removed herself from the mother-daughter identification and has even resisted Kikuji. But Kikuji finds that this resistance does not come from the girl: it comes from the "cleanness" itself.

This is only one of the moments when action cannot be interpreted in our familiar psychological terms. Kikuji's night with Mrs. Ōta, his sense of repose, even his drifting willingly on "the wave of woman," are fairly straightforward. The merging of identities is made specific by the translator: "If Mrs. Ōta had made her mistake when she saw Kikuji's father in Kikuji, then there was something frightening, a bond like a curse, in the fact that, to Kikuji, Fumiko resembled her mother: but Kikuji, unprotesting, gave himself to the drift."

But this only partially interprets the strange relationship between Kikuji and the woman who had been his father's mistress at the time of his death. The Shino water jar serves as a focusing symbol: Kikuji sees Mrs. Ōta in the jar, "like a dream of woman." This phrase lacks the ambiguity in English that is inherent in the Japanese, where "dream of woman," like "wave of woman" (lacking either article or number), may indicate that Kikuji is dreaming of the woman Mrs. Ōta, of any woman, or of all. The jar itself, however, seems to Kikuji to have a surface as voluptuous and soft as Mrs. Ōta's skin had been. This amazingly sensual jar is a masterpiece; so, too, was Mrs. Ōta and hence "nothing unclean."

The growing attraction of Fumiko and the blending in turn of the mother-daughter identities is accomplished through the jar. Kikuji looks at it: and he now wants to see the daughter. When he invites Fumiko, though, she comes bringing her mother's little Oribe tea bowl (the one she will later break). As to Fumiko's own nature: Kawabata comes no closer than a description of tea bowl and water jar, in which he suggests their relative strength.

Difficulties also arise because the Western reader tends to

find only positive connotations in Kikuji's relationship with Mrs. Ōta: in their lovemaking, which happens naturally, in her softness, her warm flesh, and her "wave of woman." When Chikako speaks of Mrs. Ōta in terms of "witch" or "curse," the words seem evidence of Chikako's psychopathology. Even the eerie qualities of Kikuji's dream embrace with Mrs. Ōta and the lure of her pliant body can be Freudian clues. To the Western reader, references to guilt invariably suggest the Puritan ethic.

But this is not the Puritan world. It is profoundly Buddhist in thought, as close reading of its allusions will show. Spirits, ghosts, and meetings that could not occur in this world hint at the otherworldliness, the ineffable quality expressed in the term *yūgen*. The continuity of the articles used in the tea ceremony—the very ceremony itself—is an expression of the Buddhist view of time and of man-and-nature.

Nor are Fumiko's "intolerable shame," her apologies, and her pleas for her mother's forgiveness gestures from our own psychoanalytical couches. For Kawabata, Mrs. Ōta is a woman who can be described in the Japanese idiom as one "departing from the right human path" in order to gratify her own whim. Fumiko assumes the burden of her mother's actions and therefore must inevitably live "a pathetically pure life" (points made in Kawabata's *Who's Who Among Japanese Writers*). These are attitudes rooted in the Japanese ethic and notions of duty and responsibility.

The concept of happy endings is as foreign to the Japanese as the complexities of *giri* (that untranslatable web of obligation, duty, and honor) are to us in the West. Life itself has no point, existence is a continuum, and experience is permeated with a sense of the incompleteness of things. Thus Kawabata shows Kikuji's position in relation to three women: Chikako, who had been his father's mistress briefly and now tries to manage his affairs; Mrs. Ōta, who had replaced Chikako in a long intimate relationship with Kikuji's father and is briefly linked with Kikuji himself; and her daughter Fumiko, who breaks the cup and symbolically seems to end these reincarnations of love. The girl of the thousand cranes in this context is scarcely a character: her rare appearances and the use of images of light hint at her role—to illuminate the relationships that *are* the narrative.

Events so slight as those outlined here could not draw to a formal conclusion—even if Japanese fiction encouraged endings. Fittingly, the concluding sentences of *Thousand Cranes* offer an open end . . . hinting that another segment would be added at some future date, as Kawabata added to *Snow Country*. We see Kikuji making his way outside "the dark ugly curtain" of the Ōta-Fumiko associations. He reflects that only Chikako is left, and as he does so he seems to spit out the "poison." Yet Fumiko, who has "brought him to life," is gone from the scene in cold images suggestive of death. Kikuji moves off not into the light of the thousand cranes "cure" but into another darkness represented by the shades of a park. Publication of *Nami Chidori* (Wave Plovers) in 1953 only deepened the mystery. The characters reappeared, seeming to presage a full sequel: yet at the time of Kawabata's death, the story was still incomplete.

The Sounds of Memory: Death and the Lonely Dance

Kawabata asserted after the Second World War that he would write only elegies, although he later qualified that statement. In his essay "Undying Beauty," he explained that "sadness" is a word having close affinities with beauty in Japan, and in the postwar years he felt it more appropriate to write of the sadness. This is the delicate Japanese sense of *aware* (or *mono-no-aware*): the sense of transience and the response to a fleeting perception of sound, season, gesture. This is the context in which we must understand Kawabata's elegaic mood—a mood, moreover, that is evident even in his earliest work.

It would be easy to link Kawabata's treatment of loneliness, sickness, and death with his personal childhood experiences.[18] Kawabata has written and spoken of his early "orphan's sorrow," which lasted until he was about twenty-four years old, and he has described his period of "emotional sickness." Later, however, Kawabata came to regard this sorrow as "childish sentimental play" (*Abura* [Oil], 1921) and "rhetoric" (*Yugashima de no Omoide* [Memory of Yugashima], 1925). A perceptive illumination of Kawabata's lonely boyhood can be found in a gentle reminiscence, *Jūrokusai no Nikki* (Diary of a Sixteen-year-old), written before his grandfather's death but not published until 1925. In these biographical notes, as in Kawabata's fictions, the feeling is profoundly Buddhist, and Kawabata's psychologically valid perceptions of loneliness, separation, and death gain strength from this underlying, and usually unvoiced, philosophy.

Many of Kawabata's early works are specifically concerned with death.[19] His first publication was the essay "Carrying My Teacher's Coffin on My Shoulder" in 1915. The story that won Kikuchi Kan's praise was *Shōkonsai Ikkei* (*Shōkonsai* is a memorial service for the war dead) in 1921. Titles such as *Kaisō no Meijin* (An Expert in Attending

[18] His father died when Kawabata was three years old, and his mother the next year. Kawabata's sister was sent to live with an aunt's family in Osaka but died a few years later; Kawabata went to stay with his grandparents in Mishima-gun, Osaka Prefecture. The grandmother died when Kawabata was seven, and his grandfather died in May 1914. Then Kawabata went to live with an uncle, staying at the dormitory of Ibaragi Middle School from January 1915 until his graduation in 1917.

[19] Kawabata is not alone in writing of death, of course. Among his contemporaries the theme of death is so commonplace that a random examination of titles (in the Kokusai Bunka Shinkōkai synopses, for instance) will reveal *Shi ni Shitashimu* (1923), Tokuda Shūsei's *Becoming Familiar with Death*, and many others. One of the earliest treatments of death and loneliness among the moderns is Natsume Sōseki's *Kokoro* (1914). Most such works, however, while revealing Japanese attitudes toward death and even occasionally making use of Japanese symbolism, seem to lack the poetic dimension that gives Kawabata's stories their lyrical tone.

Funerals, 1923) and *Shitai Shōkainin* (The Corpse Introducer, 1929) indicate the frequency with which death in
name or in fact appears in his essays and fiction. But whether
the death is that of a tubercular husband in "The Moon on
the Water," a mystical figure such as Yōko in *Snow Country*,
or the drugged girl lying beside an old man in *House of the
Sleeping Beauties*, death always has richly poetic implications in Kawabata's work, in contrast to the meticulously
clinical deteriorations in Tanizaki's novels and the murderous destruction in Mishima's.

Other stories are filled with sadness, as in the autumn
mood of even the title in *Ochiba to Fubo* (Fallen Leaves and
Parents, 1925). *Kinjū* (1933), translated as "Of Birds and
Beasts,"[20] is also a metaphorical expression of transient life,
and *Shiroi Asa no Kagami* (Mirror of a White Morning), that
first part of *Snow Country*, is a title suggesting the link between white and death (although white here is primarily a
simple description of silvery frost and white snow). *Kinjū* is
also a story beginning and ending in death, opening with a
chirping of birds while the protagonist's taxi is delayed by a
funeral procession. That chirping sound is a literal reference
to the cageful of birds to be released at the funeral, as well as
symbolic allusion to the man's preference for birds and
beasts. As in so many of Kawabata's stories, however, the
sound is more: it is an echo, a memory, leading us back to the
deaths of the man's birds at home and forward to the dance
recital given by a woman he once loved (Chikako). It is a
sound subtly linked to the man's glimpse of Chikako's face

---

[20] *Kinjū* means "birds and beasts" or "animals" and is used in a Japanese phrase expressing "inhumanity." In his *Bungakuteki Jijoden* (Literary
Autobiography, 1934), Kawabata referred to the "perversity" of this particular story. The perversity—in spite of references to cruelty—seems
rather a litany of the lonely, middle-aged man's losses, memories crowding
upon him, as each image recalls another (a shrike, an owl, a Doberman
bitch's mongrel litter), the significance lying more in the feeling of loss
than in cruel action.

beneath the makeup man's hand—an image that in turn recalls a dead girl's diary and the note by the girl's mother in
which the young face is seen "made up for the very first time,
like a bride."

At one level, *Kinjū* would seem no more than a rather unpleasant study of a man whose quest for "something living
and moving" has led him to keep many birds and beasts. The
story is enclosed by the occasion of Chikako's dance recital
—opening with his journey there and ending (after his recognition that Chikako no longer has her former "savage
strength") with his brief backstage glimpse of her deathlike
face being made up. But the real action of the story is in his
memory, a series of movements enriched by layers of implication and symbolic meaning. Once again no summary can
do justice to the profound meditation concealed in a series of
(unpleasant) incidents.

For instance, the man has kept a pair of birds. One escaped, and as replacement he could buy only another pair—
seemingly so affectionate (occasioning a symphony of images
of lovers) and yet involved in an ambiguous night incident
that left the old female and the new male as lone survivors.
The "chrysanthemum" crown of these birds deepens the note
of (autumn) sadness. Later, distracted by sights and sounds of
other birds and beasts, he neglects this pair, leaving them too
long in their bath. His frantic efforts to revive them (even putting their feet in his mouth) are linked with memories of other
creatures, with other deaths, with other interpretations of
cruelty, with the man's reasons for living as he does.

Through sounds, through similarities of appearance,
through shared experiences, through associations of ideas, we
hear the music and watch the movements of this lonely
dance: the visual qualities as well as the rhythm of the ad-
vance and retreat of memories. A recollection of a Doberman
bitch recalls a Boston terrier that smothered its puppy. The
joyous but unknowing face of that terrier calls up an image
of Chikako's face; the dog scampers across this memory of

Chikako, its (past) movement carrying us back to Chikako (the present) again. Through all of the memories, as through the memories of the father-in-law in *Sound of the Mountain*, we see the image of a woman moving: in each memory a little different, a little older, and showing us indirectly something of the loneliness of the bird-and-beast keeper.

It is worth noting that Chikako is only one of many dancers and entertainers in Kawabata's work. The Western reader might expect such figures to appear in essentially cheerful contexts, although the Japanese reader recognizes traditional implications. For these entertainers belong to the "floating world" of pleasure (*ukiyo:* "the world" and "fleeting life"). However amusing *ukiyo-zōshi* (tales) may be in detail, the inherent sadness of the floating world is always present, as it is in Kawabata's *Izu no Odoriko* (1926), translated as *The Izu Dancer* although the title actually makes an important distinction: *odori-ko* is specifically a dancing girl of eleven to fourteen years old, an essential aspect of the story.

The Izu Dancer is a beautiful expression of unfulfilled love. The time is autumn, again the sad season. A young student's longing for the thirteen-year-old dancer seen on his travels (a girl who at first seems much older and thus a possible sexual companion) is expressed in images of incompleteness: an unfinished story, partially heard drumbeats and voices, the girl waving something white (color of mourning), and the final lyric passage in which the boy floats in "beautiful emptiness." Aboard the ship returning him to his Tokyo world, he feels tears falling "as though my head had turned to clear water . . . soon nothing would remain."

In *Asakusa Kurenaidan* (The Kurenaidan [Scarlet Club] of Asakusa, 1929–1930), the characters themselves are incomplete. Neither Yukiko nor Oharu is a true woman fulfilling the ideals of womanly nature. Kawabata in this story writes of the sorrows rather than the gaiety of the Asakusa pleasure quarters, perhaps expressing an intensely personal memory of death. When some of the brothels burned down in the fire that followed the 1923 earthquake, Kawabata himself traveled with a friend from the university dormitory to the devastated area, where he looked at the terrible, charred bodies for one reason only: "A writer must train [his] unfeeling eyes."[21]

Dancing figures—expressions of loneliness or focusing a sense of loss—move through *Onsen-yado* (A Hotspring Inn, 1929) as through *Snow Country*; through *Niji* (The Rainbow, 1934), through *Hana no Warutsu* (Flower Waltz, 1936), and even through *Funa Yūjo* (Boat Prostitute), a play that had its premier at Tokyo's Kabuki-za in October 1970. Written originally for dance master Nishikawa Koisaburō and adapted for the Osaka stage as *Biwa Monogatari* (Tale of the Biwa or Lute), this is in some ways reminiscent of *Izu no Odoriko* in its interweaving of journey, longing, and loss.[22]

Its source is in the tales of Heike warrior Kagekiyo (subject of Nō and Kabuki dramas, too).[23] After the Heike defeat, in-

---

[21] According to Kon Tōkō in an interview with the Japanese press widely quoted after news of Kawabata's Nobel Prize. It is a pity that *Asakusa Kurenaidan* has not been translated, for it shows both Kawabata's linking technique (especially, here, the color scarlet: of an obi, of a club of naughty girls, of a modern entertainer) and his poetic transformations of basically unpoetic materials. When a fourteen-year-old girl is "sold" by her parents, there is a question of buying the girl a kimono: it is suggested that the (unspoiled) narrator buy it for this (fundamentally unspoiled) girl. Similarly, in *Sound of the Mountain*, an ugly news item about pregnant teenagers is transformed to pure love in Shingo's dream and into a benevolent mood when he wakens. In *Beauty and Sadness* the ugly aspects of a premature and illegitimate baby's death are tempered in a simple description of Oki tenderly performing rather unpleasant nursing tasks for the girl-mother, and the ugly events are the inspiration for the beauty of Oki's subsequent novel.

[22] Especially in the subplot with young Tokimaru (parting from Murasaki as he leaves to become a priest); the sound of his flute brings hints of loss comparable to those of the father's lute.

[23] Kawabata's play does not resemble these versions. In the Nō version, the blind impoverished father and his daughter meet at his place of exile, weep tears of joy, but ultimately part. The Kabuki repertory of *Jūhachiban*

structed in the dance by her dying mother (Kuretake), the girl Murasaki travels the country seeking her father. But she does not recognize him in the blind old man with a lute. He hears that a girl has been singing of a lost child—words he had taught his wife Kuretake—but by the time he looks for Murasaki, she has left. In the final scene, though father and daughter do meet and Murasaki hears the old man sing her mother's song, she is now a prostitute (the result of her poverty in the aftermath of the Heike-Genji wars). Their recognition is both unspoken and deeply moving, and it ends with parting.

Whether or not this recurrent, lonely dancing figure is related to the Michiko of Kawabata's 1921 diary entries is a question similar to the problems of his early experiences with death.[24] Again, whatever the experience was, it has clearly been transmuted into poetic and sensitive perceptions of feelings that must not be reduced to a clinical statement of Kawabata's "longing" for virgins (Mishima's suggestion). Michiko and Kawabata were engaged for a few weeks in 1921, and Kawabata has recorded his plans for living with her in Kikuchi Kan's house. (They were not yet planning to be married, and in any case the house was not vacated, and the episode ended). Later entries in the *Literary Autobiography* show how he saw this figure on trains, on theater posters, in front of a café. And the figure of a young girl much like the Izu dancer can be found in *Kagaribi* (Fishing Fire, 1924), in

---

(Eighteen Best Plays [of the Ichikawa family], collected by Danjurō VII) includes *Kagekiyo* and *Gedatsu*. *Kagekiyo* features a notable torture scene in which the recently defeated warrior is not cowed even by the spectacle of wife and daughter undergoing terrible punishment. In *Gedatsu* (Buddhist term for "release" of spirit), the ghost of Kagekiyo saves his daughter and her lover from their captors; and this angry ghost is "released" from passion and hate with the aid of a garment belonging to a saint (a Taira clan relative).

[24] *Yugashima de no Omoide* (Memory of Yugashima; written in 1925) gives autobiographical clues that suggest possible origins of *The Izu Dancer*.

Hijō (Emergency, 1924), in *Arare* (Hail Storm, 1928; but first entitled *Bōryokudan no Ichiya*), and in *Nanpō no Hi* (Fire in the South, 1923). In *Nanpō no Hi* the 23-year-old man thinks 16-year-old Yumiko will, as his bride, bring back his own "boy nature," a childhood happiness he had never known.

Loneliness, death, and figures moving through the "floating world" (whether read as the Gay or Pleasure Quarters, or in the philosophical sense of transience) come to rest in *Nemureru Bijo* (Sleeping Beauty or Beauties; unfortunately translated as *House of the Sleeping Beauties*, although Kawabata is concerned not with the *house* but with the richly poetic implications of beauty and with fresh explorations of the traditional linking of beauty and sorrow). As already noted, there is an ambiguity in his title—"beauty" is written with the two ideograms for beautiful *(bi)* and woman *(jo)*. Since the Japanese language does not distinguish number, the title simultaneously suggests several women, a woman, or even Woman.

More than one woman is involved, and the sleep itself is neither natural nor the enchantment of fairy tale. The familiar Sleeping Beauty wakened by her Prince is far indeed from the beauties who lie in this strange house. It is an establishment maintained for elderly gentlemen: they can spend the night with young girls who are most conveniently drugged. But it should be noted that for all of them the physical pleasures of sex are now replaced by dream and reverie.

The protagonist, Eguchi, comes again and again: his memories (rather than the sleeping beauty) are awakened. His experiences in the present are linked through sights, scents, and sounds with memories of the past. At one point, envying the girls' deep sleep, he asks the woman who manages the establishment for some of the "medicine" for himself: she tells him that it is too potent for old men. (Ironically, he alone of the visitors still has the capacity for full enjoyment of the girls, although that would break the house rules.) At the end, he lies between two young girls. But he wakes one morning to find one of them already dead and cold. When he rings for the madam, she calmly has the girl carried off, after telling Eguchi he might as well go back to bed with the second girl —it is too early in the morning for him to leave.

Once again, however, this bare outline gives little idea of the real nature of Kawabata's novel. Again there are flashes of light and dark, repeated sounds, changed patterns, symbolic hints given through season and setting or through phrases of dialogue that take on meaning with each repetition. Once again details are linked in delicate associations of barely perceived images. For instance, the opening scene is of an unmarked inn, a room decorated with an autumn scene, but offering Eguchi no clue to its hidden nature. Only the woman in charge suggests a concealed horror: a hint of death in the whitish color of her obi and a feeling of disquiet that comes to Eguchi from the qualities of the eyes and feet of the bird decorating her obi.

Eguchi is told to listen to the waves and the wind. And these are the sounds that mark his strange progress from the first girl—lovely in her setting of crimson curtains, representing "life itself," and emanating the milky scent of a nursing baby—to the unvoiced horrors of the conclusion. Like Eguchi, we hear the wash of the waves, sometimes loud, sometimes receding, their rhythm linked with the music of his feelings. The reader finds in the lyrical rendering of Eguchi's heart going out to the girl something quite different from Tanizaki's boy seeking his stepmother's milky breast in "Bridge of Dreams"; we are reminded of an entry in Kawabata's diary for 1924: "Love is my only lifeline." The milky scent brings to Eguchi other memories—so that once more we move back in time from the sounds and scents of *this* moment to moments in the past (sometimes unpleasant, sometimes matching the beauty of his perceptions of this girl).

In this scene, Kawabata's technique of composite images and linked memories is beautifully demonstrated as the roar of waves sounds against the cliff. The ocean echoes in the girl's body: it is the rhythm of life pulsing at her wrist. With his eyelids closed, Eguchi sees the image of a butterfly, its movements simultaneously set to the music of the waves and of life. But its color is white. This whiteness dissolves to the white cap worn by the baby of another girl, bringing recollections of the time when Eguchi ran off to Kyoto with that girl (a girl who said that the baby was not his).

Other stories, too, present dreams or reveries in which memories of past experience offer hints of present meaning (especially *Sound of the Mountain*). But we must remember that actions in real life, as in dreams, are often incomplete, although Kawabata may fill in details at least partially during later episodes. In the second episode, thinking of various flowers, Eguchi remembers his daughters, especially the girl who had lost her virginity to one suitor but married the other. He remembers her through a 400–year-old camellia tree they had seen together, and its various qualities suggest the girl, her troubles, and his own feelings. (The camellia symbolizes bad luck in the manner of the flowers' falling "like severed heads"—a more precise clue than in *Snow Country*, where a meeting between Shimamura and Komako in the Camellia Room was no more than a subliminal hint of coming misfortune.) As Eguchi remembers the tree, he hears a sound like a faint roar: the faint roar inside that remembered tree (perhaps a swarm of bees) hints at the sound of the waves that are now outside the window of the room where Eguchi lies with a sleeping girl.

But the reverie or dream of the tree was set in motion by Eguchi's response to this second girl's "rich" scent. The hints of enchantment accompany an overflowing sensuousness— and here Kawabata displays his customary subtlety in conveying sexuality. Flower images become more erotic and more sensual than any of Tanizaki's accounts of warm flesh and seductive toes.[25] Kawabata is using the familiar Japanese

---

[25] In this scene, the scent of the girl's arm comes to Eguchi through his closed *eyelids*, bringing images of winter peonies, white camellias, wis-

hana (flower), a synonym for girl and feminine beauty and found in countless "flower" phrases. In other stories, the scent of a white peony, the golden and feminine petals of a flower, the quality of magnolia petals, simultaneously suggest the deep attraction of Woman and the aroused passions of the narrative's particular man.

This richly seductive quality in Eguchi's second girl is linked with a mystery—hinted in signs that she is dreaming and also suffering nightmares during their hours together. In contrast, the third girl is inexperienced and small. She is also frightened and had wanted a companion to share her night of sleep: Eguchi's comment that "two would not be so bad" foreshadows his final visit. The first girl suggested life, the second in various ways hinted of qualities not human, the third is wild and undeveloped. Yet again the novel's ending is foreshadowed in hints that we only begin to understand after the final episode is over: Eguchi's wish for a drugged (death-like) sleep beside the girl who lies as though dead, associated with memories of a satisfied woman in the past, one who also slept soundly (as though dead). He has a sense of fleeting happiness; but he also has a momentary impulse to strangle this girl.

Simultaneously, Eguchi has a sense of something wrong— as his own conduct progressively breaks the rules of the house. This third girl's tongue protruding from her mouth reminds him of a young prostitute long ago; at the same time it stimulates him to an act more exciting than simply putting his finger to her tongue. Yet he also thinks of her in terms that recall earlier allusions, as he remembers stories in which prostitutes and courtesans were Buddhas incarnate. The sense of touch and barely perceived scents here bring *visual* memories. With eyes again closed, Eguchi sees golden arrows

---

taria, and other symbolic blossoms, as well as the petal-dropping camellia associated with that one daughter. These several flowers bring fleeting memories of all three daughters—but the ultimate focus is the daughter seen through three pages describing the life, movement, texture, warmth, and even sounds of the *camellias*.

and deep purple hyacinths, while waves can be heard sounding gently against the cliff.

With the final episodes, symbols again crowd too thickly for annotation. The autumn scroll of maples has been changed at his fourth visit: the scene is of winter snow. Again in the use of *shi* there are hints of four and of death, although the fourth girl is warm and the sweet scent of Woman is stronger than before. Her skin is white, and the warmth that envelops Eguchi is reminiscent of scenes with Komako in *Snow Country*. The white butterfly of Eguchi's first "sleeping beauty" now becomes two butterflies seen by his closed eyes, these two becoming two pairs, then five, and finally a swarm (a link with the swarm of bees sounding in the camellia tree and thus an unvoiced memory of his youngest daughter, while we also remember that the sound of the bees was likened to the sound of the waves and is therefore doubly linked with that rhythmical accompaniment to Eguchi's visits and his memories). Behind Eguchi's closed eyelids this swarm of butterflies becomes a field of white flowers: once more, white carries hints of death, while the flowers give subliminal clues that a girl will be dead at the novel's end.

The final episode is the fifth: two girls—one dark and cold and the other of shining beauty in the tradition of Kawabata's complementary pairs, with hints of *in'yō* contrasts of dark and light and the number five of mystic harmony. To the continuing rhythm of the ocean's sounds, with subtle changes in that rhythm, Eguchi's memories and his present actions merge, separate, flow gently far back in time, and return to now. He remembers the man who died at this inn, but he finds "life itself" in the dark girl (who is modern and slightly foreign in size and figure); there is an oily quality to her flesh that is wild and pungent. He then turns to the small-boned and sweetly scented second girl. But it is impossible to render in English the delicacy with which Kawabata shows Eguchi lying between the dark and light girls, gently clasping one breast of each.

Now Eguchi's thoughts glide back to memories of his

mother's death and forward to contemplation of his own. At the same time, the skin of the dark girl takes on a strangely unpleasant quality. In his nightmare of flowers—looking like great red dahlias that seem to bury the house to which he had brought his bride—there are links with earlier fancies of blood and a preparation for his forthcoming waking nightmare: the discovery that the dark girl is dead. The woman of the house comes in response to Eguchi's call. There are hints recalling the earlier moment when Eguchi thought of strangling one of the sleeping girls: but Eguchi assures the woman that he has done nothing wrong (and in any case, she keeps denying that the girl *is* dead). Told to go back to sleep, Eguchi hears the woman dragging the dark girl downstairs; and he turns back to the form of the fair girl "in shining beauty."

But as he does so, there are sounds to provoke more memories: a car drives away, recalling the elderly client who died at this house and whose body was tactfully taken to a nearby inn. The girls in their deathlike sleep, however, were a dream of life for the men who came to lie with them. Eguchi's own clinging to life is suggested in each episode, as in the first, where the girl's pulse was linked with the rhythm of life, the waves of the ocean (perhaps linked with "wave of woman" in *Thousand Cranes*), and Kawabata's own references to the "lifeline of love."

Whether he is dealing overtly with death or with life, Kawabata uses both symbolism and allusive language in ways that should delight admirers of Henry James. Yet the commentator who spoke of the affinity of James and Kawabata neglected several important differences—especially the ways in which Kawabata *hints* of emotion (rather than James's verbal dissections of feelings and relationships). The economy of words in Kawabata, moreover, is very far from the convoluted Jamesian syntax and narrative. Even to speak of narrative in the Kawabata context is to miss the point, and the reader of translations must continually be alert to the fact that relative pronouns, definite verbs, and statements of intention are generally the translator's interpretation of suggestions that are beautiful in Japanese but chaotic if forced into literal English "equivalents."

Sometimes, of course, a desperate translator is forced to insert explanatory phrases lest the Western reader misinterpret Kawabata's hints and symbols—and the unwary reader may then assume that Kawabata's style has undergone a radical transformation. Moreover, the profoundly Japanese contexts of Kawabata's fictions sometimes prevent the Western reader from responding to the foreshadowings and subliminal clues that are one of the pleasures of Kawabata's work. Subtleties of word and gesture, as in Tanizaki's pages, may carry the allusive links; and the fine distinction (as when the girl in *Beauty and Sadness* decides which lover shall touch her right breast and which the left) can easily be missed. Lesbian lovers and an "enchanting" but vengeful, jealous girl are not lapses from Kawabata's characteristic subtlety. They belong in the Japanese context (attitudes toward sexual behavior and traditional tales of ladies driven mad for love and seeking revenge), although for the Western reader their meaning may be just as obscure as the delicate allusion to Teika's Pavilion of the Autumn Rain (intended to convey the autumnal sadness) or the hint of approaching death in a traditional white kimono and a modern white bathing suit. The reader alert to the existence of such clues, however, will derive much richer pleasure from all of Kawabata's short stories and novels.

Kawabata's technique can be studied at its best in *Sound of the Mountain*. A situation changes with time, as the participants change and develop, although the (open) end of each episode is usually no more than a subtly shifted perspective.[26]

[26] At the outset, it is also necessary to correct the misunderstandings that may result from Seidensticker's assertion (in offering translation in *Japan Quarterly* 11, of sections one, two, and six [partially], followed by fourteen through sixteen in a later issue of *Japan Quarterly*) that a reader who had missed the untranslated intervening sections would not be handicapped in approaching the last three. He speaks of Kawabata's techniques as "a

There is a delicate web of symbol and allusion, reminiscent of the finely woven imagery in *Snow Country* and the subtle textures of tea ceremony accessories and implications of *cha-no-yu* ritual in *Thousand Cranes*. Layers of allusion in *Sound of the Mountain* are evident even in the title, in the section headings, and in the names of the characters, carefully creating the atmosphere in which we glimpse Shingo, a man in his sixties, and his wife Yasuko, a year older.[27]

Shingo is first seen trying to *remember*—and memory and time are linked with feelings of loneliness. At one level there is Shingo's feeling that he is closer to his daughter-in-law

---

stringing together of little vignettes with no regard to overall form"—as though one might arrive in time for the coda in the third movement of Brahms' Violin Concerto in D and disregard opposing melodic and rhythmic themes of the opening movement, for instance. The translator also claimed that the core of the book is Shingo's fondness for Kikuko, dislike of his own children, and lack of feeling for his wife.

[27] The sound *(oto)* of the title carries limited meanings in English, but the Japanese word can be read as many different kinds of sounds: a roar, a boom, a wash (of waves), a crash (as of something breaking), splashing, the sound of gushing water. It can also signify "fame" and is found in words (including a number of poetical terms) to be translated as "message," "news," and so on. *Onto (on* being another reading of the *kanji* for *oto)* is used for "voice" and "tone," and there are many terms in music (such as *onchō* for "melody") that use the same ideogram. Kawabata's chapter headings are linked by parallel construction (unfortunately not preserved in the translation) giving the visual link of *no* ("of") as well as links of meaning (*yama no oto, semi no hane, kumo no hono'o*, and so on). In addition, Kawabata deliberately links the names of the son's wife (Kikuko) and his mistress (Kinuko), although unfortunately the translator persuaded Kawabata to let him use the shorter "Kinu" for the mistress's name in the translation lest the similarity prove "confusing" and "troublesome" *(sic)* for the Western reader! Wife and mistress are linked in other ways too: both become pregnant (although it is the *wife* who has an abortion). He links Shingo's daughter with the son's mistress: both want to open shops, for example. And Kawabata offers many other symbolic pairs, including the foreign homosexual and his Japanese boy, and a man and a girl who at first seem to be father and daughter (a clue, perhaps, to the future of Shūichi and of his mistress's child).

than to his own daughter Fusako or his son Shūichi. Kikuko, however, is very different from the daughter-in-law of Tanizaki's *Diary of a Mad Old Man.* She is Shingo's window "looking out of a gloomy house." And she is more than that: she is a window to memory and meaning and life itself. There are also delicate nuances of sentiment in tactfully symbolized links between Kikuko and the wife's sister—a girl whom Shingo had loved, but whose death let him drift into marriage with Yasuko.

This situation is the occasion for meditation, dependent on subtle connections of remembered images and phrases and the context of allusive gestures. The way in which time itself is treated in this novel is especially important. Often a scene is rendered in terms delicately reminiscent of earlier moments yet differing in some tiny detail (whether of fact or of implication). The meaning of time is examined indirectly, as through various references to a news item concerning an ancient lotus seed and its eventual germinating.

Time passes. The seasonal signs in each section change . . . as the complexity of time is rendered in part through a calendar of seasonal images. It is also suggested in an apparently simple, historical moment: the occasion when the reckoning of time shifted from the old Japanese system (in which the child is one year old at birth and two years old at the first New Year's Day) to the familiar Western mode. Yasuko comments in surprise: "It gives you a strange feeling, doesn't it? [Our grandchild] should be five this year, and all of a sudden she's three." The new system even changes the relative ages of Yasuko and her husband, since her birth month falls after his. Meaning here clearly reaches much deeper than the date of a birthday celebration: it delves into the nature of time itself.

In comparison with Kawabata's use of memory, a Proustian remembrance of things past seems no more than a beginner's exercise. The sound of the mountain is a multiple rendering of days and events and actions that dance back and forth in time, spanning the years between a girl's death and a man's dying memories. The sound is also transformed, gathering new clusters of associations, new images, in the course of the narrative—the sound of one train, of other trains; the voice of a beloved woman, or children's voices; a fall of snow—a memory both auditory and visual that is linked with a flash of light and a rush of echoes.

The significance of the sound emerges from a "forgotten" incident, a dim remembrance, an echo of long-ago associations, a shadow of an earlier scene. We hear it first during Shingo's wakeful night: a mysterious sound like the wind, far away, with a depth of rumbling in the earth "as if a demon had passed." It brings a "death chill" to Shingo. But at this time, Shingo had forgotten its significance. It is only later that his daughter-in-law reminds him that he had heard it before—just before his wife Yasuko's sister died.[28]

The specific sound of the mountain recurs throughout the story, sometimes (as in the sixth episode) as raging sea, mountain downpour, and a "roaring in the depths of the storm" that may only be the sound of a train in the not-too-distant tunnel. This moment is to be remembered later, as in the fifteenth section, where the roar of a train links the relationship of a homosexual couple (through Shingo's perception of the foreigner "using" the sickly Japanese boy) with other sterile relationships, among them the marriages of his own children;

[28] The sound is further linked through physical and emotional resemblances between Kikuko and the dead sister. Other sounds reinforce the hints of sexuality. Kikuko returns from staying with her parents, for example, and in proper Japanese fashion carries *omiyage* (the gifts that homecoming travelers always bring). For Shingo she brings an electric shaver—seemingly a very modern gift but in Kawabata's hands a traditional symbol, as Shingo reads the instructions and discovers that it can be used to shave the hair at the nape of a woman's neck (suggesting that seductive aspect of Japanese feminine beauty: the neck rising from the back collar of a kimono). Later Shingo gives her a return present (the exchange of gifts that is customary): a vacuum cleaner! Sounds of shaver and vacuum cleaner then mingle—a hint of erotic feeling, perhaps, but also an image of Life.

there is even a hint of the difference between his marriage with Yasuko and the delicately implied perfection of his love for the dead sister. The sound that may only be the roar of a train in the sixth section is followed by a voice that recalls the loved sister. Yet the voice, seemingly so real at this instant, may after all only be the voice of a child among a group on their way to school.

Echoes of the mountain's sound are picked up and carried in other images: when the roar of the storm merges with the sound of the train, it permits later sounds of water and later journeys to convey hints of the original image. Often the sounds—however tenuously linked with the mountain roar—hint of the association of *aware* with significant sound. We hear the fall of a chestnut: there is a delicate hint of a flawed marriage. We hear, too, the chirp of small birds; the whistle of a train; voices piercingly sweet, too loud, snoring, husky, seductive, singing; the rattle of a matchbox; the sounds of a bird (a black-eared kite) moving about on the roof or the wings of pigeons in flight; bells of distant temples, bells at Kamakura, bells signaling closing time at the Shinjuku Garden that Shingo visits with Kikuko. And the novel ends with an intensely modern sound, the sound of dishes being washed by the daughter-in-law (yet even this is a multiple sound, for it echoes an earlier scene, with the crash of dishes flung into the sink by Shingo's daughter).

Then there are insects: bell crickets, pine crickets, cicadas offer the range of sounds still appreciated in modern Tokyo. Today's insects may be bought in plastic cages, but their sounds were heard by long-ago poets—as when a lady mistakes the bridle-bell insect's cry for the sound of her homecoming husband. Kawabata's poetic ear is tuned to these traditional sounds; but he also makes them function in a modern context, so that the disorders of Shingo's world are rendered in subtle shifts of insects that variously screech, rasp, sing, and whirr. This sensitivity to the *quality* of sounds may be found in Kawabata's use of sounds as gentle as the

dripping of dew from leaf to leaf and as harsh as a fishmonger's knife rasping against a shell (this last a hint of the
disorders in son Shūichi's marriage).

Not that sound is the only linking device. Glimpses of colors, especially yellows, reds, and whites, and the quality of
colors (glowing, fresh, strong)—all play their part. The
gingko reappears in various contexts as leaf, nut, and tree; it
is contrasted with the cherry; and it reappears as the carved
hairstyle of a Nō mask. Two Nō masks in turn appear in different scenes, linked with their original owner (one set of
memories), with perceptions of Beauty (another set), and so
on—simultaneously carrying hints of both sexuality and
death. Various objects reappear in new settings as clues to
old memories. There is a *furoshiki* carried by daughter
Fusako, its significance at first not remembered but later re-
called: it carried a dwarf maple (a link with Yasuko's sister).
It is also the *furoshiki* in which Yasuko carried "something"
at the time of her marriage.[29]

This weaving together of time and emotion is part of a
symphony of memories. But there is a counterpoint of symbolic forgetfulness—and this ranges from the deeply significant sound of the mountain itself to Shingo's momentary
"unawareness" of his wife and an absentminded inability to
fasten his tie. This is the associative technique of poetry, not
of psychoanalysis, although Kawabata puts traditional allusions into contexts for modern and lonely men and women.

[29] Many links both auditory and visual cannot be found in the translation. For instance, the "cluster" or "swarm" of mosquitoes in section fourteen (*mure:* cluster) is a term often used in referring to a cluster of stars.
Thus there are recollections of section one, where Shingo saw a cluster of
stars through the mountain trees just after he had first heard the sound of
the mountain. Other links are taken from traditional Japanese symbolism:
the twin pines Shingo sees from the train are a specific symbol for conjugal
love and fidelity—thus underscoring the irony of Shūichi choosing this moment to tell his father that Kikuko has had an abortion. There is even an instance of the flower-in-the-mirror image when Shingo glimpses cherry
blossoms reflected in a pond.

Also, as in so many of Kawabata's stories, memories merge with dreams.

There is a dream in the fourteenth section, "A Swarm of Mosquitoes," the mosquitoes linked with emotions Shingo felt as he lay beneath an oppressive mosquito net, for instance. In his dream, Shingo cuts at the insects with his sword: flames shoot from his uniform—recalling the flames around the moon in the section *Kumo no Hono'o.* A blaze of light around the moon then had made Shingo think of the flames behind Acala in the painting and of coiling clouds of a fox spirit (hints of the enchantress of Japanese legend). In this earlier scene, the moon had seemed dimmed by the blaze of cloud and Shingo had felt autumn (sadness). His dream includes Yasuko's dead sister again, but he wakes to the sound of rain. With that sound, we return once more to an earlier scene, when the sound of rain had been ambiguously merged with the sound of the mountain.

Fragments of each of these memories are included in other memories, taking on new connotations at each appearance yet never losing the original significance, until the sixteenth and final episode, when Shingo (still troubled by "forgetting") cannot remember how to knot his tie. His daughter-in-law tries to help and fails; then wife Yasuko steps forward. As she tilts his head, he closes his eyes; and as he does so, Shingo sees a golden mist, an avalanche in sunlight. This impression is accompanied by a dimly perceived roaring—that sound again—and the sound is here accompanied by a remembrance of Yasuko's sister knotting his tie (a gesture linked with hints of his masculinity—it was at the time when he discarded his school uniform).

The sixteenth section has other such moments of gathering together fragmentary recollections from earlier episodes. On the train, Shingo sees men with maple branches returning from an excursion. This suggests his family home, and hence the sound of the remembered mountains, although Kawabata does not emphasize this memory. These maples are more than a link with Shingo's childhood home: the men with their branches remind Shingo of a potted, crimson-leaved maple among the memorial tablets when Yasuko's sister died.

In the final part of this section, Shingo also recalls that Yasuko's sister interested him in writing haiku: he recalls a trout verse. This fish in turn has its own set of symbolic associations moving in and out of the earlier sections. There is, for instance, an echo of a scene in the first section, in which Shingo paused at a fishmonger's. His purchase of shellfish then served as a delicate statement of the deteriorating relationship between his son and daughter-in-law. An overheard conversation between two "new-style" prostitutes at the fishmonger's could be taken as a subtle comment on other new-style women in later episodes—including war widows such as the son's mistress. A *smell* of cooking fish when Shingo visits this mistress, Kinuko, is also a link with the fishmonger scene. (Its conversations, and the picture of those earlier girls, in turn throw light on Shingo's perception of Kinuko's apartment with its Occidental plants and magazines and its soiled *tatami*.)

In the closing section, lotus seeds, sunflowers, an insect wing, a wish for death, a meditation on sickness, all reappear. We see again images that carry psychological meaning, as in the second section, "The Wings of the Locust" (*semi:* usually translated as *cicada*). In that section, Kawabata described how the granddaughter learned to ask to have the cicada's wings clipped off. This insect with its clipped wings offered a symbolic reference to the faulty relationship of the child's parents (a use of symbol reminiscent of Kawabata's technique in "The Mole" and in *Thousand Cranes*). The ambiguous "father and daughter" on the train (who turn out to be strangers) focus memories of other couples, including the foreign homosexual who seemed to Shingo a distorted image of himself. At the same time, as already noted, the supposed father and daughter provide hints of a future in which son Shūichi will not recognize his own illegitimate child.

Images of death have threaded through the *Sound of the Mountain*, too. For all its mystical associations, that sound is, after all, linked with a love that has vanished with death; and Shingo's unvoiced sense of loss is beautifully expressed in one recollection where he would have run toward the lovely sister if only she had appeared in life instead of a dream. Shingo's other dreams include dead friends; he is invited to visit dying friends and attend funerals; and even the tea he drinks has its link with death (it was a "return gift" following a friend's funeral). The number of butterflies (four) naturally stimulates thoughts of dying. The body of a cicada is eaten by ants. Death at all levels in fact permeates Shingo's waking and sleeping life: in news items, such as the account of a grandfather strangling a sick boy; in the presence of various widows, among them the war widows Kinuko and Mrs. Ikeda, as well as the friend's widow who sells her husband's Nō masks; and in episodes of suicide and near-death— whether immediate (as when Shingo takes his granddaughter to a celebration at Kamakura and a dancing girl is almost run over) or remote (in allusions to a tea ceremony master who died by suicide or a painting by a man who took his own life).[30]

Even the closing scene with its trout haiku offers lines on the trout's death. The novel ends after the fish that occasioned these memories has been eaten (three fish: linking with the early episode in which three fish were both a literal and a symbolic statement of Shūichi's relations with his wife). Daughter-in-law Kikuko has arranged red gourds while Shingo watched. Throughout, there have been hints of her sexuality in moments of "coloring" and in the way Shingo responds to her. There are tenuous links between Kikuko and the lovely sister of Yasuko (even a thought that Kikuko's lost,

[30] This extensive catalogue identifies only about a third of the overt links with death in *Sound of the Mountain*. Almost every page refers to death in some way or carries the reader back to the sound of the mountain: that echo of (dead) love.

aborted child might have been Yasuko's sister reborn). Other hints of sexuality are given in sounds that range from the strangely erotic duet of shaver and vacuum cleaner to the nuances of Kikuko's voice in song and speech. At the same time she provides a window out of the dead world of dreams and a second-best marriage.

These hints of promise, however, come to rest in a tragic moment of disappointment that is masked by a seemingly prosaic comment: "Kikuko, your gourds are sagging" (*Kikuko, karasuuri ga sagatte kiteruyo. Omoi kara ne.*).[31] These reddish gourds are visually linked with the red maples associated with the mountain's sound. They are doubly linked with autumn sadness—*karasu* (crow) and *uri* (gourd) both being autumn images. They are also linked with the mountains glimpsed from Shingo's window (and it should be remembered that Kikuko is a "window" too). Thus, in spite of the moments when Kikuko's steps seemed to move closer to Shingo (in a remark that seemed to him like a hint of passion), his attempts to communicate with her must inevitably fail. As Shingo calls to Kikuko about the gourds, his voice remains unheard. The sound of his voice is lost not in the roar of the mountain, with which Kikuko has been continually linked both in poetic and in subtly sexual ways, but in the sound of dishwashing.

Perhaps the dream is shattered, as the poetic memories

---

[31] This episode is also filled with traps for the unwary reader of the translation. In his first (partial) translation, Seidensticker used "snake gourds" for *karasu-uri* but changed this to "crow gourds" in the complete version. Although most dictionaries give "snake" gourd, the Japanese reader sees only the crow *(karasu)* of the *kanji*, and the gourds have no snake association for him. Yet the Western symbol hunter would discover a link with Shingo's dream of eggs (a *snake's* egg and an ostrich egg), in which he could not tell which one represented his son's wife and which the mistress. There would also appear to be a link with the green snake seen by Kikuko in an earlier scene. But for once the Western reader would be "seeing" much more than his Japanese counterpart and would be creating links that Kawabata did not intend.

and lyric recollections are lost in the everyday sound. Yet echoes of Shingo's symbolic dreams remain. Such dreams in Kawabata's work do not yield readily either to Freudian or to Jungian interpretation, although Western symbolism often seems to reinforce the intensely Japanese dreams of his fictions. Moreover, the dreams tend to be fragmentary and to communicate *feelings* rather than meanings. For instance, Shingo retains a memory of the emotional response of his dreams but usually cannot recall the plot. He remembers sensations (of cold, or dread, or pleasure) while being quite unable to recall the face of a beautiful girl. And the dreams of Kawabata's stories lack the truly sensational qualities that are apt to appear in the dreams and hallucinations of the "aesthetic" writers to whom Mishima is partially indebted.

One apparently hallucinatory story of Kawabata's is available in English, however, and it requires considerable annotation for the Western reader. This story is "One Arm" (*Kata-ude*, 1963–1964). At first, it might seem to fit in with early neo-perceptionist interest in hallucinatory states. But here the hallucination is merely a vehicle carrying typical Kawabata meanings. At one level, it could be read as a play on the expression "I'd give my right arm." The story further includes atypical New Testament allusions (in contrast to Kawabata's usually Buddhist phrases). The silver thread is cut, the golden bowl destroyed. "Whom seekest thou?" is misquoted—to suggest how the words might be applied to either man or woman.

These elements, however, must be approached in the tone of the opening passage: " 'I can let you have one of my arms for the night,' said the girl. She took off her right arm at the shoulder and with her left hand, laid it on my knee." Here are mystical hints, essential to interpretation of subsequent actions. Perhaps there is a hint of the story of Kannon "renting out" her arms in time of need; at least this would be closer to Kawabata's story than such Kabuki horrors as the demon of *Ibaraki* coming to retrieve her arm from the warrior who cut it off. Repeated allusions to gestures of right and left recall esoteric Buddhist symbolism, and these hints are further developed in Kawabata's use of groups of five (as in the number of lights) and hints of *in'yō* symbolism (thus setting "One Arm" in Kawabata's customary philosophical context after all).

The story's atmosphere of fog and darkness with flashes of color—vermilion, faint purple, lavender—enfolds a dream-world as the narrator carries the treasured arm home to his lonely room. The arm is a symbolic hint of the sad incompleteness of a man alone—a point made specific in the narrator's conversation with the arm and in the way it becomes a presence: a girl speaking to, touching, and for a while completing the narrator. The roundness of her shoulder after it is attached to his own makes him think of the roundness of her breasts. There is a quietness when her blood flows into his, and he enjoys "sweet" sleep. Yet he wakes screaming to the repulsive feel of his own (detached) right arm. Hastily he snatches off the borrowed arm and flings it away, replacing his own proper limb. He feels this gesture, however, as an act of murder—and the separation is accompanied by sadness, the sense of loss made visible in the discarded arm that now lies white and unmoving.

The sexual nature of dream and reality in *Kata-ude* is never far from the surface, yet always handled with the delicacy of *waka* and *renga* and a beauty of form recalling the tea utensils of *Thousand Cranes*. The quality of the girl's flesh is conveyed by the texture of a bud in a glass vase, the impossibility of the dream seen in the premature fall of the bud's petals. There is delicate eroticism in the way the girl's fingers curl around the stamens or pistils (the Japanese language does not distinguish between them). We find an intensely Japanese perception of beauty recurring, as in the graceful line of the girl's neck. The darkness hints of sexuality, while homonyms also link the darkness of night with the world outside the window and with the relationship of the

man to the girl whose arm he bears. The closing words delicately express sexuality through a traditional phrase: "If the
dew of woman would but come from between the long nails
and the fingertips . . . ."

Given a couple of detached arms, thoughts of breasts, and
a man in a lonely room, Mishima would whip up a neat little
episode of butchery. But Kawabata maintains his delicate
tone. There are sounds as subtle as those in *Sound of the
Mountain* and as mysterious as the roaring of the earth in
Snow Country. In this story, as in others, the Japanese aesthetic, and images as deep as the moon-in-the-water of *Suigetsu*,
are used to enrich Kawabata's own intense perceptions of
relationships and feelings. Similarly, his seasonal images go
far beyond those of Heian literature and haiku to function
both aesthetically and psychologically, even in the most modern settings.

Only occasionally are these modern settings given a place
and time limited by history, however. For Kawabata, "contemporary problems" are those of the individual, especially
his loneliness. One story published soon after the war's end is
anchored to current events, but these are a vehicle for exploring the territory of individual isolation and the search for
love (and life). In "Reencounter" (*Saikai*, 1946), Yūzō reencounters Fujiko: at the end of the brief narrative they are
walking together through the rubble as he reencounters
Woman and feels that lifeline of love that Kawabata has described in his diary and his literary autobiography. And as in
so many stories, this awakening is accompanied by a sound:
the sound of breaking wood.

The cast includes American bandsmen playing on the
sacred stage of a shrine dedicated to Hachiman, the Japanese
god of war. There is a scene of Japanese soldiers stretched,
suffering, on a station platform. This story is unusual, too, in
its occasional commentary, as when Yūzō perceives the
American "defiling" of the shrine platform but also thinks:
"What a bright and cheerful country America must be." Yū-

zō sees Japanese girls in inappropriately bright kimono. He compares the calamity of nature (the Kantō earthquake) with the holocaust of war and speculates on the symbolic quality of the war wounded ("pure" or "poor" in the translation). These comparisons, however, are but variations in Kawabata's familiar pattern of Japanese allusions, as when Fujiko seems "foxlike," linking her with tales of enchantment.

It would be a pity if the Western reader were distracted by the "quaintness" of enchantment, or of dancing maidens, tea ceremony, and geisha. These cultural memories are becoming increasingly remote even from the younger Japanese reader, who may miss the full richness of poetic hints but can still appreciate the delicate feelings that are conveyed.

In the early *The Izu Dancer*, for instance, the rain stops, the moon comes out, the autumn sky is washed by rain. Or a flock of small birds fly up beside a bench, and in the quietness there is a rustle as they land among the dead leaves. The phrases echo from a thousand years of refined perceptions: from centuries of *aware*. There are hints of the Buddhist sound-and-silence, as in Bashō's much-quoted haiku of a pond and sound-of-frog-jumping-in.

But in *The Izu Dancer* these details suggest the intensity of a modern boy's emotion, the fragile quality of his feelings rendered by two light taps of his fingers upon a dancer's drum. It is the birds of our time that now start up in alarm. Enriched by echoes of the past, Kawabata's psychological insight here renders with great tact the responses of an inexperienced student: the boy's repeated trips to the bath in hopes of encountering the girl; his suspense when her drum falls silent (implying her closeness to some patron perhaps); his restless night at chess with a fellow guest; even his relief, as though fresh water flowed over his body, when he discovers that Kaoru is no more than a child.

Some critics speak of Kawabata's sensitivity to "feminine psychology," but *The Izu Dancer* indicates how much wider his range of understanding is, and how universal. The young man Kikuji in *Thousand Cranes*, like the narrator of "One Arm," is ultimately to be understood in the framework of Japanese culture. Yet both are valid in modern psychological terms. For instance, in identifying with his father Kikuji "sees" the elder Mitani "biting at Chikako's birthmark with dirty teeth"—and this vision becomes the figure of Kikuji himself. Kawabata also renders admirably the possible effects on the eight-year-old Kikuji of seeing his father's mistress, her breast uncovered, trimming whiskerlike hairs from the ugly mole. But he makes no explicit statement of cause and effect, preferring to convey meaning through Kikuji's tendency to use words that spoil his relationship with Mrs. Ōta, to hint at Kikuji's moments of cruelty, and to record Kikuji's attempt to vindicate himself.

The plump Shimamura with his middle-aged posturings in *Snow Country* is in many respects a rather esoteric figure. Yet he is also sadly universal, as in the evaluation of his self-published books. (In all likelihood they would contribute nothing to the Japanese dancing world: but they would bring aid and comfort to Shimamura.) Even the doubts of the sixty-year-old Eguchi trying to survive and reconstruct the ruins of his life with the aid of comatose virgins in *Nemureru Bijo* reveal a finely drawn "masculine mystique"—and the tender appreciation of love and loneliness characteristic of Kawabata's writing.

Kawabata can also convey the loneliness of marriage—as when Shingo in *Sound of the Mountain* realizes that he reaches out to touch his wife only when she snores (and he tweaks her nose to stop *that* sound). He shows the loneliness of parents intensely aware of a distance from their children that they cannot bridge, or of a loss of feeling that extends even to the next generation: to the little girl's footsteps that do not bring feelings of tenderness to her grandfather.

Some critics seemed to find *The Lake* different from other Kawabata stories when it was translated in 1974, speaking of the surprise Western readers might feel at the "brutal sensu-

ality" of several scenes. But of course the scenes are not brutal; and the sensuality, though not so evident in other translated works, has always been a characteristic of Kawabata's
writing. The sensuality or eroticism in Kawabata's work,
however, is carried in poetic images rich with symbolic clues,
as it is in this story of Gimpei—reminiscent of the lonely man
in "Of Birds and Beasts," of the night wanderer in "One
Arm," even of old Eguchi and the sleeping girls (although
Gimpei is identified as a man only thirty-four years old).

Gimpei too has his fantasies. And like the old father-in-law
of *Sound of the Mountain* and the young student of *The Izu
Dancer*, Gimpei has a dreamlike longing for the unattainable
—symbolized in fresh-faced girls—while a more intimate relationship with one of his students leads to Gimpei's dismissal
from his teaching job. The narrative opens with Gimpei in a
Turkish bath (inevitably associated in Japan with a rather
low class of sexual encounter). Yet even here interest is not
focused on the bathhouse girl, from whose barely covered
breasts Gimpei specifically shrinks. It is to the *sound* of her
voice that Gimpei responds: the voice of Woman. (One thinks
of Komako in *Snow Country*; and this girl, too, is from Niiga-
ta in Japan's "snow country.") The sensuality of the encounter is conveyed through images with traditionally erotic
meanings (such as the nape of the girl's neck), mirrored in the
pale colors of the bath, or suggested in the leaves of a garden
glimpsed through the window.

Here, as in other scenes, sensuality, whether linked to flesh
or to memory, is conveyed through skin delicately coloring
(the traditional erotic hint). Gimpei's responses are rendered
in such images as the shadows cast by gingko trees, the feeling of fresh, damp grass (when Gimpei is relieved that an encounter does not lead to consummation), the experience of
swimming in a deep black lake. The glow of fireflies in the
cage Gimpei hangs on Machie's dress is a reflection of his
glowing heart.

As in other Kawabata stories, the narrative is most slight

and moves in the familiar way, back and forth in time through associative images. Many of these are mirrored: reflections in an ice-covered lake, in a florist's window, in bathwater, in a mirror set into a hot-spring brothel's bath, the sky reflected in Gimpei's own eyes, wild cherry blossoms glimpsed in the waters of a lake. There are opposites or contrasts, too, especially between the lonely Gimpei, with his ugly feet, and the various feminine figures he encounters—not all virginal students, as some of the reviews implied, but including the young mistress of an old man, a prostitute remembered from Gimpei's schooldays, and a filthy woman discovered among the vagrants of Tokyo's underground passages.

The narrative thread runs from the Turkish bath of the opening scene to our last glimpse of Gimpei's feet as he inspects the reddened area where the ugly, drunken woman had flung a stone at his ankle. Between those moments, time past, time present, and even time future brought details of Gimpei following the young mistress Miyako; of his involvement with Hisako, a pupil in one of his classes; of his memories of beautiful cousin Yayoi beside the lake; of the girl Machie with her dog; of his mother; of street girls and prostitutes; and ultimately of the ugly woman to whom he gives a meal and sake, but from whom he runs at the entrance to a cheap hotel.

These figures are intertwined: the dog of the girl Machie recalling memories of the cousin's dog and a mouse (the mouse later appearing in other contexts); the massaging hands of the girl in the bath becoming the purse thrown at Gimpei by Miyako; Miyako, the girl with the purse, linked to the girl with the dog through Miyako's younger brother. Watching Machie and the boy, Gimpei is awakened from his reverie by the remembered sound of cousin Yayoi's voice. Lying in the grass watching a beautiful girl is linked with memories of Gimpei hiding in a thicket, hoping to discover his father's murderer. Sometimes these figures are intertwined through dream and fantasy: a baby seems to crawl on the grass, there is a memory of a prostitute abandoning her baby at student Gimpei's lodgings, the (widowed) ugly woman of the final scenes lives alone with a daughter.

Occasionally the dream fantasy brings thoughts of violent death—some linked with Gimpei's memories of his father being drowned, perhaps murdered, in the lake near his mother's home. Lost in a girl's dreamlike beauty, Gimpei is so weighted down by the beauty that he feels like dying . . . or like killing the girl. But the cause of that fleeting response is his *sadness*, not the cruel sexuality of Mishima's pages. At the moment when Hisako's mother discovers Gimpei in his student's bedroom, he fantasizes a bullet that will pierce mother and daughter. But the blood will flow over his ugly feet, turning them to mother-of-pearl; and perhaps he too will enter the world of beauty, for here is the traditional linking of beauty with feelings of sadness that is so characteristic of Kawabata's work.[32]

[32] Beauty and sadness are in fact linked in the title *Utsukushisa to Kanashimi to*, a novel that—like *The Lake*—seemed to surprise some Western readers by its sensuality and frankly described sexual encounters. Even the moments of lesbian lovemaking, however, are treated with restraint (especially in comparison with the sweaty encounters of Mishima's *Temple of Dawn* or Honda treating lesbian love as spectator sport in *Decay of the Angel*). Blood that flows here is not a prelude to the butchery of Mishima's scenes but a pouring forth of passion; and as with the homosexual pair glimpsed aboard a train in *Sound of the Mountain*, there are deeper meanings. Explicit scenes of Otoko with Keiko snuggled beside her—or of that same young girl in turn beside Otoko's former lover and the lover's son— are not a catalogue of perversity but Kawabata's symbolic rendering of transience, ambiguity, and the lifeline of love. Significance may be as ambiguous as the way in which artist Otoko sees her admiring and sexually exciting young Keiko not only as the portrait of a saintly Buddhist figure but also as a seductive young Kabuki actor (saint and actor alike being figures of appropriately ambiguous sexual significance in Japanese tradition). Yet whatever the terms, this is primarily another of Kawabata's windows on loneliness, beginning with the opening scene in which we glimpse Oki traveling to Kyoto to hear the New Year bells. These are not the simple

Some of the dream quality of this novel lies in the fragments of memory and meaning—half-developed, unexplained gestures such as Miyako's (did she drop or throw the purse—and why?), the antics of children, the relationships of scarcely glimpsed couples, the fate of a prostitute and the reasons for her actions. The ambiguities are not to be resolved.[33] For this is not so much a novel as a window on loneliness: Gimpei's longing for "clean" beauty, his responses to "pure" voice, his profound sadness even as he feels a girl's delicate skin, his memories of a hand held long ago. Such dreams cannot be reduced to simple meaning.

When Tanizaki's father-in-law reaches for those seductive toes in *Diary of a Mad Old Man*, we react with sympathy to

---

"temple bells" of the translated version, however, but specifically *joya no kane* (*joya:* New Year's Eve)—one hundred and eight strokes of a heavy wooden beam upon each great bronze bell, in symbolic midnight casting out of the 108 "evil desires" of Buddhism, to start the New Year clean. The empty ever-turning seat aboard the train in that opening scene is a focus for Oki's memories of death, loss, and separation. As in other novels, characters and episodes, sounds and objects, recall earlier scenes even as they foreshadow the shifting patterns of the future. Time is rendered through a calendar of seasonal allusions, while the feeling of sadness permeating the narrative is intensified by the recognition that only one beauty remains unchanged by time: the girl in the pages of Oki's book. But that girl is now the older woman playing with beautiful young Keiko just as Oki once delighted to play with her. Episodes of finger-nibbling or hints of cruelty should not distract the reader from deeper, philosophical implications, however, as the participants are carried back and forth in time and memory. This is a meditation not only upon love, loneliness, and loss but also upon the nature of Time itself, expressing Kawabata's recurrent theme of beauty's close links with sadness, the traditional association that he has identified as the very heart of Japanese poetic sense (the feeling of *aware*).

[33] As in other stories, the links are much too numerous for annotation. Some are no more than hints of (untranslatable) meaning, as in the glimpses of Gimpei "hidden in the grass" watching a young girl or even embracing his student. Fortunately, the translation provides a clue in the explanation that the phrase also refers to one who is dead, "hidden" in the ground. This hint adds another dimension to our view of lonely Gimpei separated from life (as in the taxi-window imagery noted above).

the distance between his dream and the reality, but ultimately Tanizaki's ironic tone encourages us to laugh with him over this preposterous pretense. The reader who laughs over the old men in *House of the Sleeping Beauties* or suspects Shingo of plotting to seduce Kikuko, however, has surely experienced neither loss nor love. Nor have other modern Japanese writers—even when using the themes and symbols we find in Kawabata's work—quite succeeded in matching his delicacy of sentiment. Other writers, for instance, have shown devoted wives nursing husbands dying of tuberculosis, as in Nogami Yaeko's *Kitsune* (The Foxes), a "beautiful portrayal of conjugal affections" according to Japanese critics. But in *Kitsune* these affections are verbalized and tied to the mundane business of a fox farm. There is none of the poetic richness we find in Kawabata's use of a similar situation in "The Moon on the Water."

Unlike the Meiji writers, who tended to deny their tradition even while their work shows how far they were from escaping it, Kawabata responds to the past proudly and without excuse. Not that he is confined by tradition: he responds to each new—and sometimes seemingly trivial—detail with the true delight of the artist.[34] At the same time, he can appreciate the visual charm *(en)* of beauty and convey the deepest mystery of *yūgen*. Instead of Tanizaki's irony, he has that

[34] Some commentators stress Kawabata's early wish to be a painter, although we have clear records that he turned to a writing career while still in Middle School. But his images are not limited to the visual: scents and sounds are more important than his rather limited palette of red and white and greens and yellows—with a perception of the *qualities* of colors ("dusky," "fresh," "clean") that suggests both painter and writer. In his public lecture at the University of Hawaii in May 1969, Kawabata spoke of the beauty to be found in reflections of light from tumblers stacked on the breakfast tables. In speaking of these mundane Western objects, he showed a Japanese preference: "Many stars [of light] gleaming may seem more beautiful than only one, but as far as I am concerned, the beauty I sensed when I first saw only one star is far greater. Surely this is true in both literature and life."

gentle perception, the smile of *okashi*. And above all he has
expressed in countless ways the sensitive, reflective tone of
the thousand-year-old aesthetic: *aware*, the traditional linking of beauty and sorrow.

All these links with traditional aesthetics, with Buddhist
thought, and with ancient Japanese literary forms and symbols should not, however, obscure Kawabata's timely psychological insight. Nor should emphasis on his poetic method
obscure the erotic and the sensual qualities of most of his
work. Because of cultural differences, the Western reader
cannot always share nuances of gesture and feeling; and the
specific sexuality, even when rendered with technical cor-
rectness in the translation, will often have quite different connotations. It should therefore be stressed that while explicitly
sexual descriptions surprise Western readers of *The Lake*,
Japanese readers find these quite natural extensions of the
quality of eroticism characteristic of Kawabata and his rich
sensual imagery: qualities that should have been apparent
even in translation.[35] Nothing in his work, however, gives
clues that would explain Kawabata's suicide on 16 April
1972.

Kawabata had in fact often spoken out against suicide.

---

[35] An exception to the poetic eroticism and sensual qualities in most of
Kawabata's work is *The Master of Go (Meijin*, 1954). Kawabata described
this as a "chronicle-novel": it focuses on an actual match, which Kawabata had reported for a newspaper, the *Nichinichi Shimbun*, in 1938. (The
translation is made from a shortened version, published in 1954, in Kawabata's *Zenshū*.) Many Western readers—and quite a few in Japan, too—
find the story tedious. Those who do not play go are bored by the details of
the games; those who do play object to the translation, which they claim
uses outdated and even inaccurate terminology. Certainly even the esoteric
tea ceremony of *Thousand Cranes* is more accessible to the foreign reader.
The master, his followers, the attitudes of the participants, and the stifling
atmosphere of hotel rooms provide little of the delicate beauty that charac-
terizes other Kawabata works. Nor does the master—a fictionalized version of the one playing the original match—display the qualities that make
Kawabata's other lonely, aging men such memorable figures.

Even in his Nobel Prize acceptance speech, Kawabata said: "However alienated one may be from the world, suicide is not a form of enlightenment. . . . I neither admire nor am in sympathy with suicide." At the time he was speaking of fellow writers as well as of figures in Japan's medieval past. Later, his shock following Mishima's suicide was even more profound.

The actual circumstances of Kawabata's own death merely added to the mystery. For that intensely Japanese writer, so finely attuned to traditional Japanese aesthetics, committed suicide with a gas hose in his mouth and an empty whiskey bottle beside him. Moreover, he carried out the action in the modern mansion apartment he had recently purchased, for ten million yen, as a place where he sometimes liked to work. And he was dressed in Western polo shirt and trousers, not the dark kimono in which he was so often photographed.

Friends, family, other writers, foreign scholars—none could explain Kawabata's death. Some found clues in a painful illness. Others related the death to Kawabata's sadness following the bloody suicide of his protégé Mishima. Many blamed the physical and emotional strains Kawabata had experienced as a public figure in the months following his Nobel Prize.

The mystery remains. Mishima's suicide could be seen as the inevitable result of his bloody aesthetics. But the manner of Kawabata's death seems utterly irrelevant to both his own delicacy of feeling and the sensitivity to beauty revealed in his writing. Although the qualities of Kawabata as man and artist can be fully appreciated only in the Japanese context, even the pale words of translation reflect the qualities of beauty and sadness that characterize his work.

We can perceive these qualities only dimly—but then dimness is a virtue to the Japanese eye. The lyrical language does not quite survive the hazards of translation. Kawabata's technique and images sometimes require a sensitivity as subtle as that of the moon-viewing cult itself. Yet, as in *Suigetsu*, the dim reflection has its own beauty: the pale light in Kawabata's mirror reveals a more richly erotic image than the glowing figures of Tanizaki's world or the gaudy actors on Mishima's stage. Perhaps there is even a fine poetic justice in the knowledge that Kawabata's work reached the Nobel Prize Committee through the mirror image of English translation. Looking at his name written in *kanji* provides a pictorial clue: *Kawa-bata*—the River-bank—forever reflected in the mirror of the moving water. In its lyric beauty, as in *Suigetsu*, there is a new world created, and as we flow with its unfamiliar images, it does indeed come to seem like the real world of that "moon in the water."

Works Available in English

Beauty and Sadness (Utsukushisa to Kanashimi to, 1961–1963) Translated by Howard Hibbett. New York: Knopf, 1975.

The Existence and Discovery of Beauty (Bi no Sonzai to Hakken, 1969). Translated by V. H. Viglielmo. Tokyo: Mainichi Newspapers, 1969.

House of the Sleeping Beauties (Nemureru Bijo, 1960–1961) *and Other Stories.* Translated by Edward Seidensticker, with an introduction by Mishima Yukio. Tokyo: Kōdansha, 1969.

The Izu Dancer (Izu no Odoriko, 1926). Translated by Edward Seidensticker. *Atlantic* 195 (January 1955):108–114. [Also in *Fifty Great Oriental Stories*, edited by Gene Z. Hanrahan (New York: Bantam, 1965) and in *The Izu Dancer and Others*, annotated by Shonosuke Ishii (bilingual Modern Japanese Authors series) (Tokyo: Hara, 1964).]

Japan, the Beautiful, and Myself (Utsukushii Nihon no Watashi —sono Josetsu). Nobel Prize acceptance speech, 12 December 1968. Translated by Edward Seidensticker. Bilingual edition. Tokyo: Kōdansha, 1969.

Note: An explanation of seeming discrepancies in dating in both bibliography and chronology is to be found in the preface.

The Kurenaidan [Scarlet Club] *of Asakusa* (*Asakusa Kurenaidan*, 1929). Summarized in *Introduction to Contemporary Japanese Literature*. Tokyo: Kokusai Bunka Shinkōkai, 1939.

The Lake (*Mizuumi*, 1954). Translated by Reiko Tsukimura. Tokyo: Kōdansha International, 1974.

The Master of Go (*Meijin*, 1954). Translated by Edward Seidensticker. New York: Knopf, 1972.

"The Mole" (*Hokuro no Tegami*, 1940). Translated by Edward Seidensticker. *Japan Quarterly* 2(1955):86–93. [Also in *Modern Japanese Literature*, edited by Donald Keene (New York: Grove Press, 1956), and *The Izu Dancer and Others*.]

"The Moon on the Water" (*Suigetsu*, 1953). Translated by George Saitō. *Asia* 8(1956). [Also in *Modern Japanese Stories*, edited by Ivan Morris (Tokyo: Tuttle, 1962), and *The Izu Dancer and Others*.]

"Of Birds and Beasts" (*Kinjū*, 1933). In *House of the Sleeping Beauties and Other Stories*, translated by Edward Seidensticker. Tokyo: Kōdansha, 1969. [Also in *This Is Japan* 17(1970):59–65. Tokyo: Asahi Shimbun, 1969.]

"One Arm" (*Kata-ude*, 1963–1964). Translated by Edward Seidensticker. *Japan Quarterly* 14(1967):60–70. [Also in *House of the Sleeping Beauties and Other Stories*.]

"Reencounter" (*Saikai*, 1946). Translated by Leon Picon. *Orient West* 8(1963). [Also in *The Izu Dancer and Others*.]

Snow Country (*Yukiguni*, 1935–1937, 1947, 1948). Translated by Edward Seidensticker. New York: Knopf, 1957.

The Sound of the Mountain (*Yama no Oto*, 1949–1954). Excerpts translated by Edward Seidensticker. *Japan Quarterly* 11(1964):304–330 and 446–467. [The complete novel was published by Knopf in 1970.]

Thousand Cranes (*Senbazuru*, 1949–1952). Translated by Edward Seidensticker. New York: Knopf, 1958.

"Undying Beauty." *This Is Japan* 17(1970):57–58. Tokyo: Asahi Shimbun, 1969.

Who's Who among Japanese Writers (with Aono Suekichi). Tokyo: UNESCO/PEN Club, 1957.

A Partial Chronology

1899   11 June: Born in Osaka.

1915–   Attended Ibaragi Middle School.
1917

1915   First magazine publication: *Kuraki Sensei no Sōshiki*, published in *Danran* (Osaka). Titled *Shi no Hitsugi o Kata ni* (Carrying My Teacher's Coffin on My Shoulder) in *Tōkō Shōnen* (1949). During this period, a number of pieces were published in *Keihan Shimpō*, a small local newspaper. Titles include: *H-chūi ni* (To Lieutenant H.); *Awayuki no Yoru* (Night of Light Snow); *Murasaki no Chawan* (Purple Teacup); *Aoba no Mado Yori* (From the Window of Green Leaves); and *Shōjo ni* (To a Little Girl). Several of Kawabata's tanka (31-syllable poems) were published during this period, too.

1917   Entered First Higher School.

1920   Entered English Department, Tokyo Imperial University.

1921   Transferred to Department of Japanese Literature because attendance requirements were less strict and he wanted to write. (There is an interesting account of Kawabata's university experiences in vol. 4 of his *Zenshū* [Collected Works].)

        April: *Shōkonsai Ikkei* (Memorial Day Scene; sometimes referred to as "A Scene from the Requiem Festival") appeared in *Shinshichō* (published with friends at Tokyo University). This piece impressed Kikuchi Kan.

        Abura (Oil) published in *Shinshichō*.

        December: First paid article (ten yen)—*Nambu-shi no Sakufū* (Mr. Nambu's Literary Style), a book review—published in *Shinshichō*.

1922   4 April: Diary entry reveals that Kawabata doubted his literary ability.

        Translations of Galsworthy and Chekhov for *Bunshō Kurabu*.

July: *Kongetsu no Sōsakukai* (Literary World This Month), a series of eight pieces of literary criticism, published in *Jiji Shimpō*.

1923 May: *Kaisō no Meijin* (An Expert in Attending Funerals) published in leading literary magazine, *Bungei Shunjū*.

July: *Nanpō no Hi* (Fire in the South) published in *Shinshichō*.

1924 March: *Kagaribi* (Fishing Fire) published in *Shin-Shōsetsu*.

Graduated from Tokyo Imperial University.

September: Beginning of *Bungei Jidai* (Literary Age) with other writers (including Yokomitsu Riichi). This literary magazine became the focus for the *Shinkankaku-ha* (neoperceptionist group).

December: *Hijō* (Emergency) published in *Bungei Shunjū*.

1925 February: *Ochiba to Fubo* (Fallen Leaves and Parents) published in *Shinchō*. Title sometimes given as *Ochiba to Chichi* (Fallen Leaves and Father) and later as *Koji no Aijō* or *Koji no Kanjō* (Orphan's Love or Orphan's Feelings).

June-August: Wrote *Yugashima de no Omoide* (Memory of Yugashima)—a "memory" that reveals the source of *Izu no Odoriko*.

August and September: *Jūrokusai no Nikki* (Diary of a Sixteen-year-old) published in *Bungei Shunjū*. Title also given as *Jūshichisai no Nikki* (Diary of a Seventeen-year-old).

December: *Arigatō* (Thank You) published in *Bungei Shunjū*.

Contributed to *Shinshin Sakka no Shinkeikō Kaisetsu*, manifesto of the *Shinkankaku-ha*.

1926 February and April: *Izu no Odoriko* (The Izu Dancer) published in *Bungei Jidai*.

June: First book: *Kanjō Sōshoku* (Sentimental Decoration), a collection of thirty-five stories, *Tenohira no Shōsetsu* (Stories on the Palm [of the Hand]; that is, very short pieces). Also note title *Tanagokoro* (Palm of the Hand) *no*

Shōsetsu, one hundred "palm-sized" stories written between 1922 and 1950.

1927   March: Collection of short stories published by Kinseidō with the title *Izu no Odoriko.*

Umi no Himatsuri (Sea Fire Festival) serialized in *Chūgai Shōgyō Shimbun.* Kawabata's diary entries include an account of his borrowing money on this manuscript.

1928   May: *Bōryokudan no Ichiya* (later title *Arare:* Hailstorm) published in *Taiyō.*

1929   January-October: *Bungei Jihyō,* a series of literary criticism for *Bungei Shunjū.*

March: *Kyūchō no Tantei* (The Class Chairman's Investigation) published in *Shōnen Kurabu.*

April: *Shitai Shōkainin* (The Corpse Introducer) published in *Bungei Shunjū.*

August: A volume of Kawabata's work appeared in the series *Shinshin Kessaku Shōsetsu Zenshū* (Complete Collection of Recent Novels) published by Heibonsha.

October: *Onsen-yado* (A Hotspring Inn) published in *Kaizō.*

1929–   12 December 1929: *Asakusa Kurenaidan* (The Kurenaidan
1930   [Scarlet or Crimson Club] of Asakusa) begins in serialized form in Tokyo *Asahi Shimbun.* Also published in *Kaizō* in September 1930. Published as a book by Senshinsha in 1930. Other Asakusa pieces: *Asakusa no Onna* (Woman of Asakusa), published in *Shinchō* in February 1931; *Asakusa no Kyūkanchō* (Asakusa Hill-Myna), published in *Modan Nihon* in June 1932; and *Asakusa Shinjū* (see *Niji,* 1934–1936).

1930   November: *Hari to Garasu to Kiri* (Needle and Glass and Fog) published in *Bungei.*

1931   January: *Suishō Gensō* (Crystal Fantasy) published in *Kaizō.* Published by Kaizōsha in April 1934.

1932   February: *Jojōka* (A Lyrical Poem [*jojō:* lyricism, personal feelings]) published in *Chūō Kōron.* Book published in December 1934.

1933   July: *Kinjū* (Birds and Beasts; translated as *Of Birds and Beasts*) published in *Kaizō*. *Kinjū*, a collection of short stories, appeared as a book published by Noda Shobō in May 1935.

December: *Matsugo no Me* (Eyes on the Deathbed) published in *Bungei*.

1933–   November 1933–May 1934: *Chirinuruo* ("The leaves have
1934   fallen . . .": allusion to a famous *waka*) published in *Kaizō*.

1934   May: *Bungakuteki Jijoden* (Literary Autobiography) published in *Shinchō*.

1934–   *Niji* (The Rainbow) published: *Niji* in *Chūō Kōron*, March
1936   1934; *Odoriko* (Dancing Girl) in *Bungei*, April 1934; *Natsu* (Summer) in *Bungei Shunjū*, June 1934; *Shichiku* (Four Bamboos) in *Chūō Kōron*, October 1935; *Asakusa Shinjū* (Asakusa Love-Suicide) in *Modan Nihon*, April 1936.

1935   *Junsui no Koe* (Pure Voice) published in *Fujin Kōron*.

1935–   *Yukiguni* (Snow Country) included two versions of the first
1937   part: *Yūgeshiki no Kagami* (Mirror of the Evening Scene), published in *Bungei Shunjū* in January 1935, and *Shiroi Asa no Kagami* (Mirror of a White Morning), published in *Kaizō* in January 1935. Other sections: *Monogatari* (Story or Tale) and *Torō* (Futile Efforts), published in *Nihon Hyōron* in November and December 1935; *Kaya no Hana* (Miscanthus Flower), published in *Chūō Kōron* in August 1936; *Hi no Makura* (Pillow of Fire), published in *Bungei Shunjū* in October 1936; *Temariuta* (Handball Song), published in *Kaizō* in May 1937. Several Japanese scholars have attempted to trace the various revisions and additions (the entries for 1937 and 1947, for instance). A "complete" *Yukiguni* was published in 1948, but yet another revised version was discovered at the time of Kawabata's suicide in 1972.

1936   January: *Itaria no Uta* (Song of Italy) published in *Kaizō*.

1936–   *Hana no Warutsu* (Flower Waltz) published in *Kaizō* in
1937   April and May. *Bikko no Odori* (Lame Dance) published in

Bungakukai in July. *Saigo no Odori* (Death Dance) published in *Kaizō* in January 1937. A collection of short stories with the title *Hana no Warutsu* was published by Kaizōsha in 1936.

1937   June: *Yukiguni* (Snow Country) and other stories published by Sōgensha.

1940   January: *Haha no Hatsukoi* (Mother's First Love) published in *Fujin Kōron*.

March: *Hokuro no Tegami* (The Mole's Letter; translated as "The Mole") published in *Fujin Kōron*. Title also given as *Hokuro no Nikki* (The Mole's Diary) and in earliest version titled *Akusai no Tegami* (Bad Wife's Letter).

November: *Yukuhito* (A Leaving Person) published in *Fujin Kōron*.

1941   December: *Aisuru Hitotachi* (Lovers), a collection of short stories, published by Shinchōsha.

1942   *Bunshō* (Prose Style), a collection of essays, published by Tōhō Shobō.

1943   August and December: *Yūhi* (Evening Sun) published in *Nihon Hyōron*.

1943–   May 1943–June 1944: *Koen* (The Old or Former Garden)
1944   serialized in *Bungei*.

1944   April: Awarded Kikuchi Kan Prize for *Yūhi*.

1945   Established Kamakura Bunko, a publishing house, with friends at Kamakura (later moved to Tokyo).

1946   February: *Saikai* (Reencounter) published in *Sekai*.

1947   October: *Zoku Yukiguni* (Continuation of Snow Country) published in *Shōsetsu Shinchō*.

Sorihashi (Arched Bridge) published in *Fūsetsu*.

1948   January–May and August: *Saikonsha* (Remarried Person; also *Saikonsha no Shuki*) published in *Shinchō*.

May: *Shōnen* (A Boy) published in *Ningen*.

June: Elected chairman of Japanese PEN Club.

December: Complete *Yukiguni* published by Sōgensha.

1948–
1954

May 1948–April 1954: *Kawabata Yasunari Zenshū* (Collected Works) published in sixteen volumes by Shinchōsha. Postscripts added to stories in the *Zenshū* provide valuable information on Kawabata's ideas and life.

1949–
1952

Senbazuru (Thousand Cranes) published: *Senbazuru* published in *Jiji Yomimono*, May 1949; *Mori no Yūhi* (Grove in the Evening Sun) published in *Bungei Shunjū*, August 1949; *E-Shino* (Figured Shino) published in *Shōsetsu Kōen*, January 1950; *Haha no Kuchibeni* (Mother's Lipstick) published in *Shōsetsu Kōen*, November and December 1950; *Nijūsei* (Double Star) published in *Bungei Shunjū*, October 1951. Published as a book with parts of *Yama no Oto* by Chikuma Shobō in February 1952. Sequel (not included in translated version): first installment, *Nami Chidori* (Wave Plovers), published in *Shōsetsu Shinchō* in April 1953.

1949–
1954

Yama no Oto (The Sound of the Mountain) published: *Yama no Oto* published in *Kaizō Bungei*, September 1949; *Semi no Hane* (Wings of the Locust) or *Himawari* published in *Gunzō*, October 1949; *Kumo no Hono'o* (A Blaze of Clouds) published in *Shinchō*, October 1949; *Kuri no Mi* (The Chestnut's Fruit) published in *Sekai Shunjū*, December 1949; *Onna no Ie* (The Woman's House) published in *Sekai Shunjū*, January 1950; *Shima no Yume* (Dream of Islands) published in *Kaizō*, April 1950; *Fuyu no Sakura* (Winter Cherry) published in *Shinchō*, May 1950; *Asa no Mizu* (Morning Water) published in *Bungakukai*, October 1951; *Yoru no Koe* (Night Voice) published in *Gunzō*, March 1952; *Haru no Kane* (Spring Bell) published in *Bungei Shunjū*, June 1952; *Tori no Ie* (The Kite's House) published in *Shinchō*, October 1952; *Kizu no Ato* (The Scar) published in *Bungei Shunjū*, December 1952; *Miyako no Sono* (Garden in the Capital; later *Midori no Sono* published in *Shinchō*, January 1953; *Ame no Naka* (In the Rain) published in *Kaizō*, April 1953; *Ka no Yume* (Dream of Mosquitoes; later *Ka no Mure:* Cluster of Mosquitoes) published in *Bungei Shunjū*, April 1953; *Hebi no Tamago* (Snake's Egg) published in *Bungei Shunjū*, October 1953; *Hato no Oto* (Sound of the Dove) or *Aki no Sakana* (Autumn Fish) published in *Ōru Yomimono*, April 1954. Complete *Yama no Oto* published by Chikuma Shobō in April 1954.

1949   December: *Aishū* (Sorrow), a collection of stories and essays, published by Hosokawa-shoten.

1950–   March 1950–April 1951: *Niji Ikutabi* (How Many Times,
1951   The Rainbow) serialized in *Fujin Seikatsu*. Fourteen parts: *Fuyu no Niji; Yume no Ato; Hono'o no Iro; Kyō no Haru; Kuro no Tsubaki; Hana no Kagari; Katsura no Miya; Sei no Hashi; Gin no Chichi; Mimi no Ushiro; Niji no E; Aki no Ha; Kawa no Kishi; Niji no Michi.*

November 1950–March 1951: *Maihime* (Dancing Girl) serialized in *Asahi Shimbun*.

1952–   January-November 1952 and January-May 1953: *Hi mo*
1953   *Tsuki mo* (Days and Months) serialized in *Fujin Kōron* in sixteen parts: *Kōetsue De; Aki no Fukiyose; Atatakanaru Yōni; Tsubaki Motsu Hito; Nami ni Yūhi; Haru no Yume; Musume no Ima; Chichi no Ato; Jigoku no Kabe; Rusu no Kyaku; Kami no Ke; Shinjitsu, Suzu Furi; Haha to Ie; Yūbae no Ato; Onna Dakega; Kitayama Shigure.*

1953   April: *Nami Chidori* (Wave Plovers) published in *Shōsetsu Shinchō* (see 1949–1952 entry).

November: *Suigetsu* (The Moon in the Water; translated as "The Moon on the Water") published in *Bungei Shunjū.*

Shōsetsu no Kenkyū (Studies of the Novel) published by Kaname Shobō.

1954   Awarded Noma Literary Arts Prize for *Yama no Oto.*

Elected to the Japan Academy of Arts. Received award for *Senbazuru.*

Meijin (translated as *The Master of Go*) published, based on Kawabata's reports for newspapers in 1938. Translation uses a shortened version of the 1954 text (published in Kawabata's Collected Works).

January-December: *Mizuumi* (The Lake) published in *Shinchō*. Published as book by Shinchōsha in 1955.

1955   *Tokyo no Hito* (The People of Tokyo) published in four volumes by Shinchōsha.

1956–   *Onna de aru Koto* (To Be a Woman).
1957

1957   German and Swedish translations of *Yukiguni.*

       Who's Who among Japanese Writers (compiled by Aono Suekichi and Kawabata) published by UNESCO/PEN Club.

       Visited Europe as PEN Club delegate and met François Mauriac, T. S. Eliot, and others.

1958   January: *Namiki* (Roadside Trees) published in *Bungei Shunjū.*

       Yumiura-shi (Yumiura City) published in *Shinchō.*

1959–   November 1959–August 1961: *Kawabata Yasunari Zen-*
1961   *shū* (Collected Works) published by Shinchōsha in twelve volumes.

1960–   *Nemureru Bijo* (Sleeping Beauty or Beautiful Women
1961   Sleeping; translated as *House of the Sleeping Beauties*) serialized 1960–1961. Book published by Shinchōsha in 1961.

1961   Awarded Cultural Medal.

1961–   January 1961–October 1963: *Utsukushisa to Kanashimi*
1963   *to* (Beauty and Sadness) serialized in *Fujin Kōron* in segments titled *Joya no Kane, Sōshun, Mangetsu-sai, Tsuyuzora, Ishigumi-Karesansui, Kachū no Renge, Sensuji no Kami, Natsuyase*, and *Kosui.* The chapter headings in the translation do not always carry the associations of the original: *Joya no Kane* (specifically the midnight bell(s) of New Year's Eve *[joya]*, with all their rich associations) is translated simply as "Temple Bells"; *Natsuyase* (specifically a term for "summer loss of weight,") is translated as "Summer Losses." Complete *Utsukushisa to Kanashimi to* published in February 1965 by Chūō Kōronsha.

1961–   8 October 1961–27 January 1962: *Koto* (Ancient City:
1962   Kyoto) published in *Asahi Shimbun.* Book published by Shinchōsha in June 1962. Translated into German as *Kyōto* by Walter Donat, 1968.

1963–   August 1963–January 1964: *Kata-ude* (One Arm) pub-
1965   lished in *Shinchō*. Book published by Shinchōsha in
        October 1965.

1968   *Kawabata Yasunari Senshū* (Selected Works) edited by
        Yoshiyuki Jun'nosuke.

        12 December 1968: Awarded Nobel Prize in literature.

1969   Nobel Prize acceptance speech published by Kōdansha as
        Utsukushii Nihon no Watashi—sono Josetsu (Japan, the
        Beautiful, and Myself).

        Public lectures delivered at University of Hawaii on 1 May
        and 16 May. Later published as *Bi no Sonzai to Hakken*
        (The Existence and Discovery of Beauty), translated by
        V. H. Viglielmo and printed in a bilingual edition (Tokyo:
        Mainichi Newspapers).

        "Undying Beauty" published in *This Is Japan* 17(1970).
        Tokyo: Asahi Shimbun, 1969.

1970   Preface to Okada Kōyo's *Fuji*.

        October: Dance-play at Kabuki-za: *Funa Yūjo* (Boat Pros-
        titute). Originally written for dance master Nishikawa
        Koisaburō and performed in recital; later Iwaya Shinichi
        adapted Kawabata's dance-drama into a play, *Biwa Mo-
        nogatari*, performed first in Osaka (1956) and subsequent-
        ly in small Tokyo theaters before the October 1970 open-
        ing at Kabuki-za.

1972   16 April: Kawabata committed suicide.

        Posthumously awarded First Class Order of the Rising Sun
        (the first Japanese novelist ever so honored).

Unfinished manuscripts discovered after Kawabata's death included *Tanpopo* (Dandelion), a novel about a girl (Ineko) and her illness
after her father's death; another revised manuscript of *Yukiguni*;
and the preface for a collection of essays and novels by Okamoto
Kanoko.

4
Mishima Yukio

*M*ishima Yukio's tragic act of *seppuku* on 25 November 1970 tempts us to begin an examination of his work with an explanation of his death.[1] But that would be a disservice to this consummate actor—as though we were to read his curtain line without first appreciating his careful choice of words and his skillfully directed significant gestures. We should, however, recognize at the outset that Mishima's death was his ultimate statement of tragic theory, the only possible expression of a view of the beauty of life and art that is found in every aspect of his work. Mishima believed that the profoundest depths of the imagination lay in death, and he spoke of "burnishing" the imagination for death in an image significantly linked with his obsessively symbolic sword. Death by the sword was a beautiful death; the act of *seppuku* the ultimate Beauty.

The Body and Its Masks

Mishima Yukio fits no categories, follows no single tradition, writes in dizzying profusion. He is a literary sport of such he-

[1] *Seppuku* is the proper term for which we in the West usually substitute the vulgar equivalent reading *harakiri* (as Mishima himself often did when addressing Western audiences—for example, in the film of "Patriotism," *Rite of Love and Death*). Traditionally, after a warrior committed *seppuku* a loyal follower decapitated him.

roic proportions that no one yet seems to have taken his full
measure. Born in 1925, after both Tanizaki and Kawabata
were established on the literary scene, he managed to share
with them the honor of Nobel Prize nomination (1965). Although he was not successful in the Nobel competition,
Mishima was no stranger to prize-winning, having received
the Emperor's Award as the highest-ranking student when he
graduated from Gakushūin (the Peers' School) in 1944 and
winning the Shinchōsha Prize for Literature in 1954, the
Kishida Prize for Drama in 1955, the Yomiuri Prize in 1957
and 1962, and the Mainichi Prize in 1965.

Mishima earned a law degree from Tokyo University in
1947 and worked very briefly for the Finance Ministry. He
had already published short pieces in the Gakushūin school
magazine and in *Bungei-bunka. Hanazakari no Mori* (Forest
in Full Bloom, 1941) was reprinted three years later as the title piece of his first collection of short works. Kawabata was
much impressed by his writing, and on Kawabata's recommendation Mishima's story *Tabako* (Cigarettes), written in
1944, was published in the literary magazine *Ningen* in
1946.

Mishima later traveled widely in Europe and in North
America, contributed articles to American magazines, wrote
modern Nō plays as well as plays for the Kabuki, the Bunraku puppets, and the modern theater. He produced a total of
about two hundred and fifty separate works, including twenty novels, more than thirty plays, all kinds of travel pieces
and literary criticism, and scripts for a number of films. Mishima adapted one of his short stories, "Patriotism"
(*Yūkoku*, 1960), as a film script, and then produced, directed, and himself played the part of a soldier committing
seppuku. He played other film roles, too, even a part in a
yakuza (gangster) movie. He appeared in musical comedy
and nightclub acts and wrote several songs, including one for
his female-impersonator friend Maruyama Akihiro. At the
end of the performance of this number, Mishima—dressed in
a sailor suit—hugged and kissed his friend. He worked on

translations of works by Yeats and Cocteau, and he lectured classes of young Kabuki actors. Nor was that all. He also formed his own army, the Tate no Kai (Shield Group), mostly university students, in 1968. Five years before his death, he even wrote what he claimed was a new literary form: *Taiyō to Tetsu* (*Sun and Steel*, 1965–1968): "confidential criticism"—his unique exploration of life and art.

Neither his followers in Japan (those to whom he has seemed a postwar hero-spokesman) nor his admirers abroad have been able to find a helpful approach to all his works—as comments by his critics and translators made painfully clear in November 1970. When one considers the range of • Mishima's writing, this is not surprising: modern adaptations of ancient Nō dramas on one hand and science fiction (*Utsukushii Hoshi:* Beautiful Star, 1962) on the other; the idyllic novel *The Sound of Waves* (*Shiosai*, 1954) and a play that focuses on *Madame de Sade* (*Sado Kōshaku Fujin*, 1965); stories and plays based on material that ranges from episodes in Japan's history to the Greek myths of Hercules and Medea; even a play entitled *My Friend Hitler* (*Waga Tomo Hittora*, 1968). Mishima's earliest four-part work was written in the centuries-old language of the traditional Nō (*Chūsei:* The Middle Ages, 1945–1946). His last, completed on the eve of his suicide, presents Mishima's own Aesthetic of Beautiful Death in the context of Time itself: the tetralogy *Hōjō no Umi* (*The Sea of Fertility*, 1965–1970), a mythic rendering of Reincarnation, rich in elements of Hindu and Buddhist philosophy.[2]

---

[2] In addition to the titles known in Western translation, Mishima wrote an extraordinary quantity of material for the popular press, including newspapers and weekly magazines for girls. Writing travel pieces for the *Asahi Shimbun* in 1952 had been a way of earning foreign exchange and traveling abroad during a time when it was almost impossible for the average Japanese citizen to do so. Other "popular" writing is less easy to explain, even on financial grounds, since Mishima's income was already high (his books regularly sold around 100,000 copies before paperback editions and translations). Magazine (serial) publication is of course a fact of the

A neglected clue to Mishima's precise literary posture, however, is to be found in the title of a book for which he wrote the introduction: *Taidō—The Way of the Body* (*Young Samurai*, in the United States), 1967. One would not ordinarily expect to find interpretations of works of literature through a volume devoted to the art of body-building. Nevertheless, in his introduction to this book of photographs, Mishima makes explicit the very attitudes (and even a personal philosophy) that had been implicit in all his works.[3]

It is essential to understand that Mishima regards this *Taidō* body as one ideally Greek of the heroic age. Moreover, his "way of the body" seems—in spite of his attempts to link it with the samurai code, and in spite of the fact that homonyms include *taido* ("demeanor") and *taidō* ("moral law" or "universal principle")—profoundly un-Japanese, although in his other writings Mishima urges a rekindling of traditional Japanese spirit.

Mishima's philosophy of the body offers a new salvation: and it is viewed in terms of "splendor," "melancholy," and "the poetry of the male physique." This physical perfection is

---

Japanese literary scene, and most novels—including works by Tanizaki and Kawabata as well as Mishima—first appeared in this form. But Mishima also produced a number of very lightweight pieces, tales of housewives and office girls that lack the literary values of his better-known works. Such magazine publication does boost the income of many other Japanese authors, apparently: as many as seven out of the ten highest incomes in Japan in recent years have been those of writers. Few examples of this popular writing are available in English. Genji Keita's stories, cited above, give some idea of the humorous tales that take the "salary man" (office worker) for subject matter. There is only one popular anthology that samples the genre: *Ukiyo*, edited by Jay Gluck (New York: Grosset's Universal Library, 1963); Mishima is represented by *Fukushū* (Revenge, 1954).

[3] Mishima's body-building aesthetic and its link with Bushido (the Way of the Warrior) is further developed in his *Sun and Steel*. Mishima designed the cover for *Sun and Steel*, using a photo for which he posed clad in a loincloth and with sword in hand; the stylized background of waves hints of the symbolic waters that flow through Mishima's work—especially his recurrent sea.

in his view linked to Greek wisdom (mentioned again in his last novel), defined as "recognizing the supreme human worth of an equilibrium of spirit and body." Mishima speaks of the time when samurai lore was not a matter of empty forms but was "intimately connected with his conscience and his code of ethics." He concludes that Japan today has lost the external rules of conduct and at the same time an essential "wardrobe." The vanished cloak can, in Mishima's view, be restored by "the powerful, sturdy male body."

This classical male body is the dominant figure in all of Mishima's works, including his final tetralogy: plays, novels, short stories, essays, films. Its personal importance is hinted not only by Mishima's body-building philosophy as expressed in *Taidō* but also in such details as the gigantic statue of Apollo displayed in his Tokyo garden.

The body assumes a hundred masks: the Great Priest of Shiga, the fisher-boy on the fairy-tale island of *The Sound of Waves*, the schoolboy hero of *Confessions of a Mask*, even the Japanese lieutenant of "Patriotism." This is the figure whose reincarnation provides theme and characters for *The Sea of Fertility*, where the beautiful Kiyoaki of *Spring Snow* reappears in *Runaway Horses* as the noble *kendō* swordsman Isao, and even takes feminine form in *The Temple of Dawn* as the lovely little princess Jin Jan (Ying Chan), before the final signs of "weakening" appear in the beautiful but flawed young signal keeper, Tōru, of *The Decay of the Angel (Tennin Gosui:* the five signs [*gosui*] of [physical] weakening observed in dying *tennin*, the celestial beings of Buddhist cosmology).

The varied settings of *The Sea of Fertility*—from Tokyo in the early years of the twentieth century to distant scenes of a gleaming temple in Bangkok, the funeral pyres of far-off Benares, a cave at Ajanta—are typical of Mishima's work too. His settings are exotic and often esoteric: backstage at Kabuki, behind the blinds of the Great Imperial Concubine, on the blood-soaked *tatami* of a heroic act of *seppuku*, on a

South American coffee plantation, at the Khmer court of the Leper King, even aboard a flying saucer. Yet the scenes are just as likely to be commonplace: the tearoom of a Tokyo department store, a San Francisco coffee shop, the beach of a popular resort. And through these scenes move minor characters who may be tricked out in disguises that range from a clubfooted student and an airline steward to a golden-haired foreign homosexual laying five eggs from his remarkable "chicken's cloaca."

None of the disguises of ancient court robes, schoolboy uniforms, and aloha shirts, however, can conceal the classic Greek body that Mishima lauds in *Taidō*. No matter what the context, the ideal male is there in his heroic glory. And even at the moment when her husband is preparing for *seppuku*, Reiko in "Patriotism" perceives that his is "masculine beauty at its most superb." Male breasts are invariably visualized as a pair of (Greek) shields.[4] The fisher-boy untying his loincloth in *The Sound of Waves* stands in the firelight "like a piece of heroic sculpture." Even the geometry instructor in *Confessions of a Mask* appears as a "statue of the nude Hercules."

There is, however, a paradox to be understood at the outset. Behind the masks and within the heroic Greek body, Mishima always remained intensely Japanese. Whatever our reactions to Mishima's ultimate, tragic gesture of *seppuku*, it is essential to remember that he regarded himself as perform-

---

[4] Mishima's private army was called the Shield Group (Tate no Kai). Mishima's enthusiasm for the Greek body can be found in all of his works: sometimes it is specific—as in his odd dramatization of the Hercules myth, *Suzaku-ke no Metsubō* (Downfall of the Suzaku Family, 1967), reset in the 1940s—and sometimes it is more thoroughly disguised by contemporary Japanese costumes and settings in *Shizumeru Taki* (Submerged Waterfall, 1955), where the protagonist Noboru works at a remote dam construction site. The ideal male figure even appears incongruously in an essay on Kawabata's work, where Mishima identifies Kawabata's "failure" to interpret the world, saying that this is the "opposite of the will of the Greek sculptor" (in *Eien no Tabibito*, 1956). The heroic figure also provides a simile for the play of sunlight on Mount Fuji's snows in *The Temple of Dawn*, resembling "the fine play of lean muscle."

ing a noble action designed to stimulate a return to Japan's)
heroic virtues. To read Mishima's death as an example of fa-
natical nationalism is to distort an ethical and aesthetic statement into a political gesture.[5]

Mishima died according to Japanese tradition, his final
words a plea for the revival of Japan's ancient spirit and a)
salute to the Emperor. Yet his literary works are often self-
consciously Greek. Sometimes, too, he fumbles flesh with the
gestures and vocabulary of pre-*Esquire* rather than post-
Playboy man. Yet the difficulties usually stem from Mishima's tendency to do what Japanese writers have been doing
since they first began adopting the trimmings of Western
literature. In his comments on the "Greek" balance of intellect and flesh, for instance, Mishima neglected to mention
Japanese treatises on the oneness of body and mind—a tradition going back to such medieval works as *Shōbō Genzō Zui-
monki*. Thus, like his Meiji predecessors, Mishima declared
he was walking in a Western way. But his Greek body casts a
very Japanese shadow.

Mishima's essay in *Taidō* typifies this. Modestly describing
himself as the "upside-down pillar" (in Japanese housebuild-
ing this deliberate imperfection is designed to discourage evil

[5] It is impossible to understand Mishima's references to the Japanese
spirit and his pleas for action unless one examines several works written
during the last five years of his life. In addition to *Taiyō to Tetsu*, already
cited, these include *Eirei no Koe* (Voices of the Spirits of the War Dead,
1966); *Hagakure Nyūmon* (Guide to *Hagakure* [Fallen or Hidden Leaf],
1967), i.e., a guide to the samurai code written by Yamamoto Jōchō
(1659–1719)—a work that was very popular during the Second World
War but was banned by the occupation authorities; *Kōdōgaku Nyūmon*
(Guide to Actionism, 1969–1970); *Bunka Bōeiron* (Defense of Culture,
1969), in which he urged a revival of traditional Japanese values; *Shōbu no
Kokoro* (Heart of Militarism, 1970), a series of interviews; various brief
essays; and of course the *Geki* (Appeal) made just before he committed *seppuku*. Most of these works have not been translated, although the translated *Geki* and excerpts from some of the other works cited here can be found
in *Japan Interpreter* 7(Winter 1971):71–87. Most critical discussions of
Mishima that refer to these works unfortunately tend to cite only a few
phrases, taken out of context and hence apt to be misleading.

spirits) of the bodies photographed, Mishima is adopting a typically Japanese "humble posture." Yet even as he does so, he flexes his muscles in imitation of heroic Greek statuary. He bemoans the "dehumanization" of modern Japan: he excuses his words with the expression, "I am not drawing water for my own rice-field." This paradox may leave the reader wondering about Mishima's similarly contradictory fictions. Is this upside-down pillar of a man intent on demolishing his cultural house? Or is he sincerely trying to renovate it by means of the classical style of a Western ideal?

The answer is as complex as the man himself, and it can come only after close reading of his work—and then only tentatively. It is clear, for example, that Mishima is ever alert to the conventional phrases and gestures of Japan, mockingly deflating sea gods and arranged marriages alike. His artistry in snatching the mask from the ritual figure cannot be denied. Whether it is the *onnagata* (the man playing women's roles in Kabuki), or a group of housewives acting out a travesty of social face-saving in "The Pearl," or the patriotic lieutenant insisting that his young bride witness his *seppuku*, Mishima manages to juxtapose the unemotional ritual phrases and the terrible realities of the actual deeds. In so doing, he gives voice to the doubts of a generation that found themselves no longer in touch with the ancestral gods, with earlier concepts of patriotism, and with ancient manly arts. Even those martial arts—linked with Japanese ethics for centuries and also associated with such artistic refinements as the philosophy of *cha-no-yu* (tea ceremony)—had in Mishima's time been proscribed by the occupation forces.

The negative vision that emerges from Mishima's fictions, however, often seems to belie his own pleas for the "new ethic" that he claimed to find embodied in the beautiful male form. The paradox approaches dangerously close to artistic betrayal sometimes. And given Mishima's statements in the introduction to *Taidō*, his handling of the beautiful male body in his fictions seems perverse.

In *Taidō*, he asserts that the "powerful, sturdy male body," a body overflowing with strength, can become an external standard substituting for lost values. We shall expect to see the "poetry" of the male physique and to find admirable qualities in the Japanese youths whose bodies conform with the aesthetic standards of ancient Greece (a point also made in *Taidō* by Takeyama Michio). Perhaps Mishima's view of the Greek aesthetic is as uncertain as that in *Forbidden Colors*, where a Shakespearean play is defined as one in which "a human banquet at midnight might become . . . a banquet for ghosts [in the final act]." In his *Watashi no Henreki Jidai* (My Wandering Years, 1963), Mishima admitted: "My view is not necessarily a correct interpretation of ancient Greek thought, but in it I have discovered the Greece I sought." In that Greece, "the Gods mounted guard against a disrupture of the human equilibrium." The world was one in which "ethical standard" was synonymous with "physical beauty."[6]

Given the remarkable consistency of Mishima's view of this profoundly Greek salvation, one would expect something positive to emerge when he offers us a Grecian hero rising godlike from the sea, a bronze Apollo, an ancient Greek sculpture, a figure of gentle beauty with soft, broad chest. This is Yūichi, the "god" of *Forbidden Colors* (*Kinjiki*, 1951)[7]—but the heroic effect is flawed. For the observer is a 65-year-old writer, one whom the reader has already seen in

---

[6] Quoted in the anonymous "Faces of Japan: Yukio Mishima, Novelist," *Asia Scene* 11(March 1966):34. This is the theme repeated so often in Mishima's essays and fictions and made even more explicit in *Sun and Steel*.

[7] The erotic hints of this title are discussed in chapter 1. In view of the complexities of Mishima's vocabulary and his fondness for the obscure, as in *Gogo no Eikō* (translated as *The Sailor Who Fell from Grace with the Sea*), it should be noted that the original meaning of "color" *(iro/shiki)* is "the phenomenal world," and the famous line "all colors are empty" provides a mocking allusion to the theme of this novel—and perhaps another footnote to the empty garden at the close of the novel Mishima completed just before his suicide.

a ridiculous pose, dandling 19-year-old Yasuko on his neuralgic knee. Shunsuke, this specifically ugly old man (we are told that he is so pictured on the cover of his recently collected works), moreover, is one with an acute deficiency in objectivity. His "wild ability to handle abstractions" is coupled with a monumental inability to establish any sort of relationship between his inner world and the outside—perhaps explaining why he views Yūichi as "beautiful nature" and himself as "ugly spirit."

Had the perspective remained that of the author Shunsuke, or even moved consistently between Shunsuke and the god-hero Yūichi, something heroic might have emerged. Unfortunately, the ugly façade of Shunsuke (behind which his readers insist on detecting spiritual beauty) is one destined to lie in ruins, while Yūichi's ideal beauty of form covers a distinctly hollow core. Mishima adds to this chaos and ruin by moving his peeping lens somewhat arbitrarily not only between Yūichi and Shunsuke but also behind the emotional attitudes of the wife Yasuko, the conventions of Yūichi's mother, and the various distortions of half a dozen other characters, among them the ambidextrous Count Kaburagi.

As far as the narrative is concerned, four hundred pages might be reduced to three or four sentences: author Shunsuke, after three unhappy marriages, finds that lovely little Yasuko (his tenth love affair) wants to marry a beautiful boy. The boy turns out to prefer other boys. But Shunsuke decides that this will be his perfect opportunity for an exquisitely artistic creation. Yūichi shall be his work of art, and through him Shunsuke will achieve vengeance against the women who have humiliated him. His plot begins with the marriage of his characters, Yūichi and Yasuko; the outline includes the involvement of Yūichi with the women who have rejected Shunsuke and with the boys for whom Yūichi has until this time merely yearned.

This particular fiction is the first real passion of Shunsuke's life. It turns out, however, that this young god is not quite the simple figure for whom Shunsuke would play aesthetic father. So Shunsuke commits suicide, bequeathing his ten-million-yen fortune to Yūichi to provide his protégé with "a nameless freedom."

To flesh out this skeleton: Shunsuke's three wives had been in turn a thief, a madwoman, and a nymphomaniac. He has kept a diary in French that (in spite of repeated assurances that his interests are quite normal) includes notations about woman "smelling like a pig" (this being cited as the reason for the masculine invention of perfume); her coquetries are described as evidence that she is fundamentally of no use; and she lacks a soul, for she is a "self-made tapeworm" who merely disgraces man's spiritual powers. In spite of Shunsuke's repetitious dialogues on Art, Beauty, and Truth, he merely dabbles in Byron for amusement, self-consciously displays Beardsley prints, marks Pater's passages on the Apollo, and introduces Yūichi to esoteric Buddhist works on the refinements and vocabulary of "The Art of the Catamite." Moreover, unlike Tanizaki's would-be artists, Shunsuke fashions his "work of art" (Yūichi) out of his own ugly motives, and with a design for corruption.

It might be claimed that in *Forbidden Colors* Mishima is attempting to show the debasing of the heroic figure—what happens when Shunsuke forces Yūichi to be "faithless to himself." At least one reviewer fell into this trap and described the novel as depicting the gradual destruction of a young man by the cynical, corrupt life of postwar Tokyo. There are certainly hints of a tragic descent: from the heroic figure emerging godlike from the foam to a clever young man pausing to get a shoeshine while he figures out how to spend his newly acquired fortune. Mishima continually emphasizes the crumbling fabric of Yūichi's morality, detailing the descent from a pinnacle on which he unwittingly exercised the "Greek options" of athletics and mathematics and seemed to be in a state of grace (practicing the conventional gestures of the dutiful son).

In spite of this promising beginning, however, Mishima soon reveals that Yūichi is in reality no such heroic figure. The dutiful son whose marriage appears to be for the benefit of his ailing and impoverished mother has already prostituted himself for Shunsuke's "marriage portion" of five hundred thousand yen. That is his price for playing the avenging son in Shunsuke's scheme, although Shunsuke also sees it as a gift for "the most beautiful youth in the world" and even as a reward to Yūichi for not loving women. Yūichi for his part accepts the money partly to purchase a ticket to his own world of forbidden colors. All too soon, however, Mishima shows that Yūichi will not give Shunsuke fair value for his money. Moreover, the moral ruin of Yūichi is not caused by his world. It lies within his own nature, as Mishima hints in Yūichi's first homosexual encounter—where Yūichi begins contemplating the end of the relationship even before he is out of bed.

Nor are the moments of "enlightenment" to be taken at face value. Later in the narrative, in a riot of sadomasochistic imagery, Father Yūichi watches his wife delivering their daughter (he has succeeded in this particular obligation by various kinds of role-playing). In this moment—so we are told—he "sees." Perhaps it is intended as a glimpse of salvation when Yūichi later turns down a homosexual invitation in favor of a visit to his wife and the new baby daughter. But the evidence is against such a reading. Yūichi later advances to innumerable new forms of betrayal, including the episode with high-school-innocent Minoru (not too innocent, perhaps, since he too has a protector). Judas-Yūichi returns to Minoru's protector the money the boy had stolen in a romantic dream of their elopement—a dream, moreover, that Yūichi himself had encouraged right up to the moment when he smugly handed over the cash.

Shunsuke's discussions of art do nothing for Yūichi's human problems; and for much of the novel, Mishima's art in depicting Yūichi's world does little for the dimensions of characterization. These are puppets, popping in and out of public toilets, prancing through dark parks, preening and posturing in a mockery of the beauty they are all supposed to admire.

Nor does Mishima's art here do much for his own Greek idols and ideals. The few glimpses of "tender," "sweet," and occasionally lyrical moments in *Forbidden Colors* are obscured by clouds of "common truth" (an idea mentioned repeatedly in the novel). This truth provides the information that "a multitude of men who love only men marry and become fathers" (a message followed by the gratuitous footnote that they make "self-sufficient" and "cruel" husbands). It is accompanied by a deliberately sensational exposé of relationships that are commercial, short-lived, and for the most part entirely narcissistic. Passages on the "metaphysics of homosexuality" sound odd in this context. Mishima's samurai-homosexual comparisons break down. He speaks in other contexts of their shared belief that manliness is not an instinctive quality but is to be gained only from moral effort. Yet such comparisons are given the lie in *Forbidden Colors:* Mishima portrays a world in which the only value seems to be the sensation of the moment.

Mishima's citing of Lafcadio Hearn in *Taidō* becomes a gloss on the world of *Forbidden Colors*, where the old writer Shunsuke sits in his study reading classical "poems about beautiful boys" in Straton's *Musa Paidica* (in French translation!). Hearn had described the Japanese as the Greeks of the Orient: to Mishima, the bodies of Japanese youths conform to the aesthetic standards of ancient Greece. Shunsuke, in turn, finds that the second-century Romans such as Straton dreamed of possessed an ideal youthful beauty distinctly "Asian in nature": black hair, "honey-colored" skin, and jet-black eyes.

If the Mishima:Hearn:Shunsuke reading of this ideal is correct, it seems a pity that Mishima offers only a study of the negative aspects of homosexuality in his novel *Forbidden*

Colors. We wonder why even the heroic, godlike figure of Yūichi must be given feet so claylike—at least, clad in those prosaic shoes he insists on having shined at the novel's end. It seems that Mishima wants to show that even the beauties he equates with salvation can only prostitute themselves, as Yūichi is continually acknowledging he does in relationships with wife, lovers, and patrons. The commercial aspects are intrusive: questions of which partner shall pay for the taxi and the "avec" hotel; the relative generosity of patrons—Japanese and foreign alike—in providing wardrobes for beautiful boys; even the reassuring thought that reports of houseboys studying abroad should generally be interpreted as indicating that the boy has a homosexual foreign lover.[8]

It is further remarkable that in a country noted for its relaxed attitudes toward homosexuality, a writer extolling the Greek way and the "poetry" of the male body should insist on the terminology of ugliness instead of beauty. Lady Murasaki's Genji and Saikaku's Yonosuke found nothing incongruous in frolics with boys: the lyric qualities of the one and the humor of the other remain uniform whether the beloved is male or female. In Mishima's work, it is the ugliness that is uniform: Yūichi's impressions of a world of "unclean, putrescent sweetness" in which we see a depressing parade of squirming five-minute kisses, boys "bathing" each other in moist glances or burying their faces in each other's breasts (always *sweatily*), damp handshakes, "sticky" winks, probing tongues, even blood-letting bites.

---

[8] Mishima's use of the *abekku* again shows him at odds with the contemporary scene. Most Japanese accept these hotels (for a lover *avec* [*abekku*] partner) as a natural and useful place for a few hours of privacy in an overcrowded land. Sometimes known also as Romance Hotels, they offer all the comforts not found at home for brief, inexpensive "rest periods" of two or three hours, frankly advertised ("A Course" or "B Course") outside. Furnishings include a refrigerator (well stocked to fuel the fires of passion); and the management serves green tea to arriving patrons. This straightforward approach does not seem to be part of Mishima's world.

To evalute Mishima's tone correctly, the reader can make comparisons with other treatments of homosexuality—not only in such earlier works as Saikaku's *Danshoku Ōkagami* (Great Mirror of Manly Love, 1687), dealing with pederasty among samurai and Kabuki actors (two groups in which homosexuality was most common)—but also among his contemporaries. When the treatment is not humorous, as in the Mad Old Diarist's experiences with an *onnagata*,[9] it is still generally treated no differently from heterosexual love. Or, as in Kawabata's work, homosexual episodes or themes are rendered in traditionally poetic and allusive terms. Kawabata's diary entry of June 1922, for example, describes his first love—a boy in the fifth year of Middle School. Kawabata wrote:

> We go to bed together. I take hold of his warm arms, hold his body, and hug him around the neck. He dreamingly pulls my head toward his face. My cheek is laid on top of his. My dry lips kiss his forehead and eyelids. I feel sorry that my body is cold. He innocently opens his eyes once in a while and embraces my head. I gaze at his closed eyelids. This goes on for about half an hour. I ask for no more. He does not expect more either.[10]

In a postscript added to this entry in the 1948–1954 *Zenshū* (Collected Works), Kawabata wrote that he had never again experienced such love.

Although it is as a poet of heterosexual love that one thinks

---

[9] The diarist first compared the experience with a night spent with a geisha in the usual way, but added that the *onnagata* was in fact a splendidly equipped male, although "he made you forget it." For contrast, there are the hints in Ōe Kenzaburō's "The Catch" (*Shiiku*, 1958) of the boy's barely perceived response to the Negro captive. Or there is Ōe's "Sheep" (*Ningen no Hitsuji*, 1958), in which United States servicemen on a bus force male passengers to bend over and expose their buttocks.

[10] My translation from a passage quoted in Yoshiyuki Jun'nosuke, "Life of Kawabata," in *Kawabata Yasunari Senshū* (Tokyo, 1968).

of Kawabata, there is also a passage in *Sound of the Mountain* that shows the difference in tone between Mishima, the avowed admirer of the male body, and Kawabata, whose sensitivity (according to some critics) focuses on very young and virginal girls. In *Sound of the Mountain*, Kawabata is describing a young male prostitute. The boy's gestures (in touching the foreigner's palm, for instance) are rendered with the delicacy of a Japanese dance movement—delicate, yet still erotic, and suggesting "a satisfied woman."

The specifically coarse features of Kawabata's foreigner, and that foreigner's insensitivity in response to the emaciated boy, are nevertheless far indeed from Mishima's squirming "putrescence." The couple are both an aesthetic and a metaphysical statement. "That such a man should come to a foreign country and appropriate a boy for himself" is not a moral judgment. It is a thought that brings to Shingo the feeling that he is faced by a monster—but a monster, a hairy-armed foreigner, in whom he sees himself. The reader who has followed Kawabata closely will then recall Shingo's earlier meditations on harmony, his memories and his fears, and his hints of death. The symbolic "sound of the mountain" links with various occasions on which Shingo hears sounds of trains, so that Kawabata's clustered images with their rich levels of meaning come to rest momentarily in the foreigner. And the associations are tactfully closed with the scene's final words, describing "a foul ditch beside the tracks . . . an unmoving train."

Similarly, in treating the flesh, Kawabata can convey the deeply erotic with partial images and unfinished phrases—as he does in showing the response of a young boy to the dancing maid of Izu. In *Sound of the Mountain*, Shingo responds to the young breasts of an office girl ("barely big enough to fill one's cupped hands") and is reminded of a print by Harunobu. Such a print (like the scrolls and haiku images and season words in all of Kawabata's work) offers ever-widening ripples of association that can convey more feeling, whether of flesh or of spirit, than a dozen of Mishima's encounters with "the icy play of sensuality."

As a method for cataloguing grotesques, Mishima's technique in *Forbidden Colors* is effective, although monotonous in its infinite variety. Foreigners in eggshell suits and bright bow ties; foreigners—fat, balding, "foolishly" Boston-accented, hailing from the City of Brotherly Love; counter-intelligence agents and transvestites; Germans, French, Lebanese. Or Japanese office workers—clay-faced, lipsticked, clothed in strange garments; the count who has been intimate with a thousand boys; Jackie, the Japanese whose naked and holly-bedecked portrait presides over a travesty of Christmas celebrations. All revolve around the god who has emerged from the sea.

But such a god: glimpsed in his final ten-million-yen freedom, pausing for a shoeshine. *Forbidden Colors* may be intended, as the narrative implies, to show what happens to those who have "larcenously and violently torn beauty from the arms of ethics" (and this of course is the idea restated in *Taidō* and *Sun and Steel*). Yet there is no evidence that beauty and ethics could ever be linked in the world of this novel. It seems more a betrayal of his own ethic when Mishima unmasks his Grecian hero. For this mask is no more to be trusted than the false, smiling faces of the apologetic ladies in "The Pearl." All men are beasts. The only consolation seems to be that women are beastlier.

Thus the glorious god-hero who emerges from Mishima's richly symbolic sea is revealed as no more than the blighted youth of ancient times (to use Shunsuke's phrase). For contrast, we can turn to another youth of mythic beauty in Mishima's fictions: the young fisher-boy of *The Sound of Waves* (*Shiosai*, 1954). In this novel, Mishima offers the idyll of a boy and a girl and the sea, with a fairy-tale series of trials for the fisher-boy and his "princess."

Shinji, son of a poor-but-honest widow, experiences the hardships of a fisherman's life. Into his island world comes the beautiful fairy-tale princess Hatsue (actually, the newly returned daughter of the owner of two coasting freighters), who is later locked up in her fairy-tale tower (that is, the upstairs bedroom of her father's house). There is, of course, a wicked-prince figure: the crafty Yasuo, son of a leading family, and red-faced in the manner of a Kabuki villain. There is even an ugly sister—a part given to the lighthouse keeper's jealous daughter.

Setting is deliberately evocative of the legendary past. Not only are there pines and butterflies, seasonal kimono, and scenes that occasionally suggest the delightful *michiyuki* of Kabuki.[11] There are also wartime memories of soldiers who blamed lost supplies on a phantom badger; and schoolboys tell of "seven pure-white sharks" miraculously appearing in the island's three-tiered cave at the full of the moon. The sea and sky, the scents and sounds of the enchanted island, are beautifully evoked in language reminiscent of the harmony of old Japan: bonito boats decked with red banners are bound for Ise; shrines shelter the protective gods; a legendary prince's burial mound lies beneath mysteriously shadowing seven pines; men confront the mythic sea. This is, moreover, a world of traditional duties and obligations, where even the drawing of water has its appointed hour.

The quality of innocence is nicely rendered: in boyish games, in childish secrets (notes exchanged by Hatsue and Shinji through a hiding place beneath the lid of a water jar), even in the first direct glance of childlike curiosity that Shinji gives the lovely Hatsue. Nor is the island's innocence confined to the terms of a lyric past. In modern terms, too, it is

----

[11] *Michiyuki* are journeys, usually by lovers. In the poetic descriptions of the places on their route (each scene with its own clusters of literary and poetic associations—a lake, or beach, or mountain linked with an episode or a character in earlier poem, story, or legend), the audience may perceive a reflection of the emotions of the traveling couple. Tanizaki used the technique in creating the delicate atmosphere of his short story *Ashikari* (the opening passage of the narrator's journey).

unspoiled—lacking, for instance, the ubiquitous Japanese *pachinko* (a kind of pinball) parlor and the movies that show urban boys "the ways of love."

Opportunities that in *Forbidden Colors* would have led to a sticky tangle of flesh preserve a delicate innocence in *Sound of Waves*. Drying herself, naked before a fire, Hatsue finds Shinji waking and observing her. Momentary embarrassment will be forgotten if only he too will be naked before the fire. Mishima shows the boy casting off his loincloth and standing before her like the statue of yet another Greek hero. In spite of the judgment of the (ugly) world: "Nothing happened." Yet knowledge has come to this Hellenic paradise.

The hero must go out in a Herculean test of strength: in part a moral struggle in which his sincerity is to be measured against the laziness of the villainous Yasuo. The challenge is met with appropriately heroic physical endurance: swimming through the mountainous seas, Shinji makes the lines fast, thus saving his typhoon-buffeted ship. He is rewarded with his princess, Hatsue, whose father had put the two boys aboard his vessel for the classic test. Like a true fairy-tale princess, Hatsue too has performed an impossible task—diving for a record number of abalone, followed by a victory gesture in which she lays her trophy (a handbag!) at the feet of Shinji's mother.

Once again, though, Mishima seems reluctant to grant full points to the heroic tradition he so admires. In *Thirst for Love*, life on an island is identified as "life in an ideal form," and Mishima has asserted that *Sound of Waves* was a deliberate evocation of Hellenic beauty. Although it is not purely Hellenic, Mishima's island does blend elements of universal fairy tale, of the Greek hero-against-the-sea, and of a Japanese past of gods, the valiant legendary Peach Boy, and a medieval prince. Yet after setting up the idea of Hatsue and Shinji existing within a finely delineated moral code ("never once having doubted the providence of the gods"), Mishima quietly leads the reader to the last words. Even as Shinji gives thanks to the god of the sea for a safe return, and even as he stands with his beautiful princess beside him, he reflects on the night of his heroic trial: it had been *his own strength* that tided him through. Presumably this is intended as justification for the self-sufficiency and nobility of Man Alone. We are to see that Shinji has mastered the unknown, symbolized by a white freighter. Mishima, however, also seems bent on sardonic demolition of many of the values that at first appear positive in the context of *Sound of Waves*.

The white freighter is presented early in the narrative as it sails off into the unknown world-beyond-the-island. It is part of the two contrasting views from the island, views symbolizing the worlds of past and present. On one side, there is the view from the shrine: the safe past, a place for prayers and talismans, from which one can glimpse the enfolding shores "cradling with their arms the unchanging Gulf of Ise." The other view offers the restless modern world: steep cliff, powerful whirlpools, the scientific precision of an unmanned beacon, and the sweeping illumination of the lighthouse. The idyllic island is further linked with the reality of the outside world by a ferryboat—the boat that brings in the "ugly sister" daughter of the lighthouse keeper and takes Shinji's brother off into a brief excursion to the modern world.

The idyllic world is not entirely cut off from the disruptive present, although those who go away generally forget the streetcars and the factories and the movies once they return to their island. Nor is the idyllic without flaw: those festive bonito boats are crowded with men gambling and drinking. *The Tale of Genji* is updated: the boy betrays his presence to Hatsue not with a poem but with a whistle. A boyish game in the mythic cave is marred by the whispered word *omeko* (in *Kansai-ben*, "fuck") that offers a coarse comment on the "innocent" beauty of Hatsue and Shinji's relationship. The idyllic implications of Hatsue going to fetch water at the wellspring are flawed, too: the orderly roster merely provides a handy timetable for the villainous Yasuo's attempt at rape.

All this might be cited as evidence that the forms and phrases of tradition are as nothing without the moral and physical vigor on which Mishima insists. Yet there are subtle undercuttings even of the heroic image of young Shinji. Such undercutting is already hinted in the opening scene: we have a picture of peach blossom and a boy carrying a fish—suggesting the legendary Peach Boy Momotarō perhaps. But we are not permitted to preserve this illusion for more than a moment: the figure is revealed as an ordinary boy carrying a halibut to the lighthouse keeper. There would seem to be no myths and no gods in this world: only the self-reliant and ultimately commonplace boy.

By contrast, the boy of *Confessions of a Mask* (*Kamen no Kokuhaku*, 1949) is far from ordinary—and far from the mythic grace of young Shinji. Mishima's narrator introduces himself as pallid, an "unchildlike" child whose fantasies begin with what he believes to be a memory of his birth: an utterly impossible recollection of tongue-tips of water lapping the basin in which he took his first bath and of golden reflections from its rim. He is snatched away by his grandmother, raised in strange isolation from his immediate family (although in the same house), in an atmosphere "perpetually closed and stifling with the odors of sickness and old age."

At one level this is, as some observers have noted, a case history of inversion. As such, it might not be much more interesting than the tags and names dropped by the narrator—Stefan Zweig, Hirschfeld, Whitman, Proust, Michelangelo, Count von Platen. More than a simple case, though, *Confessions* reveals a strange world of fantasy, symbolism, and sadomasochism behind the mask worn in the "reluctant masquerade" of social conformity. Words, gestures, and even "an adolescent's thoughts" are practiced with a group of cousins, for instance. Meanwhile, the parents' wish to keep their son from "learning bad things" (as when they hid photos of female nudes) is ironically frustrated by the boy's discovery of that ubiquitous Ideal Male.

The associations that later relate to what the narrator terms his bad habit are rendered for the most part with great sensitivity, no mean task when one considers the details. *Confessions of a Mask* begins with an early memory of an odorous night-soil carrier in tight trousers—a figure descending a slope and eventually linked with the sweaty odor of passing soldiers and the heroic knight who turns out to be a woman, Joan of Arc (this last being the narrator's first experience of "revenge by reality"). Other preludes lead to his first climax (inspired by the picture of St. Sebastian): a brief period of dressing up as a woman, first as Tenkatsu, the female magician, and then as Cleopatra. Additional memories cluster around the princes of fairy tales—especially those "murdered or fated for death."

Death:night:blood—the cluster of images appearing in all of Mishima's fiction in an odor of male sweat and accompanied by a ripple of muscles—is established before the narrator even enters school. His encounter with the hidden book reproducing "Greek" statuary gives his vague feelings their lifelong focus: the figure of St. Sebastian (Guido Reni's painting, not a Greek statue)—a beautiful male body, but one tortured, its sides pierced with arrows, blood running down the white flesh.[12]

At fourteen, the Mask (never really revealing his name, even on the two or three occasions when he is addressed by the diminutive Kō-chan) adds to these stimulating but untouchable figures a real boy, Ōmi. Physically and socially mature, Ōmi's attractions range from black footprints in the snow to hairy armpits and a "savage melancholy . . . not

---

[12] Mishima demonstrated the personal significance of the St. Sebastian image not only in other references scattered throughout his work but also in the melodramatic pose he assumed for a photograph widely reprinted in the popular press after his death and earlier displayed in a Tokyo department store's special exhibit. In this picture Mishima assumes the St. Sebastian pose: complete with loincloth, arms tied above his head, arrows piercing his sides and armpit, "blood" running from the wounds.

tainted in any way with intellect." The narrator at this point knows love only as "a dialogue of little riddles." Yet he recognizes his feeling for Ōmi as "connected with the desires of the flesh." It is also "the pattern of that forgotten perfection which the rest of us have lost in some far distant past"—a phrase suggesting the heroic Greek past of Mishima's own ideal. Later, when he is alone on a beach, the sense of solitude, the feeling for Ōmi, and the image of St. Sebastian merge in another sexual experience, one that is "washed away by the sea."

This is not a proper moment of symbolic purgation, however, in spite of the lyrical qualities that Mishima frequently gives to his seascapes. For the narrator goes on to memories —whether real or imagined is deliberately questioned—and to fantasies that include a "murder theater" with arrows, daggers, and spears. He also experiences love for younger boys as well as for youths. He adds love for "the graceful and the gentle" to his earlier preferences for the savage. Nevertheless, he also enjoys his "murder theater" fantasy: a particularly muscular fellow student is served up on a foreign-style platter, surrounded with salad greens, while the narrator's knife raises a fountain of blood as he begins to carve the breast into delicate thin slices.

If this is intended as humor, it is dark indeed. It is far, too, from the delicately allusive sexuality of Kawabata's poetic images and from the fondness for plump flesh (especially toes) in Tanizaki. Yet, unlike *Forbidden Colors*, *Confessions* avoids physical contact. More often, the narrator watches his young sailors, toughs, and fishermen from afar, not even speaking to them. There are only tentative moments—as in episodes relating to Ōmi's two pairs of gloves—dark, snow-wet leather, and "fingers fitting closely inside the white gloves."

In contrast to the dream quality of his homosexual life, the Mask's attempts to practice heterosexual social gesture are direct—and disastrous. There is a clashing of teeth in a (literally) feverish encounter with a distant relation. Visiting a prostitute results in failure: they achieve only one moment of contact, during which her tongue protrudes "like a stick." A semblance of conventional heterosexual contact—with the seventeen-year-old piano-playing sister of one of his friends— is accompanied by whispers, bicycle rides, and intertwined arms: but this is a self-conscious role playing that brings neither applause nor satisfaction.

The memories of the girl Sonoko, though, offer strange counterpoint to the Mask's homosexual theme. Although she is introduced first as the *sound* of piano music, she is most significantly seen when she descends a staircase, deliberately contrasting with that earlier encounter with the night-soil collector descending the slope. Also, in contrast to the earlier odor and the stirrings of the flesh, this descent offers (through the boy's relationship with Sonoko) a feeling that he is "purified." But whatever happiness he feels is inseparable from sensations of remorse and of grief. The relationship is clearly ephemeral—a specifically "platonic" concept that is masked by the tentative words, gestures, and even dreams of a "normal" boy. (At one point, the narrator decides that he can love a girl without feeling any desire; he enjoys strangely asexual dreams of "the lovely bride I had not yet seen.") He even feels —or perhaps only enacts—"ecstasy" at receiving his first "love letter" (although the ecstasy is quickly deflated by the contents: a pack of "mission school" postcards and a neatly businesslike note). Sonoko for her part appears often in red, and at one point she plucks the boy's sleeve in what seems to be a parody of the customary erotic gesture.

The relationship may seem no more than a fantasy and a masquerade. The narrator continues to eye sailors and soldiers and to dream of the lithe bodies of simple young men— inevitably associated with fountains of blood and the familiar complex of arrows, spears, and daggers. Sonoko appears also as the incarnation of the narrator's love for "everlasting" things. Yet in spite of later meetings (tentative, unfulfilled, with hints of a partially opened door, after she has married someone else) the narrator must inevitably return to his own world of boys and blood. Half an hour before they are due to separate, he takes Sonoko to a suffocating dance hall. Already he feels the distance between them as permanent. Then his eye falls on the customary muscled and sweating tough. Boy and girl part as *Confessions* ends. The narrator glances at the empty table where the youth had been sitting: spilled liquid throws back glittering, threatening reflections.

It is in this final symbolic moment that the full significance of *Confessions of a Mask* becomes apparent. Questions as to whether this novel is autobiographical are really irrelevant.[13] The Mask is, after all, never completely lifted; the

[13] Henry Scott-Stokes even states: "My study of Mishima's early life relies heavily on a single source, his autobiographical masterpiece" (in *The Life and Death of Yukio Mishima* [New York: Farrar, Straus and Giroux, 1974], p. 56). From some of the details in their essays and interviews, including their conversations with biographer John Nathan, it has also seemed as though the Hiraoka family when pressed for the facts of his childhood found it convenient to retreat behind Mishima's fictional Mask. Nevertheless, Mishima repeatedly denied its autobiographical aspects during his lifetime. Of course, he does seem to have taken perverse pleasure in sharing many details of his own childhood, education, and interests with the Boy in the Mask (even the name Kō-chan can be a diminutive of Kōi, the "Chinese" reading of the name Kimitake—Hiraoka Kimitake being his own name before he adopted the pseudonym Mishima Yukio). But I do not believe that exercises in reading *Confessions* as autobiography really shed light on either the life or the artistry of Mishima. Nor do we need to ask whether such details as the relationship between Kiyoaki and Satoko in *Spring Snow* really came from Mishima's life (a link forged from the shaky evidence that he had a *miai* [preliminary meeting for a projected arranged marriage] with the girl who—according to some accounts—later married the Crown Prince). A psychoanalyst or a gossip columnist may enjoy such tidbits, but the general reader and the scholar alike will find more valuable insights through the imagery of *Confessions*, with its early hints (made explicit in *Sun and Steel*) of the association of sea and sweat, butchered bodies and romantic Ideal, *seppuku* as an act both heroic and erotic, tattooed chests and obsessive tufts of underarm hair. Mishima has made clear

voice issuing from it remains disembodied and almost nameless. But the novel is a sensitive and highly personal account of interwoven fantasy and fact. The fictional character himself even seems more real in the world of his dreams than in the world of his family. Family members, for instance, are for the most part only dimly perceived, except at moments when they impinge on the narrator's sexual fantasies: the mother pops her head up from among plants in the garden to discuss a letter from Sonoko's brother (in which he asks the narrator's intentions); the "minx" of a sister teases him about Sonoko ("When will you marry?"), but the death of this minx is disposed of in a one-line reference.

Whatever its links with Mishima's own life, the symbolism in *Confessions of a Mask* is specific and provides valuable footnotes to all of Mishima's work. Like *Forbidden Colors* and *Sound of Waves*, it also serves as commentary on his "Greek Way." These three novels are of course only a tiny fraction of his monumental output. Nevertheless, they reveal all the obsessive symbols and recurrent themes of Mishima's literary universe, as well as his rich vocabulary and virtuoso technique. In all three we can also observe his use of sardonic comment. Unfortunately the tone—as in *Forbidden Colors*—tends to demolish the heroic statuary and reduce Mishima's poetry of the male body to the prosaic.

---

in many of his (untranslated) essays and conversations that characters should speak with the voice—or at least with what he referred to as the "knowledge"—of their creator. But he spoke disparagingly of the rawly autobiographical I-novel form. And a number of his essays emphasize the way in which his work grew from the tension—the fundamental difference —between life and letters. Apart from the material in *Sun and Steel* and various interpretations and misinterpretations by Western scholars, Mishima's theories of fiction remain untranslated. The essays referred to include interviews and book reviews in *Mishima Yukio Senshū* (Selected Works, 1957–1959), *Hyōron Zenshū* (Collected Essays, 1966), and *Shōsetsu towa Nanika* ("What Is the Novel?"—the discussion being serialized at the time of his death and reprinted in the special Mishima issue of *Shinchō* in 1971).

The Actor Speaks: Lessons in Voice and Gesture

In spite of the difficulties of Mishima's often gaudy vocabulary and a style that he himself described in *Sun and Steel* as "on the verge of noncommunication," one cannot blame the problems of tone on awkward translation.[14] Many of the difficulties of tone result from Mishima's theories of fiction—for even if Mishima's characters are not (autobiographical) extensions of his own personality, he insisted that they should speak not out of their own "ignorance" but with the author's "knowledge." As a result, characters frequently deliver quasi-philosophical commentary, and the narrator—or Mishima—continually interrupts the narrative with extended interpretations.

The actors wearing Mishima's masks, for instance, have a very nasty habit of offering asides in oddly aphoristic terms. "Everyone has his own way of looking at things," in *Dōjōji*. "Funeral offerings are always larger when the head of the family, who can still provide, is a survivor than when it is his funeral," in "Death in Midsummer." Mishima's one-liners sprinkle his narrative until the reader wishes he would remember Lady Shōnagon's commentary in the *Pillow Book:*

[14] Mishima's style and his often exotic vocabulary obviously cannot be given precise English equivalents. Few of Mishima's writings on the theory or craft of fiction are accessible to readers lacking proficiency in Japanese, although Miyoshi's comments in *Accomplices of Silence* and Nathan's in *Mishima: A Biography* can be helpful. Alas, the reader without a knowledge of Japanese cannot appreciate Mishima's early examples of supposed *Rōman-ha* (Japanese romantics) influence or evaluate a later style that Mishima himself compared with that of Ōgai. (Mishima claimed, for instance, that in *The Temple of the Golden Pavilion* he was combining the styles of Mori Ōgai and Thomas Mann!) Similarly, the reader requires a very discriminating knowledge of Japanese, and of French, to trace the resemblances to Mauriac that Mishima identified as being in his *Thirst for Love*. There are, moreover, problems of untranslatable vocabulary—ranging from obscure *kanji* and intensely Japanese connotations to colors selected from a mixed and gaudy palette of Wilde and Akutagawa.

"If one tries to describe what one feels in words it becomes commonplace."

The commonplace itself, though, is an aspect of Mishima's technique of aphorism. "Death in Midsummer" (*Manatsu no Shi*, 1952) is an excellent example. Mishima describes the comfortable living standards of a family whose two children have just drowned (their aunt then collapsing from a heart attack) and adds: "There was no pressing need to cut the family down by three." Throughout the story the horror of events is intensified by the businesslike attitude of the bereaved father, expressed in neat little tags: "Incidents require money." His emotions are rendered as being "like dismissal from a job"; and actions such as traveling to the scene of the tragedy are compared with a detective on his way to the scene of a crime.

Similarly, the frugal calculations of the "affectionate" couple in the story translated as "Three Million Yen" (*Hyakuman-en Sembei*, 1960)—budgeting for electric appliances, discussing the price of cucumber, and considering the cost of powdered milk for a baby they plan to have ten years hence, as well as the wife's embarrassment in the tunnel-of-love atmosphere of a ride "Twenty Thousand Leagues under the Sea"—all take on horrifying implications when their profession as "exhibitionists" is revealed.

Granted there is humorous intent. Mishima does offer amusing moments in his pages, as when "bad boy" Yasuo in *Sound of Waves* tries to seduce the maiden-at-the-well and ends up getting stung by hornets in all the appropriate places. More often, though, the humor is of the variety found in some of the grotesque predicaments of the homosexuals in *Forbidden Colors*, reaching a climax when the count's wife (who had been hoping to peep in and glimpse dreamed-of-as-lover Yūichi talking business with her husband) discovers instead her would-be lover and her not-so-loving husband in flagrante delicto.

Mishima also has an annoying trick of playing the intrusive author in a self-defeating style that suggests "camp" before that term became fashionable. Thus in *Forbidden Colors* the author pops in to announce that "italics were often a sign that [Shunsuke] was speaking ironically," somewhat spoiling the effect of interior monologue. Similarly, in *Sound of Waves*, the boy's youthfully eloquent thoughts of Hatsue are shattered by the author, who cleverly points out that these are not really the boy's words (he would not be so articulate). In *After the Banquet* (*Utage no Ato*, 1960), Mishima is not content to let the reader observe Kazu's relationships but insists on pausing to discuss her "complicated psychology."

In "The Priest [of Shiga Temple] and His Love" (*Shigadera Shōnin no Koi*, 1954), Mishima even offers a sort of running commentary to make things "clear to the reader" as he explains the Imperial Concubine's motives. The intention is again mocking, but one cannot help wishing that Mishima would occasionally trust the reader as Tanizaki does, or as Kawabata does in offering meaning through symbol and allusion. One longs for Kawabata's felt experiences and apprehended reality—especially in *Forbidden Colors*, where the demands of characterization or meaning would still seem a poor excuse for some of Mishima's expository passages. "Shunsuke" (Mishima's voice?) offers tiresome essays on aspects of homosexuality, packed with quotations and with a not-always-accurate name-dropping that ranges through the literature of Winckelmann, Pater, Wilde, Gide, and the Ancients themselves to the "Alexandrian purifications" of Eastern theology and the esoteric aspects of Buddhist writings on "The Art of the Catamite."

This urge to force a point is evident in symbolism, too. In *After the Banquet*, a scrap of cloud—its shape suggesting a gravestone and therefore already sufficiently allusive to Kazu's usual excitement in response to the Noguchi death-benefits (discussed below)—is footnoted by a passage in which the clouds turn the color of ashes. Kawabata would be content to describe a "smoke-wisp of cloud"—alluding to phrases for death in Japanese literature (the smoke itself, even in contemporary fiction, usually being a sufficient hint of the Japanese custom of cremation). Mishima in *After the Banquet* also offers a running commentary (at least partially ironic in intention) on Kazu's flower arrangement of water lilies. He tells the reader that the water symbolizes people going to vote, the blossoming water lilies are Noguchi, and the water's only function is "to crave the favor of the lily blossoms and reflect them."

Elsewhere, Mishima gives long quasi-philosophical passages to somewhat unlikely characters, as in *The Sailor Who Fell from Grace with the Sea* (*Gogo no Eikō*, 1963), where the thirteen-year-old gang leader discourses precociously on "the chaos of existence," using terminology that includes references to the "Roman mixed bath" of a "meaningless" society. Sounding more like a casebook than a well-characterized adolescent, this boy goes on to an analysis of fathers, his conclusion nicely rendered by the translator as: "Filthy lecherous flies broadcasting to the whole world that they have screwed our mothers." Such passages may be intended to provide horrifying contrast with the more familiar adolescent activities, such as Noboru making red-inked charges against Tsukazaki Ryūji or the assertion by their "chief" that his gang members are all geniuses. But the technique is again apt to be self-defeating.

Once again Mishima ties on a little tag at the end. The sailor has now fallen from grace—descended from sea-going dream-hero to the "filthy" role of father. We are privileged to share the boys' plans for poisoning and dismemberment of the grace-less sailor Ryūji. We are led gently through Ryūji's dreams of the lost sea and permitted to share his marginal perceptions of rubber gloves, trembling hands, and other evidence of the forthcoming horror. Then, "still immersed in his dream, he drank down the tepid tea." That ought to be sufficient. But we must also be told: "It tasted bitter." And in case we miss the significance of that, Mishima pins on his antimoral: "Glory, as anyone knows, is bitter stuff."

The "aside" and the "explanation" that often seem to defeat Mishima's ironic intention are only two of his many anti-heroic devices. He also juxtaposes prosaic and sensational, as he does in "Patriotism," where the meticulous care with which the young couple bolt their door, the husband shaves, and the wife wraps little mementos for their friends all contribute to the horror of their suicidal intention. One is reminded of the line in *Confessions of a Mask:* "In spite of the identical nature of the physical action, there was a profound difference so far as mental objects."

In the same way, the businesslike details already noted in "Death in Midsummer" intensify the appalling and senseless tragedy. The familiar *haramaki* (bellyband) and soiled shirt of the innkeeper are further clever touches in Mishima's examination of tragedy. But much of Mishima's tragedy—and his comedy—can be understood only in the context of his intensely personal sensationalism.[15]

The sensationalism requires annotation because the values that Mishima attaches to his sensational elements are often at odds both with his own explicit attitudes and with the values commonly found in Japanese life and literature. Attitudes are notoriously hard to pin down, but the reader unaware of the "expected" responses of Japanese life will miss many of the subtle implications of Mishima's gestures and will fail to appreciate his particular tone.

Yūichi's mother in *Forbidden Colors* might be taken as offering a conventional Japanese response. At Rudon's homosexual bar she is shocked not by the (sensational) relationships of boys but by behavior that is an awful example of bad manners or poor upbringing. Nice people simply do not kiss and pet one another in public places: the sex of the couples is quite irrelevant. This is different from the frequent Western

[15] Perhaps there is a clue in the interview with Ishikawa Jun, published posthumously (*Chūō-Kōron,* December 1970), in which Mishima described himself as a tragedian doing his best to make people cry—only to have them burst into laughter.

response (at least until very recently): indulgent smiles for "young lovers" turn to snarls or sniggers if the young lovers happen to be of the same sex (especially two men).

The traditional attitude of Yūichi's mother is close to that alluded to in Tamari Hitoshi's essay, "Bodybuilding in Japan," in *Taidō*. Tamari speaks of the "discourtesy" of exposing one's body in a place that is *inappropriate*. The gloss relating this attitude to the "prudery" *(sic)* of Confucianism, and Mishima's words about Puritans and Victorians in his introduction, strike knowledgeable readers as deliberately perverse.

Mishima asserts there that the Japanese are "the original Victorians . . . [who] put drawers on nude statues" from motives related not to the teaching of Western missionaries but to their own prudery. This is a distortion both of Japanese and of Western attitudes. The Japanese objection was not to the body, that "sinful" instrument of our own Puritan Ethic, but to the bad manners—to conduct (undressing) appropriate not to the public square but to the public bath. Even today, the average Japanese man at a Ginza girlie show is not responding to the naked breasts and bottoms that he could just as easily study in the remaining coeducational public baths (where he would tend to look but not see): he is still Meiji Man experiencing simultaneously the odd wickedness of the foreigner and a marvelous lapse in his own sense of decorum. The reader doubting this point could find an enlightening contrast in the sleazy atmosphere of Western porno shows (or earlier burlesque) and the noisy good humor of the Japanese male at live "exhibitions" and the kind of movies described in Nozaka's *The Pornographers*.

Tanizaki's sensitive rendering of the flesh should provide useful comparisons in evaluating Mishima's oddly self-conscious fascination with the flesh itself, especially as in *Confessions of a Mask*, "flesh not tainted . . . with intellect" (an idea repeated in his *Sun and Steel*). For Mishima's fictional world is ripe with the smells of zoos, bodies, toilets, and even (in "Thermos Bottles") "a peculiarly American odor, half the hygienic smell of medicines, half the sweet clinging odor of bodies." At some point in every narrative, at least one of Mishima's characters is beaded, or pearled, or just plain dripping with sweat—indiscriminately the result of passion, fear, or exercise.

In proletarian literature, sweat was at least functional, an essential aspect of the sufferings of the workers. In the works of "sensationalist" Akutagawa, sweat, smells, and blood have a metaphysical implication and are rendered with the stylized gestures of a Kabuki performance and in the glittering tones favored by the writers who called themselves aesthetes. But in Mishima—at least until his final tetralogy—the fascination seems to be with the sweat itself, and meaning is to be found in the night-soil-and-soldiers-and-beloved-Ōmi association of *Confessions of a Mask*. Always with sexual implication, sweat nevertheless is as likely to be occasioned by the uphill puffing of a middle-aged lover as by the walk through a cemetery of young, bereaved parents. The cause may be the heroic effort of impending *seppuku*, where the smell of armpits is equated with the "essence of young death." It is not until *The Sea of Fertility* that sweat is finally revealed as the esoteric sign of decay—copious perspiration being one of the five signs of the physical weakening of *tennin* (heavenly beings). Thus in *The Decay of the Angel* (*Tennin Gosui*, 1970), the sexual connotations of Ōmi's sweating armpits in *Confessions of a Mask* take on metaphysical significance.

In earlier works, however, the sweating of Mishima's characters is no more than the aftereffect of psychological or physical exertion—perhaps only a game of tennis. This may be linked with Mishima's attitudes toward the body as expressed in *Taidō*. Certainly his characters, whether male or female, are apt to be shown in loving contemplation of their own flesh. While this may be appropriate in *Forbidden Colors*, where Yūichi's narcissistic aspect is stressed, it scarcely seems fitting in other contexts, and is certainly at odds with customary Japanese attitudes toward the body. In "Death in

Midsummer," Yasue looks at her shoulders and breasts, pinches her own flesh, enjoys the warmth of flesh and sun—and in this brief moment finds that her nephew and niece have disappeared beneath the apparently gentle waves.

Elsewhere breasts appear in images of jellyfish and fangs. They jiggle, bounce, cavort "like young animals," "roll in waves" beneath a lemon-colored sweater, "dance about," squirt milk into ceremonial tea bowls, and offer honey-colored or dark flesh in images that might suggest a parody-ing of Western attitudes but in context do not. The average Western reader, raised on maidenform dreams, served by topless waitresses, and contemplating playmates and bun-nies, may not find anything strange in the jolly rivalries in breast development of the diving girls in *Sound of Waves* or in young Tōru's selection of maids with the largest breasts in *The Decay of the Angel*. But as already noted, the breast is not considered one of those traditional nine points of beauty in Japan. Japan's ingenious plastic inflations and the sponge falsies worn in *Forbidden Colors* are generally found more among foreigner-pleasing bar hostesses and entertainers than on housewives and office girls. Yet flesh seems so attractive to the actors in Mishima's dramas that even a fly is moved to "caress" a girl's breast (in *The Temple of the Golden Pavilion*). In *After the Banquet* a maid finds Kazu's skin so lovely that "even a woman [would] want to pounce on you." And the ultimate example is the perverse banquet of *Confessions of a Mask*, where a boy's breast is indeed "good enough to eat."

Not that flesh is always handled sensationally. In *The Temple of the Golden Pavilion*, for instance, Mishima is tact-ful in his handling of the mosquito net incident.[16] The boy,

---

[16] Understanding this incident naturally presumes knowledge of Japa-nese sleeping customs. In Japan, a number of people may quite properly occupy the same room, each with his or her individual *futon* quilts and sometimes under a communal mosquito net. Such an arrangement is not limited to groups of students or family members: it may simply be the eco-nomical traveling plan of a group of office workers.

one of four people under this net, speaks only of "the thing I now saw," rendering it in terms of a billowing net, a rumpled expanse of sheet, partly perceived sounds, and the hand of his father blotting out the actions of his mother. That tactful hand, though, is later referred to as "fetters" from which the boy had to be freed.

In *The Sailor Who Fell from Grace with the Sea*, a youth's first encounter with a woman (a Hong Kong whore) is handled well. Her lower body, "like a hibernating animal," moves;[17] he senses the stars tilting as they "slanted into the south, swung to the north, wheeled, whirled into the east, and seemed finally to be impaled on the tip of the mast. By the time he realized this was a woman, it was done." Emotions too are subtly rendered in this novel, as when the changed quality of the sailor Ryūji is revealed in Mishima's description of his telling yet another sea story: "The tone of his voice reminded Noboru of a peddler selling sundry wares while he handled them with dirty hands."

The tone of Mishima's own voice, especially in his rendering of sexuality, requires a special note. Again Mishima has made explicit statements that demand unusual attention. For instance, he has been quoted as saying: "In Japan, only descriptions of normal sex relations cause problems. . . . I don't think abnormal relations have much impact on the Japanese at large."[18] In an interview with Abe Kōbō, author of *The Woman in the Dunes (Suna no Onna)*, he said that he was determined to go beyond the "conformity" imposed by Freud. Moreover, the reader of Mishima's works cannot escape the universally sick relationships, whether homosexual or heterosexual. Narcissism is a recurrent theme, not only in *Forbid-*

[17] The female body is often seen in animal terms in Mishima's work—and the animal (or insect) is apt to be dead or in the process of destruction (including sexual "death"). Examples include a butcher-shop carcass in *Forbidden Colors*, a hungry bitch and a mosquito in *Thirst for Love*, and a dead fish rotting on the beach in *The Temple of Dawn*.

[18] Quoted by Leon Zolbrod in a note to his translation of "Love in the Morning," *The East* 2(ii)(1965):36.

den Colors but in *Dōjōji*, for instance, where there is a hint
that the girl's lover was driven to death because his own
beauty was "all that he could stand."

Mishima's interest in the ideal Greek body and the homosexual hero is already clear. But what of attitudes toward heterosexual love: is "sympathetic" treatment precluded by the
homosexual bias? Apparently heterosexuals and homosexuals
are fundamentally alike: the relationships in all of Mishima's
work, with the possible exception of the fairy-tale couple in
Sound of Waves, are sick, sterile, and mutually destructive.[19]

In "Love in the Morning" (*Asa no Junai*, 1965), Mishima
shows a couple at dawn "in a warm embrace." They are soon
exposed as two people attempting to preserve their youthful
passions forever with the aid of a young couple they pick up

[19] Many of Mishima's studies of love are not available in translation. He
offers other unlovely views of the postwar generation in *Ao no Jidai* (Blue
Period, 1950) and *Junpaku no Yoru* (Snow-white Nights, 1950). In *Shizumeru Taki* (Submerged Waterfall, 1955), a frigid (married) woman drowns
herself in the waterfall at the damsite where her engineer lover Noboru
(who really loves only stone and iron) has been working: when the dam is
completed, the waterfall will be submerged. In *Bitoku no Yoromeki* (Tottering Virtue, 1957), another bored housewife has an affair. In *Kyōko no
Ie* (Kyōko's House, 1958–1959)—a four-part novel that Mishima claimed
reflected postwar social problems—a rich divorcée is seen in a series of
barren encounters with her four friends: this Mirror Girl *(Kyō-ko)* is very
different from the Kyōko of Kawabata's lyrical "Moon on the Water."
Nikutai no Gakkō (School of Flesh, 1963) features yet another divorcée—
this one with a cold, homosexual friend. Occasionally there are glimpses of
seemingly average lives—as of the young couple in *Ai no Shissō* (Scamper
of Love, 1962). More often, the lovers are in an ugly relationship—though
rarely as unpleasant as the female vampire of *Inochi Urimasu* (A Life for
Sale, 1968) or the fellow who fantasizes the violent killing of a young girl
after her mother (his sex partner) lies dead. Invariably, death and destruction are in store for those who love, and disillusion is the reward for lovers.
(John Nathan's biography offers some valuable excerpts and commentaries. Unfortunately, it was published too late for me to include the variant
English titles Nathan uses; but the reader using the *rōmaji* versions found
in my Bibliography and Chronology will be able to identify, for example,
Nikutai no Gakkō as the work he indexes under *Body School*.)

(separately) and, after suitable preliminaries, take home. But the details are saved for the second part of the story, a deliberate reduction of the first impression of a lyrical dawn-embrace.

The second part (a dialogue with the figure that had brushed against the couple in the opening segment) reveals in detail the ways in which the couple used the youth of the boy and the girl to (re)create their own illusion. Already exhausted, in spite of poetry, drama, and dreams, the couple attempt to regain their lost dream. The husband takes the girl on one side of the room; the wife enjoys the unknowing boy in the nearby darkness. Next morning, as the couple enjoy their passionate, tongue-kissing embrace, they are knifed by this boy: apparently as much because of their "porcelain beauty" as because they have used the two young lovers. The middle-aged couple are twice described as "the real thing": surely in a context to make the true Jamesian wince.

The love in *Thirst for Love* (*Ai no Kawaki*, 1950) might also seem heterosexual. This novel appears to be the story of young widow Etsuko, her wrinkled old father-in-law Yakichi, and other members of the household. Its "story" is her attraction to the young gardener Saburō, whom she eventually kills with a sharp garden tool (reminiscent of the weapons in *Confessions of a Mask*) and buries with Yakichi's help. In details, however, this "heterosexual" story continually reminds the reader of the homosexual attractions of Mishima's other work, and especially of the *Confessions*. We are fooled neither by the scene-shifting (to Osaka—although Mishima both by birth and by temperament is very much the Tokyo man) nor by the casting of Etsuko in the lead role. In spite of her "pregnant" walk, in fact, it is tempting to see her as the Masked Confessor, this time masquerading in women's clothes.

This is especially clear in the terms in which her attraction to Saburō is rendered. At our first glimpse (and hers), the sleeping young man has been reading a samurai adventure.

She notices his tanned, muscled arms; and his way of speaking reminds her of military usage. Then there are references to the smell of young animal lingering in his bedding. And in a later encounter her mounting excitement is linked with his faint odor of perspiration. We find ourselves back in the familiar world of musky-odored and half-naked young men, especially in the climactic fire festival scene. We are back with the festival celebrants of *Confessions.*

The fire festival scene of *Thirst for Love* is prefaced by the father-in-law's thoughts about night soil (although it is Etsuko who is sexually excited as they climb *this* slope, leading to the festival). "Animal" shouts and the thundering crowd are reminiscent of the Mask's boyhood memory, while the movement of the young men's bodies (and of the dragon's head darting above them) is rendered in terms of Mishima's recurrent sea imagery.

Firelight, sunset color, the perspiration of the young men, the musky odor, thoughts of death, and Saburō's back seen as the "ocean depth" (and associated with death) are a kaleidoscopic prelude to the inevitable moment of bloodletting. The crowd pushes against excited Etsuko, and her fingernails gouge Saburō's back, so that she sees blood dripping between her fingers (and later licks some of the blood from her fingernail as she looks at the maid, just revealed as pregnant with Saburō's child).

Nor is this the only moment in which sexual excitement is rendered as a form of butchery. When Etsuko meets Saburō at night and he obligingly (but mindlessly) finally reaches for her, she screams. The alarmed Yakichi (who had picked up a mattock on his way to look for the missing Etsuko) arrives on the scene, but stands irresolute. Etsuko promptly seizes the tool and brings it down upon Saburō's white flesh (on the nape of his neck: ironically, that erotic focus of *woman's* beauty). The reader cannot escape memories of the boy banquet in *Confessions.* Similarly, the repeated references to cruelty, Etsuko's "jealousy" of her husband's death, a burst of sunlight that provides a kind of epiphany after his death, and the idea that words "stood between them" (Etsuko and Saburō) are aspects of the *Confessions* and of Mishima's direct statements in *Sun and Steel*, where his own yearning for a "simple soul in a simple body" is made explicit.

Love, homosexual or heterosexual, is apt to be specifically like a fever (perhaps helping to account for the profuse perspiration of Mishima's characters). Or it may be a "thirst for revenge"; and Mishima's couples are more often bound by sexual loathing and hate than by love. Count Kaburagi and his wife in *Forbidden Colors* have not slept together for ten years, but they remain partners in crime. The "love" of the couple in "Three Million Yen" is exploited in the exhibitions they put on for well-to-do women (and men), who find the pair's apparent fondness for one another "an added attraction."

Mishima's own shock tactics often seem to be just such exercises in exhibitionism. They may be regarded as appropriate techniques in a satirist's work, where a picture of the ideal would be out of place. But in fiction, essay, drama, and interview, Mishima continually insisted that he wished to restore the ideal state. He proffered his own replacement for the lost "cloak" of Japanese etiquette (and the samurai code), planning to cover his nation's contemporary state of moral "nudity" and to achieve national salvation through the naked ideals symbolized in Greek male bodies of perfect beauty. Unfortunately, Mishima's "nihilism" (the word he favored in describing his intentions and his fictional worlds) offers few clues to the attainment of his Ideal.

The aesthetic reveals flawed beauty, and the bodies of Mishima's earliest characters already show the signs of decay. In contrast to the subtly drawn figures of Japan's poetic past (as in hints of "the dew of woman"), to the warmly appreciated flesh of Tanizaki's fiction, and to the lyrically erotic hints of his master Kawabata, Mishima makes of the body not only an object of wrinkled, sweating, and smelling flesh but also quite often an object of unprecedented physical loathing. His attitude frequently makes it well-nigh impossible for even the most reluctant reader to avoid casebook terminology and psychopathological criticism in examining Mishima's imagery.

A closer look at the imagery underscores the difficulty. In the context of *Forbidden Colors*, for example, the imagery of Yūichi's delivery-room experiences may be appropriate, although rather too deliberately sensational. To Yūichi, Yasuko's lower body moves like the mouth of a person vomiting; urine and mercurochrome "ooze" and "drip"; scalpel and shears flash; and his wife's "complicated" and crimson "interior" flesh appears in dissecting-room detail. This is but an extension of an earlier vignette, in which Yūichi saw the gynecologist's examining table as a torture machine, seemingly symbolic of his relations with his wife.

This birth is presented as a moment of truth, Mishima's honest recording of changes in Yūichi. We are told that this young man can no longer treat his wife's flesh as inanimate (a point that had been stressed by Shunsuke's earlier comments on inanimate flesh, when he urged Yūichi to accept marriage and to act as though his bride were a butcher-shop carcass or a cushion). Yet later events do not bear out the promise that "Narcissus had forgotten his own face" in contemplating the "scarlet flesh" linking him to his wife.

Nor is the imagery of the butcher confined to *Forbidden Colors* and the boy-banquet fantasy of *Confessions of a Mask*. In *After the Banquet*, Kazu feels the words of the crowd dripping like red meat in the sunshine. In *The Temple of the Golden Pavilion*, the sound of flowers being cut is not linked with the usual gentle philosophy of the art of flower arranging: instead, flower arranging suggests "the dripping of blood." In *The Sailor Who Fell from Grace with the Sea*, the boys are spattered with the blood of a kitten as they dissect it with a pair of scissors (the mother-of-pearl loveliness of its exposed insides appearing "not at all repellent"). Similar images appear even in Mishima's final tetralogy, with a murder theater even uglier than the one in *Confessions:* in *The Temple of Dawn,* fantasies of sexual murder are consummated in cannibalism. The "lovely" image of intestines recurs there, too: the colors of human intestines are "spread over the entire sky."

One very brief story, "Swaddling Clothes" (*Shimbungami,*[20] 1955) even features a newspaper-wrapped newborn bastard who is linked through images of knives and butchery to a newspaper-covered figure on a bench beneath the cherry blossoms. In a gesture far removed from the customary poetic associations of cherry-blossom viewing, a strong hand reaches out from this second bundle. We are spared the details this time, but the presumably bloody encounter between the concealed figure and the sensitive Toshiko is a scene that has already been foreshadowed in the fantasies of Toshiko, wife of a busy and insensitive Tokyo man.

Occasionally, of course, when knives flash and blood drips the actions and imagery are appropriate to the theme. In the context of Mishima's play *Madame de Sade* (*Sado Kōshaku Fujin,* 1965), for instance, the ladies' preoccupation with blood and flesh is understandable.[21]

But the supreme example of Mishima's butchery is surely the story "Patriotism" (*Yūkoku,* 1960). Here Mishima forces the reader step by step through the *seppuku* ritual to the reali-

[20] There are alternative readings of the *kanji* used in writing the Japanese title, but Mishima indicated that he intended the reading *gami (kami),* emphasizing that this is waste, dirty, useless newspaper (giving a rather different impression from the translator's "Swaddling Clothes").

[21] Again Kawabata offers a contrast. In the untranslated story *Asakusa Kurenaidan* (The Scarlet [or Crimson] Club of Asakusa, 1929 and 1930), Kawabata has a woman, Yumiko, whose ways are compared with the sharpness of a cutting tool. Hence her admirer Umekichi is shown wanting to make his living in a profession where he can experience the sensations such a tool provides (as a surgeon, a barber, or a cook). When blood actually flows, as in Kawabata's *The Lake,* it does so with the delicacy of the mother-of-pearl image cited elsewhere.

ty of pain: through blood that forms pools, stains the *tatami*, splashes upon a white kimono, drenches the wife's clothing so that she feels "damp in the region of her thighs." Here, too, we see fat clinging to the sword blade, entrails bursting forth as though a wound "vomited," and a meticulously minute recording of vomit, retch, and stench.

There is a critical question of intention here, especially in the light of Mishima's extensive commentary on "Patriotism" and of his widely quoted assertion that it is a story of happiness. It is essential to examine the details closely, considering Mishima's personal involvement with the story, the subsequent film, and his own eventual death by the sword in ritual suicide, as well as the prevalence of *seppuku*, swords, and suicide in all of his work.

To begin with the story itself: Its "occasion" is the incident of 26 February 1936, in which military extremists conspired to assassinate government leaders.[22] The young Lieutenant Takeyama Shinji is supposed to lead a detachment against his rebellious friends. He will not, although the refusal to carry out orders is a betrayal too (of his military ideals and loyalty to the Emperor). Thus the lieutenant comes home to his young bride Reiko and to death, the warrior's honorable *seppuku*.

---

[22] Mishima also used the 26 February incident in his 1961 play, *Tōka no Kiku* (often referred to in English as "The Day After the Fair" but literally "Chrysanthemum on the Tenth [of September]," meaning anything past its time, since the chrysanthemum is the flower for a festival on 9 September). In his *Eirei no Koe* (Voices of the Spirits of the War Dead, 1966), the ghosts of the heroes of the 26 February incident—as well as those of the kamikaze pilots of the War in the Pacific—continually ask why the Emperor has declared himself to be no longer Divine. Mishima referred to the incident in numerous other essays, interviews, and fictions as well. The date even takes on special significance in *The Sea of Fertility*, where Kiyoaki, making his futile last effort to see Satoko, struggles to Gesshūji on 26 February. That fevered journey leads to his death. The date thus marks the beginning of the tetralogy's reincarnations, and the *seppuku* of swordsman Isao provides a particularly fitting conclusion to the second volume.

The perfection of the heroic ideal is stressed—given visual intensity by a wedding portrait in which the bride holds her fan with a hand delicate as "the bud of a moonflower." Reiko pledges her wifely duty on the wedding night: by placing her own dagger on the *tatami* opposite her husband's sword to show that she is ready if necessary to join him in death. Their lives are lived "beneath the solemn protection of the gods," as in the idyll of *Sound of Waves*. Their marriage is "harmonious" in the spirit of the moral injunctions of the Imperial Education Rescript.

When Shinji comes home to die, the horror of the physical fact of *seppuku*, usually masked by noble sentiments, is underlined by the awful precision with which the couple prepares. The relentless steps of their evening ritual will end this time in death: the bath, the drink of sake, glimpses of the keepsakes Reiko has wrapped for friends, the retiring to bed at the regular hour. The ritual steps also serve as a prelude to the last taste of passion. But once again Mishima's voice breaks into this lyrical scene with an aphoristic interpretation: "urges of his flesh and the sincerity of his patriotism . . . [are] parts of the same thing."

The tragic shadow deepens as Mishima dwells on the familiar details of the couple's routine and on the subtle deviations from the familiar, as when the lieutenant helps to put away the bedding (the folding Japanese *futon*)—not one of the traditional husbandly duties. Inexorably, this "heroic" couple marches on to the moment when the gods must weep. The husband takes his final bath, the ritual preparation for death, while his wife sets out paper for farewell notes and prepares the ink (here making a properly domestic gesture).

So far, the tragic irony is restrained. It remains muted as the couple place themselves one mat apart in their room with its scroll saying "Sincerity." But the peace of that momentary pause in the action is wickedly shattered as the husband for the first time shows his "public" (soldier's) self to his wife. Mishima spares no detail of the sensational, from the moment when the sword is first "entangled" with the lieutenant's entrails to the time when its blade emerges tipped with fat—and even beyond, when Reiko, in *tabi* (socks) slippery with blood, walks downstairs to unfasten the bolt on the front door in order to make sure that their bodies will be discovered before they putrefy.

Our final vision is of wife Reiko's suicide, as she considers that she will now taste for herself "the true bitterness and sweetness of that great moral principle in which her husband believed."[23] Earlier in the story, the lieutenant and his wife were described as "this heroic and dedicated couple" whose last moments would "make the gods themselves weep." But our tears are not necessarily to be shed for precisely the same reasons.

Mishima's intention in writing this story is as deep and ambiguous as the narrative itself. The subsequent two-character film, with Mishima producing, directing, and even acting the part of the lieutenant himself, only creates more puzzles. The film is linked with Mishima's various Nō plays by his choice of set: a Nō stage. The film is given a heavily symbolic cast not only by its title (in English versions, "Rite of Love and Death") but also by the closing scene in which the two bodies (all blood miraculously vanished) lie together in a tranquil composition in a garden of raked sand, suggesting a place of Zen meditation.[24]

[23] Note that "great moral principle" is *Taidō*; and this is the title of the volume in which Mishima expresses his "Way of the Body" (also read as *taidō*).

[24] The mystery is further deepened by the strange use of a Nō stage for this film: a tranquil stage usually associated with *inner* action rather than with bloodshed. Perhaps it is related to Mishima's comments linking the Nō with Beauty and Death. In "The Japan Within," (in *This Is Japan* 18 [1971]) Mishima even declares that Nō cannot begin until "after . . . beauty lies in ruins"; and he links this "necrophilous" *(sic)* aesthetic rather self-consciously with Poe's Ligeia and Berenice. Moreover, in spite of Mishima's assertions that this was a story of "happiness," in his introduction to *New Writing in Japan* Mishima pointed out that the title *Yūkoku* "conveys

Accounts of faintings in the audience during the *seppuku* scene were by no means entirely the invention of press agents. In spite of the beauty of the preceding segment (the rite of love enacted on a dais that serves as stylized version of the customary *futon*), the heaving, frothing mouth of the lieutenant, the blood that gushes forth and lies deep on the *tatami*, and the close-ups that transform the noble connotations of *seppuku* into the reality of a vile tangle of bloodied gut—all offer an ugliness that seems to negate the beauty of the tradition. But Mishima at no time admitted any but the most noble and heroic intentions.

The profound implications of *seppuku* for Mishima became clearer in his later writings, especially *Sun and Steel*—the ideas and ideals of *seppuku* expressed in a ghastly reality five years after Mishima had mimed the act on film. A closer look at Mishima's earliest writings, however, reveals the prevalence of *seppuku* as theme and image, while hinting at his later description of suicide as "the apex of freedom" (in *Shōbu no Kokoro* [Heart of Militarism], 1970). In the early *Confessions of a Mask*, specifically sexual stimuli include samurai committing *seppuku*, and the narrator later visualizes a dagger going into the torso of a young man in a dance hall —the last in a series of images of beautiful male bodies pierced and bleeding.

Mishima also performed *seppuku* in the movie *Hitokiri* (Assassin, 1969) based on the life of a notorious nineteenth-century swordsman and assassin (hired by revolutionary forces to dispose of the opposition). In his short story *Onnagata*, Mishima alludes to *Imoseyama*—a Kabuki play with a famous *seppuku* scene. His own Kabuki play *Chinsetsu Yumiharizuki* (1969) dramatizes the *seppuku* and subsequent *kaishaku* (ritual beheading) of the warrior Minamoto no

more than a hint of melancholy: the word *yū* is related to the verb 'to feel grief' and grief is the emotion sustaining this story." (Translated by Mishima's coeditor, Geoffrey Bownas, this introduction was published posthumously: *New Writing in Japan* [Baltimore: Penguin Books, 1972].)

Tametomo and even includes the *seppuku* of a child. At the time of his death, Mishima was working on a long Bunraku play adapted from this successful Kabuki drama at the request of the National Theater and the Bunraku Association of Osaka.[25] In this play, the hero Tametomo is obliged to behead his son Tameoki after the son has committed *seppuku* following the Genji defeat. Then Tametomo himself dies by *seppuku*. By the play's end, ten men and women have died —seven of them by *seppuku*. And even this score is exceeded by that of the novel *Runaway Horses*, where there are a dozen such deaths in the account of Otaguro's unsuccessful rebellion of 1877 and the last act of the "beautiful" young Isao is *seppuku*, linked as so often in Mishima's works with images of sunrise and sea.

These are by no means Mishima's only examples of death by the sword, although the boy suicide in the untranslated *Ken* (Sword, 1963) is rather ambiguously found with the bamboo practice sword used in *kendō*, not the sharp weapon that usually brings death in Mishima's pages. Even when death comes by some other means, it is usually violent: like the poison in *The Sailor Who Fell from Grace with the Sea*. And sharp weapons—whether scissors employed on a kitten or a garden tool murderously descending on a young man's seductive neck—are the rule. For Mishima, violent death is both the norm and the ideal, whether of man or beast, if we are to judge by the slaughter of the flock of birds in his short

[25] The projected drama would have been the longest puppet play in two hundred years. Mishima had finished the first act on 20 November 1970, and Bunraku's Tsuruzawa Enzo was providing the musical setting. According to some reports, Mishima had made a recording of the script, playing all the parts (about forty) himself. The play was finally presented as part of the National Theater's fifth-anniversary program (the first new Bunraku play ever presented there). Mishima adapted the romantic novel written by Bakin (Takizawa or Kyokutei Bakin) in 1806–1810, instead of presenting the historical Tametomo (whose twelfth-century role is recorded in the *Heike Monogatari* [The Tale of the Heike], source of so many Kabuki and Nō plays).

story *Kujaku* (Peacocks, 1965). But it is suicide that Mishima identifies as the "apex of freedom." And the finest manifestation of "beautiful" death is *seppuku:* the death by the sword that was the culmination of Mishima's Aesthetics of Death.

These are the deaths in *Hōjō no Umi* at the end of his career and *Confessions of a Mask* at the beginning; of suicides in *Ao no Jidai* (Blue Period, 1950) and in "Patriotism"; of blood flowing in short stories, plays, and novels alike. They seem to lead inevitably to Mishima's own death poem (written just before his *seppuku*) on valor "nourished by the sword." The puzzle, however, is not his theme—linked with a noble ideal—but the way in which he exploits its "beauty."

Mishima is by no means the first Japanese writer to delight in the sensational or to linger upon details of the flesh, although even Tanizaki in his supposedly "demonic" early period offers nothing as gratuitously ugly as Mishima's account of the lieutenant's death throes. A number of Meiji writers and their literary descendants embarked on grotesqueries that they attributed to the influence of Poe.[26] But many were updated versions of the grotesque, macabre, and ancient ghost tales of Japan—filled with lank-haired and one-eyed horrors of ghastly pallor. As already noted, such tales were traditionally told during the summer as a way of keeping cool; they are still offered in the summer programs at the Kabuki-za as a way of combatting Tokyo's humid summer weather.

Such horrors, however, are to be visualized in the terms of those "gruesome" and "immodest" puppet plays described in Tanizaki's *Some Prefer Nettles.* In *The Lady of Tomano*, for instance, the nine-tailed fox not only kills the lady—he eats her entrails right on stage. But these are wads of red cotton, not the meticulously anatomical details of Mishima's kit-

---

[26] One writer even adopted the name Edogawa Rampo. Mishima adapted an Edogawa Rampo short story for the stage: *Kurotokage* (Black Lizard, 1961), a three-act play.

ten in *The Sailor Who Fell from Grace with the Sea,* whose "immaculate" bowels are unwound, its colon sliced as prelude to the squeezing out of "a broth the color of lemons." Nor are they the length of (animal) gut crudely spilled from Mishima's abdomen in the film of "Patriotism."

It would be difficult to compare Mishima's sensational elements with that master of the bizarre, Akutagawa Ryūnosuke, whose vast output of "morbid" and of "macabre" tales was not flawed by the obsessive symbolism of Mishima's constellation of ugliness. In "Kesa and Moritō," for instance, Akutagawa shows Moritō planning "for the sake of the woman I don't love . . . [to] murder the man I don't hate." We see Kesa sitting and deciding to substitute her own body for the husband Moritō plans to murder. But Akutagawa does not invite the reader to participate in the butchery. Having built up the suspense, he ends with Kesa blowing out the light, the sound of a shutter opening, and "a shaft of pale moonlight" striking the curtains.

When Akutagawa in "The Robbers" describes the putrid liquid of a dead snake, green flies, and the glittering oil oozing from the snake's entrails, he is offering a carefully constructed symbolic link. The woman plague victim gnawed by dogs, the decomposing bodies of children, the ugly old woman—actions and states of man, beast, and child—are to be viewed in relation to that snake. The one-eyed wanderer does not dwell on the dead with sadistic fervor. On the contrary, he reflects that "they revealed to him his own future." Even the horrors of "Hell Screen," with its ghostly elements and lurid colors, are a way of visualizing the "arrogance" and "shamelessness" of the artist Yoshihide and a commentary on the paradoxes of artistic creation. The punishment of "the perversity of the artist" is inherently horrible: he insists on a living model for his scene of hell—and is obliged with the spectacle of his own daughter being consumed in a fiery carriage. Unlike Mishima, transforming the beauties of flesh and spirit into images of ugliness, however, Akutagawa converts the occasion of horror into the haunting beauty of snow-white skin colored by fire.

The total aesthetic effect in Akutagawa is right: the girl in the fire "like gold leaf on a brown screen" merges with a painted figure so exquisitely beautiful that even a priest is moved to say: "Well done." In Mishima's pages, the aesthetic effect of even the most brilliant images tends to be flawed by his insistence on instructing the reader—whether on the "Six States of the Sphere of Illusion" or the funnel markings of international cargo vessels. There is a lack of restraint in achieving the effects of Mishima's horrors, too. In contrast, Akutagawa employs theatrical colors and the intensely dramatic gestures of his fictions to give the horrors the distance of a Kabuki performance.

The distance of such a performance from all Mishima's here-and-now horrors can be further gauged by comparing the *seppuku* scenes in such Kabuki classics as *Kanadehon Chūshingura* or *Imoseyama Onna Teikin* with Mishima's renderings in print and on film of tangled intestines and putrescent flesh. In Japanese literature, moreover, details of putrescence are not usually part of some psychopathological condition, as they frequently are in Mishima's pages. On the contrary, as in Tanizaki's "The Mother of Captain Shigemoto," there is a profound philosophical meaning embodied in the decaying flesh—meaning that is self-contained and not dependent for gloss on essays, the content of other fictions, or even on the final action of the author himself. In Tanizaki's story, the rotting, bloated corpse of a young girl, with its crawling maggots and putrefying flesh, is part of a Buddhist practice in which the priest's approach to Buddha-hood may be accomplished through "a sense of foulness" (a point made clear within the context of the story). Tanizaki also keeps his "modern" perspective by permitting the son to resent the father's contemplation of that ugly, loathsome corpse instead of preserving the memory of his mother's beauty.

It is true that Tsubouchi, early in the Meiji Era, decried

the prevalence of "bloodthirsty" works. Neatly packaged heads, stylized tortures, and dramatic battles abound in Kabuki plays even today. The blood in such works, however, is more often a symbolic commentary on the ideals of the samurai, on broken taboos, or on the merits of devotion to duty. *Seppuku* is generally rendered with tact as great as that shown in *Imoseyama*,[27] and death may be dramatized in a single scarlet thread running down a white kimono.

The foregoing examples are intended merely to assist in evaluating the tone of voice and the meaning of the gestures of Mishima's characters. These details also point up the element of the unnecessarily unpleasant in Mishima's work. There are, for instance, such minor details in *Forbidden Colors* as Yūichi drinking down a lemon peel around which is twisted a hair that reminds him of the count's wife. Or there are Shunsuke's wife and her lover, washed up after their suicide in a horrible mass "like wet tissue" so that they have to be pried apart. Then we see Shunsuke pressing a Nō mask (representing a beautiful woman—doubly unpleasant when

[27] *Imoseyama Onna Teikin* (1771) makes a particularly instructive comparison, since this is one of the plays alluded to in Mishima's story *Onnagata*. In a scene of balanced harmony (characteristic of its author's work), there are two houses, one on either side of a river. In one house, Koganosuke commits *seppuku* as an honorable alternative to serving the tyrant Iruka; in the other, the mother of his beloved Hinadori lops off the girl's head to save her from becoming the tyrant's concubine. The daughter's head is later floated across the river for token "nuptials." Yet although Koganosuke's father in turn cuts off the young man's head (thus the two lovers are finally united), and in spite of the fact that Koganosuke has been bent over his (presumably bleeding) abdomen for an extraordinarily lengthy scene, the only indication of blood is in the father's gesture of wiping his sword, and the only sign of suffering is in various tense body poses and the cry of two companions who see the headless body of Hinadori (concealed from the audience behind a screen). The scene in *Imoseyama* referred to in Mishima's *Onnagata*, however, is one in which court ladies treat a discarded woman with unbridled cruelty. This scene is especially appropriate in the Mishima context, because the court ladies are played by "actors of minor male roles" and speak in male voices instead of the feminine tones prescribed for conventional *onnagata* roles.

we consider Mishima's lyrical enthusiasm for the beauty of Nō, as expressed in "The Japan Within") down on the bloated face of his wife until the flesh buckles like overripe fruit—apparently one aspect of Shunsuke's "unyielding resentment against the vagina." To say, as so many scholars both Japanese and Western have said, that in such description Mishima "expresses postwar nihilism" is simply to beg the question.

In *Madame de Sade*, however, there are two significant lines that might be used in footnoting Mishima's ambiguous tone, although they are offered as commentary on the marquis. We are now, according to Renée, living in a world created by the Marquis de Sade, who has (paradoxically?) built for himself, and presumably for us, a "back stairway to heaven." Perhaps we are intended in a world of lost values to find a new aesthetic in the "beautiful" horrors of Mishima's pages.

The beauty of much of Mishima's earliest work was apparently deliberately in the manner of the Japanese romantics, although his obsessive color is the blood-red so appropriate to his own preference for raw flesh. He uses red and white to great effect—perhaps a cliché in the marquis emptying a cask of wine over a field of white lilies in *Madame de Sade*, but also strangely lovely in his "blood coursing down a forsythia stem in the rain" (although this is applied to the sadomasochistic spectacle of the marquise's naked body). Such imagery is very different from the delicate red and white of Kawabata's *Snow Country*. But then Mishima's colors are often hard and glossy, like the enamel clouds in *The Sailor Who Fell from Grace with the Sea*. His colors appear in strange, glittering combinations, too, as in the peacock imagery of *The Sea of Fertility*. Sometimes greens shade into lavender and vermilion with color changes that have the qualities of nightmare. And Mishima shares with his forebears of the decadent and neo-romantic schools a rich palette of vermilion, scarlet, and golden yellow.

Red is appropriate to Mishima's scenes of bloody swords

and knives. There are also the shades of a night sky vermilion or apricot-striped; dresses of pink, salmon, cinnabar; sweaters of canary yellow; hands that glow like agate. This palette is the one used in *Confessions of a Mask* and in *Sun and Steel* alike, as well as in the crimson mountains, vermilion silk kimono lining, and Chinese red tiles of *The Sea of Fertility*. These are the colors of his fire imagery: a shower of sparks, a flaming golden pavilion, the inevitably golden body. Often Mishima's colors glow in response to the light of his (symbolic) sun, although in *The Temple of Dawn* we are given hints that there is "no substance in the evening glow." A green forest absorbs light, becoming rich emerald. The sun illuminates clouds that become orange or purple. And there are finely detailed contrasts of light and shadow—whether in the face of a girl chewing gum or the cheeks of women delicately shadowed by wistaria blossoms.

In *Sound of Waves*, there are stark contrasts of black horrors and blinding white light. Rich blue-green waters are transformed into a black-and-white symphony, the black eyes and dark skin of the fisher-boy are set against the glowing "princess," and touches of black mar the idyll—perhaps the darkness symbolic of sex and reminiscent of the black footprints and underarm hair of Ōmi in *Confessions*. The shadow of a black butterfly falls, a policeman drowned on a Black Isle, black smoke attracted enemy planes to the boat on which the fisher-boy's father had died on decks awash with blood. Dark whirlpools and stormy waters hint at mystic depths of the past, while foaming water, white freighter, and brilliant beams of lighthouse and beacon suggest the hero's conquest, "by his own efforts" alone, of a threatening universe.

All the brilliance of Mishima's universe is not confined to his colors. Odors, too, have the opulent and decadent qualities of dream and nightmare. The bodies so often drenched in the "dark" odors of sweat—or enshrouded with odors that range from Lysol to the reek of urine—are also at times redolent of jasmine and of pomade. Lovers exchange kisses tasting of peppermint, seaweed, and sweets; in *The Temple of the Golden Pavilion*, young Mizoguchi thinks of the *touch* of a girl's flesh as "a scent like that of pollen."

To these sensory impressions Mishima adds his own somewhat repetitive symphony of sounds: the screeching fire engines of dream and reality in *Forbidden Colors*, such odd notes as the "flute" sound of a typhoon, and the piano music of *Confessions of a Mask*, where the quality of the sound is used to suggest the psychological progress of the pianoplayer.[28] A dog's bell, a ship's horn, less often the notes of samisen or flute—closer analysis reveals that the sounds of music in Mishima's work are also the sounds of *sex*, although in *Confessions of a Mask* they appear to hint at another interpretation, merging with the footsteps of disease.

It is not surprising that Japanese critics—including his mentor Kawabata—use such terms as "ornate" and "gorgeous" in describing Mishima's language. But they are also referring to those untranslatable elements already noted. Some of the obsolete *kanji* and unfamiliar words and phrases can be rendered into suitable English equivalents—as in the oddly "stridulous" blast of a ship's horn. Some of his metaphors have been rendered in felicitous English, as in the description of Noboru's heart in *The Sailor Who Fell from Grace with the Sea:* "a large iron anchor . . . sinking polished and indifferent through heaps of broken glass, toothless combs, bottle caps, and prophylactics into the mud at harbor bottom." Alas, Mishima's images are not always so successful: the glimpses of ships at Yokohama in *The Decay of the Angel* include a freighter "napping with its private parts exposed to the forbidden gaze of landsmen." In *The Sea of Fertility*, comparisons seem to be continually straining their

---

[28] In the untranslated *Ongaku* (Music, 1964), there is a rather Freudian image of a frigid girl unable to hear music. In *Runaway Horses*, Isao's memories of Makiko are linked with echoes of piano music.

way into English in this fashion. Within fifty pages of *The Decay of the Angel*, these include a walk as irritating as a hangnail, lips like red-black bits of apple beginning to rot, chestnut stuffing with the saccharine taste of hypocrisy, and women "chastity-eaters" who are compared to hens "warming the eggs of sin . . . less interested in hatching the eggs than in cracking the heads of young roosters."

Mishima often uses the language of fantasy and dream, sometimes in the context of his character's dreams (as in the fantasy-dream of *The Temple of Dawn*, where Honda sees the little Thai princess flying overhead on a peacock and urinating a cloud of golden rain). But he also puts his language to more conventional uses, employing the devices of puns, homonyms, and other ambiguities of Japanese. It would be tiresome to annotate all of them, although the richness of meaning already noted in the title *Forbidden Colors* is typical.

The title of "Patriotism" *(Yūkoku)* might even suggest "Pleasure Quarters" *(Yūkaku)* to an ear finely attuned to punning, although the written characters *(kanji)* provide no visual links. Shinji in *Sound of Waves* has a name that plays on *shinjin* (new man); there is a hint of *shinwa* (myth), especially appropriate in this mythic context; and there are echoes of "god," "heart," "spirit," "truth," and "reality." But the reader should be warned against excessive ingenuity in hints of multiple meaning: there are more than sixty different ideograms that can be read as *shin!* Mishima's own ingenuity in naming his characters, however, is a subject that has not yet received much attention—although Shunsuke in *Forbidden Colors* is a particularly intriguing example. His surname is Hinoki, meaning "cypress," but also known as "the tree of fire"—and this hints of his association with the "fire of darkness" (an allusion to "The Art of the Catamite").

Forbidden Colors is only one among many of Mishima's titles offering symbolic commentary on the story's content. The ambiguity of number and article in Japanese gives

Kamen no Kokuhaku a range of interpretations inevitably lost in our English restrictions of number and insistence on article: *Confession*(s) *of* (a) (the) *Mask*(s). In Japanese, it can be one specific confession or many, the multiple nature of the mask(s) being implicit in *Kamen.* The Japanese characters for "wearing a mask" *(kamen o kaburu)* are also read as "playing the hypocrite"—and not quite identical with our allusions to "mask" and "persona."

In "The Priest and His Love," we lose the implications of Mishima's *Shigadera Shōnin no Koi*, for *Shōnin* refers not simply to a priest but particularly to a saintly person or holy man. And *The Sailor Who Fell from Grace with the Sea* is a figure departing most radically from the hints of the Japanese *Gogo no Eikō*, meaning "towing in the afternoon." "Towing" indicates the dragging of a boat by power other than its own—but the reader is not presented with a simple identification of either boat or power. There is wordplay here, too, since a different ideogram read as *eikō* means "glory," and another *eiko* refers to the vicissitudes ("ups and downs") of life.

More difficult than the vagaries of exotic or hard-to-translate language for the Western reader, however, are the vagaries of thought. In trying to interpret the significant gestures of Mishima's characters, the reader is continually confronted with figures whose attitudes deviate from those in their own culture but are equally ambiguous in the context of Western thought. Mishima's maverick statements about Japanese thought and tradition, as in his commentary on the body beautiful and the Greek Way, complicate the task of interpretation. When Mishima speaks of a "classical" theme, moreover, he is less likely to be thinking of the classics of the Heian period than of the poetic bodies of his Greek statuary.

Mishima worshipped at the Greek temple while urging, right up to the moment of his *seppuku*, a revival of the Japanese spirit. And his postures before the temples and shrines of Japan are apt to seem mocking in their ambiguities. Does he, like the couple in "Patriotism," wish to observe the ritual gestures before the *kami-dana* (god-shelf, or home altar) dedicated to the Shintō gods? Was the samurai's profoundly Buddhist and Confucian philosophy a fundamental aspect of Mishima's attitude toward *seppuku?* In much of his fiction, it would seem that the answer is no, both at the apparent and at the deeper symbolic levels.

Mishima uses characteristically mocking tones in speaking of Shintō and Buddhist beliefs alike—and the heaviest irony of all comes in the ending of *The Sea of Fertility*, where all the philosophical explication and carefully structured accounts of reincarnation are resolved in an *empty* garden. Mishima's statements on his own beliefs are similarly ambiguous. He showed little enthusiasm for his family's Zen Buddhist affiliation. And when he writes of the soul of Japan, as in *Kōdōgaku Nyūmon* (Guide to Actionism), he refers to "national spirit."[29]

Mishima's mocking tone toward conventional religious postures intrudes even during the "introduction" to "The Priest and His Love" (*Shigadera Shōnin no Koi*, 1954). The catalogue of the joys of Pure Land Buddhism (ordinarily to be understood in terms of ineffable beauty rather than material benefits) is deflated with the author's commentary: "However sweet their voices may sound [that is, the indescribable sweetness of mythic birds], so immense a collection of birds must be extremely noisy." There is, too, a constant

---

[29] Mishima has made many statements—not all of them consistent. He notes that his family was Zen but asserts that his only personal experience with this Buddhism was in memorial services for his grandparents. He has also made many mocking allusions to the American professors who spent an entire lunch hour discussing Zen (although one may suspect that in this instance he was provoked because they were not discussing his writing!). But Mishima's comments on religion—like those on national spirit—cannot be adequately treated in the context of his fictions or without extensive annotation of Japanese traditions that Mishima may (or may not) be handling ironically.

perverting of the Buddhist ideal through the person of the Great Imperial Concubine, whose "faith" is tied to the thought that the Great Priest has excelled all her previous lovers in his sacrifices: *he* has given up these Ineffable Beauties. Moreover, there is a sardonic dimension to the conclusion, a hint of self-delusion (planted through an earlier comment that the Great Priest was "at the very boundary of oblivion"—not knowing whether he awaited the Great Imperial Concubine or the Future World).

The actor Mishima, speaking from behind these many masks, seems often to be mocking the tradition, the reader, and himself. In his fictions, Mishima displays his ingenuity— designing sets, creating characters, and inventing oddly disturbing actions that can be transferred with minimal alterations to the stages of Japan's theaters. But the world of his Nō, Kabuki, puppet, and modern plays is always closer to the familiar *inner* vision of Mishima's fictions (and essays) than to the conventions of the theatrical forms he is employing.

In Mishima's *Modern Nō Plays*, as in his Kabuki play *Yuya*, religion offers no comfort. In *Yuya*, we see the concubine who is forced to dance for her lord when she would prefer to travel homeward to comfort her dying mother.[30] In the traditional versions, both the Nō and the Kabuki, the lord Munemori is moved by beauty—by Yuya's poem saying that she would be sad to leave the cherry-viewing but "if the flower in the East [her mother] should fall. . . . " Whether she then arrives in time is irrelevant. In Mishima's version, the girl dances to the ironic counterpoint of the priests' chanting (before dancing at the cherry-viewing party, she had gone to

[30] Mishima's version of the ancient Nō drama was published in 1955 and 1956. It was performed by Utaemon at a dance recital in 1955 and was added to the regular Kabuki-za program in April 1957. Another notable Kabuki-za performance was given in 1965, again with Utaemon (the *onnagata* who was Mishima's special friend). *Yuya* and the 1953 performance of his Kabuki drama *Muromachi Hangonkō* at the Meiji-za are part of the firsthand experiences reflected in Mishima's short story *Onnagata*.

pray for her mother). Munemori is moved to send her, not by subtle poetry but by dancing with her—a physical response that seems a parody of a famous Kabuki play, *Dannoura Kabuto Gunki*, in which the tyrant is *spiritually* moved by Akoya's virtuoso performance on koto, samisen, and kokyū. Mishima's Yuya, moreover, is speeded on her way by a friendly priest who chants: "Too late, too late."

Traditionally, the Nō drama is profoundly Buddhist in meaning, its "action" being a gloss on or atonement for actions or events occurring before the play opens. The means of communication are both intensely formal and richly symbolic: a single step may signify a journey completed: in the traditional *Aoi no Ue*, a folded kimono symbolizes the suffering lady. In Mishima's *Aoi no Ue* (translated as *The Lady Aoi*), on the other hand, there is a ghastly scene in which the lady suffers on a real hospital bed (complete with bedside lamp and telephone).

Paradoxically Mishima—who filmed his ugly version of *seppuku* on a Nō-like set and put an exquisite Nō mask in Shunsuke's contaminating hands in *Forbidden Colors*—insisted: "For me, the Nō theatre is a temple of beauty." Choosing for his example the Nō play *Kayoi Komachi*, he adds that Komachi is the "embodiment of the eternal aspect of time," obliterating the whole world "beneath a single consistent beauty."[31] Yet when Mishima wrote his modern Nō play

---

[31] These remarks were made in "The Japan Within" in *This Is Japan* 18 (1971), but this volume was actually published several months before Mishima's death in 1970. In this essay, Mishima also writes of the moment-to-moment evocation of beauty in the Nō and says that the essence of beauty lies in prescribed form. Praising the traditonal Nō mask, movement, and voice, he sees in the Nō his "perfect image of beauty." In the Nō drama *Kayoi Komachi*, the spirit of the poetess appears to a priest with daily offerings of wood and fruit; he goes to her grave, and the ghost of her lover Fukakusa appears to tell of his ninety-nine visits. In the traditional Nō version of *Sotoba Komachi*, a "beggarwoman" sitting on the grave marker (*sotoba*: stupa) is possessed by Fukakusa's ghost and her words include learned Buddhist quotations.

Sotoba Komachi he depicted Komachi as an old hag gathering cigarette butts. The questioning priests of the traditional *Sotoba Komachi* are replaced in Mishima's version by Tokyo transients. And in Mishima's Nō plays Death (a poetic prelude to traditional Nō) invariably becomes a physical and even ugly reality, as in his rendering of *seppuku* on film—a very strange expression of his remarks about the "necrophilous aesthetic" of Nō.

The gestures of Mishima's actors continually reveal perversions of spiritual tradition in his fiction too, and sometimes the accompanying attacks on social conventions appear to be unduly harsh. The middle-aged ladies of "The Pearl" (*Shinju*, 1963) are deservedly mocked for their terrible preoccupation with form. Mishima catalogues the lying, the cheating, and the stealing so often concealed by the masks of social usage in this account of housewives going to ridiculous lengths to avoid the "bad manners" of telling the truth, speaking the unpleasant, or losing face. This is a legitimate aspect of Mishima's attacks on hypocrisy.[32] Yet we wonder if it is also necessary to mock Shinji's mother in *The Sound of Waves*, when she bows repeatedly to the postmaster's wife at the public bath. The bow is a ritual social gesture expressing thanks for the safe delivery of a letter from her son: but are her thanks less genuine because she expresses her gratitude with ritual gestures?

In spite of his admiration for the ritual gestures of Nō, Mishima continually uses ironic tones to describe the prescribed

---

[32] This attack on hypocrisy is also linked to Mishima's final action. For in discussing his "action philosophy" (*Kōdōgaku Nyūmon:* Guide to Actionism) and telling of Ōshio Heihachirō (who committed suicide after the uprising on behalf of famine victims in 1837), Mishima claimed that Ōshio was "hurling himself bodily against hypocrisy." The line is echoed in Mishima's *Geki* (Appeal) as he prepared to commit *seppuku*. To the listening Ground Self-Defense Forces he cried: "Is there no one who will die by hurling his body against the Constitution . . . ?" (For Mishima the U.S.-inspired Constitution symbolized the loss of Japan's heroic spirit.)

gestures of shrine worship, of tea ceremony, of memorial services. Thus, in *After the Banquet*, a ritual gesture degenerates into this view: Kazu is holding up a basin into which her gargling husband spits, and she is described as "like a priestess at a shrine . . . [in] a posture of service and self-sacrifice openly offered." Sometimes Mishima offers the formal gesture as a fine lesson in perception—as in the tea-and-milk ritual in *The Temple of the Golden Pavilion*. But his is not the technique of delicately repeated symbol and gesture found in Kawabata's *Sound of the Mountain* or *Thousand Cranes*.

In Mishima's tea ceremony, a woman squirts milk from her breast into the man's traditional tea bowl. This seemingly beautiful and mystic moment is progressively stripped to a harsh and ugly reality. First perceived by the innocent Tsurukawa and Mizoguchi, it seems a mystery: they interpret it as a woman's farewell gesture to the father of her child. Later "explanations" in adding to the so-called facts also add the bias of the beholder. A girl assures Mizoguchi that the woman had not had a single love affair since that day— although Kashiwagi asserts that she had been constantly running after men. To Mizoguchi, the beautiful image had been defiled not just by Kashiwagi but by "knowledge." The image is shattered when the lady of the ritual is seen close up, smashing Kashiwagi's perfect flower arrangement. Its final meaning is suggested when she offers that same mystic breast to Mizoguchi, who is then overcome by dizziness. At that moment, once again the golden image that has dominated his vision since childhood comes to remind Mizoguchi that what is seen "too carefully and too completely" is no more than a "meaningless fragment."

Beauty and Tradition: Clues to Meaning

Images of breast and temple merge in Mizoguchi's unhappy moment of intimacy with that figure from the ritual picture. As they do so, Mishima hints at the theme of *The Temple of*

the Golden Pavilion (Kinkakuji, 1956).[33] In this novel,
Japanese tradition fares badly. The tea ceremony, flower arrangement, and garden viewing provide occasions for acts of
sadism, arson, and treachery. Autumn grasses, cherry blossoms, the ancient sword, the mirror, and even the moon in
the water recall centuries of allusive imagery. But to what
purpose! At the moment of the perfect flower arrangement,
the symbols that for centuries have represented the beautiful,
the ineffable, the evanescent, are deliberately contrasted with
the ugliest of actions, tangled with suspect motives, and
placed in a world of lost ethics and perverted values.

The "lost ethic" is of course Mishima's obsessive theme,
but criticism of this novel usually focuses on the character of
the protagonist, Mizoguchi. Critics have asserted (as in the
foreword to the English edition of the novel) that Mishima
appears chiefly interested in the imaginative recreation of a
psychotic acolyte's obsession. Readers encountering Mishima
for the first time in this work tend to dwell on the novel's supposed hints of revolt against the Buddhist tradition, find in
the narrative an expression of postwar nihilism, or dissect the
elements of what they regard as a study in evil.

It is true that Mishima here took a news item concerned
with a disturbed acolyte who did indeed burn down the Kinkakuji in 1950. It is true that Mishima recreated actual
events, too. But it is important to observe the kinds of
changes he made in the factual material. For example, in
spite of his numerous discussions of "heroic" suicide and the
prevalence of suicide in his work, Mishima replaced the attempted suicide of the real-life acolyte with a quite different

[33] *Kinkaku,* "golden building," is also sometimes read as "beautiful
building," giving the title an added dimension. As a pleasingly ironic
touch of wordplay, two other characters read as *kinka* are the term for a
fire in one's neighborhood. For most Japanese, as for Mizoguchi, *Kinkakuji* is visualized as a lovely, golden pavilion in a Kyoto garden and reflected
in a pond (perhaps with snow on the pavilion's roof, as in so many post-
card renderings)—although the reality looks more brown than golden.

scene. At the end, Mizoguchi throws away his arsenic and knife and feels "like a man who settles down for a smoke after finishing a job of work." Mishima's acolyte wants to *live*.

The Temple of the Golden Pavilion does offer a study in psychopathology. It can be read as yet another of Mishima's many casebooks of death wishes, childhood trauma, and delusions of power. The novel is also appropriately rich in details of Zen ritual. There may even be a hint of Mishima's other allusions to the breakdown of traditional values, as in the comment on former times, when "the Zen religion had not yet been captured by convention and when the spiritual awakening of the individual was valued above all else." Yet here a word of caution is in order: we should be as wary of traps laid by hinted "Zen" readings of the novel as is the Zen novice faced with traps of Zen *kōan* (riddles defying rational answers and filled with paradox).

A more helpful approach to the novel is to be found in the development of Mizoguchi's *perception*, for like many other Mishima characters he is concerned with a personal aesthetic and puzzled by the nature of Beauty. Explicitly, Mizoguchi tells us that his first real problem was that there is "nothing on earth so beautiful as the Golden Temple." The theme of Beauty—its relation to reality and to the power of the imagination—is the one unifying principle in *The Temple of the Golden Pavilion*.[34]

Such disparate elements as the girl on the bicycle, Uiko; Mizoguchi's relationship with the clubfooted Kashiwagi; the

---

[34] In a number of interviews, Mishima has been quoted as saying that the man's character defect made him jealous of beauty. Mishima's remarks on the beauty of Nō in "The Japan Within" offer additional clues to meaning, for he said that "true beauty is something that attacks, overpowers, robs, and finally destroys." *The Sea of Fertility* further develops the theme of Beauty. In *The Temple of Dawn*, where "Beauty renders human endeavor completely futile," several passages are reminiscent of *Kinkakuji* and various characters speak Mishima's own lines.

harmony of friendship with Tsurukawa; even the acolyte's hatred of his mother—all are related to the perception of beauty and its mirror-image of ugliness. The temple offers a transcendental beauty: Uiko is the boy's first experience of beauty—an experience shattered in the dark reality of their confrontation, just as the boy's dream of the golden pavilion is first shattered when he confronts it in the Kyoto garden.

Beauty has its "sterile and frigid characteristics"—an idea echoed in *After the Banquet*, where Kazu finds beauty threatening in a vista of "vast, beautiful, inorganic presence" (inevitably, if not ironically, this is the distant view of the U.S. base at Tachikawa). But such distance is essential. One feels that Mishima was early impressed with the idea of Eliot's lines: ". . . human kind/Cannot bear very much reality." As the demented Mizoguchi sees it, the law of distance regulates; the shadow is "more beautiful than the building itself." Too close an approach to the beautiful—as when Mizoguchi confronts that white breast (a breast rich in poetic possibilities when viewed from afar)—reduces it to that "meaningless fragment"; the golden phoenix of the pavilion is revealed as a dark crow; harmony is transformed into restlessness and disharmony.

In *After the Banquet*, also, Kazu preferred to view things from a height, lest "an aged couple out for their melancholy stroll [should] . . . be transformed into a picture too ugly to bear contemplation." Such reality is apparently always "unbearable"—as when the boy in *Confessions of a Mask* is frightened by the reality of Kusano's rough hands. This does not mean that reality is to be equated with ugliness, however. For in "Love in the Morning" the boy who had been exploited by two middle-aged lovers killed them only when he saw them standing in that embrace reminiscent of porcelain figures. They were then "the real thing" . . . and "too beautiful."

The pavilion is also "too beautiful," and its destruction can be read in terms of aesthetics rather than psychopathology. Mizoguchi does not want his destructive deed "to be explained away as having been actuated by some established philosophy," and we are assured that his weakest subject at the university was logic. These are two clues that we should avoid reading the novel in terms of a specifically Zen aesthetic. Mizoguchi wants to "rob [the pavilion] of its arrogance" and "rule" it so that it can never again get in his way. Only through its destruction will he be free to act. And in spite of its sexual symbolism, the temple's "interference" is not so much a psychological block as an aesthetic one: its tendency to interpose its form between Mizoguchi's imagination and life.

Repeatedly the acolyte is seen groping for definitions of beauty—trying to reconcile dream and reality, yet unable to see except through the eyes of his pavilion. In the opening pages of the novel, the reader shares this boy's dreams, the golden light shed on his drab and impoverished world by a golden mirage fashioned from his father's words and his own need. The first confrontation with that sublime temple of the imagination, however, is a disappointment. The boy wonders if he suffers from a deficiency in "aesthetic appreciation" or whether the golden pavilion itself is practicing some sort of deception, a defense to hide its "truth."

The real pavilion is a disappointment, a beautiful dream reduced to peeling gold leaf, sooty images, and dark spaces. At this point "a perfect little image" of the pavilion (a model in a glass case) seems preferable to the actual building. Now Mizoguchi feels truly free to dream—his imagination is released from the reality of faded beauty and can range to ever-smaller pavilions or pavilions great enough to envelop the world. Back in Yasuoka, though, the boy finds that the temple has now become *more* beautiful: what had been nurtured in his dreams has now become "real."

This perception of "reality" is essential to understanding the remaining narrative. What is ultimately "real" is that which is "solidly" and "deeply" *within* him. Here there are hints of other Mishima characters confronting the claims of beauty and reality: the fantasies of the narrator in *Confessions of a Mask*, the failures in the world of *Forbidden Colors*, the longings of the boy in *The Sailor Who Fell from Grace with the Sea*—and of Mishima himself in *Sun and Steel*.

Mizoguchi confronts his pavilion again and again: its remembered or imagined beauty, its actual form, its aesthetic and even metaphysical significance. At one time it is "transformed into a symbol of the real world's evanescence." At another, it is an intermediary between the unlovely Mizoguchi and the very essence of Beauty. Sometimes the boy wishes to be forever freed from the shadow of his dream: he wishes for a bomb that will consume the pavilion in eternal fire. When the war ends, the relationship between Mizoguchi and his pavilion has undergone a change: its beauty transcends the entire world of reality, rejecting every sort of meaning. The earlier bond between boy and temple has been cut, and the gold of the earliest image merges subtly with hints of the glitter of evil: "The very fact that the temple should have struck a young boy as so incomparably beautiful contained the various motives that were eventually to lead him to arson." The motives and the meaning, however, are ultimately contradictory and baffle the reader.

Whatever its eventual significance, the golden pavilion—real or imagined—encompasses the whole narrative, just as it "engulfs" the uncertain and ugly figure of the acolyte Mizoguchi. Mizoguchi's perception of this beauty (a beauty found eventually both in the temple and in the dark night enfolding it), and of Beauty imagined and within himself, is further defined by the deliberate contrast between his view of beauty and that of Kashiwagi, though the clubfooted boy's "theory" sometimes seems to Mizoguchi more accurate than his own. It should be noted that Kashiwagi's "beauty" is not that of the illuminating imagination: Kashiwagi's gestures are reminiscent of the falsities practiced by the Mask. The music

Kashiwagi plays upon the flute, like his flower arrangements that fade, shows his dislike of lasting beauty. He loathes architecture and literature and prefers a beauty that will leave him "unmarked."[35]

Kashiwagi enjoys momentary control of his transitory flowers. Elsewhere Mishima condemns such control, as in Shunsuke's allusions to the abstract garden of the Daigoji in *Forbidden Colors*. There is a description of the garden "so packed with artificial winter, so controlled, so abstracted, so composed . . . that there was no space for real winter to enter": this is condemned and described as "the most direct statement of aesthetic Japanese thinking," its extreme artificiality being judged a "betrayal" of nature. In *The Sailor Who Fell from Grace with the Sea* the murderous boys attempt to restore beauty to their universe by means of control —they will master death, a mastery practiced on kittens and on grace-less sailors.

In one of his short stories, "Onnagata" (*Onnagata*, 1957), Mishima further explores the union of dream and reality—in the person of this man playing women's roles. But he describes the union as "illicit" there. A young graduate in classical Japanese literature, Masuyama, enters the esoteric backstage world of Kabuki. He sees in the *onnagata* Mangiku a rare figure of "aloof beauty," one who still follows the advice of an eighteenth-century manual to live offstage ("in real life") as the woman he portrays in the theater. Nowadays, *onnagata* are usually family men, whose sons in turn may follow the *onnagata* tradition. But Mangiku is a figure from the past, acting, living, and thinking the role "Woman."

Mangiku also substitutes art for life. It is fitting that on stage he should be an exquisite Yukihime in the play *Kinka-*

---

[35] Kashiwagi's name sounds like another Mishima joke and another example of his paradoxical treatment of the "ideal male beauty" he continually lauded. For it is Kashiwagi who is the lover of shining Prince Genji's young wife, and who fathers a child by her, in Lady Murasaki's long-ago *Tale*.

kuji or bewitch the audience with a single feminine glance as he plays Omiwa in *Imoseyama*. But when Mangiku falls in love—with a newly imported "modern play" director—his love is predictably drawn from these dramatic "experiences." Masuyama himself is caught up in the illusion, unwittingly assuming a role as minor villain while apparently acting as go-between for Mangiku (who wants to take the unsuspecting Kawasaki, the director, to dinner). Yet as Mangiku and Kawasaki walk off under a black umbrella, the illusion is finally shattered. At this moment, with snow falling upon the black umbrella, we might be looking at a specific haiku or *senryū* (humorous verse) commenting on the loneliness of "one" observing "two" lovers beneath an umbrella. But we are left with no sweet evocation of the past. All that remains is Masuyama's jealousy and his dread of where this new emotion will lead.

This Kabuki interlude might, of course, be taken as another manifestation of the deadening effect of tradition. Certainly any character who follows "tradition" in Mishima's work is inevitably doomed, and bound for tragic death, like the patriarchal president of the spinning company in his *Kinu to Meisatsu* (Silk and Insight, 1964), although Mishima seemed to regard that president as heroic. Or at best, like Masuyama, they can be sure of disappointment. The girls of "Seven Bridges" (*Hashizukushi*, 1956) are an ironic statement of this concept. They set out to pray in silence under the moon, observing a ritual of "double seven," praying at either end of each bridge (yet not above a modern shortcut of counting a Y-bridge as two).

Their project is obviously doomed in the modern world: Kanako drops out with stomachache; Koyumi is accosted by an old friend; clouds gather, rain falls; Masako is assailed by doubts—and a policeman pounces, assuming that she is contemplating suicide. Yet there is a fourth and unwanted member of this group, the unthinking maid (sent along to act as their chaperone). She alone plods on and completes the round that for her apparently had no meaning. Nevertheless, she refuses to reveal the secret of her prayer. The story ends with Masako poking the maid's shoulder and feeling "heavy flesh" repel her nails.

The "tradition" in which these girls are involved is only a superstition, a crude response rather than one in the aesthetic tradition of moon-viewing. But Mishima shows no more patience for the "aesthetic" moonlight: the light that shines over his world is more likely to be the beam of a beacon, the flashing colors of a neon sign, or the work of a newly repaired generator. Nor does Mishima waste much time on the traditional symbolism that undergoes such rich transformations in Kawabata's work, although on a number of occasions Mishima offers his own version of the moon-in-the-water image.

In "Seven Bridges" there is a brief hint of this image as the maidens approach their first bridge. But in a world so prosaically rendered in terms of neon signs and concrete pillars, it serves as no more than a smirking allusion to the Buddhist paradox of "the impossible" (so gracefully hinted in Kawabata's story). Mishima's image is as empty of meaning as the Tokyo riverbank on which willows, ostensibly "faithful to tradition," tremble in the sterile city air.

In *The Temple of the Golden Pavilion*, Mishima uses words quite close to Kawabata's, as the golden pavilion is reflected in the water and the evening sky is "different from the one above our heads . . . clear and filled with serene light." The moon-in-the-water and the temple-in-the-water, however, are ominous images. Rather than *suigetsu*, Kawabata's lovely water-moon, in Mishima's image it is *suihyō*, the duckweed that lies thickly on the surface of the pond. Even when the image does offer a momentary beauty, he quickly shows it "crumbled" by Tsurukawa's tossed pebble and "shattered" by Kashiwagi's flute playing.

Similarly, Mishima delights in shattering other familiar images of haiku, chronicle, and drama. He cannot tolerate "the flowers of the season," and he reduces "autumn geese" to the sounds of "babies crying at night." In *After the Banquet*, Kazu feels the autumn winds pierce through her sleeves to the base of her breasts, not the usual delicate, seasonal sadness. It is a typically Mishima association—she thinks of the thief who might have touched her body (flesh instead of poetry, again); and this thought is followed by an ugly premonition of the "incipient decay of her flesh." Gazing at a landscape in this context becomes "a political act," while the seemingly beautiful imagery of mountain fire ceremonies is reduced to the reality of flames from the municipal crematorium. Nor are "cranes across the sky" the customary delicate allusion to the autumn flight of birds: they are prosaic machines, and they mark the sites of modern building construction.

Mishima's mirror symbolism in particular measures his distance from the tradition—and from his master Kawabata. *Forbidden Colors* appropriately offers a whole world of mirrors: the mirrors of Narcissus, preludes to seduction, a mask behind which the count approaches his beautiful boy, a metaphor for lovers and protectors who simply mirror one another. At the beginning of *Forbidden Colors*, Yūichi is attracted by his reflected image and tastes the "mystery" of that beauty. Later, he is continually "in need of a mirror," whether to stand between himself and his wife or to lure him into experiencing desire and fulfillment. (There are also hints that Yūichi hates beauty in men, so that we wonder whether his reflection actually helps him practice self-hatred or self-love.)

In *Forbidden Colors* there are vaguely symbolic moments: the pregnant wife seems to hold a mirror on her abdomen (but this proves to be only the reflection of sun on a red dress). The mirror at home is broken—"perhaps a sign that the beautiful youth had been released from the legendary power of the mirror." Later, he has been set free from a childish ambition, his dream that society might supply an image to substitute for the one the mirror reflected. But the mirror wavers, distorts, and shatters. It is, after all, only the rear-view mirror of a car on the way to a *"Gei Pā-ti,"* reflecting the foreign homosexual winking at Yūichi as he kisses the mirror and leaves his lipsticked mark.

In *Thirst for Love,* Etsuko's elegant mirror with its red brocade back is a striking contrast to Kawabata's mirror in "The Moon on the Water." Etsuko's mirror does not reflect a beautiful world. It shows only the lips of her husband—dead from typhoid: "Fringed with whiskers and pouting [they] appeared in the mirror bright and clear." "Losing oneself in a mirror" in "Death in Midsummer" is similarly neither poetic nor metaphysical. "The moon after rain" in "Patriotism" is no longer an exquisite expression of the Japanese preference for subtly veiled beauty: in the context of death and destruction, the effect is satiric.

At other times, Mishima fastidiously picks up the conventional symbols just for the pleasure of dropping them in the dust. When he waves the familiar pine branch, it is only to hit the reader—"Slap!" as the dirt and sand tumble down on Masaru's carefully pressed trousers. Or the snow (an image of beauty in Japanese poetic tradition) is reduced to a "dirty bandage" that hides a city's "open wounds," and the context is a setting for riot and revolution. A pellucid picture in *The Temple of the Golden Pavilion*—pine forest, shining reflection, river, hills, azaleas—is deliberately set up to be shattered by Kashiwagi's ugly actions. A fluttering moth is not a delicate allusion to a line in Bashō or evocative of loss as in Kawabata's *Snow Country:* instead it is a glimpse of a homosexual waiter. Autumn fruits are "cold as corpses"; autumn grasses are no more than "an exquisite work in plaster of paris."

No one would be inspired to address haiku to the moon in such settings: for the moon is after all only "a drawing pin stuck in the wall" (in *After the Banquet*). When the seasonal symbols are not "cold," they are foreign: like the epigraph of

"Death in Midsummer," taking its seasonal words not from linked verses but from Baudelaire. And for the delicate hints of loosening or unwinding the obi, Mishima substitutes the "shriek" of Etsuko's (an obi later untied by her withered father-in-law, to whom she seems a "beautiful" skin disease in *Thirst for Love*).

Often Freudian symbolism substitutes for the traditional: the tie on the portrait of the homosexual Jackie, or the tie that Yūichi "whips" against the hotel balcony on his wedding night. A piece of strawberry shortcake is demolished by Yūichi's white teeth—and friend Eichan feels as if his own body is being swallowed. In *After the Banquet*, tie and strawberry shortcake merge when Yamazaki gobbles up a helping and Kazu is reassured to see "a ruddy-faced man, necktie firmly in place, eat a big piece of cake."

This of course is one of Mishima's jokes, as is Fusako's cherry pit that the sailor Ryūji picks up from an ashtray and pops into his mouth. Mishima also occasionally makes rather amusing use of Japan's traditional erotic symbolism. In "Thermos Bottles" (*Mahōbin*, 1962), for instance, Kawase thinks of Asaka's rustling paper handkerchiefs *(hanagami)* while they are dancing: this is an allusion to those "spring pictures" in which the hero's prowess and enjoyment beneath the *futon* covers is indicated by the quantity of *hanagami* scattered about. In "Thermos Bottles," too, Mishima has a delightfully original symbol in his squeaky bottles. Two children (Shigeru, son of the wife, and Hamako, daughter of the mistress) are shown in mortal fear of the sound of air escaping 'round thermos-bottle corks. This somewhat unlikely symbolic sound—and eventual breakage of the bottle itself—hints at the nature of the relationship between Kawase and his wife, Kawase and the former geisha, and ultimately between the wife and a young co-worker of Kawase's.

Mishima's frequent symbolic associations of fire and desire—as in *Sound of Waves* or *The Sailor Who Fell from*

Grace with the Sea—are not exactly original, but at least in Mishima's work the variations include an ironically timely fire engine. In *Forbidden Colors*, Yūichi sees flames on his wedding night; fire images and the sirens of fire engines, perhaps only dreamed, accompany his first homosexual encounters. He hears the sirens again when he is alone with Mrs. Kaburagi and when he is on his way to his wife's delivery of their daughter. Later, recalling sirens, Yūichi thinks that his innocence must pass through fire in order that his guilt become pure, immune to fire. Then, as Yūichi heads to his final confrontation with Shunsuke, he passes a big cabaret fire, tricked out with details of three fire engines and spraying fire hoses.

In *Forbidden Colors*, "the fire of darkness" is also a term taken from an esoteric Buddhist volume about "The Art of the Catamite" (the "engine" or "instrument" of the homosexual partner taking the male role). Buddhist "flames of lust" seem relevant in the context of *The Temple of the Golden Pavilion*, just as flames of Christian hell are correct for *Madame de Sade*. But Mishima's use of fire-and-water imagery is not quite so far from Japanese tradition as the reader might suppose. It is found in the Japanese and Chinese tradition of *in'yō* (yin and yang), the ancient harmony of woman and man, of water and fire.

The water found most often in Mishima's world is the sea, and in his obsessive imagery the sea—frequently mirroring the fiery colors of sunset—is given sexual connotations. In *Confessions of a Mask*, the soldiers' odor of sweat is compared with a sea breeze and linked with air burned to gold above the seashore. Such a lyrical flow of color and movement may serve as prelude to the appearance of a hero-god, as in *Forbidden Colors*. Yet in "Death in Midsummer" a brilliant view of blue-green waters (though reminiscent of the idyllic setting of *The Sound of Waves*) serves as prelude to horror. And although the sea is a symbol of power and of peace, it is the source of both life and death.

The waters that flow in the four-part *Sea of Fertility* recall the "unearthly" blue of the sky reflected in the sea of *Confessions of a Mask* twenty years earlier. That color was identified with the color "mirrored in the eyes of a person on the verge of death." In the novel that Mishima completed on the eve of his own death, Honda does not fear the "five signs of debility" (the *gosui* of the title *Tennin Gosui*) because he has recognized that even an old man forgotten by society possesses the absolute power of destruction called death.

In *Confessions of a Mask*, restless green ocean swells are related to the "razor-keen blade of the sea's enormous axe . . . ready to strike"; and this "dark blue guillotine" as it falls sends up a "white blood splash" in the moment of the Mask's climax. Similarly, a tide of blood seems to sweep across the sea of "Sea and Sunset" (*Umi to Yūyake*, 1955), an odd story with a thirteenth-century setting in Kamakura. Here the caretaker Anri with his limpid blue eyes tells his tale to a boy whose eyes seem to mirror what he wishes to say. But the boy is deaf and dumb. Anri tells of his boyhood—a disillusioning experience with the Children's Crusade. Then "the sea did not divide"; the beautiful boys were sold into slavery in Egypt, and Anri eventually came to his master Daigaku. More interesting than the tale itself—yet another example of romantic Ideal Male betrayed (complete with the ever-present bare and youthful breasts)—is the imagery. We find ourselves back with the sunset sky, "fire blazing on the sea."

This image punctuates the narrative and is linked with memories of golden-haired children on that ill-fated crusade when they seemed "crowned with helmets of fire." The sea "burns" in the sunset, until the "tide of blood" sweeps the sea, inevitably recalling the significance of similar images in *Confessions of a Mask* and "the flame of the flesh" in *Sun and Steel*. Now, however, the temple bell sounds. Anri closes his eyes and listens: sounds dissolve time and "carry it away to eternity." He opens his eyes in darkness; the sea has turned gray. "The sunset was over," and as he turns to beckon his deaf-and-dumb "audience," Anri discovers that the boy is asleep. Again, in contrast to Kawabata's sounds, we find that the sounds of Mishima's world bring disillusionment instead of enlightenment.

Yet the sun continues to illuminate Mishima's meaning—to be ultimately glimpsed in the sunlight of the garden at the end of *The Decay of the Angel*. Like the flower image opening that novel's seascape, *Sun and Steel* has red lilies: reflections from the surface of the sea dyed crimson by the sunset, staining a sea of clouds with red flowers (imagery linked with the lily-shaped stadium of an earlier passage and with a description of "semen-white" clouds). It was into these clouds that Mishima penetrated in a riot of sexual imagery: "Erect-angled, the F104, a sharp silver phallus, pointed into the sky. Solitary, spermatozoon-like I was installed within. Soon I should know how the spermatozoon felt at the instant of ejaculation." In *Sun and Steel*, we leave Mishima simultaneously about to "pierce" the sky and to take "a great bite" out of it. Significantly the book ends with a poem, "Icarus," that includes the "burning rays" of reason and the "single, blue space" of an idea.

This appears to be another reference to life's "eternally transparent blues and greens," another link between Mishima's sea and sunset, between fire (whether of sun or festival) and a primeval water that identifies the odor of sweat with both sea and night soil. Night soil, the blackness of hairy armpits, and the "darkness" of the festival *mikoshi* (as well as the sky reflected in the eyes of *mikoshi*-bearers in *Sun and Steel*) can also be linked with that black-and-white sea imagery of *The Sound of Waves*. Thus, like the image of clouds to be pierced by Mishima-spermatozoon—but also "a snake encircling the globe" in *Sun and Steel*—the image "bites its own tail." We are back with *The Temple of the Golden Pavilion*, where Maizuru is "a sort of generic name for the sea that cannot be seen" and the black-and-white sea is sometimes "full of rage," appearing beside the temple itself in a pond that is "a symbol of the sea." We are also in the world of the sea and the sunset glimpsed throughout Mishima's final tetralogy, where the symbolic sea is given ironic resolution in that arid sea of the moon from which *Hōjō no Umi* takes its title: *The Sea of Fertility* so different from cosmic implications of references to the churning (Hindu) Sea of Milk in *The Decay of the Angel.*

The Sailor Who Fell from Grace with the Sea (*Gogo no Eikō*, 1963) provides additional clues to symbolic meaning. At the same time, it adds to earlier treatments of beauty and definitions of art some comments on the role of the imagination. The story deals with thirteen-year-old Noboru and his widowed mother. This boy dreams of some day having an anchor tattooed on his chest. He also spies on his mother in her bedroom, as she sits naked, with feverish eyes and "scented fingers rooted between her thighs." Through the boy's preoccupation with the sea that stretches beyond the windows of their Yokohama house, he and his mother meet Second Mate Tsukazaki Ryūji—a hero figure who has indeed stepped from the sea. In a variation of the hero in *Forbidden Colors*, Ryūji seems to Noboru "a fantastic beast that's just come out of the sea all dripping wet."

Squeezing his sweaty body into the chest that conceals the spy-hole, Noboru *hears* his mother's obi unwinding in that familiar erotic gesture. He also smells her "musky fragrance" and sees the naked Tsukazaki Ryūji, a prototypical Mishima hero combining in his person earlier associations of sweaty male flesh and golden pavilion: broad shoulders, "square as the beams in a temple roof"; hairy chest, a body golden with light reflected from sweat; muscles like twists of rope; flesh like a suit of armor; and finally, "rippling up through the thick hair below the belly, the lustrous temple tower soared triumphantly erect." To complete the picture, Ryūji's ship, too, is a "shining pagoda of steel."

In this novel, the sea's reflected light is not so innocent as that surrounding the island of *The Sound of Waves:* for it is reflected sunlight that first shows Noboru the spy-hole through which he can watch his mother and the sailor. In part, the sea in this novel is a hackneyed image of Woman: "Nature surrounds the sailor with all these elements so like a woman and yet he is kept as far as a man can be from her warm living body." Once again, the sea has its nightmarish powers, associated with "the dark passions of the tides." It also has its mundane aspect: "like all sailors" Ryūji belongs neither to sea nor to land; and for all his youthful dreams of palm trees and faraway places, the sea is for the most part "just a job."

There are, however, deeper meanings, symbolized in a ship's horn with its "thirst for the dark nectar in the little room" (not the mother's bedroom but the "pitiful little vacant house" of her vagina). The recurrent sound of this horn is one through which Noboru perceives his own "universal order and circle of life linking him through mother and man to the sea." Later the horn "probes" Ryūji and rouses his "passion for the Grand Cause," while the sea itself is for Ryūji "a glistening green drop" in contrast to the "putrid" odors of landsmen. The landsman is also associated with the "stench" of death.

This landsmen's "stench" does not have the positive (and sexual) connotations of the "sweating armpits" sea imagery that Mishima associates with heroic deaths (of the lieutenant committing *seppuku* in "Patriotism," for example, or of knights in armor in *Confessions of a Mask*). Ryūji identifies the sea with death and glory in Mishima's familiar cluster of images, however—and this cluster is related to his remote sea life and an existence that impels Ryūji toward "the pinnacle of manliness." Although this is ostensibly an account of heterosexual love, moreover, Mishima's hero again cannot separate sex and death. His concept of ideal love is that a man encounters the ideal woman only once in a lifetime and in every case death (an "unseen Pandarus") intervenes, "luring them into the preordained embrace."

In spite of the occasions on which we peer through Noboru's spy-hole at the embraces of Ryūji and Fusako, they are apparently only "captives" of this seeming tenderness, and Ryūji apprehends his sexual desires as "pure abstractions." He is, too, a hero in the quasi-mythological tradition. Noboru and his teenage gang regard death as the only means by which Ryūji can be restored to his heroic glory after he has sacrificed his heroic (homosexual) purity at the altar of (heterosexual) marriage. His fall from heroic grandeur is further compounded of lost illusions. When Noboru is caught spying, the sailor's commonsense reaction constitutes a tragic fall: his "unearthly brilliance" is forever dimmed, just as his imaginative powers of transformation have been lost by his coming ashore to the mundane land.

Fusako, unaware of Ryūji's fantasies of glory, love, and death, had admired his "plainness." Her son, however, found in the (unfallen) sailor "the medium without which his imagination had been helpless." There is also a continual tension between the homophones "glory" *(eikō)* and the passive "towing" *(eikō)*, as well as between the heroic ideal ("the splendid hero who once shone so brightly") and the world of everyday land routine (its epitome being the fashionable foreign accessories in the shop run by Noboru's mother). At the same time, there is Mishima's familiar undercutting of the heroic—as when Ryūji, close to his last moments, speaks again of the Grand Cause but reduces it to "another name for the tropical sun." At the end, the sea appears in shades of Prussian blue, the sea-land dichotomy expressed in an "ocher net" of water spreading out from the dirtied shore.

The filth of the land has contaminated the heroic sea animal, although as in *Forbidden Colors* there seems to be ample evidence that the hero's downfall is self-determined and that his unheroic deed—like the heroic accomplishment of the fisher-boy in *The Sound of Waves*—is achieved "by his own strength," or lack of it. But Ryūji's fall is accomplished in Mishima's familiar terms of paradox and disappointment.

At the close of the novel, Ryūji reflects: "I could have been a man sailing away forever." He meditates on his recurrent "vision of death," thinking it now eternally beyond his reach —even as the boys are preparing a "heroic" death to be achieved through the medium of poisoned tea. The boys-in-the-machine who plan to drain the sailor's lifeblood to "transfuse the dying universe" are, however, a little too pat either for the heroic vision or antiheroic deflation. The commentator who read this story as "a Japanese *Lord of the Flies*" seems to have missed the point. And that concluding tag—"Glory, as anyone knows, is bitter stuff"—tends to annoy rather than illuminate.

A different kind of tension operates in *After the Banquet* (*Utage no Ato*, 1960), another novel in which Mishima showed his interest in the personalities behind the masks of public life.[36] The protagonists here are an elegant political figure in his sixties, Noguchi Yuken, and Fukuzawa Kazu, proprietress of the Setsugoan restaurant—a woman with a man's resolution and a woman's reckless enthusiasm, preferring to love rather than be loved. She is now past fifty, it is a long time since her last love affair, and she is "unshakably convinced" that she is "proof against all manner of dangerous sentiments." Kazu is certain that there is no ambiguity left in the world: the insides of other people's minds are now "transparent" before her eyes. Thus she is introduced to the reader at what appears to be a pinnacle of potentially tragic pride.

Into the magnificent Setsugoan, favorite of the Conservative Party, come a group of doddering former ambassadors. One collapses, and across his body she sees Noguchi, the only

---

[36] Mishima's probing in this instance led him into the law courts—in the celebrated "privacy trial" of 1964, Arita Hachirō, ex-foreign minister and candidate for the governorship of Tokyo, was awarded a judgment of 800,000 yen (about $2,200 at that time) against Mishima on 28 September 1964, setting off a great outcry in Japan on the relative rights of "privacy" and "art."

member of the group who strikes her as being still alive. One reviewer made a serious error in evaluating the relationship that develops between Kazu and Noguchi. He described it as a conflict of two cultures, identifying them as "the austere aristocracy" and the "pleasure-loving young." That is an oversimplification, as well as a distortion of the Japanese context. It is also a distortion of a relationship in which "at dawn a man over sixty and a fifty-five-year-old woman slept in the same bed." Noguchi and Kazu experience a tragic fall, rendered in the context of a mismatched marriage, a disastrous political campaign, and a mortgaged restaurant. This Japanese restaurant and Noguchi's Persian-carpeted house symbolize the true nature of the conflict, however, and the novel ends inevitably in divorce.

At the end of the novel, Kazu reopens her restaurant, having chosen that life in preference to the recurrent thoughts of the Noguchi family's burial place. We see Kazu reading a letter from Yamazaki—her own and her husband's advisor in the political campaign, a man who had cooperated with Kazu in her financing of the illegal preelection activities (activities that Noguchi himself would not have countenanced). Kazu has made various seemingly frank gestures to Yamazaki, but Mishima stresses that for her such gestures are possible only in relation to a man she does *not* love. Yamazaki in turn writes that she is probably right to "return to warm blood and a human vitality." He will be delighted to come to her banquet, a "back in business" celebration.

Although it is true that Kazu increasingly perceives Noguchi as an old man, this is not the real focus of their difference. Rather, their difference is to be found in Noguchi's study full of German books: his turning for harmony not to ancient Japanese aesthetics but to Goethe's *Wanderer's Night Song*. His preference for things foreign is even demonstrated in his "English" elegance of clinging to old customs (although one would have expected the Japanese tradition of clinging to old customs to have filled his need). But his habits

of frugality are "Confucian," and in spite of his foreign tastes
and furnishings he is annoyed by Kazu's unconventional
behavior. He emphasizes the *forms* of behavior continually,
while speaking pompously of the "substance" of the intellect.
Noguchi's world has no place for real passion—only for
the conventional sentiments. He is described as "the incarnation of the old moral virtues," with a logical passion for the
impossible and a tragic blindness toward human nature. This
blindness is exhibited both in his political campaign and in
his view of Kazu. He can perceive Kazu only in his own
(illusory) terms, whether the point at issue is her taste for soy-
beans or her conduct on the political platform. After years as
foreign ambassador, he cannot escape hints of condescension
in his attitude toward Kazu. Nor can he escape from the
belief that there is no room for divergence in human conduct,
whether in politics or love. He is sure that all human actions
are "based on the same principles . . . [and] governed by
fixed laws." When Noguchi does show emotion, as in his
postelection tears, Mishima makes it plain that these are "un-
mistakably oriental theatricality" (although Noguchi is a
man usually not at all theatrical). Noguchi's "feelings" at
this seemingly emotional moment are merely related to "the
old-fashioned rhetoric of Chinese poetry."

Kazu, by contrast, is prejudiced against the intellectual
life. She has always been a woman of flesh, of passion, and of
unbridled fancy. In delineating her role as mistress of the Setsugoan, Mishima shows a fine sensibility in rendering the
traditional world: the old-fashioned frankness and freedom
of the geisha, the meticulously seasonal menus, the carefully
chosen kimono accessories, even the subtleties of expected
(and unexpected) behavior, and the splendid features of the
Setsugoan's vast garden ("in the Kobori Enshū style," and
complete with its own pond and even an ancient moon-viewing pavilion brought from Nara).

Old-fashioned attitudes are further reflected and help to
define Kazu's role (at least for the Japanese reader) in the

opening incident. When the old man collapses (the occasion of Kazu's first real encounter with Noguchi), the man's wife makes clear that she would rather her husband died as a result of being moved to a hospital than lived only thanks to the hospitality of a place of entertainment. Yet this is a Japanese restaurant with *tatami*-matted rooms that could easily provide accommodation for the man. And in spite of the doctor's recommendation and Kazu's generosity, Mishima makes clear in this passage the great social gulf between Kazu's world and Noguchi's—since he is one of the group to which the dying man belongs. Mishima presumably does not expect the reader to share the "proper" wife's judgment of Kazu; yet he does offer hints that Kazu's passions and her fancies are flaws, and certainly not symbolic of "youth."

To begin with, Kazu is a woman of "romantic dreams." Her tears fall with equal abandon in response to the yelping of research dogs, the gestures of Kabuki actors, and the anger of a husband whose political principles she has violated. It might seem a virtue when she is spoken of as being close to ordinary Japanese people. But her actions are sometimes "superstitious" actions—the striking of good-luck flintstones—reminiscent of those praying girls in "Seven Bridges." Moreover, when she uses haiku to lure Noguchi into bed, she is far from the poetic declarations of love in Heian times. Rather than a delicate allusion inscribed on a fan, as in *The Tale of Genji*, she offers a verse on the lining of her coat: "As long as you know / I am waiting, take your time, / Flowers of the Spring." Mishima's irony here is inescapable.

Mishima adds: "Through no design of Kazu's, men generally went down in the world once they met her." Like Noguchi's, their downfall is accomplished by way of the *tatami*. Kazu, of course, is more comfortable when she sleeps on the *tatami*, and this further defines her true distance from Noguchi—at whose house she has to learn to sleep on twin beds. Kazu's preference for old-style sleeping arrangements might at first appear a virtue: yet Mishima makes it clear that her attitude toward marriage hardly qualifies her for a role as ideal Japanese wife. She lives in her husband's home only at weekends, although she recognizes that it is "wrong" when a married couple can talk only on the phone. And rather than being truly helpful, she is self-willed and deceitful in her misguided, seemingly generous attempts to promote Noguchi's political candidacy.

In addition, the relationship between Kazu and Noguchi, like so many in Mishima's work, is a partnership in death. Even at their marriage ceremony, she thinks: "Now I'm sure to be buried in the grave of the Noguchi family! At last I've found some peace of mind." Later, her fears of loneliness after death (the thought that she will have no family to tend her grave or put her memorial tablet on the family altar) provide more powerful motivation than any argument of intellect or physical passion. She prefers the small, moss-encrusted tomb of the Noguchi family to the Setsugoan.

The narrative of *After the Banquet* serves as a vehicle for Mishima's sardonic comments on Japanese politics as well as on the conventions of marriage, social usage, and even death itself. Mishima shows Kazu praying to her predecessor (the late, first Mrs. Noguchi) for help in her husband's political campaign. Here he makes a mockery of Japanese attitudes toward the dead. When Kazu sends "offerings" (two dozen foreign oranges!) to the departed ambassador of that early Setsugoan scene, it is only a gesture of spite toward the widow who would not accept her hospitality for the ailing man.[37]

The supposedly noble sentiments of the posturing politicians are reduced to the judgment expressed by the "wise" and winning conservatives (old-fashioned Noguchi is ironically the candidate of the opposition). The conservatives

[37] The Japanese reader would recognize the (excessive) quantity of Kazu's oranges as inappropriate. Another flawed memorial appears in *Thirst for Love:* instead of buying fruits to offer in memory of her husband, the widow purchases two pairs of socks for young Saburō (whom she would like to take as a lover).

believe that the important things in the election are "money" and "feelings"—both tied to the idea of exploitation. We are told that the politician has an affinity with the geisha (although in context the act seems rather to be one of prostitution) and hence with Kazu's world of the Setsugoan.

After the Banquet has other aspects that require close attention. For example, Mishima here uses his device of repeated symbols to suggest disillusioning alterations in perspective or in character, as he did in the milk-and-tea ritual of *The Temple of the Golden Pavilion*. An orchid is first seen in the restaurant where Kazu meets Noguchi for their first date. Her lack of response to Noguchi's enthusiasm for orchids on that occasion already hints at the weakness of their relationship. The orchid reappears in the guise of one of the "four gentlemanly flowers" of Noguchi's door-pull: the sleepless Kazu compares it with a hard, fastidious face. It is finally brought by Noguchi as a potted gift, after the fiasco of the election: "His dried-up old hands . . . playing a kind of trickery intended to win her over . . . coquetry on the part of a self-satisfied old man."

These are of course different from the allusive repetitions of Kawabata's lightly sketched details of red and white reflections in a mirror, flashes of reminiscent light, softly beating insect wings, or echoes of long-ago sounds. Mishima's repeated symbols seem rather to take on the obsessive quality of psychopathology—a point that can be made clear if the reader now returns to *Confessions of a Mask*.

Whether or not Mishima was truthful in denying that *Confessions of a Mask* was autobiographical, it does include images and incidents that re-form and reappear in all of Mishima's subsequent writing. Moreover, the ideas and ideals of the Greek heroic experience hinted in *Confessions of a Mask* have since been made explicit, as in the passages of *Taidō* already cited; while its epigraph from *The Brothers Karamazov*, beginning with, "Beauty is a terrible and awful thing!" could be applied to all of Mishima's work. These are

the ideas ultimately finding expression in the book he
describes as his "kind of hybrid between confession and
criticism . . . 'confidential criticism' ": *Sun and Steel.*[38]

In *Confessions of a Mask*, we find the associations later
represented by the fire, gold, and phoenix constellation in
The Temple of the Golden Pavilion. The sweaty universe of
Mishima's fiction is traced back to a childhood encounter
with a night-soil collector—a memory linked with the Mask's
later responses to armored heroes and male bodies. The linking of the odor of sweat with seascapes and the air "burned
to gold" in *Confessions* are specifically images of "sensuous
craving," later transformed into that sweaty scene of a fire-
man's festival—an occasion on which the phoenix atop a festival *mikoshi* (portable shrine) sways and rocks in sea images,
as it does in the festival scene of *Thirst for Love,* while
Mishima's favorite colors of vermilion and gold dominate the
picture. A specific symbol of the Mask's childhood years is a
chant that sounds like "lamentation for the extremely vulgar
mating of humanity and eternity." Significantly, this is the
chant of the firemen at the summer festival.

Those of us who saw Mishima himself sweating during his
participation in a festival some years ago cannot help recalling the symbolic associations of such a scene in his novels.
Whatever biographical implications are here seem to have
been made explicit in *Sun and Steel,* in Mishima's account of
his own literary-psychological development. He speaks of his
boyhood, of a time when he watched young men carrying a
mikoshi and saw the sky reflected in their eyes. The perception associated with this episode is linked with his later
search for "a language of the body." Mishima then details his
growing interest in sunlight and in implements fashioned of

[38] The *tetsu* of Mishima's title *Taiyō to Tetsu* is usually read as "iron";
here it alludes to the iron used in body-building weights (cf. the weight-
lifting of the *Taidō* photographs). But *tetsu* is also used for "steel" and thus
provides a dual reference: to Mishima's advocacy of swordsmanship and
to his obsessive images of sharp weapons.

tetsu (both iron and steel), linking a "fetishism" of the body with a "fetishism of words." He finds "identical origin of the formal beauty in the wordless body and the formal beauty in words," converting his apparently psychological statement into a system of aesthetics.

Marking off the stages in his own life in relation to encounters with the sun (in 1945 and 1952), and offering a somewhat opaque account of his literary style at the same time, Mishima speaks of an existence that could be "finally endorsed only by death," identifying his own illusions with those of the warrior. He speaks of his boyhood hypocrisy ("wearing a mask" is a term for hypocrisy) toward the "purity" of the body. Mishima also speculates about the relationship of these ideas, his "difficult metaphysical problem," to the "distant martyrdom of Saint Sebastian" (another link with his symbolic scenes of butchery). The sexual stimulus of *seppuku* in his *Confessions* and the heroic *seppuku* of "Patriotism" also reappear in *Sun and Steel*, now in the guise of the "young heroes" of Etajima, the wartime kamikaze pilots.

In the "beauty" of the suicide squad, which he believes to be generally recognized not only as heroic but also as "ultraerotic," Mishima even finds yet another link with his beloved Greek ideal, another expression of his repeated desire to live and die beautifully.[39] Mishima compares the nobility of these pilot-heroes and the beauty of their death with that moment of ultimate Beauty described in his many essays on the Way of the Warrior. This was the ultimate Beauty that Mishima himself sought on 25 November 1970.

There is a confusion of the Mask's "sensual desires with a system of aesthetics" in *Confessions of a Mask*, and it seems that *Sun and Steel* is Mishima's attempt to resolve that confusion. He speaks of his early plan for a union of art and life, of

[39] The reader seeking a comparative view of these pilots might well read Umezaki Haruo's *Sakurajima* (1946), reprinted in *The Shadow of Sunrise*, edited by Saeki Shōichi (Tokyo: Kōdansha, 1966), where the narrator depicts these same pilots as a group of swaggering, loud-voiced roisterers.

style and "the ethos of action" (see his *Guide to Actionism*).
Rather oddly, he adds that the function of style is "to restrain
the wayward imagination": and one is also faced with the
anomaly of a writer who seeks "a reality without words."
But this is only one of the many paradoxes that for Mishima
were an expression of life itself.

Sun and Steel also amplifies the hints for a postwar code
that Mishima gives in his essay in *Taidō*, that we find in his
guide to *Hagakure* and his theory of "Actionism," and that
recur in his *Bunka Bōeiron* (Defense of Culture, 1969). In *Sun
and Steel*, Mishima declares that this is the time for reviving
the old Japanese ideal of a combination of letters and the
martial arts: art and action. This is the traditional linking of
"arts" and "letters" in Bushido, the Way of the Warrior.[40]
And through such close reading of *Sun and Steel* we discover
Mishima's Way of the Body made explicit as a literary—and
even a life—style.

At times his aesthetic offers oddly distorted echoes of the
acolyte's visions of Beauty in *The Temple of the Golden Pavilion*. Often, too, the words resemble those of apprentice homosexuals, thirteen-year-old philosophers, aging authors,
and even that once-heroic sailor. This apparent confusion between the voices of Mishima's essays and his fictions, however, is an essential aspect of his literary theory. Characters
express not their own ideas but the author's, often by way of
asides that the reader finds irritating. And as in *Forbidden
Colors*, where the voice of the author mingles with the babel
of homosexual and heterosexual lovers, attitudes become
blurred—not with the vagueness of Kawabata's rich possibil-

---

[40] This is the aspect of Mishima's theory that is misunderstood by those
who read a sinister kind of (aggressive) "militarism" in his ideas. This mis-
reading of an ethical and aesthetic principle as perverse "nationalism"
was typical of even the most perceptive foreign analyses of the plea for
"action" in Mishima's curtain speech. Typically, one found references to
the "aesthetic *and [sic]* the martial" aspects of Mishima and of Japan,
whereas Mishima's use of the term *bumbu ryōdō* shows that these "two"
parts are really one (*bumbu:* literary and military arts).

ities but with the contradictory claims of a dozen insistent voices. This may be the weakness that Mishima had in mind when he admitted to John Bester that his work lacked the essential *yohaku:* the "unfilled space" or "remaining white" so essential in Japanese (and Chinese) art.[41]

Certainly, this characteristic "babel" should serve as warning to the reader expecting to find a consistent whole philosophy in the fictions. In *The Sailor Who Fell from Grace with the Sea*, for instance, Mishima moves back and forth between the boy's world and the sailor's world of sea and dream, with effective lapses into the commonplace landsmen's world of the mother. At the same time, he will not forego the already-noted comments on glory being "bitter stuff," and he cannot resist putting some of his own idiosyncratic philosophy into the mouths of the adolescent idealists who seek beauty-through-destruction.

Mishima's talents do *not* include firm control of point of view. He prefers the technique of aphorism and the role of omniscient author. But even with the guidance of *Sun and Steel*, there are ambiguities in *The Sea of Fertility*, as there were in *Forbidden Colors*. Who is to say whether we are listening to the voice of Mishima himself or to Shunsuke when Shunsuke (described as "out of touch with reality") declares: "The profession of the novelist is the worst [rubbish] . . . for the expression of beauty," and adds that his work is "the most bungling and low-class of professions." We wonder if we are to assume that Mishima's sharp tongue is here offering an echo of Shunsuke's distorted reality or his own version of the old Truth and Beauty argument.

Paradoxically, the characters whose thoughts we read most intimately in Mishima's fictions still remain no more than masked figures. The reader troubled by apparent failures of characterization in his work may perhaps find a hint

[41] John Bester, "The Magnificent Egocentric," *This Is Japan* 18(1971): 53–54. Contrast this with Kawabata's comments on the need for such "space."

of an explanation in his play *Tropical Tree* (*Nettaiju*, 1960). In his notes,[42] Mishima asserted that he wished his stage to be peopled by passions only: passions "clothed in words." The passions in this play are apt to leave the audience unmoved, the characters being so self-consciously symbolic and so clearly related to their obsessively imaged cousins in Mishima's other works as to be near-failures in dramatic terms.

According to Mishima's notes, Ikuko is a girl with "an air of completely unsullied purity" who at the same time is a woman "of passion and daring . . . [hoping for] a thorough purification" of the world in which she and her brother live. Having first glimpsed Ikuko in an unpleasant scene in which she is planning to strangle her eighth "little birdie" (while she enjoys the prospect of a puzzled family coming to sing funeral songs), the reader of the script may be forgiven for requesting more convincing evidence—especially after she and brother Isamu have been glimpsed in various moments of

---

[42] The notes accompany the translation by Kenneth Strong in *Japan Quarterly* 11(1964):174–210. The play is typical of Mishima's "hybrid" aspects, as his commentary makes clear. The "source" was a news item about murder and incest in France (reported to him by a Japanese student who had been living in Paris), but he describes the play as a "distillation" of his own memory (recollections of a dead sister, a flame tree he had seen in the Dominican Republic, the reclaimed lands of Shibaura, and so on). The scarlet flame tree, rather than having the "color" *(iro)* of Japanese tradition, is "evil" in the Western sense. The character named Isamu (meaning Courageous) is a coward. In addition, the play is simultaneously a "modern" version of Chikamatsu's "sweet inducements to death" (reference to the love-suicide plays) and one employing the "classicism" of Aristotelian unities, he says. Finally, Mishima describes this three-act play as a tragedy in which motives are "a single-minded and uncomplicated version of the original 'Greek myth for money' "—and a "Japanese Electra." Such contradictions should remind us of the dangers of trying to reconcile all Mishima's claims to Greek and samurai ideals. We are reminded of the Mask's assertion that his ideas concerning human existence came from "the Augustinian theory of predetermination" and Mishima's own admission that his "Greek" way was not necessarily a true version of the original. We might also remember generations of other Japanese writers claiming to be in the tradition of such Western authors as Poe and Wilde.

death, murderous intent, and incest. As they ride off toward the sea, accompanied by the sound of a bicycle bell, however, we realize we are again listening to the *Confessions of a Mask*.

These are the same sounds that we shall hear in *The Sea of Fertility*. Once again we shall find moments of profound psychological awareness—apt both in the particular context of the fiction and in its universal application. The four novels, like others in Mishima's rich output, sometimes reveal the universal sources of insecurity. There are glimpses reminiscent of the fears of the guilt-ridden family shown so economically in "Revenge" (*Fukushū*, 1954). Or we recall Mishima's perceptions in showing the jealousy of the lighthouse keeper's daughter in *Sound of Waves*, where he was able to preserve both a Japanese concept of responsibility and a Freudian sense of guilt.

But in the grand sweep of four novels in which Mishima attempts to cover sixty years of Japanese history, generations of social change, journeys to Bangkok and the holy cities of India, and ethical and philosophical questions of great complexity: problems of interpretation abound. Once again, the prevalence of Mishima's hybrid personal symbolism leaves the reader uncertain of the correct context in interpreting Mishima's fictional—and philosophical—approach to Reincarnation. Like the characters in Mishima's play *Dōjōji*, we are faced with sounds simultaneously identified as Nō chant and "a noisy factory." We only know that we are participating in Mishima's "beautiful, sweaty, intricate choreography of death."

"This Beautiful, Sweaty, Intricate Choreography of Death"

In *Runaway Horses*, this beautiful death is glimpsed only when sunlight is reflected from the golden chrysanthemum crest of the Emperor. Elsewhere in Japan "the rays of the sun were blocked." The words, however, might serve as a description of all Mishima's work, especially *The Sea of Fertili-*

ty. For as Mishima told many of his friends, he had included in this tetralogy "everything I felt and thought all through my life." He declared that he would finish the tetralogy on the day of his "action" and would thus "realize my *bumbu ryōdō*"—that is, his unity of "spirit and action."[43]

Mishima also said that once his tetralogy was completed he would have nothing left either to do or to say. The first installment of *Spring Snow* was published in September 1965. The last words of *The Decay of the Angel* were written only hours before his death. During those five years, Mishima wrote—and talked—about his work in progress. Some of his comments seemed to assert his belief in a radical separation of life and art. Others echo the body-and-words philosophy of *Sun and Steel.* But in view of the care with which Mishima completed his manuscript hours before the action of his *seppuku*, we are surely justified in seeking clues to his death by sword in these four novels. At the same time, the tetralogy reexamines Mishima's earlier literary preoccupations, ideas beautifully and ironically resolved in that area of the moon from which the novels take their name, the arid *Sea of Fertility.*

In these four novels, familiar Mishima settings, recurrent characters, and obsessive themes, symbols, and images all make their final appearance. The recurrent image of sweating flesh is even elevated to a metaphysical sign foreshadowing decay—just as these four novels foreshadowed Mishima's

[43] Mishima used similar words in writing to all his closest friends. His untranslated essays include a number of references to the unity of thought and action (Wang Yang-ming concept), although many of his remarks seem contradictory. In *Shōsetsu towa Nanika* (What Is the Novel?), reprinted in a special Mishima Yukio number of *Shinchō* (January 1971, although serialization had begun before his death), Mishima wrote about keeping art and life separate, but he also wrote that he could not imagine (living in) a world where the (world of the) novel *Sea of Fertility* had ended. My interpretation makes use of this essay, and of interviews, personal communications, and conversations in Japan, where I had been living since 1963.

own death. Perhaps some future scholar will annotate *The Sea of Fertility* much as Ivan Morris added to our enjoyment of the classical *Tale of Genji* with his *World of the Shining Prince*. In the meantime, readers can find in the translation at least some clues to the images of blood and perspiration, of flashing swords and heroic male figures, of gold and vermilion fire, and of Mishima's "churning sea" of memory and meaning.

At the simple narrative level, *The Sea of Fertility* presents a four-part chronicle of the reincarnation of a beautiful boy, Kiyoaki, marked with a constellation of three moles. In the first volume, *Spring Snow (Haru no Yuki,* 1965–1967), set in the second decade of the twentieth century, the narrative focuses on Kiyoaki, one of Mishima's many male figures of exceptional beauty. Son of an aristocratic Tokyo family afflicted with "the virus of elegance," Kiyoaki is a student at Gakushūin, the school of Mishima's Mask (and of Mishima himself). Kiyoaki is alienated from his surroundings and always at a distance from others—including his friend Honda. Some of the alienation is reminiscent of the *Confessions*, though without the overtly homosexual bias.

Much of the action in *Spring Snow* concerns the always-frustrating encounters between Kiyoaki and the tempting Satoko—a relationship bitterly fulfilled as Satoko becomes pregnant *after* she had agreed to marriage with an Imperial prince. An abortion is arranged. And Satoko retreats to Gesshūji, a Buddhist temple whose aged abbess had delivered sermons on *yuishiki* ("awareness only") in the opening scenes. Continually repulsed in his efforts to see Satoko once more, Kiyoaki contracts pneumonia and dies, leaving his school friend Honda a "dream diary" and a promise that they will meet again "beneath the falls."

In the second volume, *Runaway Horses (Homba,* 1967–1968), the young Honda of *Spring Snow* has become a successful judge in Osaka, but his barren marriage is yet another example of Mishima's various heterosexual disasters. True to the prophecy, Honda sees the reincarnation of Kiyoaki—recognizing the three moles on the body of a beautiful youth beneath a waterfall. He had already seen this boy Isao as a figure of manly and perspiring virtue in a *kendō* (Japanese bamboo "sword") match.

Concerned—like Mishima himself—with the "corruption" of his nation's noble ideals, Isao plots the destruction of enemies of the Japanese spirit (inspired by a book detailing earlier rebellion). Failing, he is arrested for his part in the political conspiracy. Honda resigns his judgeship to defend Isao in the ensuing trial. Isao, however, finds no pleasure in acquittal (the verdict, it should be noted, is *not* "Not Guilty" but remission of punishment). Isao will not be thwarted: in the closing chapter he succeeds both in destruction of the enemy who had been tarnishing the Ideals of Japan (Isao's weapon is a dagger) and in his own suicide. On a cliff above the sea, he performs *seppuku*.

In the third volume, *The Temple of Dawn* (*Akatsuki no Tera*, 1968–1970), Isao's dream—of a rose-hued landscape —is fulfilled through the figure of the Thai Princess Ying Chan (Jin Jan): Princess Chantrapa, sometimes rendered literally as "Princess Moonlight." Mishima opens the narrative with a meticulous guidebook-detailed description of prewar Bangkok. To this setting of exotic colors and tropical images, Honda has come on business.

Just as Isao had been doubly linked with Kiyoaki through an earlier figure (his father Iinuma, who had served as houseboy-tutor to Kiyoaki), so the Princess is revealed as the daughter of Prince Pattanadid, who had been at school with Kiyoaki and had shared with Kiyoaki and the young Honda views of the night sea at Kamakura. Seven years old, Jin Jan (Ying Chan) is regarded as quite demented, since she repeatedly claims to be Japanese. Honda uses his earlier friendship with her father to contrive a visit to the Rose Palace, where he puts a series of testing questions that reveal the Princess's strange knowledge of Kiyoaki's life and death. But Honda can find no way to expose the telltale moles.

It is only many years later, after Princess Ying Chan (all memories of her Japanese "existence" now erased) comes to Tokyo to study, that Honda gets his opportunity. By this time Honda and his wife—described as a pair of bored parrots on a perch—are building a new country house. Eventually, Honda manages to see the three distinguishing marks (through a peephole, reminiscent of the boy's spy-hole in *The Sailor Who Fell from Grace with the Sea*). Once more, though, the cosmic moment is rich in irony: at the moment of discovery, Honda is spying on Ying Chan while she lies in (sweaty) embrace with a lesbian neighbor. As in *The Temple of the Golden Pavilion*, destructive fire intervenes. As in *The Temple of the Golden Pavilion*, the image of the burning building is reflected: in a swimming pool, instead of the pavilion's pond, with floating embers replacing the earlier images of floating duckweed. Honda's house is destroyed, but Princess Ying Chan survives and returns to Thailand—where she is killed by the bite of a cobra, dying as both Kiyoaki and Isao had done at the age of twenty.

In the fourth volume, *Tennin Gosui* (1970), translated as *The Decay of the Angel*, the "heavenly being" *(tennin)* bearing the significant signs is Tōru, an orphaned boy working at the signal station of the port of Shimizu. Alas, he clearly displays at least one of the five *(go)* signs foreshadowing the (physical) deterioration of *tennin:* copious perspiration. Honda (now an old man of seventy-six) discovers this "beautiful" and "immaculate" figure (possessing the muscles, firm flesh, and other qualities of Mishima's recurrent hero) and adopts Tōru. Honda plans to save Tōru by educating him, teaching him to march in step with the crowd.

Much of the action—some of it conveyed through a central section written in the form of Tōru's diary—is oddly reminiscent of Shunsuke's discovery of the pure, godlike, beautiful Yūichi in *Forbidden Colors* and of Shunsuke's role as artist-creator of "work of art" Yūichi. Just as Yūichi proved less than ideal, so too Tōru is "cruel," eventually turning on the old man. Tōru attacks Honda both physically and psychologically, until neighbor Keiko (the lesbian whose embrace had exposed Princess Ying Chan's three moles) exposes the mystery. She tells Tōru the story of Kiyoaki and explains Honda's plan to "save" Tōru by destroying the boy's "pride" or "spirit."

Tōru's first response to knowledge is in terms of murder. He imagines himself shoving Keiko's head into the flames, while blood "pours from his self-respect." Back at home, Honda reluctantly lets Tōru read Kiyoaki's diary—reluctantly, for he already thinks of Tōru as "counterfeit," not the real thing. Doubt has been cast on *this* reincarnation by uncertainties about the precise date of Ying Chan's death. (It is said that the spirit lingers for only a few days: if Tōru was not born within that critical period, he cannot be what he seems, in spite of the three moles beneath his armpit, though unlike his predecessors Tōru had thought of these marks as symbols of his own "élite" quality.)

After reading the diary, Tōru attempts suicide—with poison, the weapon used in the death of that earlier Sailor who fell from grace. Tōru does not die, but he loses his sight. Our last glimpse shows him truly decayed: wearing a white kimono (the color of death) and revealing all of the five signs. The immaculate Tōru is now soiled; he is surely "no longer happy in this place"; the heavenly being not only sweats copiously—Tōru now also smells. He even has the wilted flowers in his hair—placed there by the ugly madwoman he has recently married and who (with heavy Mishima irony) imagines herself to be exquisitely beautiful. Moreover, the immaculate and once-unspoilt figure has fallen from grace: his lunatic wife appears to be pregnant.

The ailing Honda has learned that he has a tumor of the pancreas. He determines to make another pilgrimage to Gesshūji (where he had once pleaded Kiyoaki's case). He will tell Satoko what has passed in the intervening years. At this point, Mishima creates wonderful suspense—forcing the reader to share Honda's suffering as he sweats up the hill to the temple entrance (underscored by a setting filled with hints of death and decay). Satoko, now Abbess of Gesshūji, responds to Honda's narrative with a denial that she had known Kiyoaki: "Don't you suppose there was no such being from the beginning, anywhere . . . "—apparently denying the very existence on which the narratives of reincarnation have been built.

Yet like other figures in the tetralogy, Satoko is an image of continuity, if not of reincarnation. As the present, aged abbess of Gesshūji, robed in white and cloaked in purple, she inevitably recalls the aged abbess who had visited Kiyoaki's garden in the opening passages of *Spring Snow*. At the end of that novel, the abbess had refused Honda's pleas to let Kiyoaki have one last meeting with Satoko, who had just entered Gesshūji. But at the end of *The Decay of the Angel*, Honda stands in an empty garden.

Brief summaries of the four narratives making up *The Sea of Fertility* give no more clues to meaning than the titles of T. S. Eliot's four poems give to his *Four Quartets*. It is impossible to read these novels in the simplistic terms of plot: ultimately, the reader must face the metaphysical implications.[44] At the same time, the novels of the tetralogy are linked—by character, symbol, and incident—to earlier fictions, essays, drama, even musical comedy lyrics. Mishima did indeed include everything of his life and thought in *The Sea of Fertility*.

Even the nagging voice of the pedagogue-author occasionally seems to be that issuing from behind the masks of earlier characters. Once more, Mishima's characters are not permitted well-developed individualized voices; the reader may

[44] The ambiguity of these hints is evident even in Honda's last agonizing journey to the temple. Images of decay (abandoned tea bushes, a fallen tree, wilted flowers) are accompanied by hints of life (delicate young leaves, contrasted with others that are black with "malice," for instance) and a pine tree that clearly retains its essential quality (pine-ness) in spite of the surrounding signs of decay and death.

well grow tired of the excess of aphoristic commentary. To replace such earlier (and unlikely) mouthpieces as a thirteen-year-old boy discoursing on "the chaos of existence" in *The Sailor Who Fell from Grace with the Sea*, Mishima produces extraordinarily varied figures in his final work, however.

Mishima's earlier tetralogy, *Kyōko no Ie* (Kyōko's House, 1958–1959), had failed largely on account of its excess of philosophy over (literary) art. To Mishima, that novel had been "a study in nihilism," and he published an extensive account of his intentions and of the disappointing achievement. He had seen *Kyōko no Ie* as a kind of summation of his earlier work, too—and a means of expressing his ideas through an artist, an actor, a boxer, and a businessman—each representing a specific quality (such as "self-awareness" in the actor). Alas, the readers just did not like Kyōko and her four cardboard lovers. And the reader not inclined to philosophical speculation finds much of *The Sea of Fertility* as arid as its namesake on the moon.

In *The Sea of Fertility*, the reader is offered a four-part education not only in reincarnation but also in the meaning of Free Will; in Hindu belief (including the bloody rites in honor of Durga); in esoteric elements of Buddhist belief, such as the sermons by the old abbess of Gesshūji in *Spring Snow*, as well as later disquisitions on *yuishiki* ("awareness only" or "subjective awareness"), the fundamental doctrine of the Hossō sect; in the Sutra of the Peacock Wisdom King; in a world survey of theories of transmigration, with long passages on samsara and a good deal of name-dropping (Aphrodite, Pythagoras, Heraclitus, Dionysus, *et al.*). The fourth volume adds glimpses of the Diamond and the Womb mandalas, as well as an extended explanation of the Signs of Decay (not one but several versions of the Buddhist belief—especially, of course, the "sweat of armpits").

Not all of the philosophy appears in straight lecture form. Following Mishima's theories regarding the "knowledge" of characters, the ideas are expressed through talk with Siamese princes; in the plotting of students; in the chatter of party guests; over cups of coffee in Tokyo basements; in Tōru's diary; in the voices of Indian guides and Japanese business-men overseas; and of course in Honda's words and thoughts. In *Runaway Horses*, Mishima uses the device of a pamphlet that has inspired Isao and that he lends to Honda. Amounting to more than one-tenth of the novel, this is appropriately a treatise on the sword and military ideals, describing a nineteenth-century "patriotic action" by brave men, some of them young. It includes a score of not-always-so-noble ex-amples of *seppuku*.

Mishima's instructions-to-the-reader are not limited to Buddhist thought and noble examples of valor, however. As in other novels, he offers what often seems like a gratuitous display of knowledge (not always accurate). In *The Decay of the Angel*, such instruction includes the duties of signalman Tōru's work (all the reader ever did *not* want to know about the funnel markings of freighters, the routine of ships' arriv-als and departures, harbor activities and signals, and the role of various port officials). Other instructive notes tell us about fashions in stock portfolios and the characteristics of liberal economics. In Tanizaki's fictions, details of medicine label or taste in food enrich characterization and offer clues to inter-pretation. When Kawabata identifies a particular bird or flower, symbolic or literary allusion replaces conventional narrative. But in Mishima's pages, the naming of objects and the excesses of information rarely function in terms of the fic-tion.

Often *The Temple of Dawn* is a tourist's guidebook—first to Bangkok and later to such Indian exotica as the Durga (Kali) Festival and the cracking of bones on the funeral pyres of Benares. Trivial and profound are inextricably tangled (as in life?), and seemingly insignificant details link with earlier (or later) incidents to produce ambiguous "meanings." For even as Honda-the-tourist relishes the beauty of Marble Palace and the rotting flesh of beggars, he continues to reflect

on the old abbess's sermons. When he does so—recalling her
views of the doctrine of reincarnation as expressed in the
Laws of Manu, for instance—the critic could well complain
that narrative and literary values are suspended. Yet Reincarnation *is* the narrative, providing theme, action, setting,
and characters. Hints found in the words of the abbess in the
opening volume lead inevitably to the silent garden at the end
of the fourth: a garden that is an appropriate setting for the
concept that all existence is based on subjective awareness.[45]

Whatever the meaning of *The Sea of Fertility* as a whole, it
is appropriate that the most insistent of the recurrent themes
is *seppuku*, the action with which Mishima achieved his
bumbu ryōdō. Seppuku—"beautiful" death by the sword—is
muted in the first volume, where Kiyoaki specifically reacts
against "militarism." In the second volume, sword and *seppuku* and the ideals of past warriors provide a gloss on all of
Mishima's work. There are links not only with the treatment

---

[45] The "meaning" of this garden involves questions of Buddhist belief
—and of Mishima's—beyond the scope of the present study. Some of the
Japanese commentaries on Mishima fault him for garbling various aspects
of Buddhist thought or point out (as in an essay included with the Japanese
edition of *Tennin Gosui*) ways in which Mishima's view differs from or resembles the Buddhist view of man as a tiny grain in the thick stream of
time. Translation of the concluding description as "the garden was empty," however, seems to founder on the ambiguous Japanese tense. My own
reading is similar to that in Miyoshi's *Accomplices of Silence*. And the
question of "memory" versus "memories"—like that of Beauty versus
Beauties in the title of Kawabata's novel—is another difficulty of interpretation that is related to differences between English and Japanese language. The sound of the cicadas may be interpreted by way of the Buddhist
association of "significant sound" and "awareness." But whereas the
sound of insect or bell is of profound meaning in Kawabata's work, the
reader should remember that conventional symbolism more often takes on
negative aspects in Mishima's. Whatever the ultimate meaning, though,
the reader will find it more useful to substitute for the Seidensticker
translation ("The garden was empty . . .") these words: "There is nothing
in the garden . . . no memory. . . . The garden is in silence, bathed in full
summer sun."

of *seppuku* already noted in his films, dramas, and fictions, but also with his discussion of the samurai code in *Hagakure Nyūmon*, the voices of spirits of the war dead in *Eirei no Koe*, and other untranslated discussions of the Japanese Spirit (see footnote 5). Many of the words in the "little book" that inspires Isao in *Runaway Horses* are identical with those Mishima had used in expressing his own ideas and ideals. The translator shirks the Western connotations of kamikaze pilots by referring to the group in *Runaway Horses* as the League of the Divine Wind. But Mishima uses the term kamikaze (divine wind) deliberately: in *Sun and Steel*, *Eirei no Koe*, and other contexts, he made specific reference to the heroic qualities of the wartime pilots, as well as to the origins of the term in Japan's medieval past (when the "divine" wind had driven back the ships of would-be invaders).

Deaths by sword are appropriate in the context of *Runaway Horses*, but the reader cannot avoid identifying Isao's friends and the men of the earlier league too with Mishima's own army, the Tate no Kai. As the catalogue of *seppuku* and other deaths by sword continues (especially in the earlier uprising described in Isao's pamphlet), the reader hears echoes of Mishima's voice in a hundred other settings. Isao declares: "Once the flame of loyalty blazed up within one, it was necessary to die"—the words sound like a preliminary script for Mishima's own death-scene *Geki* (Appeal). References to disemboweling and a dagger in the throat described as "graceful" or "brave" further suggest the language of "Patriotism." And when even the rather phlegmatic Honda dreams of "the supreme bliss of the moment of suicide," we hear once again the voice not of created character but of creator-author.

A substantial portion of *Runaway Horses* is a treatise on "lost" Japanese values as well as on the sword and noble death—again reminiscent of Mishima's aesthetic and his repeated references to the role of the sword in exalting the Japanese spirit. We are told that at the moment a samurai fell, his blood-smeared corpse became at once "like fragrant cherry blossoms." Here is the traditional comparison of cherry blossom and warrior. Here, too, is a visual link with the concluding scene of the film of "Patriotism," where Mishima transformed the bloody act of *seppuku* into a lyrical glimpse of a garden of raked sand.

In *The Temple of Dawn*, however, death by sword takes its metaphysical aspect from the ritual slaughter of goats, sacrifices to the Hindu Durga (Kali). And images of beautiful death by sword cannot convey the theme of decay in the final volume. In the account of *The Decay of the Angel*, with its metaphysics of sweating flesh, the noble image of suicide is flawed by such details as the strange parable told by Tōru's tutor. Furusawa asks Tōru if he has thought of suicide and then tells of the mouse who thought himself a cat (cf. Mishima's death speech?)—a concept resolved by suicide (mouse thus retaining his self-image as "cat"). Writing of Beautiful Death in his diary, Tōru quotes a Greek verse (cf. Mishima's Greek hero-samurai analogies). Tōru believes he will find true perspective "on the far side of death"; he thinks of the sexual fullness of love-suicide and foresees death in terms of pain. Mishima's words, perhaps—but ambiguous, especially when we consider Tōru's signs of decay.

The theme of beautiful death is also carried in imagery of swords—whether in a "sharp" blade of grass or the "stabs" of a cold shower. Tōru even has a fantasy of his car as shining blade, cutting through the crowds and splashing blood. When Tōru is faced with the difficulties of Momoko's "love," his response is partly expressed in the thought that he must provide her a blade with which to cut herself. Similar examples occur in all four novels.

But there is another, related theme, found not just in references to beautiful death but in examinations of the quality of Beauty itself. In particular, there are passages reminiscent of *The Temple of the Golden Pavilion*. Fire and Beauty appear in similar relationship in *The Temple of Dawn*, where Honda sees a temple in terms of soaring and fire images. White birds fly up like particles of soot, the birds and the golden flame-color of sun on marble appearing and reappearing in shifting images that merge with temple carvings. But "beauty renders human endeavor completely futile." And Honda thinks that Ying Chan must exist beyond the reach of his desire for perceiving: "The minute he attempted a violation, beauty could no longer exist in this world." Honda's many views of Mount Fuji provide another parallel, as he sees the mountain glowing like rain-soaked brick, crimson in the sunrise, the snow rose-tinted by the sun, or "flushing," changing to a rich shade of purple, seeming "a Japanese Temple of Dawn." Honda even perceives dual images: "in addition to the real image, an essence of the mountain, pure white"; or he regrets that Fuji-san is "almost too visible." The reader may be reminded of the soaring Golden Pavilion of Mizoguchi's imagination, especially when the Fuji image seems to take on an obsessive quality. And the mountain of Honda's imagination has its own symbolic values in *The Decay of the Angel*, where a glimpse of Fuji coincides with Honda's first awareness of the tower in which Tōru works.

Early in the narrative of *Decay*, the reader is told that "seeing went beyond being," transporting Tōru to a realm visible to no one, where beauty was "a sea never defiled by being . . . a realm of solid, definite indigo, where phenomena and consciousness dissolved." There are further links to Honda's earlier reluctance to visit Gesshūji (the temple playing such a deeply significant role in Kiyoaki's death). Honda's reluctance had been that of someone denying beauty—beauty that is "certain to bring destruction." We are back once more with Mizoguchi's vision in *The Temple of the Golden Pavilion*.

At the end of *The Decay of the Angel*, when Keiko tells Tōru about the reincarnations, she also says that he will be denied the beautiful death of Kiyoaki, Isao, and Ying Chan. He will suffer premature senility, and he (his thoughts? his words?) will "never be at one" with his *actions*. Tōru's murderous response—he contemplates her death in terms of an *iron* weapon (the poker), blood spurting, and fire imagery—inevitably leads to his attempted suicide, and so to his blindness. But the meaning of this blindness has been hinted in an earlier passage, where Tōru reflected that the ultimate vision would be *the eye's denial of self* (a thought coming to him as he contemplated his image in a mirror).

The mirror image is significantly linked with both fire and sea. When Tōru was tired of looking at the sea, we are told he looked at himself in a mirror. Honda's obsession, in turn, is like "fire reflected in a mirror." Other hints are contained in Honda's soliloquy on the eye of awareness and his thoughts of cutting time short at the "pinnacle" (beauty, radiance, and waterfall imagery)—especially his thought that "endless physical beauty" is the special prerogative of those who cut time short (as Mishima himself did?) when that "radiant pinnacle" lies just ahead.

Throughout *The Sea of Fertility* such images of beauty and beautiful death are linked to the ideally beautiful male figure that moves through all of Mishima's fictions. In *Spring Snow*, Kiyoaki is described in terms that show he is exceptionally beautiful, a doomed figure with "smooth" back, "grace," and "firm masculinity." He might have stepped out from behind the Mask of the *Confessions* or emerged from the sea of *Forbidden Colors*. Once again, we meet a man "afflicted" by true beauty, with a predilection for suffering and an incapacity for friendship that similarly recalls both the Mask and the flawed Yūichi.

The second volume, *Runaway Horses*, creates Isao in a St. Sebastian (sexual) image—and Honda first sees Iinuma's son as one with a pain "as though an arrow had pierced his breast." In this volume, focusing on the sword and on martial spirit, it is appropriate that Mishima includes among the secondary figures yet another portrait of the ideal warrior, one reminiscent of the lieutenant in "Patriotism."

The lieutenant of *Runaway Horses* is first seen relaxed in kimono: but young Isao wishes that Lieutenant Hori had greeted the boys "dressed in khaki uniform that gave off the scent of spring and of manure, a gleeful flash of red and gold at the shoulders and collar." This heroic figure of firm body, straining muscles, and military bearing seems to be a composite drawn from *Confessions of a Mask*, where that exciting figure smelling of night soil (manure) had so affected the narrator and was linked with fire festivals and other recurrent Mishima images. Like Mishima himself, and like the hero of "Patriotism," Lieutenant Hori speaks of the difficulty of beautiful death. At the same time, the lieutenant's admirer Isao (again like Mishima and the figures of his other fictions) has this for his greatest wish: "Before the sun . . . looking down on the sparkling sea . . . to kill myself."

His wish is fulfilled, though flawed in detail, and as the blade pierces his abdomen and a symbolic sun image appears behind his closed eyelids, Isao has found his beautiful death. But death by sword would be inappropriate for the Princess of *The Temple of Dawn*, where images of beauty and death are more properly found in the funeral pyres of Benares or the image of those fires reflected in the river. Yet though Ying Chan's death by cobra bite is scarcely the noble ideal, she is permitted a personal beauty rarely found in the women of Mishima's work—a beauty that reflects her role as reincarnation of the exquisite Kiyoaki.[46]

[46] Usually, the (rare) glimpses of feminine beauty in Mishima's work are obscured by a sense of incompleteness, by flawed perceptions, by ugly and even immoral actions, with perhaps one exception in the fisher-maid of *The Sound of Waves*. Satoko in *Spring Snow* is more representative: one of many girls and women leading lovely men to disaster. At one point, Satoko had seemed like Woman to Honda—but the image carried none of the promise found in the Woman of Kawabata's *Snow Country*. Honda's "bloated" and "sour" wife seems closer to the Mishima norm, especially when she is perceived as a fish cast up by the sea and rotting on the shore (doubly unpleasant in comparison with terms used to describe Kiyoaki-in-feminine-form, Ying Chan). Lesbian Keiko, thrashing about with Ying

It is worth noting, however, that Princess Ying Chan is also seen in terms reminiscent of Mishima's descriptions of classic (male) statues, as well as in tones appropriate to the "rose sunshine" of Bangkok. Her skin is like polished Chinese quincewood and smooth with "the moistness of amber orchid petals." By way of contrast, Kiyoaki had seen Satoko in terms of greenhouse atmosphere and dying flowers—especially ironic in the Japanese context, where "flower" *(hana)* is a synonym for "woman," especially to signify "woman's beauty."

Images of beautiful death are oddly resolved in the final volume with the Beauty—and Decay—of Tōru, another of Mishima's many sea-linked hero-gods. Tōru is linked with the sea at the most literal level: through his dead father (captain of a freighter) and through his work (at the Shimizu signal station). Beneath this simple "factual" surface, however, are layers of symbolic meaning. Tōru is a boy who *thinks* in sea images—of himself as sea, harbor, ship; and even of love as a form of seasickness. It is fitting that this sea god should be discovered by Honda: Honda is the unifying figure who moves through each narrative to simultaneously identify the lovely Kiyoaki and speak the words of Mishima's philosophy. And in some ways Honda is an uncomfortable parody of the earlier Shunsuke in *Forbidden Colors.*

As *Decay of the Angel* begins, the beautifully detailed descriptions of the sea inevitably recall the sea from which Shunsuke's lyrical vision of a god had emerged. The shining

---

Chan, and later (in *Decay*) playing a dual role as Honda's traveling companion and a wealthy fancier of beautiful girls, is a typical Mishima grotesque (especially in a vignette where she enjoys a lovely maiden in one bed while Honda comes from his adjacent bed to fondle the girl's foot: a nasty parody of amusing Tanizaki scenes, perhaps). Heterosexual couples in the tetralogy—from Kiyoaki's parents to the guests whose odd habits result in the burning of Honda's house—all experience the disappointments, frustrations, and ugliness typical of Mishima's heterosexual (and homosexual) lovers.

sea in Mishima's last novel, however, is described in threatening images of "thorns" and "spikes" of light, with a sur-
real promise of bloody death—especially in the image of sea-
and-flower sunrise that Tōru watches. As Tōru watches the
sunrise and seascape, the surrealistic flower also recalls the
sexual connotations of the skies in *Sun and Steel*, where
Mishima's awareness of his own body and of the Ideal Male
merged with an image of Mishima as Primeval Spermatozoon.[47]

In *Confessions of a Mask*, the sea had provided a "guillotine" splash of waves as image for the Mask's sexual climax.
In *The Decay of the Angel*, the waves rise and break, the crest
falling like a severed head. There are similar hints in
Runaway Horses, where "purity" is a concept that recalls
flowers, blood, swords cutting down iniquitous men, and
blades slashing down through the shoulder to *spray* the air
with blood. Earlier in that novel, Isao's pamphlet had included Otaguro's "glinting swords cutting down the wicked,
blood spilling . . . [and] beyond the blood, what was pure,
just, and honest took form, like the blue line of the distant
sea."

Sexual and cosmic seas merge, and the Night Sea of Eternity in *Spring Snow*—perceived even in the gold-flecked black
pool of an ink-stone—is little different from the actual night
ocean that Kiyoaki and Honda watch at Kamakura. Kiyoaki's thoughts move like the sea; while actual waves in turn
stimulate Honda's memories and speculations. In *Runaway
Horses*, black night waves crash on the sand, as they had in

[47] In *The Decay of the Angel*, the image—at first beautifully rendered in
vivid colors, rose form, and glittering detail—deteriorates into an ugly car-
mined "smile." The sea's evil quality is also suggested in black-green color
combinations, sometimes with similes of disease and cancerous growth. At
the same time, the sea here is specifically linked with the (Hindu) Sea of
Milk rather than with the arid image of the tetralogy's title. It is only in the
awesome emptiness of the garden at the novel's end that the full irony of
this "fertile" sea becomes apparent.

Spring Snow, although these waters are at other times the "shining" sea associated with Isao's *seppuku*. These are the symbolic seas and familiar ocean colors of *The Sailor Who Fell from Grace with the Sea*, *The Sound of Waves*, "Death in Midsummer," and "The Sea and the Sunset." But in *The Decay of the Angel*, Mishima amplifies his earlier cosmic implications.

All the rivers that feed Mishima's oceans now clearly become part of a universe in which every being moves constantly like a violent stream, and "everything is in constant flux like a torrent"—as when Honda meditates on *yuishiki*, recalling the cascade of the Matsugae garden, the waterfall where he had recognized Isao's signs, and the Ajanta waterfalls. The waterfall is a philosophical statement, made most clearly in *The Temple of Dawn* (especially in this lengthy passage). Here Mishima brings us lessons in the interpretation of Mahayana Buddhism, especially the *yuishiki* school, which interprets the world as torrential and swift rapids, a great foaming white cascade, world-as-waterfall. As he reflects on the cascade of "ever-different" water, Honda repeatedly thinks: "The world MUST exist." Yet if reality "is" in the present only, he faces a paradox.

Honda's thoughts on suicide here may hint of a deeper symbolism in Mishima's many deaths by water—whether the multiple tragedy of "Death in Midsummer," the heroine's plunge into the sea in *Muromachi Hangonkō*, or the leap into the waterfall of *Shizumeru Taki*. Through Honda, Mishima suggests that Time should be cut short just before the waterfall's plunge—at the pinnacle of physical beauty. There are hints, too, in the flowing *shiki*, of "all colors [*shiki*] are empty"—and thus of that empty garden, bathed in sunlight, at the end of the tetralogy. In the imagery of a man "flowing to the fall(s)," or to the cosmic ocean, are clues to Tōru's longing for liberation in a realm (of uncertainty) beyond *this* world, where phenomena continually flow over a metaphysical waterfall.

Sometimes actual waterfalls recall scenes in earlier fictions, such as the fall "submerged" by the dam built in *Shizumeru Taki*. In the tetralogy, the waterfalls help to carry both narrative and philosophical speculation: discovery of the dead dog in *Spring Snow*, a glimpse of Isao's identifying moles in *Runaway Horses*, a hint of lost Kiyoaki's presence in the Ajanta caves of *The Temple of Dawn*, the "Waterfall of Awakening" in a Tokyo garden in *The Decay of the Angel*. Multiple meanings flow through all these waters, from the sacred Ganges to the Thai Princess's bathing place.

Water imagery reinforces these hints. Even Tōru's three moles are seen as resembling black pebbles in a cascade. But these moles are also associated with images of blood, as well as with those other dominant colors in Mishima's universe: the brilliant reds and gold of sun and fire. When Keiko told Tōru about the reincarnations—and he realized that he might *not* be the élite being he had supposed because of his moles—he responded with fantasies of murder and images of blood spurting on golden chair and doors. The imagery of blood dominates the narrative, sometimes occurring even in the sound of roosters in *Runaway Horses*, where the cry of birds sounded as if the dark throat of night had been burst asunder and was spurting blood. In that novel, even the red ink of Makiko's seal seems like a splash of blood to Isao. Such images are of course especially appropriate in the context of *Runaway Horses*, with its theme of purity symbolized by the sword.[48]

---

[48] Actual blood—like that in the film of "Patriotism"—forms its own rivers in this odd universe. In *The Temple of Dawn*, Honda is entranced by the blood of sacrificial goats at the Durga festival, and Mishima lovingly details an old woman plucking the entrails (reminiscent of the boys with kitten entrails in *The Sailor Who Fell from Grace with the Sea*). Predictably, this passage includes admiration for the young assistant's skill with the sword. But the hints of blood are often forced; as in the references to Momoko's menstruation in *The Decay of the Angel* (a hint that she was menstruating at the time of a photograph in which she is seen in the

The dominant colors of blood, sun, and fire had been muted in *Spring Snow*—as in the golden sheen and scarlet reflections of the mother's fan. Garden settings in that novel provided a traditional (red) flower-in-the-mirror or moon-in-the-water image, too: the reflection of red maple leaves in the pond (although, as so often in Mishima's fictions, that image set up ripples of disquiet). In *Runaway Horses*, the blood red of heroic death is linked with the vermilion and gold of the symbolic sun, the "true image of His Sacred Majesty." For the roseate light of Bangkok and the parched scenes of bloody death in India, shades of red are essential. And red-gold even provides an exotic dream sequence in *The Temple of Dawn*, when the little princess—riding on the back of a peacock—flies high above the crowd and anoints Honda with that golden shower of urine.

But both the rose light of *The Temple of Dawn* and the splendor of the sun blazing behind Isao's eyelids in *Runaway Horses* are linked to the other, earlier scenes of sun-drenched seascapes, sometimes coupled with scenes of bloody death and always reminiscent of the sun that had been Mishima's source of strength and meaning, according to his *Sun and Steel*. In *The Decay of the Angel*, Mishima uses the same palette: golden petals, young bamboo leaves; red tree trunks, lilies, roses, hollyhocks, candles, lips ("red-black bits of decaying apple"). The Robe of Feathers myth blazes with golden fire imagery, as Honda meditates on the *tennin* and the Five Signs of Decay. And the fire—like the sea—merges with images of cruelty and with sexual associations even while it hints of metaphysical meaning.

Fire, blood, and sea are simultaneously setting and sym-

---

reflected light of a bonfire). Or an elderly pervert inflicts a knife wound on a woman in a park (an incident unmasking Honda as the long-time voyeur). At other times, blood provides brilliant images—blood and pus are "carried like pollen by thousands of fat, shiny, green-gold flies" in *The Temple of Dawn*. Yet it also offers the unpleasantness of life viewed as an accumulation of used bandages, "soiled with layers of blood and pus."

bol. So too the metaphysical sweat that marks the decay of the heavenly being is accompanied by real sweat throughout the entire tetralogy. In *Spring Snow*, Iinuma's sweaty kimono and chest hair are described in terms reminiscent of Ōmi in *Confessions of a Mask*, while his flesh is "a distastefully coarse and heavy vessel." The traditionally erotic image of feminine neck gracefully arched above the neckline of a kimono takes on a different dimension in Mishima's pages, where the necks of women at a festival are beaded with sweat. Honda sweats, too. Only Count Ayakura has "a profound aversion to human sweat."

In *Runaway Horses*, the military drills and heroic images of sword and patriotism provide Mishima's *erotic* sweating bodies. Even the classroom in that novel is "filled with the heavy acid odor given off by the young flesh of growing boys."

Yet sweat is not missing from the feminine atmosphere of *The Temple of Dawn*, where it may appear more delicately as bedewed amber orchid petals (the flesh of the princess) or in a grossly sexual incident: the sweaty embrace of lesbian Keiko and Princess Ying Chan, that moment when Kiyoaki's three moles are so ironically revealed.

And so the hints of sweating bodies move from erotic to metaphysical meaning again. In *The Decay of the Angel*, the sign begins as "cold sweats," with a glimpse of Tōru continually washing his armpits. Later, Honda sweats profusely as he puffs uphill to the mystic, sunlit garden. But by then the scene of Tōru's decay—the five signs now shown in his soiled, smelly appearance and flower-decked hair—has already signaled the passage into Nothingness.

Thus *The Sea of Fertility* seems to end. Yet its timing does not quite coincide with the dramatic ending of Mishima's own life, in spite of his assertion he would realize his *bumbu ryōdō* in this dual performance. For although the fourth novel opens in the year of Mishima's death, its narrative carries us into the future, four years hence. We are thus reminded of Mishima's comments on his inability to imagine a world continuing beyond the world of his novel. There is also a profound paradox: a tetralogy taking reincarnation for action, theme, characters, and imagery simultaneously presents "words" (spoken by a woman, though!) to suggest that perhaps the beautiful Kiyoaki had never "existed."

Paradoxes, however, are characteristic of all Mishima's work—including the odd "Greek" way that he identified with noble samurai ideals of his own nation's past and his search for a renewal of Japanese "spirit" by means of such foreign devices as body-building and weight-lifting. Moreover, the values that Mishima so often said that he wished to "restore" are values that receive scant support in his imagined universe.

In all his work, there are problems of setting. Even when his characters are not moving in an exotic world of Brazilian coffee plantation, ancient Leper King court, or modern political arena, they seem to be blind to the Japanese aesthetic. In Mishima's theory of fiction, dramatic necessity does not justify a character's ignorance (even of so small a matter as the correct name for traditional furnishings). Why then, is so much of his fictional world profoundly foreign? Why are his characters so consistently blind to every imaginable Japanese value?

Mishima himself attempted to revive the spirit of *Young Samurai* while living in a Western-style Tokyo house filled with Greek statuary, European furniture, and the works of foreign authors. The characters in his fictions sleep not under soft Japanese quilts *(futon)* on the *tatami* but in Western twin beds, in brass beds imported from New Orleans, or in double beds whose squeaking springs are lovingly detailed. Underfoot there is parquet flooring or Persian carpeting, while crystal chandeliers dangle from the ceiling. When lovers write, they do not inscribe poems on fans or use a brush and delicate Japanese paper: they use a ballpoint pen on stationery embossed with a design from Walt Disney.

These figures know where to get the best Florentine leather and how to distinguish various grades of Jaeger sweaters. But they have little knowledge of the culture Mishima refers to as ideal, and no taste for it either. With the exception of Noguchi—who eats rice but refuses the traditional accompaniment of a raw egg—Mishima's characters prefer a day that starts with marmalade, toast, and coffee. They quote Whitman or Wilde instead of Bashō and Lady Murasaki. Instead of a maid who can write haiku, as in Tanizaki's *Makioka Sisters*, Mishima offers a maid who can read the titles of Noguchi's German books.

As these characters smoke their brand-named American cigarettes or drive their (branded) American cars, they do indeed suffer those "symptoms of the disease of modernity" mentioned in *Forbidden Colors*. Like the boy in *The Sailor Who Fell from Grace with the Sea*, they appear to break "the endless chain of society's taboos." They reject the Japanese sense of *aware* and share with Shunsuke the experience of "Ionian melancholy."

This world seems entirely divorced from the lyrical Japanese feeling of Kawabata's. Yet when Kawabata was awarded the Nobel Prize, Mishima was there to offer congratulations: "It is almost a family joy. I feel as though my own father had won the prize." And Kawabata himself—whose praise was so important in launching Mishima's literary career—continually praised the work of his "gifted" and "nihilistic" protégé. Kawabata was also a member of two of the committees that awarded prizes to Mishima: the Shinchōsha Prize for Literature in 1954 (for *The Sound of Waves*) and the Kishida Drama Prize in 1955 (for *Shiroari no Su:* Termites' Nests).

The reader who responds to Kawabata's delicate brush strokes while being repulsed by the harsh lines of Mishima's world might at this point recall some aspects of Japanese history. For instance, readers disturbed over Mishima's enthusiasm for Western body-building techniques as a first step on the route to Japanese spiritual regeneration might well recall that Japan's traditional arts were for some years proscribed by the MacArthur regime. Along with that temporary loss of the spiritual elements of their martial arts, the Japanese also suffered a separation from Shintō (blamed for "nationalistic" fervor, although it is an inseparable element also of modern attitudes toward sex). They suffered an even more terrifying loss when their Emperor—a figure whose Divine Majesty is in direct descent from the (Shintō) Sun Goddess Amaterasu —was suddenly presented to them as a man who appeared in department stores, carrying his soft-crowned hat.[49]

This is the lost postwar world appearing in so many of Mishima's fictions. It is a world we must understand in Japanese terms if we wish to know how men as apparently unlike as Kawabata and Mishima can describe their work in terms of

[49] John Ashmead, Jr., quotes a moving description of this difficulty in "These were my Japanese Students" (*Atlantic* 204[September 1959]: 56–59). One student wrote of sharing the national dream, of being ready to lay down his own life for the Emperor, "a living god," only to find that his faith had been placed in "a mere nothing." The surrender in 1945 had ended the dream, and he felt that he was living on in the postwar world only because he dared not kill himself. Perhaps there is something of this feeling in Mishima's references to the Emperor, although it is the (symbolic) Imperial Chrysanthemum or Sun that he writes of, rather than the Emperor as individual or *man*. Mishima was educated at the Gakushūin (The Peers' School), where he received the Emperor's Prize in 1944. The "voices" of his *Spirits of the War Dead* cried out to the Emperor, asking why he had denied his divinity. Mishima's *Shōbu no Kokoro* (Heart of Militarism; or Martial Spirit) was a defense of the Emperor system. Mishima's last public words—at the end of his speech urging a return to Japan's manly ideal of art and action—were a salute to the Emperor. Mishima's last words even recall those of the lieutenant in "Patriotism," crying out "Long live the Imperial Forces!" as he committed *seppuku*. Yet whether speaking of the "dying embers of Japan's warrior spirit"—specifically the (lost) code of Bushido—or attacking the Constitution, or defending the Emperor, Mishima was not concerned with military victories. For him, the "aesthetics of destiny" had always been linked to the aesthetics (and ethics) of his Japanese tradition. And that was the source of his aesthetic of Beautiful Death.

postwar nihilism. This is the world whose inhabitants live in the "spiritual vacuum" to which Mishima so often referred in his last years—the world he described in *Taidō* as one where, thoughtless, "we are rushing headlong toward fragmentation, functionalization, and specialization . . . toward the dehumanizing of the human being."

These are the dehumanizing crannies that Mishima explores with such obsessive vigor—unmasking all the inhabitants, whether they be "respectable" ladies employing an exhibitionist couple in "Three Million Yen" or the sad Sunday homosexuals dispossessed in their wanderings by two-by-two heterosexual society in *Forbidden Colors*. He drags them out of the soft light of a moon-viewing party into the glare of neon and the brilliance of crystal chandeliers. He shows them viewing cherry blossoms that resemble "undertaker's cosmetics" or that are only discarded paper decorations and even —as in the story "Swaddling Clothes"—set the stage for a sordid crime. The cries of insects now come only from beneath the bodies of cars parked on a city street. And like Fusako in *The Sailor Who Fell from Grace with the Sea*, many families do not even have one Japanese room.

Yet the past lingers. Fusako makes her one concession—a display of old lacquer dishes for the New Year festivities, incongruous in her Western room but inescapable. Mishima and his characters alike seem to deny many aspects of their past, but they cannot escape its meaning. As in *Forbidden Colors*, the figures in Mishima's landscapes may be "careful not to disturb a particle of dust between us." When Mrs. Kaburagi uses those words, they are not in the usual context of a man complimenting a beautiful girl: she is expressing her yearning for her young homosexual "god." But however perverted the use, however different the meaning, the words of the past will not be denied.

Thus Mishima prepared for his final union of spirit and action through the writing of four novels reexamining events and meanings of Japanese history. Going back to the opening

years of the twentieth century (and through such devices as
Isao's pamphlet and Honda's recounting of myth going back
even further into the sources of Japanese thought and action),
Mishima provides for us the context in which we may understand all his work. If the conventional Japanese symbols appear but rarely in his pages, and seem to deny this past, we
should recall the seemingly flawed maple-viewing incident at
the opening of *Spring Snow*. Discovering a dead dog in the
waterfall would seem to be a disastrously "wrong" version of
autumn's traditional maple-leaf viewing. Yet it is worth
noting that for the abbess of Gesshūji this does not spoil the
occasion. On the contrary, it stimulates thoughts of *yuishiki*
—of awareness or consciousness—the thread of meaning that
runs through the bewildering reincarnations and transformations of Mishima's beautiful boy(s).

However barren *The Sea of Fertility* may seem to be, in
Mishima's version it is fed by the purifying waterfall, moves
with the passions of his sea imagery, is illuminated by the colors of sun and fire, and is part of the mythic memory of the
life-giving (Hindu) Sea of Milk. However ugly the businessmen, the politicians, the housewives, the lovers, the priests,
and however decayed the bodies of young sea gods, there is
Beauty—to be glimpsed but never grasped. It is to be found in
the Golden Pavilion of the imagination: not in the peeling
paint of a neglected and flawed building. Thus it is fitting
that Mishima's own death was a return to the past, as he performed the act of *seppuku*, the warrior's ultimate gesture.

That bloody, beautiful ritual death, however, can be understood only if it is recognized as a gesture linked with
Mishima's view of the "heroic" and "beautiful" death in *Sun
and Steel*, with his belief that the most profound depth of the
imagination lay in death. And of course the gesture takes on
added significance when it is seen as Mishima's own way of
finding that "endless beauty"—cutting time short in that instant of the "radiant pinnacle"—described in the waterfall
and flowing streams, the images of *The Sea of Fertility*.

At the same time, it should not be forgotten that Mishima staged this ritual gesture with the precision of a master dramatist: assembling his chosen group for a commemorative photograph before the event, making an official appointment at the Ichigaya headquarters of the Ground Self-Defense Forces, mailing copies of his manifesto to the news media, and finally stepping out onto the balcony he had used as a backdrop for Hitler's speech in his play *Waga Tomo Hittora* (My Friend Hitler, 1968).

Whatever the response of the gathered men, Mishima's final action was already determined. As he had written in *Kōdōgaku Nyūmon* (Guide to Actionism, 1969–1970): "Once an action is launched, it cannot stop until it comes to a logical end. . . . Once a Japanese sword is drawn from its scabbard, it cannot return until it completes its mission of cutting." He had already drawn his sword in the commander's office, when his Tate no Kai followers forced the general to provide the audience for Mishima's final drama. (It was on the general's orders that the men assembled before the balcony.)

The linking of the setting with Hitler and with Mishima's anomalous *Hagakure Nyūmon* (his guide to *Hagakure*, the celebrated interpretation of Bushido, the Way of the Warrior) should not be construed as evidence that Mishima the man of letters had been transformed into a militaristic and fascist fanatic. The correct context is found in Mishima's literary and spiritual heritage (in particular the Wang Yangming ethos and *chikō gōitsu*, "bringing 'knowing' and 'doing' together"), and his references to the Emperor remain in the context of spiritual values.

Mishima made a number of statements in which he identified the Emperor system as "the rock and center" of his aesthetics. In *The Sea of Fertility*, it is specifically the Imperial Chrysanthemum (symbol of the Emperor and of traditions stretching back to Japan's mythical past) that looks down on the "beautiful, sweaty, intricate choreography of death." In the Appeal *(Geki)* made at the time of his death, Mishima urged the listening soldiers to rise together and die as "true men and *bushi.*" He lamented that no Self-Defense Forces general had yet committed *seppuku* in protest against contemporary conditions. He even cried: "Is there no one who will [hurl] his body against the Constitution?"

But it was not political action that Mishima cried out for.[50] *Kōdōgaku Nyūmon* provides clues to the meaning of this action, as in passages where he calls upon the youth of Japan to take action instead of being "like bean sprouts." He deplores the loss of the Japanese Spirit—a term that includes love of country but also encompasses centuries of ethical and aesthetic values. This spirit is linked to the traditional Japanese culture that Mishima defended in his *Bunka Bōeiron* (Defense of Culture, 1969), the vanished ideals of the samurai (Bushido), and the "ethos of action" that Mishima described in terms of a union of art and life in *Sun and Steel.*

In 1968 Mishima had gathered about him his own Men of Action—the Tate no Kai (Shield Group), carefully selected university students who numbered almost ninety by 1970. Wearing uniforms that Mishima himself designed and paid for, and drilling regularly with Japan's Ground Self-Defense Forces, they were not the aggressors that one might have supposed from Mishima's dying references to the Japanese Constitution, even though his "actionism" at that time appeared to be a rallying cry for rebellion. On the contrary, the refer-

---

[50] Political response was in fact negligible; and the audience of Ground Self-Defense Forces responded with catcalls and laughter. There were some ritual gestures in response: General Mashita tendering his resignation, a few speeches made in the Diet, and a reexamination (token) of policy in the upper echelons of the GSDF. The ideas examined in *Runaway Horses* can give the Western reader some clues to understanding the *ethical* rather than the militaristic aspects of the warrior code. However mistaken Mishima may have been in his interpretation of that code, he saw in it beauty and strength and ideals. It is no more the advocacy of "fascist" ideas that some Western observers have claimed than his play *Waga Tomo Hittora* (set in the 1930s and concerned with power and values) had been.

ence to "wasted effort" of the "foundling" GSDF in *Sun and Steel* shows that Mishima was primarily concerned with their lost potential for glory. And "glory" in turn is a reference to Mishima's linking of heroic virtue, ideal Beauty, Confucian ethics, and the traditional association of art and action in the) code of the warrior.[51]

This is the "militarism" of his Tate no Kai, who were also an expression of Mishima's concept of group. On a number of occasions, he made it clear that "group" expressed "the principle of the flesh." The ideal group was a community of warriors. And the Tate no Kai expressed Mishima's philosophy of the Ideal Male Body as well as the general idea that a man can be associated with Beauty only through the heroic. This masculine ideal is found, in Mishima's view, in the potentially tragic quality of a *group* "open to death."

Throughout *Sun and Steel*, Mishima looked at death in its tragic and heroic forms, making explicit the symbolism of sun and sea and giving clues to his lifelong preoccupation with sharp weapons. His wish for "a union of art and life, of style and the ethos of action" reveals his act of *seppuku* as a tragically fitting expression of what Mishima called "the aesthetic demands of destiny" or the "formal aesthetic of death." Elsewhere he placed the correct distance between the meaning of his action and the kind of militarism that would justify the (false) fascist label: Literature is absolutely unrelated to the secular world of *conflicts* [my italics]. For Mishima, burnishing the sword and burnishing the imagination were synonymous.

Perhaps Mishima, like the protagonist in his story *Ken*

---

[51] The homosexual tradition among the samurai provides an interesting footnote; but it is not sufficient evidence for claiming—as one Western biographer has done—that there are hints of homosexual "love-suicide" in Mishima's death. Certain misunderstandings about the samurai code may be corrected by the statements in the pamphlet that Mishima handed out at the time of his Tate no Kai parade in November 1969 (reprinted with other relevant excerpts in *Japan Interpreter* 7[Winter 1971]:77–78).

(The Sword, 1963), believed that justice could be achieved only through his own death. Perhaps Mishima himself was unsure of his own meaning. Perhaps he did not succeed in resolving the Mask's early confusion of "sensual desires" with "a system of aesthetics." Certainly, the variety of interpretations of his death and the strange forms taken by some of the responses to his action should serve as reminders that Mishima had a splendid sense of the dramatic (and the melodramatic). We may also remember that his first great novel carried the word "Mask" in its title. He was a consummate actor who simultaneously enjoyed playing the roles expected by his friends and startling them with various unscheduled performances.[52]

[52] Some of Mishima's more startling performances received wide publicity in magazines following his death. These showed him, offstage and on, wearing the contradictory masks of a thousand roles: domestic Mishima, posed beside his wife (and a brace of stuffed animals), among his foreign artifacts, leaning against some of his Greek statuary. Wearing a sailor suit, Mishima sings in a cabaret performance. He debates with a group of rebellious students at Tokyo University. Series of photos-from-an-exhibition: Mishima committing *seppuku*, clasping a rose, as St. Sebastian, or lying naked on a beach, washed by waves, his eyes turned heavenward (presumably toward his symbolic sun). Group man Mishima sits in a Japanese bath with nine smiling young men, he chopsticks a bowlful of rice into an already full mouth, he drinks with friends, he appears with his Tate no Kai and the Ground Self-Defense Forces on "maneuvers" of doubtful authenticity. We see Mishima boxing, riding a horse, carrying a *mikoshi* in a festival parade, lifting weights, flourishing a bamboo *kendō* sword or one of his favorite sharp blades. The puzzled car-owner is seen attempting to change a tire. In another photograph he is transformed into a motorcycle policeman. His disguises include a leather jacket, turban and silken pantaloons, spy-style raincoat, evening dress, pilot's pressurized suit, loincloth, even a suit of medieval armor—but only one kimono (and his *kendō* costume). He is glimpsed backstage with a famous *onnagata* or dancing across a stage holding the hand of his female-impersonator friend (in contrast to the respected figure of the Kabuki, the bewigged and bosomed impersonator is on the nightclub stage). Spear-carrier, gangster, orchestra conductor—Mishima dodges behind his masks and we all play the part of audience.

But we should remember Mishima's words in *Sun and Steel*, where he

In *Sun and Steel*, Mishima declared that from the beginning of his career he had been concerned with methods for concealing rather than revealing himself. In the end, we can only recall how much the Masked figure of 1949 did not confess. Perhaps there are clues in one of Mishima's aphorisms: "We human beings sometimes steer off in a direction in which we hope to find something better." Whatever it was that Mishima ultimately hoped to find, we can only marvel at the intricacy and the endless variety of his work, the "beautiful, sweaty, intricate choreography" of Mishima's aesthetic of Death.

Works Available in English

After the Banquet (Utage no Ato, 1960). Translated by Donald Keene. New York: Knopf, 1963.
"An Appeal" *(Geki*, 1970). Translated by Harris I. Martin. *Japan Interpreter* 7(Winter 1971):73–77.
Confessions of a Mask (Kamen no Kokuhaku, 1949). Translated by Meredith Weatherby. New York: New Directions, 1958.
The Damask Drum (Aya no Tsuzumi, 1951). Translated by Donald Keene. In *Five Modern Nō Plays* (below).

---

wrote that he had "concerned myself from the outset of my literary life with methods for concealing rather than revealing myself." No wonder that responses to his death were so varied—and even bizarre. At one extreme: a valuable special edition of *Shinchō* in January 1971 with 250 pages of essays, interviews, and bibliographical material, as well as photos. At the other: the men's magazine *Pureibōi (Playboy)* of 18 December 1970 with an attempt to discover Mishima's feelings at the moment of his *seppuku*—by means of a séance (doubly shocking, a breach of decorum among spiritualists, who customarily observe the 49-day Buddhist mourning period). Other journals debated the technicalities of his *seppuku* with clinical vigor and presented their readers with souvenir recordings of Mishima's last words. Young men gathered for a "wake." Housewives, political figures, literary critics, and businessmen were interviewed. And the verdicts on Mishima's action were as varied among these strangers as among his self-styled "friends": to some, Mishima's death was accomplished with "nobility"; to others, it was simply "insanity."

Note: An explanation of seeming discrepancies in dating in both bibliography and chronology is to be found in the preface.

"Death in Midsummer" (*Manatsu no Shi*, 1952). Translated by Edward Seidensticker. *Japan Quarterly* 3(1956):315–340.

Death in Midsummer and Other Stories. New York: New Directions, 1966.

The Decay of the Angel (*Tennin Gosui*, 1970). Translated by Edward Seidensticker. New York: Knopf, 1974.

Dōjōji (*Dōjōji*, 1957). Translated by Donald Keene. In *Death in Midsummer and Other Stories* (above).

"A Famous Japanese Judges the U.S. Giant." Translated by Donald Keene. *Life*, 11 September 1964, pp. 81–84.

Five Modern Nō Plays (*Kindai Nōgakushū*, 1950–1956). Translated by Donald Keene. New York: Knopf, 1957.]Includes *Sotoba Komachi* (1952), *The Damask Drum* (1951), *Kantan* (1950), *The Lady Aoi* (1954), and *Hanjo* (1956). *Kindai Nōgakushū* (in Japanese only) includes *Yuya* instead of *Hanjo*.]

Forbidden Colors (*Kinjiki*, first part 1951). Translated by Alfred Marks. New York: Knopf, 1968.

Hanjo (*Hanjo*, 1956). Translated by Donald Keene. In *Five Modern Nō Plays*.

"An Ideology for an Age of Languid Peace." *Japan Interpreter* 7(Winter 1971):79–80.

"The Japan Within." *This Is Japan* 18(1971):54–55. Tokyo: Asahi Shimbun, 1970.

Kantan (*Kantan*, 1950). Translated by Donald Keene. In *Five Modern Nō Plays*.

The Lady Aoi (*Aoi no Ue*, 1954), Translated by Donald Keene. In *Five Modern Nō Plays*.

"Love in the Morning" (*Asa no Junai*, 1965). Translated by Leon Zolbrod. *The East* 2(ii)(1965):32–36.

Madame de Sade (*Sado Kōshaku Fujin*, 1965). Translated by Donald Keene. New York: Grove Press, 1967.

"The Monster" (*Kaibutsu*, 1949). Translated by David O. Mills. In *Occasional Papers, Japanese Culture*. Ann Arbor: University of Michigan Press, 1969.

New Writing in Japan (with Geoffrey Bownas, co-editor). Baltimore: Penguin Books, 1972.

"Onnagata" (*Onnagata*, 1957). Translated by Donald Keene. In *Death in Midsummer and Other Stories*.

"Party of One. Japan: The Cherished Myths." Translated by Donald Keene. *Holiday* 30(October 1961):9–13.

"Patriotism" (*Yūkoku*, 1960). Translated by Geoffrey Sargent. In *Death in Midsummer and Other Stories.*

"The Pearl" (*Shinju*, 1963). Translated by Geoffrey Sargent. In *Death in Midsummer and Other Stories.*

"The Priest [of Shiga Temple] and His Love" (*Shigadera Shōnin no Koi*, 1954). Translated by Ivan Morris. In *Death in Midsummer and Other Stories* and *Modern Japanese Stories*, edited by Ivan Morris (Tokyo: Tuttle, 1962).

"Revenge" (*Fukushū*, 1954). Translated by Grace Suzuki. Tokyo: Phoenix Books, 1954. [Also in *Ukiyo*, edited by Jay Gluck (New York: Grosset's Universal Library, 1963).]

Runaway Horses (*Homba*, 1967–1968). Translated by Michael Gallagher. New York: Knopf, 1973.

The Sailor Who Fell from Grace with the Sea (*Gogo no Eikō*, 1963). Translated by John Nathan. New York: Knopf, 1965.

"The Sea and the Sunset" (*Umi to Yūyake* [*yūyake:* sunset colors], 1955). Translated by Geoffrey Sargent. *This Is Japan* 18(1971):58–60. Tokyo: Asahi Shimbun, 1970.

The Sea of Fertility (*Hōjō no Umi*, 1965–1970). A cycle of four novels—see *Spring Snow, Runaway Horses, The Temple of Dawn*, and *The Decay of the Angel.*

"The Seven Bridges" (*Hashizukushi*, i.e., A List of Bridges, 1956). Translated by Donald Keene. In *Death in Midsummer and Other Stories.*

Sotoba Komachi (*Sotoba Komachi*, 1952). Translated by Donald Keene. *Virginia Quarterly Review* 33(Spring 1957):270–288. [Also in *Five Modern Nō Plays.*]

The Sound of Waves (*Shiosai*, 1954). Translated by Meredith Weatherby. New York: Knopf, 1956.

Spring Snow (*Haru no Yuki*, 1965–1967). Translated by Michael Gallagher. New York: Knopf, 1972.

Sun and Steel (*Taiyō to Tetsu*, i.e., Sun and Iron, 1965–1968). Translated by John Bester. Tokyo: Kōdansha International, 1970.

"Swaddling Clothes" (*Shimbungami*, 1955). Translated by Ivan Morris. In *Death in Midsummer and Other Stories.*

Tate no Kai (The Shield Society, 1969). Translated by Andrew
  Horvat. *Japan Interpreter* 7(Winter 1971):77–78.
The Temple of Dawn (*Akatsuki no Tera*, 1968–1970). Translated
  by E. Dale Saunders and Cecilia Segawa Seigle. New York:
  Knopf, 1973.
The Temple of the Golden Pavilion (*Kinkakuji*, 1956). Translated
  by Ivan Morris, introduction by Nancy Wilson Ross. New
  York: Knopf, 1959.
"Thermos Bottles" (*Mahōbin*, 1962). Translated by Edward Sei-
  densticker. *Japan Quarterly* 9(1962):201–214. [Also in *Death
  in Midsummer and Other Stories*.]
Thirst for Love (*Ai no Kawaki*, 1950). Translated by Alfred Marks.
  New York: Knopf, 1969.
"Three Million Yen" (*Hyakuman-en Sembei*: "Million-yen *Sembei*
  [Rice Crackers]," 1960). Translated by Edward Seidensticker.
  Japan Quarterly 9(1962):190–200. [Also in *Death in Midsum-
  mer and Other Stories*.]
Tropical Tree (*Nettaiju*, 1960). Play written for Bungaku-za.
  Translated by Kenneth Strong. *Japan Quarterly* 11(1964):
  174–210.
Twilight Sunflower (*Yoru no Himawari*, 1953). Play translated by
  Shinozaki Shigehō and Virgil A. Warren. Tokyo: Hokuseidō,
  1958.
"Yang-Ming Thought as Revolutionary Philosophy" (excerpts from
  Kōdōgaku Nyūmon, 1969–1970). Translated by Harris I.
  Martin. *Japan Interpreter* 7(Winter 1971):80–87.
Young Samurai: Bodybuilders of Japan (*Taidō*, 1967). Edited by
  Takeyama Michio. Photographs by Yato Tamotsu. Introduc-
  tion by Mishima. Translated by Meredith Weatherby and
  Paul T. Konya. New York: Grove Press, 1967.

A Partial Chronology

1925   14 January: Born in Tokyo. Real name: Hiraoka Kimitake
        (Kōi).

1938   *Sukampo* (Sorrel) published in March issue of Gakushūin
        (The Peers' School) magazine, *Hōjinkai*.

1941   September-December: *Hanazakari no Mori* (Forest in Full
        Bloom, or Flowering Grove) published in *Bungei-bunka*.

1944 Graduated from Gakushūin. Received Emperor's Award for highest-ranking student. Entered Tokyo Imperial University in October.

Hanazakari no Mori, a collection of short pieces including *Minomo no Tsuki* and *Yoyo ni Nokosan*, published by Shichijō Shoin.

1945– February 1945: Part 1 of *Chūsei* (The Middle Ages), a
1946 story written in language of traditional Nō plays and with Ashikaga setting, published in *Bungei Seiki*. Part 3 published in *Bungei Seiki* in January 1946. Part 4 published in *Ningen* in December 1946. Part 2 unpublished.

1946 January-June: *Tabako* (Cigarette[s]) published in *Ningen* on recommendation of Kawabata Yasunari.

November: *Misaki nite no Monogatari* (Tales at a Promontory; sometimes "A Tale at the Cape" in English discussions) published in *Gunzō*. Collection of short pieces (same title) published by Sakurai Shoten in 1947.

1947 Graduated from Tokyo University with law degree.

April: *Karu no Miko to Sotoori Hime* (Prince Karu and Princess Sotoori) published in *Gunzō*.

August: *Yoru no Shitaku* (Preparations for the Night) published in *Ningen*. Collection of short stories (same title) published by Kamakura Bunko in December 1948.

December: *Haruko* (Haruko) published in *Ningen*.

1948 Worked at Finance Ministry for eight months.

June: *Hōseki Baibai* (Precious Stone Broker) published in *Bungei*. Volume of short stories with the same title published by Kōdansha in 1949.

November: *Tōzoku* (Thieves), a novel about a couple who commit love-suicide, published by Shinchōsha.

November: *Kataku* (Burning House), Mishima's first play published in *Ningen*. Performed at Mainichi Hall (Haiyūza) in February 1949.

December: *Shishi* (Lion), a novel based on Euripides' *Medea*, published by Jokyoku.

1949   January: *Daijin* (Minister), an ironic tale, published in *Shinchō*.

February: *Magun no Tsūka* (Passing of a Host of Devils) published in *Bessatsu Bungei-Shunjū*. Collection of short stories with the same title published by Kawade Shobō in August.

May: *Tōdai* (Lighthouse), a one-act play, published in *Bungakukai*. Collection of short stories and plays (same title) published by Sakuhinsha in May 1950. *Tōdai* staged at Mainichi Hall by Haiyū-za in February 1950.

July: *Kamen no Kokuhaku* (Confessions of a Mask) published by Kawade Shobō.

October: *Seijo* (A Holy Woman), a one-act play, published in *Chūō Kōron*. Published by Meguro Shoten in April 1951.

December: *Kaibutsu* (Monster) published in *Bessatsu Bungei Shunjū* 14. Collection of short stories with the same title published by Kaizōsha in June 1950.

1950   January: *Kajitsu* (Fruit), a short story about a lesbian couple, published in *Shinchō*.

January-October: *Junpaku no Yoru* (Snow-white Nights) published in *Fujin Kōron*. Published by Chūō Kōronsha in December.

Summer: *Nichiyōbi* (Sunday), a short story about young office workers, published in *Chūō Kōron, Kaki Bungei Tokushū Gō* (special summer literature supplement).

June: *Ai no Kawaki* (Thirst for Love) published by Shinchōsha.

July-December: *Ao no Jidai* (Blue Period) published in *Shinchō*. Published by Shinchōsha in December.

October: *Kantan* (*Kantan:* title of a Nō play) published in *Ningen*. Staged at Bungaku-za Atorie (director, Akutagawa Hiroshi) in December 1950. Published in *Kindai Nōgakushū* in 1956.

1951   January-October: First part of *Kinjiki* (Forbidden Colors) published in *Gunzō*. Published as book by Shinchōsha in November 1951. (See also *Higyō*, 1952–1953.)

January: *Aya no Tsuzumi* (The Damask Drum) published in *Chūō Kōron*. Performed at Mitsukoshi Gekijō by Haiyū-za in February 1952. Published by Miraisha in October 1953. This modern Nō play was also performed in traditional Nō style at Tokyo Sankei Kaikan Kokusai Kaigijō, in 1955. Published in *Kindai Nōgakushū* in 1956.

Isu (Chair): essay/short story on relationship with mother and grandmother. Published in *Senshū* in 1957–1959. (See also *Hyōron Zenshū*, 1966.)

June: *Kari to Emono* (The Hunter and His Prey), a collection of essays published by Kaname Shobō.

August-November: *Natsuko no Bōken* (Natsuko's Adventures), a novel, published in *Shūkan-Asahi*. Published by Asahi Shimbunsha in December.

1951–
1952

December 1951: Sailed aboard S.S. *President Wilson* from Yokohama on overseas travels as special foreign correspondent for *Asahi Shimbun*. Kept a journal, "Apollo's Glass," on his travels in the United States, Brazil, England, France, Greece.

1952

January: *Sotoba Komachi (Sotoba Komachi)*, a modern Nō play, published in *Gunzō*. Performed in Tokyo and Osaka in 1952 and 1956 (Bungaku-za Atorie, February 1952; Osaka Sankei Kaikan performance by Kansai Kageki Dan, March 1956). Sung as a Western-style opera in 1956. Published in *Kindai Nōgakushū* in 1956.

October: *Manatsu no Shi* (Death in Midsummer) published in *Shinchō*. Collection of short stories with this title published by Sōgensha in February 1953.

1952–
1953

August 1952–August 1953: *Higyō* (Secret Pleasure), second part of *Kinjiki*, published in *Bungakukai*. Published by Shinchōsha in 1953.

November 1952–January 1953: *Nipponsei* (Made in Japan), a minor novel, serialized in *Asahi Shimbun*. Published by Asahi Shimbunsha in March 1953.

1953 April: *Yoru no Himawari* (Twilight Sunflower), a four-act play, published in *Gunzō*. First performed by Bungaku-za in July. Collection of plays published by Kōdansha in July.

Muromachi Hangonkō, a Kabuki drama (on General Yoshitaka, who dies in battle, and Ayoko, who drowns herself for love), staged at Meiji-za. Revived at National Theater in June 1971.

1953– July 1953–April 1954: *Mishima Yukio Sakuhin-shū*
1954 (Works) published in six volumes by Shinchōsha.

October 1953–July 1954: *Koi no Miyako* (Capital of Love), a minor novel, published in *Shufu no Tomo*.

1954 January: *Aoi no Ue* (The Lady Aoi) published in *Shinchō*. First performed by Bungaku-za in 1955. Published in *Kindai Nōgakushū* in 1956.

June: *Shiosai* (The Sound of Waves) published by Shinchōsha.

June: *Wakōdo yo, Yomigaere* (Young Men, Revive!) published in *Gunzō*. Published as book by Shinchōsha in November 1954. Staged at Haiyū-za Gekijō from November 1954 to January 1955.

July: *Fukushū* (Revenge) published in *Bessatsu Bungei Shunjū*.

October: *Shigadera Shōnin no Koi* (The Love of the Holy Priest of Shigadera; translated as "The Priest [of Shiga Temple] and His Love") published in *Bungei Shunjū*.

Awarded Shinchōsha Prize for Literature for *The Sound of Waves*.

1955 January: *Umi to Yūyake* (The Sea and the Sunset Colors; translated as "The Sea and the Sunset") published in *Gunzō*.

January-April: *Shizumeru Taki* (Submerged Waterfall) published in *Chūō Kōron*. Published by Chūō Kōronsha in April. This story (summarized in Mishima, n.19) deals with a man's philosophical self-examination as he wavers between becoming an "organization man" and adopting a nihilistic attitude toward life.

February: *Yuya* (Yuya) first performed at a dance recital by Utaemon's Tsubomi-kai group (by Nakamura Utaemon and Matsumoto Kōshirō). Mishima had written his version of the fifteenth-century Nō drama in 1949, but it was not published until May 1955 (in *Mita Bungaku*) and in *Kindai Nōgakushū* (1956). Mishima himself directed the first performance of his *Yuya* as part of a regular Kabuki-za program in April 1957; in the June 1965 performance, Utaemon played Yuya and Enjaku was Munemori.

March: *Shimbungami* (Waste Newspaper; translated as "Swaddling Clothes") published in *Bungei*.

September: *Shiroari no Su* (Termites' Nests; or Nest of the White Ants), a three-act play with coffee plantation setting, published in *Bungei*. Staged in Tokyo in 1955. Reprinted as title play in a volume of Mishima's plays by Shinchōsha in 1956.

Awarded Kishida Drama Prize for *Shiroari no Su*.

First performance of *Fuyō no Tsuyu Ōuchi Jikki* (True History of the House of Ōuchi [*Fuyō no Tsuyu:* dew on the *fuyō*—a flower—cf. "dew on the lotus"]).

1956   January-October: *Kinkakuji* (The Temple of the Golden Pavilion) published in *Shinchō*. Published by Shinchōsha in October.

January-December: *Nagasugita Haru* (Too Long a Spring), a story of a couple's "adventures" during a long engagement, serialized in *Fujin Kurabu*.

March: *Kindai Nōgakushū* (Five Modern Nō Plays) published by Shinchōsha. Includes *Kantan, Aya no Tsuzumi, Sotoba Komachi, Aoi no Ue,* and *Yuya*. (English version includes *Hanjo* instead of *Yuya*.)

April: *Hanjo* (Hanjo), a modern Nō play, published in *Shinchō*. Staged at Chiyoda Kōkaidō in June 1957.

April: *Eien no Tabibito* (Eternal Traveler), an essay discussing Kawabata Yasunari, published in *Bessatsu Bungei Shunjū*. Reprinted in *Kawabata Yasunari*, edited by Mishima Yukio (Kawade Shobō, 1962).

Kōfukugo Shuppan (Happiness Sets Sail), a minor novel, serialized.

Tōsui ni Tsuite (On Intoxication), an essay about his experiences with the *mikoshi* (portable shrine) of a summer festival.

November: *Rokumeikan* (Rokumei Mansion), a four-act play, staged by Bungaku-za at Daiichi Seimei Hall. Published in *Bungakukai* in December. Collection of plays with this title published by Tokyo Sōgensha in March 1957. Mishima appeared in a minor role in the original production.

December: *Hashizukushi* (A List of Bridges; translated as "Seven Bridges") published in *Bungei Shunjū*. Collection of short stories with this title published by Bungei Shunjū Shinsha in February 1958.

1957   Awarded Yomiuri Prize for *Kinkakuji*.

January: *Onnagata* (Onnagata) published in *Sekai*.

January: *Dōjōji* (Dōjōji), a one-act play, published in *Shinchō*.

April-June: *Bitoku no Yoromeki* (Tottering Virtue), a minor novel, serialized in *Gunzō*. Published by Kōdansha in June.

Spent six months in the United States visiting Michigan and New York (after a period of intensive English study). Delivered speech at the University of Michigan entitled "The Present State of the Japanese Literary Establishment." Also visited Puerto Rico, Haiti, Dominican Republic, Mexico. Returned to Japan in January 1958 via Rome, Madrid, Athens.

1957–   *Mishima Yukio Senshū* (Selected Works) published by
1959   Shinchōsha in nineteen volumes, including Mishima's comments on his work (some reprinted from interviews) and *Shōsetsuka no Kyūka* (Writer's Holiday).

1958   May: *Bara to Kaizoku* (Roses and Pirates), a three-act play, published in *Gunzō*. Published by Shinchōsha in May. Staged by Bungaku-za at Daiichi Seimei Hall in July 1958.

30 May: Married Sugiyama Yōko, daughter of a noted Japanese artist.

1958– *Kyōko no Ie* (Kyōko's House), a novel, written between
1959   March 1958 and the summer of 1959 (first part completed in December 1958). Published by Shinchōsha in September 1959. A diary kept while writing this novel was published in *Koe* from October 1958 to 1959. The diary, *Ratai to Ishō* (Nude and Costume), was reprinted in *Hyōron Zenshū* in 1966.

1960   January: *Nettaiju* (Tropical Tree), a three-act play, published in *Koe*. Bungaku-za performance at Daiichi Seimei Hall in January 1961.

January-October: *Utage no Ato* (After the Banquet) serialized in *Chūō Kōron*. Published by Shinchōsha in November.

July: *Yoroboshi (Yoroboshi)*, a modern Nō play, published in *Koe*.

Ojōsan (Young Lady), a novel, serialized.

Played a gangster *(yakuza)* boss in the Daiei movie *Karakkaze Yarō* (Tough Guy [*karakkaze*: dry wind]).

April: Designed sets and costumes and directed production of Oscar Wilde's *Salome* by Bungaku-za.

Hitotsu no Seijiteki Iken (One Political Opinion), an essay.

September: *Hyakuman-en Sembei* (Million-yen *Sembei*; translated as "Three Million Yen") published in *Shinchō*. Also printed in *Sutā* in 1961.

November: *Sutā* (Movie Star) published in *Gunzō*. Title story in volume of short stories (including *Hyakuman-en Sembei* and *Yūkoku*) published by Shinchōsha in January 1961.

December: *Yūkoku* (Patriotism) published in *Shōsetsu Chūō Kōron*. Also printed in *Sutā* in 1961.

1961   *Kemono no Tawamure* (The Play or Sport of Beasts), a novel about plans for murder in a "love" story.

October: "Party of One. Japan: The Cherished Myths," translated by Donald Keene in *Holiday* 30.

December: *Tōka no Kiku* (The Day After the Fair; or One Day Too Late), a three-act play published in *Bungakukai*. November performance by Bungaku-za. One of a number of works linked to the 26 February 1936 incident (Mishima n.22), but set sixteen years later; the Minister of Finance who had escaped assassination is the central character.

December: *Kurotokage* (Black Lizard), a three-act play from the story by Edogawa Rampo, published in *Fujingahō*. Performed in March 1962 at Sankei Hall.

Some of Mishima's modern Nō plays staged successfully at the Players' Theater, New York.

1962   January: *Mahōbin* (Thermos Bottles) published in *Bungei Shunjū*.

January-November: *Utsukushii Hoshi* (Beautiful Star), a science fiction story featuring a flying saucer, published in *Shinchō*. Published by Shinchōsha in October.

February: Awarded Yomiuri Prize for literature for his play *Tōka no Kiku*.

Ai no Shissō (Scamper or Stampede of Love), a minor novel, serialized.

1963   January: *Shinju* (The Pearl) published in *Bungei Shunjū*.

January-May: *Watashi no Henreki Jidai* (My Wandering Years) serialized in *Tokyo Shimbun*. Published in collection of essays with same title, by Kōdansha in 1964.

February: *Hayashi Fusao Ron* (Study of Hayashi Fusao) published in *Shinchō*. Published by Shinchōsha in August 1963.

Nikutai no Gakkō (School of Flesh; or Body School), another novel that includes glimpses of the homosexual scene, focusing on a well-to-do divorced woman and her homosexual friend.

September: *Gogo no Eikō* (Towing in the Afternoon; translated as *The Sailor Who Fell from Grace with the Sea*—a title that Mishima himself selected from a list submitted by Nathan) published by Kōdansha.

October: *Ken* (The Sword) published in *Shinchō*. Collection of stories with this title published by Kōdansha in 1963.

1964 January-October: *Kinu to Meisatsu* (Silk and Insight) serialized in *Gunzō*. Published by Kōdansha in October.

February: *Mishima Yukio Tampen Zenshū* (Collected Short Pieces: seventy-four items published by Shinchōsha.

May: *Yorokobi no Koto* (Koto of Rejoicing or Happiness), a play, performed at Nissei Gekijō.

September: "A Famous Japanese Judges the U.S. Giant," translated by Donald Keene in *Life*, 11 September.

Ongaku (Music), a minor novel, serialized.

1965 January: *Mikuma no Mōde* (Pilgrimage to the Three Kumano Shrines) published in *Shinchō*. Also title of collection of short pieces published by Shinchōsha in July.

Kujaku (Peacocks), a short story describing the slaughter of a flock of birds.

June: *Asa no Junai* (Love in the Morning) published in *Nihon*.

September: Round-the-world journey to New York, Paris (for *Rite of Love and Death* premiere), Stockholm, Bangkok, and other cities.

September: Private screening in Paris of the film *Rite of Love and Death*. This movie version of *Yūkoku* (Patriotism) was shown at the 1966 Tours Film Festival and released in Japan in April 1966. Mishima directed and starred, acting out an elaborately horrifying *seppuku*.

November: *Sado Kōshaku Fujin* (Madame de Sade) published in *Bungei*. Performed at Kinokuniya Hall. Book published by Kawade Shobō Shinsha.

"St. Sebastian's Martyrdom," translated with Ikeda Kōtaro, published in *Hihyō*.

Awarded Mainichi Prize for *Kinu to Meisatsu*.

Work considered by Nobel Prize Committee.

1965–   November 1965–June 1968: *Taiyō to Tetsu* (Sun and Iron;
1968   translated as *Sun and Steel*) published in *Hihyō*. Published
         as book by Kōdansha in October 1968.

1965–   *Hōjō no Umi* (The Sea of Fertility):
1970   Part 1: *Haru no Yuki* (Spring Snow) written between June
         1965 and November 1966; published in *Shinchō* from Sep-
         tember 1965 to January 1967. Book published by Shinchō-
         sha in January 1969.

         Part 2: *Homba* (Runaway Horses) written between Novem-
         ber 1966 and May 1967; published in *Shinchō* from Feb-
         ruary 1967 to August 1968. Book published by Shinchō-
         sha in February 1969.

         Part 3: *Akatsuki no Tera* (The Temple of Dawn) begun July
         1967; published in *Shinchō* from September 1968 to April
         1970. Book published by Shinchōsha in 1970.

         Part 4: *Tennin Gosui* (Five Signs of [Physical] Weakening
         of *Tennin* [Heavenly Beings]; translated as *The Decay of
         the Angel*) written between 1968 and summer 1970; final
         revisions completed 25 November 1970. Book published
         by Shinchōsha in 1971.

1966   January-June: *Fukuzatsuna Kare* (That Complex Man)
         published in *Josei Seven*. Title provides ironic reference to
         "simple" airline steward.

         February: *Kiken na Geijutsuka* (Dangerous Artist) pub-
         lished in *Bungakukai*.

         February-August: *Owari no Bigaku* (Aesthetics of Ending)
         published in *Josei Jishin*.

         March: *Han-teijo Daigaku* (College of Unchasteness), a
         minor novel, published by Shinchōsha.

         June: *Eirei no Koe* (Voices of the Spirits of the War Dead
         or Departed Soldiers) published in *Bungei*. Book published
         by Kawade Shobō Shinsha in June. Ghosts of the heroes of
         the 26 February incident and of kamikaze pilots cry out to
         ask the Emperor why he declared himself a (mere) man.

         July: *Watakushi no Isho* (My Last Words), an essay

quoting the words Mishima had written in 1945 in anticipation of wartime death, published in *Bungakukai*.

Hyōron Zenshū (Collected Essays) published by Shinchōsha. Includes several pieces in which Mishima discusses aesthetics, especially in relation to his own writing. Also personal pieces on his mother, grandmother, sister; and comments on his disappointment at the poor reception given *Kyōko no Ie*.

1966– September 1966–August 1967: *Yakaifuku* (Evening
1967   Dress), a novel, serialized in Japanese *Mademoiselle*. Published by Shūeisha in September 1967. Characters include various society types and former aristocrats.

1967   *Taidō* (The Way of the Body; translated as *Young Samurai*). Mishima wrote the introduction to this book of photographs (subtitled *Body-builders of Japan*). The volume includes an essay by Tamari Hitoshi, whom Mishima identifies as the one who guided him "along the body-building path eleven years ago."

Various articles written for *Ronsō* (Controversy Journal): *Nihon e no Shinjō* (Faith in Japan), *Nentō no Mayoi* (New Year's Dilemma), *Seinen ni Tsuite* (On Youth).

September: *Hagakure Nyūmon* (Guide to *Hagakure* [Hidden Leaf], the famous guide to the samurai code by Yamamoto Jōchō, 1659–1719) published by Kōbunsha.

October: *Suzaku-ke no Metsubō* (Downfall of the Suzaku Family), a four-act play based on the Hercules myth, staged at Kinokuniya Hall. Published in *Bungei* and by Kawade Shobō Shinsha.

1968   *Inochi Urimasu* (Life for Sale), a minor novel with gangsters, a female vampire type, and other disreputable characters, serialized in *Pureibōi (Playboy)*.

Waga Tomo Hittora (My Friend Hitler) published by Shinchōsha. Hitler appears as a sensitive "aesthete" given a political education and (wrongly) identified as "my friend" by Ernst Roehm, the Nazi Chief of Staff executed in 1934. When this play was staged, Mishima used a backdrop of the Ichigaya Self-Defense Forces building where he later committed *seppuku*.

18 October: *Kawabata-shi no Jushō ni Yosete* (On Kawabata's Winning the [Nobel] Prize), published in *Mainichi Shimbun*.

Wakaki Samurai no Tameni ([Spiritual] Lectures for Young Samurai) published by Nihon Kyōbunsha. Pamphlet included *Tōdai o Dōbutsuen ni Shiro* (Turn the University of Tokyo into a Zoo).

3 November: Mishima's private army (a group formed on 26 February) adopted the name *Tate no Kai* (Shield Society, referring to a "shield" for the Emperor).

1969   June: *Raiō no Terasu* (Terrace of the Leper King) published by Chūō Kōronsha. Performed at Teikoku Gekijō in July 1969. Play is built around the Khmer King Jayavarman III (Angkor Thom).

July: Played leading role in *Hitokiri* (Assassin); film released in December.

Bunka Bōeiron (Defense of Culture) published by Shinchōsha. Urges revival of traditional Japanese values.

3 November: *Tate no Kai*, pamphlet describing Mishima's private army, distributed at parade. Reprinted in evening edition of *Yomiuri Shimbun*, 25 November 1970. (Translation in *Japan Interpreter* 7 [Winter 1971]:77–78.)

Tōron Mishima Yukio Tōdai Zenkyōtō (Mishima Yukio vs. the Strike Coalition Committee of the University of Tokyo) published by Shinchōsha.

Chinsetsu Yumiharizuki (The Strange Story of Tametomo [*Yumiharizuki*—the new crescent moon that resembles a bent bow—is an allusion to the Genji warrior Tametomo, renowned as an archer]). The Kabuki play was performed at the National Theater in 1969, with *jōruri* music by Nozawa Shonosuke. Mishima's Bunraku version was one of the National Theater's fifth-anniversary presentations, in November 1971 (see Mishima n.25).

1969–
1970

September 1969–1970: *Kōdōgaku Nyūmon* (Guide to Actionism) serialized in *Pocket Punch Oh!* Published by Bungei Shunjūsha in 1970. (Excerpts translated as "Yang-Ming Thought as Revolutionary Philosophy" in *Japan Interpreter* 7 [Winter 1971]:80–87.)

1970

Shōbu no Kokoro (Heart of Militarism), a collection of interviews, published by Nihon Kyōbunsha.

Yūkoku no Genri (Theory of Patriotism), a pamphlet.

Sakkaron (Essays on Writers) published by Chūō Kōronsha.

Bunshō Tokuhon (Manual of Style) published by Chūō Kōronsha.

Gensen no Kanjō (The Deepest Feelings) published by Kawade Shobō Shinsha.

"The Japan Within" published in *This Is Japan* 18(1971 number, published in September 1970 by Asahi Shimbun) —an essay in which Mishima discusses the significance of Nō drama.

Shōsetsu towa Nanika (What Is the Novel?) serialized. Reprinted in *Shinchō*, special Mishima Yukio issue, January 1971—a volume that includes photographs of Mishima in many of his varied roles, as well as a number of discussions, interviews, essays.

25 November: Mishima committed *seppuku*. The text of Mishima's *Geki* (Appeal) was reprinted in *Sandē* (Sunday) *Mainichi*, 13 December 1970, and there is a translation in *Japan Interpreter* 7(Winter 1971):73–77.

1971

February: *Waga Dōshi Kan* (My View of Comradeship) published posthumously in *Ushio*.

Note: Other posthumous publications include *Waga Shishunki* (My Adolescence) from Mishima's reminiscences for a magazine in 1957 (the book became Number Four on January 1973 bestseller lists). Family, friends, and commentators have produced various poems and essays (some dating from Mishima's childhood). But these works—like the many minor novels and stories that Mishima himself seemed to discount—are not available in translation (and references to them in critical discussions are often inaccurate and hence contradictory).

Purported translations of biographical material should be approached with extreme caution also. Much of the material appearing in the English-language press was affected by the sensational circumstances of Mishima's death, and many self-styled authorities—with little (sometimes no) knowledge of the Japanese language or even of the contemporary Japanese scene—rushed into print. Neither of the two biographical accounts of Mishima had been published when my manuscript was completed, and I regret that it has generally not been possible for me to indicate inaccuracies in those and other volumes. The biography by John Nathan, cited elsewhere, offers few firsthand reminiscences of Mishima, but it does include some valuable excerpts from previously untranslated works, as well as the most balanced interpretation of Mishima's later years.

General Bibliography:
Selected Translations and Critical Studies in English

The following list is not intended as a complete bibliography of available translated works by major Japanese authors, but it does offer a representative selection. Critical studies vary widely in accuracy and usefulness, and I have therefore chosen only the few that I believe the reader will find helpful. For works of the three major novelists discussed in this study, see the bibliographies at the end of the pertinent chapters.

Abe, Kōbō. *The Face of Another (Tanin no Kao*, 1966). Translated by E. Dale Saunders. New York: Knopf, 1966.

———. *The Ruined Map (Moetsukita* [Burned] *Chizu*, 1967). Translated by E. Dale Saunders. New York: Knopf, 1969.

———. *The Woman in the Dunes (Suna no Onna*, 1962). Translated by E. Dale Saunders. New York: Knopf, 1964.

Akutagawa, Ryūnosuke. *Exotic Japanese Stories.* Translated by Takashi Kojima and John McVittie. New York: Liveright, 1961.

———. *Rashōmon and Other Stories.* Translated by Glenn W. Shaw. Bilingual Modern Japanese Authors series. Tokyo: Hara, 1964.

Aono, Suekichi, and Kawabata Yasunari, *Who's Who among Japanese Writers.* Tokyo: UNESCO/PEN Club, 1957.

Ashmead, John Jr. "These Were My Japanese Students." *Atlantic* 204(September 1959):56–59.

Bester, John. "The Magnificent Egocentric." *This Is Japan* 18(1971):52–53. Tokyo: Asahi Shimbun, 1970.

Boardman, Gwenn R. "Greek Hero and Japanese Samurai: Mishima's New Aesthetic." *Critique* 12(1971):103–115.

――――. "Kawabata Yasunari: A Critical Introduction." *Journal of Modern Literature* 2(September 1971):86–104.

――――. "Kawabata Yasunari: Snow in the Mirror." *Critique* 11(1970):5–15.

Bownas, Geoffrey, and Mishima Yukio (eds.). *New Writing in Japan*. Baltimore: Penguin Books, 1972.

Dazai, Osamu. *The Setting Sun* (*Shayō*, 1947). Translated by Donald Keene. New York: New Directions, 1956.

Endō, Shūsaku. *The Sea and Poison* (*Umi to Dokuyaku*, 1958). Translated by Michael Gallagher. Tokyo: Tuttle, 1973.

――――. *Silence* (*Chinmoku*, 1966). Translated by William Johnston. Tokyo: Sophia University and Charles Tuttle, 1969.

Etō, Jun. "Natsume Sōseki: Japanese Meiji Intellectual." *American Scholar* 34(Autumn 1965):603–619.

――――. "An Undercurrent in Modern Japanese Literature." *Journal of Asian Studies* 22(May 1964):433–445.

"The Faces of Japan: Yukio Mishima, Novelist." *Asia Scene* 11(March 1966):32–35.

Futabatei, Shimei. *Ukigumo* (Drifting or Floating Cloud, 1887–1889). Translated by Marleigh Grayer Ryan as *Japan's First Modern Novel: Ukigumo*. New York: Columbia University Press, 1967.

Genji, Keita (pseud.). See Tanaka, Tomio.

Gluck, Jay (ed.). *Ukiyo*. New York: Grosset's Universal Library, 1963.

Hanrahan, Gene Z. (ed.). *Fifty Great Oriental Stories*. New York: Bantam, 1965.

Hara, Tamiki. "Summer Flower" (*Natsu no Hana*, 1947). Translated by George Saitō. In *The Shadow of Sunrise*, edited by Saeki Shōichi. Tokyo: Kōdansha, 1966.

Hayashi, Fumiko. "Bones" (*Hone*, 1949). Translated by Ted T. Takaya. In *The Shadow of Sunrise*, edited by Saeki Shōichi. Tokyo: Kōdansha, 1966.

_____. *Floating Clouds* (*Ukigumo*, 1949–1951). Translated by Koitabashi Yoshiyuki and Martin C. Collcutt. Bilingual Modern Japanese Authors series. Tokyo: Hara, 1965.

Hibbett, Howard. *The Floating World in Japanese Fiction.* New York: Oxford University Press, 1959.

Ibuse, Masuji. *Black Rain* (*Kuroi Ame*, 1965–1966). Translated by John Bester. Tokyo: Kōdansha, 1969.

_____. "The Far-Worshiping Commander" (*Yōhai Taichō*, 1950). Translated by Glenn Shaw. In *The Shadow of Sunrise*, edited by Saeki Shōichi. Tokyo: Kōdansha, 1966. [Also in the bilingual *No Consultations Today* (below).]

_____. *No Consultations Today* (*Honjitsu Kyūshin*, 1949). Translated by Edward Seidensticker and Glenn Shaw. Bilingual Modern Japanese Authors series. Tokyo: Hara, 1964.

Ihara, Saikaku. *The Life of an Amorous Man* (*Kōshoku Ichidai Otoko*, 1682). Translated by Hamada Kengi. Tokyo: Tuttle, 1964.

_____. *The Life of an Amorous Woman* (*Kōshoku Ichidai Onna*, 1686) *and Other Writings.* Translated and edited by Ivan Morris. New York: New Directions, 1963.

Kaikō, Takeshi. *Darkness in Summer* (*Natsu no Yami*, 1972). Translated by Cecilia Segawa Seigle. New York: Knopf, 1973.

Kanaseki, Hisao. "Haiku and Modern American Poetry." *East-West Review* 3(Winter 1967–1968):223–241.

Keene, Donald. *Japanese Literature: An Introduction for Western Readers.* New York: Grove Press, 1955.

_____. *Landscapes and Portraits.* Tokyo: Kōdansha, 1971.

_____ (ed.). *Anthology of Japanese Literature.* New York: Grove Press, 1955.

_____ (ed.). *Modern Japanese Literature.* New York: Grove Press, 1956.

_____ (trans.). *Four Major Plays of Chikamatsu.* New York: Columbia University Press, 1961.

Kobayashi, Takiji et al. *The Cannery Boat and Other Japanese Stories.* New York: International Publishers, 1933.

Kokusai Bunka Shinkōkai (Society for International Cultural Relations). *Introduction to Contemporary Japanese Literature.* Tokyo: Kokusai Bunka Shinkōkai, 1939.

Kokusai Bunka Shinkōkai (Japan Cultural Society). *Synopses of Contemporary Japanese Literature* 2: 1936–1955. Tokyo: Kokusai Bunka Shinkōkai, 1970.

Matsumoto, Ryōzō. *Japanese Literature New and Old.* Tokyo: Hokuseidō Press, 1961.

Matsumoto, Seichō. *Points and Lines (Ten to Sen,* 1957). Translated by Yamamoto Makiko and Paul C. Blum. Tokyo and Palo Alto: Kōdansha International, 1970.

McClellan, Edwin. *Two Japanese Novelists: Sōseki and Tōson.* Chicago: University of Chicago Press, 1969.

Mills, D. E. (ed.). *A Collection of Tales from Uji.* Cambridge: Cambridge University Press, 1970.

Miyoshi, Masao. *Accomplices of Silence: The Modern Japanese Novel.* Berkeley: University of California Press, 1974.

Mori, Ōgai. *The Wild Geese (Gan,* 1911–1913). Translated by Ochiai Kingo and Sanford Goldstein. Tokyo: Tuttle, 1959.

Morris, Ivan. *The World of the Shining Prince.* London: Oxford University Press, 1964.

_____ (ed.). *Modern Japanese Stories.* Tokyo: Tuttle, 1962.

Murasaki, Shikibu (Lady Murasaki). *Genji Monogatari.* Translated by Kencho Suematsu. Tokyo: Tuttle, 1974.

_____. *The Tale of Genji (Genji Monogatari).* Translated by Arthur Waley. New York: Modern Library, 1960.

Nagai, Kafū. *Geisha in Rivalry (Ude Kurabe* [Trial of Strength], 1916). Translated by Kurt Meissner. Tokyo: Tuttle, 1963.

Nakamura, Mitsuo. *Contemporary Japanese Fiction: 1926–1968.* Tokyo: Kokusai Bunka Shinkōkai, 1969.

_____. *Modern Japanese Fiction, 1868–1926.* Tokyo: Kokusai Bunka Shinkōkai, 1968.

Nathan, John. *Mishima: A Biography.* Boston: Little, Brown, 1974.

Natsume, Sōseki. *Botchan (Botchan,* 1906). Translated by Sasaki Umeji. Tokyo: Tuttle, 1968.

_____. *I Am a Cat (Wagahai wa Neko de aru,* 1905–1906). Translated by Shibata Katsue and Kai Motonari. Tokyo: Kenkyūsha, 1961.

_____. *Kokoro (Kokoro,* 1914). Translated by Edwin McClellan. London: Peter Owen, 1957.

_____. *The Three-Cornered World (Kusa Makura* [Grass Pillow], 1906). Translated by Alan Turney. London: Peter Owen, 1965.

_____. *The Wayfarer* (*Kōjin*, 1912–1913). Translated by Beong-cheon Yu. Detroit: Wayne State University Press, 1967.

Niwa, Fumio. *The Buddha Tree* (*Bodaiju*, 1955–1956). Translated by Kenneth Strong. UNESCO Series. Tokyo: Tuttle, 1966.

_____. *The Hateful Age* (*Iyagarase no Nenrei* [sometimes given as *Age of Being a Nuisance*], 1947) [and other stories]. Translated by Edward Seidensticker and others. Bilingual Modern Japanese Authors series. Tokyo: Hara, 1965.

Nozaka, Akiyuki. *The Pornographers* (*Erogotoshi-tachi*, 1967). Translated by Michael Gallagher. New York: Knopf, 1968.

Ōe, Kenzaburō. "The Catch" (*Shiiku* [Breeding], 1958). In *The Shadow of Sunrise*, edited by Saeki Shōichi. Tokyo: Kōdansha, 1966.

_____. "A Game of Football." Translated by John Bester in three parts. *Japan Quarterly* 20(October–December 1973); *Japan Quarterly*, 21(January–March and April–June 1974).

_____. *A Personal Matter* (*Kojinteki na Taiken*, 1964). Translated by John Nathan. New York: Grove Press, 1968.

_____. "Sheep" (*Ningen no Hitsuji*, 1958). Translated by Frank Motofuji. *Japan Quarterly* 17(April–June 1970):167–177.

Ōoka, Shōhei. *Fires on the Plain* (*Nobi*, 1951–1952). Translated by Ivan Morris. New York: Knopf, 1967.

Osaragi, Jirō. *Homecoming* (*Kikyō*, 1948). Translated by Brewster Horwitz. New York: Knopf, 1955.

_____. *The Journey* (*Tabiji*, 1952). Translated by Ivan Morris. New York: Knopf, 1960.

Saeki, Shōichi. *The Shadow of Sunrise*. Tokyo: Kōdansha, 1966.

Saikaku: See Ihara, Saikaku.

Seidensticker, Edward. "Modern Japanese Literature." *Atlantic* 195(January 1955):168–169.

Sei Shōnagon. *The Pillow Book of Sei Shōnagon*. Translated and edited by Ivan Morris. Oxford: Oxford University Press, 1967.

Tanaka, Tomio. *The Guardian God of Golf and Other Humorous Stories*. Translated by Hugh Cortazzi. Tokyo: Japan Times, 1972.

_____. *The Ogre and Other Stories*. Translated by Hugh Cortazzi. Tokyo: Japan Times, 1972.

Tsuruta, Kinya. "Akutagawa Ryūnosuke and I-Novelists." *Monumenta Nipponica* 25(1–2)(1970):13–27.

Tsunoda, Ryusaku, Wm. Theodore de Bary, and Donald Keene (comps.). *Sources of Japanese Tradition.* 2 vols. New York: Columbia University Press, 1964.

Umezaki, Haruo. "Sakurajima" (*Sakurajima*, 1946). Translated by D. E. Mills. In *The Shadow of Sunrise*, edited by Saeki Shōichi. Tokyo: Kōdansha, 1966.

Yokomitsu, Riichi. *Time and Other Stories.* Translated by Edward Seidensticker and others. Bilingual Modern Japanese Authors series. Tokyo: Hara, 1965.

Index

Because of the confusing versions of titles sometimes used in referring to untranslated works, this index provides both the Japanese title (in *rōmaji*) and the English version used in this book. Titles mentioned only in the Chronologies are not indexed.

✠ Production Notes

This book was designed by Roger J. Eggers and typeset on the Unified Composing System by the design and production staff of The University Press of Hawaii.

The text and display typeface is Compugraphic Caledonia.

Offset presswork and binding were done by Halliday Lithograph. Text paper is Glatfelter P & S Offset, basis 55.